STUDIES IN INTERDISCIPLINARY HISTORY
Edited by ROBERT I. ROTBERG and THEODORE K. RABB

The Origin and Prevention of Major Wars

OTHER BOOKS IN THE SERIES

The Origin and Prevention of Major Wars

Edited by ROBERT I. ROTBERG and THEODORE K. RABB

Contributors:
Robert Gilpin
John F. Guilmartin, Jr.
Myron P. Gutmann
Jeffrey L. Hughes
Robert Jervis
Jack S. Levy
Charles S. Maier
Bruce Bueno de Mesquita
Joseph S. Nye, Jr.
George H. Quester
Gunther E. Rothenberg
Scott D. Sagan
Kenneth N. Waltz
Samuel R. Williamson, Jr.

CAMBRIDGE
UNIVERSITY PRESS

CAMBRIDGE UNIVERSITY PRESS
Cambridge, New York, Melbourne, Madrid, Cape Town, Singapore, São Paulo

Cambridge University Press
40 West 20th Street, New York, NY 10011-4211, USA

www.cambridge.org
Information on this title: www.cambridge.org/9780521370943

First published 1989
9th printing 2005

Printed in the United States of America

A catalog record for this publication is available from the British Library.

ISBN-13 978-0-521-37094-3 hardback
ISBN-10 0-521-37094-9 hardback

ISBN-13 978-0-521-37955-7 paperback
ISBN-10 0-521-37955-5 paperback

Contents

Introduction

Joseph S. Nye, Jr.

Old Wars and Future Wars: Causation and Prevention

History is the study of events that have happened only once; political science is the effort to generalize about them. These caricatures sometimes seem an apt description of mutual reactions when members of the two professions discuss the origins and prevention of major wars. It might be amusing were it not that the next major war could be the last. Nuclear war is too serious to leave to either historians or political scientists alone.

As Waltz argues below, conflict may be endemic in human behavior, but war has its origins in social organization. Nonetheless, general theories of the causes of war can be misleading. "It is assumed, for instance, that there is a class of events involving human behavior that can be legitimately subsumed under a single term 'war.' True, the events have a common observable factor—organized violence perpetrated by groups of people upon each other. But that is near the extent of the commonality."[1] This volume does not search for a common set of causes of all violence from tribal vendettas to world wars. Instead, it focuses on the upper end of the scale.

Since the development of the modern state system in Europe some four centuries ago, there have been ten general wars involving a majority of the major powers and a high level of battle deaths.[2] Some of these wars stand out in terms of their consequences for the hierarchy and structure of the system of states. In his article, Gilpin refers to them as hegemonic wars. Historians do not agree on the exact set of such wars, but at a minimum

Joseph S. Nye, Jr., is the director of the Center for Science and International Affairs and Ford Foundation Professor of International Security, Kennedy School of Government, Harvard University. He is the author of *Nuclear Ethics* (New York, 1986).

The author is indebted to Stephan Haggard, Robert O. Keohane, Charles S. Maier, and Robert I. Rotberg for comments on an earlier draft.

1 Anatol Rapoport, "Approaches to Peace Research," in Martin Nettleship, R. Dale Givens, and Anderson Nettleship (eds.), *War: Its Causes and Correlates* (The Hague, 1975), 44.
2 Jack S. Levy, "Theories of General War," *World Politics*, XXXVII (1985), 372.

most would include the Thirty Years' War (1618–1648); the French Revolutionary and Napoleonic wars (1792–1815); and the two world wars of the twentieth century (1914–1918, 1939–1945). Each of these wars is discussed below as well as the earlier wars of the Ottoman Empire for control of eastern Europe. By looking at major wars of the past, we learn about the potential causes and prevention of major war in our own time.

Historians and political scientists tend to approach this task differently. Political scientists strive to generalize and develop theory; historians probe the layers of complexity and the potential pitfalls of overly simple analogies. Each has strengths and weaknesses. Poor political science runs the risk of false simplicity; poor history describes causality through irrelevant detail and confused complexity.

Some theory is unavoidable. Like John Maynard Keynes' practical man of affairs, unknowingly the mental prisoner of some scribbler whose name he has long forgotten, so the historian faced with an infinite supply of facts must follow some general principle to select and make order of them. As Waltz argues in his article, a theory separates a particular domain (such as international politics) from its surroundings and gives a picture of the connections among its parts. Bueno de Mesquita adds that such mental constructs specify a simplified, ordered view of reality in order to reveal internally consistent and externally useful general principles.

There are different views about how to judge theory in the social sciences. The model of the natural sciences is not fully applicable where there is no laboratory to hold variables constant, and in which human choices are not fully predictable. Nonetheless, one can speak of the range and power of different theories. Theories of limited range cover a narrow domain of cases or a limited period. Their generalizations hold only within carefully specified limits. The explanatory power of a theory is a more complex concept and involves two dimensions often at odds with each other: parsimony and descriptive fit. Parsimony is the ability to say a lot with a little. It is the principle of Ockham's razor: shave away unnecessary detail. However, parsimony is only one dimension of power. Inventing parsimonious explanations is easy; inventing parsimonious explanations with a reasonable descriptive fit is rare. Explanatory power requires accounting for behavior with few anomalies. Since theory (by definition) is not pure description, there will always be problems of descriptive fit. Some anomalies are inevitable. The most powerful theories are the least procrustean in their treatment of anomalies. They also encompass more corroborated empirical content than their alternatives.[3]

Successful prediction is one sign of a powerful theory, but determining success is often ambiguous. When theories predict general categories of behavior rather than specific events, there is room for interpretation of how successful (or unsuccessful) a theory has been. For the same reasons, it is difficult to falsify such theories. Proponents challenge interpretations and introduce auxiliary hypotheses to save their theories. Yet a good theory should specify conditions which, in principle, could falsify it. For example, Darwinian theory is not good at predicting the evolution of particular species, but the discovery of mammal bones in the Precambrian strata of rocks would falsify it.

Most theories in social science are of limited range and modest power. In part the weakness of the theories reflects the nature of the domain. As a political philosopher has counseled, "A rational social scientist might well learn to relax and to enjoy the rich diversity and uncertainty that mark his calling. . . ."[4] As Maier argues below, post-Enlightenment historians do not seek to identify the constant traits sought by Enlightenment historians or by some contemporary political scientists. Instead, they map complicated and unanticipated causal chains, not foreseeable individual reactions. They see history as a temporal process of development, rather than as a warehouse of examples. This indeterminacy does not make history useless to policymakers.

> For history to provide insights applicable to present conduct, it must explain why other outcomes did not prevail—not in the sense that they could not, but in the sense that they might well have. . . .
> By exploring what conditions would have been needed for alter-

3 Imre Lakatos, "Falsification and the Methodology of Scientific Research Programmes," in *idem* and Alan Musgrave (eds.), *Criticism and the Growth of Knowledge* (London, 1970), 91–180; Harry Eckstein, "Case Study and Theory in Political Science," and Donald J. Moon, "The Logic of Political Inquiry," in Fred Greenstein and Nelson Polsby (eds.), *Handbook of Political Science* (Reading, Mass., 1975), I, 131–209; VII, 79–138.
4 Judith N. Shklar, "Squaring the Hermeneutic Circle," *Social Research*, LIII (1986), 473.

native outcomes to materialize, history can assume a heuristic role. It thereby suggests how freedom of action is foreclosed or seized.[5]

Such a method of counterfactual argument cannot assign precise probabilities, but it does raise the historian out of total immersion in the particularity of one time and place. This counterfactual reasoning is also an area of common ground with political scientists. Such "post-diction" represents a means (in the absence of a laboratory) of estimating the range and power of theories.

In practice, there is a long tradition of theorizing about international politics and the causes of war. Thucydides' *History of the Peloponnesian War* was more than a descriptive account of battles. Gilpin discusses Thucydides' interest in setting forth a general account of how such wars occur. This theory led Thucydides to select and emphasize certain facts rather than others.[6] Thomas Hobbes was indebted to Thucydides and his focus on power. Indeed, the preponderant school of thinking—both academic and practical—in modern European history has stressed the fundamentally anarchic nature of the international system and the struggles and balances of power among states that result. This "realist" tradition became dominant in the United States after 1945. Theorists such as Hans Morgenthau were well read in history and wanted to warn their countrymen against reverting to the idealism and isolationism that they believed helped to bring on World War II.

As Waltz describes in his article, Morgenthau never developed a fully coherent theory, and there are a number of ambiguities intrinsic to classical realism. Terms such as power and balance are used loosely. Some theorists hold that war is more likely when power is nearly balanced, whereas others argue that it is more likely when one side has a preponderance of power. Still others point out that the balance of power is a principle for maintaining the independence of states, not peace.[7] The first three articles in this volume represent theories which refine different aspects of the mainstream realist tradition. They all focus on states that act rationally in response to incentives created by their en-

5   Charles S. Maier, "Wargames: 1914–1919," *Journal of Interdisciplinary History*, XVIII (1988), 821.
6   Donald Kagan, *The Outbreak of the Peloponnesian War* (Ithaca, 1969).
7   Edward Vose Gulick, *Europe's Classical Balance of Power* (New York, 1955), 30.

vironment—defined as the international system of states. In that sense, they are analogous to microeconomic theories in which firms respond rationally to market incentives.

Waltz's neorealist theory portrays power as a means rather than a goal deeply rooted in human nature. It predicts that states will act to balance the power of others in order to preserve their independence under the anarchic situation in which they find themselves. It does not try to predict particular wars, but the general propensity to war. It focuses attention on the structure (distribution of power) of the system. Waltz argues that bipolar systems are more stable and peaceful because they involve less uncertainty than multipolar systems. The opponents and their relative power are clearer, and shifts in alliances make less difference.

Waltz's theory has the virtue of broad range and great parsimony, but its explanatory power is less impressive than might first appear. The theory is static. Since changes in the structure of the system are rare, other causes must be invoked to explain most wars.[8] Waltz defines bipolarity very narrowly as involving the power of the two largest states, not two tightly knit coalitions. By this definition, neither the Greek city-state system at the time of the Peloponnesian War nor Europe in 1914 was bipolar. Historians are hard pressed to find cases before 1945 to test the theory. Further, as Waltz admits, the peace of the bipolar world since 1945 owes a great deal to the existence of nuclear weapons, which he calls a feature of the units in the sysem rather than its structure. Nonetheless, because diffusion of power is occurring and a multipolar system may evolve in the future, Waltz's theory focuses attention on important questions about the propensity to make war under such conditions.

Bueno de Mesquita's theory also had broad range and great parsimony. Moreover, there is something commonsensical about an expected utility theory that says states go to war when they expect to do better than by remaining at peace. This explanation is not the same as saying that states go to war when they expect to win. As Sagan's article shows, Japan chose war in 1941 not because it expected to win, but because even a modest prospect of success was better than sure defeat if the American oil embargo

8 See Robert O. Keohane (ed.), *Neorealism and its Critics* (New York, 1986), 158–203.

was allowed to take its course. By refusing to assume that states have similar reactions to risk, Bueno de Mesquita is able to resolve differences among realists about whether a balance or a preponderance of power is more likely to produce war. Power itself is neither a necessary nor a sufficient condition for a rational realist to choose war or peace. The distribution of power (Waltz's structure) has no direct bearing on the likelihood of war independent of different utilities.

Bueno de Mesquita admits some limitations to his theory. He aggregates utilities at the level of the state, but they may not remain consistent under the pull of domestic politics. And leaders may have different psychological reactions to taking risks to avoid losses as compared with achieving gains even though the expected utility is the same. Moreover, in strategic interaction, states may bluff rather than act on their true utilities. Even more fundamental is the debate over the power of the theory. For some historians, his use of what he calls "stylized facts" compresses the temporal flow of history and represents parsimony purchased at the expense of descriptive fit. Others argue that the theory lacks power because it says so little about where utilities come from and how preferences are shaped and change over time. It says little about what variables of international politics are relevant. In a sense, it is not a theory of international politics at all, but a model borrowed from microeconomics and applied to international politics. If one believes that the rational-actor assumptions of microeconomics have not done all that well when applied to macroeconomic policy, then one might be skeptical about the promised power of the theory even if problems such as intransitive preferences and non-rational psychological responses are overcome. Nonetheless, the microeconomic metaphor directs the attention of historians to important questions about rationality and war.

Gilpin theorizes about hegemonic wars resulting from changes in the preponderance of power as a result of uneven growth among states. Essentially, he updates Thucydides' variant of realism. The theories he develops are dynamic but incomplete. They deal with wars which have major structural effects on the international system, but, as Gilpin points out, they do not specify whether the nation in decline or the challenger is likely to start the war, nor what the consequences will be. Nor is it easy to identify hegemonic wars in such a way that the argument is nontautological. Although Gilpin sees hegemonic wars occurring at roughly 100-year intervals, he is skeptical of the causation adduced in cyclical theories.

Gilpin's own argument is that states act rationally to try to change the system to advance their interests in response to shifts in the distribution of power, but unanticipated consequences can give rise to hegemonic wars that no one wanted. This admission of uncertainty improves the descriptive fit, but weakens the parsimony and overall explanatory power of the theory. Given the effects of uneven growth and the role of declining power in the onset of World War I, as described in Williamson's article, Gilpin's theory also brings attention to important issues. But a powerful theory must explain why and when dogs do not bark as well as when they do. A powerful hegemonic transition theory would explain the absence of war between the United States and Britain in the 1890s and the relatively pacific withdrawal of Spain after the seventeenth century. It would also suggest what to watch for in the relationship between the United States and East Asia in coming decades.

The articles by Levy, Jervis, and Quester concentrate on perceptions and domestic politics. They make no claims to powerful or parsimonious general theories. As Levy points out, the complexity of the linkage between domestic political factors and the causes of war has made historians feel at home with their line of work but has discouraged broad theorizing by political scientists. Marxist and liberal theories about economic structure and war have not held up well under the test of events. A version of liberal theory that explains why democracies do not fight *each other* is interesting but limited in range.[9] Scapegoat theories relating internal conflict to external conflict have generally been poorly formulated and tested.

Jervis explicitly admits that there are so many kinds of misperceptions with so many different effects that it is impossible to develop an overall theory of misperception as a cause of war. Nonetheless, he argues that misperception often plays a large role, and that certain modest propositions can be developed. Many historians agree. Blainey has argued that "it is not the actual distribution or balance of power which is vital; it is rather the way in which national leaders *think* that power is distributed. . . . War is a dispute about the measurement of power. War marks the choice of a new set of weights and measures."[10] Excessive military optimism is frequently associated with the outbreak of war. Jervis points out that it is especially dangerous when coupled with political and diplomatic pessimism. Jervis' observation makes a useful auxiliary hypothesis to the power transition theories that Gilpin addresses.

Quester's discussion of brinkmanship and crises of resolve is an illustration of how both perceptions and the logic of war change sequentially under certain conditions. Both parties may start out in a game such as "chicken," in which both are better off if there is no war. But the process of crisis escalation and the belief that war is inevitable and imminent may transform the game into one of Prisoner's Dilemma, in which it is better to strike first than to be struck first. As Quester points out, wars of attrition or contests of endurance encourage the "rationality of irrationality." Each side pretends indifference to disaster in order to win the contest of resolve in the game of chicken. But there is danger that the pretense could become reality as the game changes or unforeseen events occur. Maier and Bueno de Mesquita describe how each step in War War I seemed to be a rational choice to the participants as the sequence unfolded. As Maier puts it in his essay, "From one point of view the war was 'irrational,' risking national unity, dynasties, and even bourgeois society. Many of the European statesmen . . . claimed to understand that such long-term stakes were involved . . . they did not think they were in a position to act upon these long-term forebodings. Rather, they saw themselves confronted with decisions about the next step."[11] Although each step may be rational in a procedural sense of relating means to ends, the substantive outcome may be so distorted that one should refer to it as irrational.

None of the political theories discussed above is very powerful, but each suggests interesting questions for historians to consider as they map the complex causality of major wars and

10 A. Geoffrey Blainey, *The Causes of War* (New York, 1973), 114.
11 Maier, "Wargames," 840.

try to structure counterfactual arguments that illuminate the range of choice and the limits that statesmen face. In addition, the various theories suggest different attitudes and problems regarding the prevention of a major nuclear war.

The implications of Waltz and Bueno de Mesquita's theories are optimistic. For Waltz, the stability of the bipolar structure is reinforced by the prudence which nuclear weapons engender at the level of the individual states. In terms of expected utility theory, a major nuclear war should be very difficult to start. There would be no political goals which leaders could hold commensurate with the absolute magnitude of destruction that their nations would suffer. This situation is the crystal-ball effect.[12] In 1914, if one could have shown Europe's leaders a crystal ball with a picture of the devastation in 1918, they might have drawn back from war rather than become trapped in the sequence that Maier describes. An elementary knowledge of the physical effects of nuclear weapons serves as today's crystal ball.

Gilpin agrees that a nuclear balance of terror has created a new basis of international order among the superpowers in contrast with the earlier balance of power. But he argues that change in the nature of warfare has not necessarily altered the nature of international politics. Struggles for hegemony continue, and one cannot rule out the possibility of hegemonic war in the nuclear age. "The theory of hegemonic war does not argue that statesmen 'will' a great war; the great wars of history were seldom predicted, and their course has never been foreseen."[13] The essays by Jervis, Quester, and others tend to reinforce Gilpin's cautionary note. Misperceptions and situational irrationality can occur in the nuclear age. Crystal balls can be clouded by misperception or shattered by accident.

How likely are such dangers? Howard argues that it is difficult to find any historical cases of accidental war. Blainey argues that unintended war is also rare. It is not enough to say that "neither side wanted war." Like Bueno de Mesquita, he argues that "every preference for war or peace is attached to a price.

12 Joseph S. Nye, Jr., *Nuclear Ethics* (New York, 1986), 61.
13 Robert Gilpin, "The Theory of Hegemonic War," *Journal of Interdisciplinary History*, XVIII (1988), 611-612.

. . . What was so often unintentional about war was not the decision to fight but the outcome of the fighting."[14] In one sense, Blainey is correct. Someone decides. There are no purely accidental wars. But the important questions are how the preferences for war or peace are shaped, and how the compression of time in nuclear crises may magnify the effect of nonrational factors.

A nuclear war is unlikely to start by accident or by purely rational calculation. But the intersection of rational and nonrational factors may greatly increase risks in a crisis.[15] Nonrational factors include psychological stress clouding judgment (witness Joseph Stalin in June 1941); organizational complexity (for example, the straying of a U-2 reconnaissance flight over the Soviet Union at the height of the Cuban missile crisis); misdirected or misunderstood communications (note the examples in the articles by Sagan, Hughes, and Jervis); and accidents (which may have greater effects on perceptions in a nuclear crisis when there is less time to correct them). Under the influence of such nonrational factors, situationally constrained rationality could persuade a leader who believed nuclear war to be imminent and inevitable that it would be better to strike first than be struck first.

The fact that such scenarios are possible and that the consequences would be devastating lead one back to the proposition that major war in the nuclear age is too important to leave to the political scientists or historians alone. Their strengths and weaknesses complement each other as they turn to history as a substitute for a laboratory. Historians should pay heed to questions about rationality, perceptions, crises, and power transitions raised by some of the most interesting political theorists. Political scientists must pay heed when historians challenge their stylized facts, warn against the loss of temporal context and sequences, and point out the dangers of mistaking theory for reality. Both need to cooperate in formulating the counterfactual arguments that can illuminate the range and limits of choice for policy.

14   Michael Howard, *The Causes of War* (Cambridge, Mass., 1984), 12. Blainey, *Causes of War,* 15, 144.
15   See Graham Allison, Albert Carnesale, and Nye (eds.), *Hawks, Doves, and Owls* (New York, 1985), 206–222.

The Origins of War:
Structural Theories

Robert Gilpin

The Theory of Hegemonic War
In the introduction
to his history of the great war between the Spartans and the
Athenians, Thucydides wrote that he was addressing "those in-
quirers who desire an exact knowledge of the past as an aid to
the interpretation of the future, which in the course of human
things must resemble if it does not reflect it. . . . In fine, I have
written my work, not as an essay which is to win the applause
of the moment, but as a possession for all time."[1] Thucydides,
assuming that the behavior and phenomena that he observed
would repeat themselves throughout human history, intended to
reveal the underlying and unalterable nature of what is today
called international relations.

In the language of contemporary social science, Thucydides
believed that he had uncovered the general law of the dynamics
of international relations. Although differences exist between
Thucydides' conceptions of scientific law and methodology and
those of present-day students of international relations, it is significant that Thucydides was the first to set forth the idea that the
dynamic of international relations is provided by the differential
growth of power among states. This fundamental idea—that the
uneven growth of power among states is the driving force of
international relations—can be identified as the theory of hegemonic war.

This essay argues that Thucydides' theory of hegemonic war
constitutes one of the central organizing ideas for the study of
international relations. The following pages examine and evaluate
Thucydides' theory of hegemonic war and contemporary variations of that theory. To carry out this task, it is necessary to make
Thucydides' ideas more systematic, expose his basic assumptions,
and understand his analytical method. Subsequently, this article

Robert Gilpin is Eisenhower Professor of International Affairs at Princeton University.
He is the author of *The Political Economy of International Relations* (Princeton, 1987).

1   Thucydides (trans. John H. Finley, Jr.), *The Peloponnesian War* (New York, 1951), 14–
15.

discusses whether or not Thucydides' conception of international relations has proved to be a "possession for all time." Does it help explain wars in the modern era? How, if at all, has it been modified by more modern scholarship? What is its relevance for the contemporary nuclear age?

THUCYDIDES' THEORY OF HEGEMONIC WAR   The essential idea embodied in Thucydides' theory of hegemonic war is that fundamental changes in the international system are the basic determinants of such wars. The structure of the system or distribution of power among the states in the system can be stable or unstable. A stable system is one in which changes can take place if they do not threaten the vital interests of the dominant states and thereby cause a war among them. In his view, such a stable system has an unequivocal hierarchy of power and an unchallenged dominant or hegemonic power. An unstable system is one in which economic, technological, and other changes are eroding the international hierarchy and undermining the position of the hegemonic state. In this latter situation, untoward events and diplomatic crises can precipitate a hegemonic war among the states in the system. The outcome of such a war is a new international structure.

Three propositions are embedded in this brief summary of the theory. The first is that a hegemonic war is distinct from other categories of war; it is caused by broad changes in political, strategic, and economic affairs. The second is that the relations among individual states can be conceived as a system; the behavior of states is determined in large part by their strategic interaction. The third is that a hegemonic war threatens and transforms the structure of the international system; whether or not the participants in the conflict are initially aware of it, at stake is the hierarchy of power and relations among states in the system. Thucydides' conception and all subsequent formulations of the theory of hegemonic war emerge from these three propositions.

Such a structural theory of war can be contrasted with an escalation theory of war. According to this latter theory, as Waltz has argued in *Man, the State, and War*, war occurs because of the simple fact that there is nothing to stop it.[2] In the anarchy of the

2 Kenneth N. Waltz, *Man, the State, and War: A Theoretical Analysis* (New York, 1959).

international system, statesmen make decisions and respond to the decisions of others. This action-reaction process in time can lead to situations in which statesmen deliberately provoke a war or lose control over events and eventually find themselves propelled into a war. In effect, one thing leads to another until war is the consequence of the interplay of foreign policies.

Most wars are the consequence of such an escalatory process. They are not causally related to structural features of the international system, but rather are due to the distrust and uncertainty that characterizes relations among states in what Waltz has called a self-help system.[3] Thus, the history of ancient times, which introduces Thucydides' history, is a tale of constant warring. However, the Peloponnesian War, he tells us, is different and worthy of special attention because of the massive accumulation of power in Hellas and its implications for the structure of the system. This great war and its underlying causes were the focus of his history.

Obviously, these two theories do not necessarily contradict one another; each can be used to explain different wars. But what interested Thucydides was a particular type of war, what he called a great war and what this article calls a hegemonic war—a war in which the overall structure of an international system is at issue. The structure of the international system at the outbreak of such a war is a necessary, but not a sufficient cause of the war. The theory of hegemonic war and international change that is examined below refers to those wars that arise from the specific structure of an international system and in turn transform that structure.

Assumptions of the Theory   Underlying Thucydides' view that he had discovered the basic mechanism of a great or hegemonic war was his conception of human nature. He believed that human nature was unchanging and therefore the events recounted in his history would be repeated in the future. Since human beings are driven by three fundamental passions—interest, pride, and, above all else, fear—they always seek to increase their wealth and power until other humans, driven by like passions, try to stop them. Although advances in political knowledge could contribute to an understanding of this process, they could not control or

3   *Idem, Theory of International Relations* (Reading, Mass., 1979).

arrest it. Even advances in knowledge, technology, or economic development would not change the fundamental nature of human behavior or of international relations. On the contrary, increases in human power, wealth, and technology would serve only to intensify conflict among social groups and enhance the magnitude of war. Thucydides the realist, in contrast to Plato the idealist, believed that reason would not transform human beings, but would always remain the slave of human passions. Thus, uncontrollable passions would again and again generate great conflicts like the one witnessed in his history.

Methodology One can understand Thucydides' argument and his belief that he had uncovered the underlying dynamics of international relations and the role of hegemonic war in international change only if one comprehends his conception of science and his view of what constituted explanation. Modern students of international relations and of social science tend to put forth theoretical physics as their model of analysis and explanation; they analyze phenomena in terms of causation and of models linking independent and dependent variables. In modern physics, meaningful propositions must, at least in principle, be falsifiable— that is, they must give rise to predictions that can be shown to be false.

Thucydides, by contrast, took as his model of analysis and explanation the method of Hippocrates, the great Greek physician.[4] Disease, the Hippocratic school argued, had to be understood as a consequence of the operation of natural forces and not as a manifestation of some supernatural influence. Through dispassionate observation of the symptoms and the course of a disease, one could understand its nature. Thus, one explained a disease by recognizing its characteristics and charting its development from its genesis through inevitable periods of crisis to its final resolution in recovery or death. What was central to this mode of explanation was the evolution of the symptoms and the manifestations of the disease rather than the search for the underlying causes sought by modern medicine.

Thucydides wrote his history to fulfill the same prognostic purpose, namely, to recognize that great wars were recurrent phenomena with characteristic manifestations. A great or hege-

4 W. Robert Connor, *Thucydides* (Princeton, 1984), 27.

monic war, like a disease, displays discernible symptoms and follows an inevitable course. The initial phase is a relatively stable international system characterized by a hierarchical ordering of the states in the system. Over time the power of a subordinate state begins to grow disproportionately, and that rising state comes into conflict with the dominant or hegemonic state in the system. The ensuing struggle between these two states and their respective allies leads to a bipolarization of the system, to an inevitable crisis, and eventually to a hegemonic war. Finally, there is the resolution of the war in favor of one side and the establishment of a new international system that reflects the emergent distribution of power in the system.

The dialectical conception of political change implicit in his model was borrowed from contemporary Sophist thinkers. This method of analysis postulated a thesis, its contradiction or antithesis, and a resolution in the form of a synthesis. In his history this dialectic approach can be discerned as follows:

(1) The *thesis* is the hegemonic state, in this case, Sparta, which organizes the international system in terms of its political, economic, and strategic interests.

(2) The *antithesis* or contradiction in the system is the growing power of the challenging state, Athens, whose expansion and efforts to transform the international system bring it into conflict with the hegemonic state.

(3) The *synthesis* is the new international system that results from the inevitable clash between the dominant state and the rising challenger.

Similarly, Thucydides foresaw that throughout history new states like Sparta and challenging states like Athens would arise and the hegemonic cycle would repeat itself.

Conception of Systemic Change   Underlying this analysis and the originality of Thucydides' thought was his novel conception of classical Greece as constituting a system, the basic components of which were the great powers—Sparta and Athens. Foreshadowing later realist formulations of international relations, he believed that the structure of the system was provided by the distribution of power among states; the hierarchy of power among these states defined and maintained the system and determined the relative prestige of states, their spheres of influence, and their political relations. The hierarchy of power and related elements thus gave order and stability to the system.

Accordingly, international political change involved a transformation of the hierarchy of the states in the system and the patterns of relations dependent upon that hierarchy. Although minor changes could occur and lesser states could move up and down this hierarchy without necessarily disturbing the stability of the system, the positioning of the great powers was crucial. Thus, as he tells us, it was the increasing power of the second most powerful state in the system, Athens, that precipitated the conflict and brought about what I have elsewhere called systemic change, that is, a change in the hierarchy or control of the international political system.[5]

Searching behind appearances for the reality of international relations, Thucydides believed that he had found the true causes of the Peloponnesian War, and by implication of systemic change, in the phenomenon of the uneven growth of power among the dominant states in the system. "The real cause," he concluded in the first chapter, "I consider to be the one which was formally most kept out of sight. The growth of the power of Athens, and the alarm which this inspired in Lacedaemon [Sparta], made war inevitable."[6] In a like fashion and in future ages, he reasoned, the differential growth of power in a state system would undermine the status quo and lead to hegemonic war between declining and rising powers.

In summary, according to Thucydides, a great or hegemonic war, like a disease, follows a discernible and recurrent course. The initial phase is a relatively stable international system characterized by a hierarchical ordering of states with a dominant or hegemonic power. Over time, the power of one subordinate state begins to grow disproportionately; as this development occurs, it comes into conflict with the hegemonic state. The struggle between these contenders for preeminence and their accumulating alliances leads to a bipolarization of the system. In the parlance of game theory, the system becomes a zero-sum situation in which one side's gain is by necessity the other side's loss. As this bipolarization occurs the system becomes increasingly unstable, and a

5 Robert Gilpin, *War and Change in World Politics* (New York, 1981), 40.
6 Thucydides, *Peloponnesian War*, 15.

small event can trigger a crisis and precipitate a major conflict; the resolution of that conflict will determine the new hegemon and the hierarchy of power in the system.

The Causes of Hegemonic War   Following this model, Thucydides began his history of the war between the Spartans and the Athenians by stating why, at its very inception, he believed that the war would be a great war and thus worthy of special attention. Contrasting the beginnings of the Peloponnesian War to the constant warring of the Greeks, he began in the introduction to analyze the unprecedented growth of power in Hellas from ancient times to the outbreak of the war. Although, as we have already noted, Thucydides did not think of causes in the modern or scientific sense of the term, his analysis of the factors that altered the distribution of power in ancient Greece, and ultimately accounted for the war, is remarkably modern.

The first set of factors to explain the rise of power in Athens and the expansion of the Athenian empire contained geographical and demographic elements. Because of the poverty of its soil, Attica (the region surrounding Athens) was not envied by any other peoples; it enjoyed freedom from conflict. As a consequence, "the most powerful victims of war or faction from the rest of Hellas took refuge with the Athenians as a safe retreat," became naturalized, and swelled the population.[7] With an increase in population Attica became too small to sustain its growing numbers, and Athens began to send out colonies to other parts of Greece. Athens itself turned to commerce to feed her expanding population and became the "workshop of ancient Greece," exporting manufactured products and commodities in exchange for grain. Thus, Athens began its imperial career from demographic pressure and economic necessity.

The second set of influences was economic and technological: the Greek, and especially the Athenian, mastery of naval power, which had facilitated the expansion of commerce among the Greek states and the establishment of the hegemony of Hellas in the Eastern Mediterranean. After the defeat of Troy, Thucydides tells us, Hellas attained "the quiet which must precede growth" as the Greeks turned to commerce and the acquisition of wealth. Although Athens and other seafaring cities grew "in revenue and in dominion," there was no great concentration of power in Hellas prior to the war with Persia: "There was no union of subject cities round a great state, no spontaneous combination of equals for confederate expeditions; what fighting there was consisted merely of local warfare between rival neighbours."[8] The technical innovation of naval power, the introduction into Greece of fortification techniques, and the rise of financial power associated with commerce, however, made possible an unprecedented concentration of military and economic power. These developments, by transforming the basis of military power, created the conditions for the forging of substantial alliances, a profound shift in the power balance, and the creation of large seaborne empires. In this novel environment, states interacted more intimately, and an interdependent international economic and political system took shape. These military, technological, and economic changes were to favor the growth of Athenian power.

The final factor leading to the war was political: the rise of the Athenian empire at the conclusion of the war with Persia. That war and its aftermath stimulated the growth of Athenian power at the same time that the war and its aftermath encouraged Sparta, the reigning hegemon and the leader of the Greeks in their war against the Persians, to retreat into isolation. With the rise of a wealthy commercial class in Athens, the traditional form of government—a hereditary monarchy—was overthrown, and a new governing elite representing the rising and enterprising commercial class was established; its interest lay with commerce and imperial expansion. While the Athenians grew in power through commerce and empire, the Spartans fell behind and found themselves increasingly encircled by the expanding power of the Athenians.

As a consequence of these developments, the Greeks anticipated the approach of a great war and began to choose sides. In time, the international system divided into two great blocs. "At the head of the one stood Athens, at the head of the other Lacedaemon, one the first naval, the other the first military power in Hellas."[9] The former—commercial, democratic, and expansionist—began to evoke alarm in the more conservative Spartans. In

8   *Ibid.*, 9, 11.
9   *Ibid.*, 12.

this increasingly bipolar and unstable world a series of diplomatic encounters, beginning at Epidamnus and culminating in the Megara Decree and the Spartan ultimatum, were to plunge the rival alliances into war. In order to prevent the dynamic and expanding Athenians from overturning the international balance of power and displacing them as the hegemonic state, the Spartans eventually delivered an ultimatum that forced Athens to declare war.

In brief, it was the combination of significant environmental changes and the contrasting natures of the Athenian and Spartan societies that precipitated the war. Although the underlying causes of the war can be traced to geographical, economic, and technological factors, the major determinant of the foreign policies of the two protagonists was the differing character of their domestic regimes. Athens was a democracy; its people were energetic, daring, and commercially disposed; its naval power, financial resources, and empire were expanding. Sparta, the traditional hegemon of the Hellenes, was a slavocracy; its foreign policy was conservative and attentive merely to the narrow interests of preserving its domestic status quo. Having little interest in commerce or overseas empire, it gradually declined relative to its rival. In future ages, in Thucydides' judgment, situations similar to that of Athens and Sparta would arise, and this fateful process would repeat itself eternally.

THE CONTRIBUTION OF THUCYDIDES' MODEL   Thucydides' history and the pattern that it reveals have fascinated students of international relations in all eras. Individuals of every political persuasion from realist to idealist to Marxist have claimed kinship to him. At critical moments scholars and statesmen have seen their own times reflected in his account of the conflict between democratic Athens and undemocratic Sparta. The American Civil War, World War I, and the Cold War between the United States and the Soviet Union have been cast in its light. In a similar vein, Mackinder and other political geographers have interpreted world history as the recurrent struggle between landpower (Sparta, Rome, and Great Britain) and seapower (Athens, Carthage, and Germany) and have observed that a great or hegemonic war has taken place and transformed world affairs approximately every 100 years. The writings of Wright and Toynbee on general war are cast in a similar vein. The Marxist theory of intra-capitalist wars can be viewed as a subcategory of Thucydides' more general theory. More recently, a number of social scientists have revived the concept of hegemonic war. The "power transition theory" of Organski, Modelski's theory of long cycles and global war, and the present writer's book on international change are examples of elaborations of Thucydides' fundamental insights into the dynamics of international relations.[10] Although these variations and extensions of Thucydides' basic model raise many interesting issues, they are too numerous and complex to be discussed here. Instead, the emphasis will be on the contribution of Thucydides' theory, its applicability to modern history, and its continuing relevance for international relations.

The theory's fundamental contribution is the conception of hegemonic war itself and the importance of hegemonic wars for the dynamics of international relations. The expression hegemonic war may have been coined by Aron; certainly he has provided an excellent definition of what Thucydides called a great war. Describing World War I as a hegemonic war, Aron writes that such a war "is characterized less by its immediate causes or its explicit purposes than by its extent and the stakes involved. It affect[s] all the political units inside one system of relations between sovereign states. Let us call it, for want of a better term, a war of hegemony, hegemony being, if not the conscious motive, at any rate the inevitable consequence of the victory of at least one of the states or groups." Thus, the outcome of a hegemonic war, according to Aron, is the transformation of the structure of the system of interstate relations.[11]

In more precise terms, one can distinguish a hegemonic war in terms of its scale, the objectives at stake, and the means employed to achieve those objectives. A hegemonic war generally involves all of the states in the system; it is a world war. Whatever

10 Halford J. Mackinder, "The Geographical Pivot of History," in Anthony J. Pearce (ed.), *Democratic Ideals and Reality* (New York, 1962), 1–2; Quincy Wright, *A Study of War* (Chicago, 1942); Arnold J. Toynbee, *A Study of History* (London, 1961), III, IV; Vladimir Ilyich Lenin, *Imperialism: The Highest Stage of Capitalism* (New York, 1939). See, for example, A. F. K. Organski, *World Politics* (New York, 1968; 2nd ed.); Organski and Jacek Kugler, *The War Ledger* (Chicago, 1980); George Modelski (ed.), *Exploring Long Cycles* (Boulder, 1987); Gilpin, *War and Change*.
11 Raymond Aron, "War and Industrial Society," in Leon Bramson and George W. Goethals (eds.), *War—Studies from Psychology, Sociology, Anthropology* (New York, 1964), 359.

the immediate and conscious motives of the combatants, as Aron points out, the fundamental issues to be decided are the leadership and structure of the international system. Its outcome also profoundly affects the internal composition of societies because, as the behavior of Athens and Sparta revealed, the victor remolds the vanquished in its image. Such wars are at once political, economic, and ideological struggles. Because of the scope of the war and the importance of the issues to be decided, the means employed are usually unlimited. In Clausewitzian terms, they become pure conflicts or clashes of society rather than the pursuit of limited policy objectives.

Thus, in the Peloponnesian War the whole of Hellas became engaged in an internecine struggle to determine the economic and political future of the Greek world. Although the initial objectives of the two alliances were limited, the basic issue in the contest became the structure and leadership of the emerging international system and not merely the fate of particular city-states. Ideological disputes, that is, conflicting views over the organization of domestic societies, were also at the heart of the struggle; democratic Athens and aristocratic Sparta sought to reorder other societies in terms of their own political values and socioeconomic systems. As Thucydides tells us in his description of the leveling and decimation of Melos, there were no constraints on the means employed to reach their goals. The war released forces of which the protagonists had previously been unaware; it took a totally unanticipated course. As the Athenians had warned the Spartans in counseling them against war, "consider the vast influence of accident in war, before you are engaged in it."[12] Furthermore, neither rival anticipated that the war would leave both sides exhausted and thereby open the way to Macedonian imperialism.

The central idea embodied in the hegemonic theory is that there is incompatibility between crucial elements of the existing international system and the changing distribution of power among the states within the system. The elements of the system— the hierarchy of prestige, the division of territory, and the international economy—became less and less compatible with the shifting distribution of power among the major states in the system. The resolution of the disequilibrium between the super-

12 Thucydides, *Peloponnesian War*, 45.

structure of the system and the underlying distribution of power is found in the outbreak and intensification of what becomes a hegemonic war.

The theory does not necessarily concern itself with whether the declining or rising state is responsible for the war. In fact, identification of the initiator of a particular war is frequently impossible to ascertain and authorities seldom agree. When did the war actually begin? What actions precipitated it? Who committed the first hostile act? In the case of the Peloponnesian War, for example, historians differ over whether Athens or Sparta initiated the war. Whereas most regard the Megara decree issued by Athens as the precipitating cause of the war, one can just as easily argue that the decree was the first act of a war already begun by Sparta and its allies.

Nor does the theory address the question of the explicit consequences of the war. Both the declining and rising protagonists may suffer and a third party may be the ultimate victor. Frequently, the chief beneficiary is, in fact, a rising peripheral power not directly engaged in the conflict. In the case of the Peloponnesian War, the war paved the way for Macedonian imperialism to triumph over the Greeks. In brief, the theory makes no prediction regarding the consequences of the war. What the theory postulates instead is that the system is ripe for a fundamental transformation because of profound ongoing changes in the international distribution of power and the larger economic and technological environment. This is not to suggest that the historic change produced by the war must be in some sense progressive; it may, as happened in the Peloponnesian War, weaken and eventually bring an end to one of mankind's most glorious civilizations.

Underlying the outbreak of a hegemonic war is the idea that the basis of power and social order is undergoing a fundamental transformation. Halévy must have had something like this conception of political change in mind when, in analyzing the causes of World War I, he wrote that "it is thus apparent why all great convulsions in the history of the world, and more particularly in modern Europe, have been at the same time wars and revolutions. The Thirty Years' War was at once a revolutionary crisis, a conflict, within Germany, between the rival parties of Protestants and Catholics, and an international war between the Holy Roman

THEORY OF HEGEMONIC WAR | 27

Empire, Sweden, and France."[13] Similarly, Halévy continues, the wars of the French Revolution and Napoleon as well as World War I must be seen as upheavals of the whole European social and political order.

The profound changes in political relations, economic organization, and military technology behind hegemonic war and the associated domestic upheavals undermine both the international and domestic status quo. These underlying transformations in power and social relations result in shifts in the nature and locus of power. They give rise to a search for a new basis of political and social order at both the domestic and international levels.

This conception of a hegemonic war as associated with a historic turning point in world history is exemplified by the Peloponnesian War. A basic change in the nature and hence in the location of economic and military power was taking place in Greece during the fifth century B.C. This changing economic and technological environment had differing implications for the fortunes of the two major protagonists. The Peloponnesian War would be the midwife for the birth of the new world. This great war, like other transforming wars, would embody significant long-term changes in Greece's economy, military affairs, and political organization.

Prior to and during the Persian wars, power and wealth in the Greek world were based on agriculture and land armies; Sparta was ascendant among the Greek city-states. Its political position had a secure economic foundation, and its military power was unchallenged. The growth in the importance of naval power and the accompanying rise of commerce following the wars transformed the basis of power. Moreover, the introduction into Greece of fortification technology and the erection of walls around Athens canceled much of the Spartan military advantage. In this new environment, naval power, commerce, and finance became increasingly important components of state power. Thus, whereas in the past the nature of power had favored the Spartans, the transformed environment favored Athens and other rising commercial and naval powers.

Athens rather than Sparta benefited from this new military and economic environment. Domestically, Athens had experi-

13 Eli Halévy (trans. R. G. Webb), *The Era of Tyrannies* (Garden City, N.Y., 1965), 212.

enced political and social changes that enabled it to take advantage of the increased importance of seapower and commerce. Its entrenched landed aristocracy, which had been associated with the former dominance of agriculture and land armies, had been overthrown and replaced by a commercial elite whose interests lay with the development of naval power and imperial expansion. In an increasingly monetarized international economy, the Athenians had the financial resources to outfit a powerful navy and expand its dominion at the expense of the Spartans.

By contrast, the Spartans, largely for domestic economic and political reasons, were unable or unwilling to make the necessary adjustment to the new economic and technological environment. It was not merely because Sparta was land-locked, but also because the dominant interests of the society were committed to the maintenance of an agricultural system based on slave labor. Their foremost concern was to forestall a slave revolt, and they feared external influences that would stimulate the Helots to rebel. Such a rebellion had forced them to revert into isolation at the end of the Persian wars. It appears to have been the fear of another revolt that caused them eventually to challenge the Athenians. The Megara decree aroused the Spartans because the potential return of Megara to Athenian control would have opened up the Peloponnesus to Athenian influence and thereby enabled the Athenians to assist a Helot revolt. Thus, when Athenian expansionism threatened a vital interest of the Spartans, the latter decided that war was inevitable, and delivered an ultimatum to the Athenians.[14]

The differing abilities of the Athenians and the Spartans to adjust to the new economic and technological environment and the changed nature of power ultimately led to the war. The development of naval power and acquisition of the financial resources to purchase ships and hire sailors necessitated a profound reordering of domestic society. Whereas the Athenians had reformed themselves in order to take advantage of new opportunities for wealth and power, the Spartans would or could not liberalize due to a constellation of domestic interests and their fear of unleashing a rebellion of the Helots. The result was the uneven growth of power among these rivals that Thucydides viewed as the real cause of the war.

14   G. E. M. de Ste. Croix, *The Origins of the Peloponnesian War* (London, 1972).

The critical point arrived when the Spartans began to believe that time was moving against them and in favor of the Athenians. A tipping-point or fundamental change in the Spartan perception of the balance of power had taken place. As certain contemporary historians assert, Athenian power may have reached its zenith by the outbreak of the war and had already begun to wane, but the reality of the situation is not particularly relevant, since the Spartans believed that Athens was growing stronger. The decision facing them had become when to commence the war rather than whether to commence it. Was it better to fight while the advantage still lay with them or at some future date when the advantage might have turned? As Howard has written, similar perceptions and fears of eroding power have preceded history's other hegemonic wars.[15]

The stability of the Greek international system following the Persian wars was based on an economic and technological environment favoring Spartan hegemony. When agriculture and land armies became less vital to state power and commerce and navies became more important, the Spartans were unable to adjust. Therefore, the locus of wealth and power shifted to the Athenians. Although the Athenians lost the war when they failed to heed the prudent strategy laid down by Pericles, the basic point is not altered; the war for hegemony in Greece emerged from a profound social, economic, and technological revolution. Wars like this one are not merely contests between rival states but political watersheds that mark transitions from one historical epoch to the next.

Despite the insight that it provides in understanding and explaining the great wars of history, the theory of hegemonic war is a limited and incomplete theory. It cannot easily handle perceptions that affect behavior and predict who will initiate a hegemonic war. Nor can it forecast when a hegemonic war will occur and what the consequences will be. As in the case of the theory of biological evolution, it helps one understand and explain what has happened; but neither theory can make predictions that can be tested and thereby meet rigorous scientific standard of falsifiability. The theory of hegemonic war at best is a complement to other theories such as those of cognitive psychology and

Michael Howard, *The Causes of War* (Cambridge, Mass., 1983), 16.

expected utility and must be integrated with them. It has, however, withstood the test of time better than any other generalization in the field of international relations and remains an important conceptual tool for understanding the dynamics of world politics.

HEGEMONIC WAR IN THE MODERN INTERNATIONAL SYSTEM   In the modern world, three hegemonic wars have successively transformed the international system. Each of these great struggles not only involved a contest for supremacy of two or more great powers, but also represented significant changes in economic relations, technological capacities, and political organization. The war arose from profound historical changes and the basic incongruity between new environmental forces and existing structures. Each was a world war involving almost all of the states in the system and, at least in retrospect, can be considered as having constituted a major turning point in human history. These long and intense conflicts altered the fundamental contours of both domestic societies and international relations.[16]

The first of the modern hegemonic wars was the Thirty Years' War (1619 to 1648). Although this war may be regarded as a series of separate wars that at various times involved Sweden, France, Spain, Poland, and other powers, in sum it involved all the major states of Europe. As Gutmann points out in his contribution to this volume, the origins of the war were deeply embedded in the history of the previous century.[17] At issue was the organization of the European state system as well as the internal economic and religious organization of domestic societies. Was Europe to be dominated and organized by Habsburg imperial power or autonomous nation-states? Was feudalism or commercial capitalism to be the dominant mode of organizing economic activities? Was Protestantism or Catholicism to be the prevalent religion? The clash over these political, economic, and ideological issues caused physical devastation and loss of life not seen in Western Europe since the Mongol invasions of earlier centuries.

---

16 Summary accounts of the wars and their backgrounds are contained in R. Ernest Dupuy and Trevor N. Dupuy, *The Encyclopedia of Military History from 3500 B.C. to the Present* (New York, 1984; 2nd rev. ed.), 522–546, 730–769, 915–990.
17 Myron P. Gutmann, "The Origins of the Thirty Years' War," *Journal of Interdisciplinary History*, XVIII (1988), 749–770.

Underlying the intensity and duration of the war was a profound change in the nature of power. Although the power of a state continued to be based primarily on the control of territory, technology and organization were becoming more important in military and political affairs. From classical times to the seventeenth century, military technology, tactics, and organization had hardly changed; the pike, the Greek phalanx, and heavy cavalry continued to characterize warfare. By the close of that century, however, mobile artillery, professional infantry in linear formations, and naval innovations had come to dominate the tactics of war. In conjunction with what has been called the Military Revolution, the modern bureaucratic state also came into existence. This development greatly enhanced the ability of rulers to mobilize and increase the efficient use of national resources. With these military and political innovations, the exercise of military power became an instrument of foreign policy; war was no longer "the [unrestrained] clash of societies" that was characteristic of warfare in the ancient and medieval worlds.[18]

The Thirty Years' War transformed the domestic and international political scene. The Habsburg bid for universal empire was defeated, and the nation-state became the dominant form of political organization in the modern world. In the Treaty of Westphalia (1648), the principle of national sovereignty and non-intervention was established as the governing norm of international relations; this political innovation ended the ideological conflict over the religious ordering of domestic societies. For the next century and a half, foreign policy was based on the concepts of national interest and the balance of power; as a result, the scale of European wars tended to be limited. The commercial revolution triumphed over feudalism, and the pluralistic European state system provided the necessary framework for the expansion of the global market system.[19] With their superior armaments and organization, the several states of Western Europe created overseas empires and subdued the other civilizations of the globe.

In the closing decade of the eighteenth century, a second great war or series of wars once again transformed international

18 Howard, *Causes*, 16; Michael Roberts, *The Military Revolution, 1560–1660* (Belfast, 1956); George Clark, *War and Society in the Seventeenth Century* (Cambridge, 1958).
19 Jean Baechler (trans. Barry Cooper), *The Origins of Capitalism* (Oxford, 1975), 73–86.

affairs and ushered in a new historical epoch. For nearly a century France and Great Britain, operating within the framework of the classical balance of power system, had been fighting a series of limited conflicts both in Europe and overseas to establish the primacy of one or the other. This "hundred years' war," to use Seeley's expression, culminated in the great or hegemonic wars of the French Revolution and Napoleon Bonaparte (1792 to 1815).[20] As in other hegemonic conflicts, profound political, economic, and ideological issues were joined: French or British hegemony of the European political system, mercantilistic or market principles as the organizing basis of the world economy, and revolutionary republicanism or more conservative political forms as the basis of domestic society. The ensuing conflagration engulfed the entire international political system, resulting in unprecedented violence and the opening of a new age of economic and political affairs.

During the second half of the eighteenth and the first decade of the nineteenth century, economic, technological, and other developments had transformed the nature of power and undermined the relative stability of the previous system of limited warfare. At sea the British had gained mastery of the new tactics and technology of naval power. On land the military genius of Napoleon brought to a culmination the revolution wrought by gunpowder as the new weaponry, tactics, and doctrine were integrated. The most significant innovations, however, were organizational, political, and sociological. The conception of the levée en masse and the nation at arms made it possible for the French to field mass armies and overwhelm their enemies. Under the banner of nationalism the era of peoples' wars had arrived. The new means of military organization had transformed the nature of European warfare.[21]

After twenty years of global warfare extending to the New World and the Middle East, the British and their allies defeated the French, and a new international order was established by the Treaty of Vienna (1815). On the continent of Europe, an equilib-

20 John R. Seeley, *The Expansion of England: Two Courses of Lectures* (Boston, 1905), 28–29.
21 See Gunther G. Rothenberg, "The Origins, Causes, and Extension of the Wars of the French Revolution and Napoleon," *Journal of Interdisciplinary History*, XVIII (1988), 771–793.

rium was created that was to last until the unification of German power in the middle of the century. British interests and naval power guaranteed that the principles of the market and laissez faire would govern global economic affairs. Underneath the surface of this Pax Britannica, new forces began to stir and gather strength as the decades passed. Following a century of relative peace, these changes in the economic, political, and technological environment would break forth in the modern world's third hegemonic war.

Like many other great wars, World War I commenced as a seemingly minor affair, even though its eventual scale and consequences were beyond the comprehension of contemporary statesmen. In a matter of a few weeks, the several bilateral conflicts of the European states and the cross-cutting alliances joined the Europeans in a global struggle of horrendous dimensions. The British-German naval race, the French-German conflict over Alsace-Lorraine, and the German/Austrian-Russian rivalry in the Balkans drew almost all of the European states into the struggle that would determine the structure and leadership of the European and eventually of the global political system.

The scope, intensity, and duration of the war reflected the culmination of strengthening forces and novel forms of national power. The French under Napoleon had first unleashed the new religion of nationalism. During the ensuing decades of relative peace, the spread of nationalistic ideas tore at the traditional fabric of European society, undermined stable political structures, and set one people against another. The Industrial Revolution also had diffused from Great Britain to the Continent. War had become industrialized and fused with the passion of nationalism. An era of rapid economic change and social upheaval had also given rise to radical movements threatening revolution and challenging the domestic status quo of many states.[22] In this new environment of industrialized and nationalistic warfare, the political leaders lost control over the masses, and war reverted to what it had been in the premodern era: an unrestrained clash of societies. Nations threw men and machinery at one another causing massive carnage and social dislocations from which Europe found it difficult to

22 Robert E. Osgood and Robert W. Tucker, *Force, Order, and Justice* (Baltimore, 1967), 3–192; Halévy, *Era*, 209–247.

recover. Only mutual exhaustion and the intervention of a non-European power—the United States—ended the destruction of total war.

The terrible devastation of the war brought to a close the European domination of world politics and resulted in a new attitude toward war. The democratization and industrialization of war had undermined the legitimacy of military force as a normal and legitimate instrument of foreign policy. In the Treaty of Versailles (1919), statesmen outlawed war, and the revolutionary concept of collective security was embodied in the charter of the League of Nations. States for the first time were legally forbidden to engage in war except in self-defense and were required to join together in the punishment of any aggressor. In contrast to the other great peace conferences and treaties of European diplomacy the settlement failed to reflect the new realities of the balance of power and thereby was unable to establish a new and stable European political order.[23] This failure laid the foundation for World War II, which should be seen as the continuation of the hegemonic struggle begun in 1914 with the breakdown of the European political order.

The postwar international order has been based on American-Soviet bipolarity and the concept of mutual deterrence. Peace has been maintained and war as a means of settling conflicts between the superpowers has been stayed by the nuclear threat and the possibility of mutual annihilation. Whether or not this sytem will also one day be undermined by historical developments and utterly destroyed by a hegemonic war fought with weapons of mass destruction is the fundamental question of our time.

THE NUCLEAR REVOLUTION AND HEGEMONIC WAR   Although the theory of hegemonic war may be helpful in understanding the past, one must ask whether it is relevant to the contemporary world. Has it been superseded or somehow transcended by the nuclear revolution in warfare? Since no nation that enters a nuclear war can avoid its own destruction, does it make any sense to think in terms of great or hegemonic wars? Morgenthau was referring to this profound change in the nature of warfare and its political significance when he wrote that the "rational relationship

23   Howard, *Causes*, 163.

between violence as a means of foreign policy and the ends of foreign policy has been destroyed by the possibility of all-out nuclear war."[24]

That a revolution in the nature of warfare has occurred cannot be denied. Nuclear weapons have indeed profoundly transformed the destructiveness and consequences of a great war. It is highly doubtful that a war between two nuclear powers could be limited and escalation into a full-scale war prevented. Nor is it likely that either protagonist could escape the terrible devastation of such a great war or find the consequences in any sense acceptable.[25] In the nuclear age, the primary purpose of nuclear forces should be to deter the use of nuclear weapons by one's opponent and thereby prevent the outbreak of hegemonic warfare.

It does not necessarily follow that this change in the nature of warfare, as important as it surely is, has also changed the nature of international relations. The fundamental characteristics of international affairs unfortunately have not been altered and, if anything, have been intensified by the nuclear revolution. International politics continues to be a self-help system. In the contemporary anarchy of international relations, distrust, uncertainty, and insecurity have caused states to arm themselves and to prepare for war as never before.

To be able to say that nuclear weapons have changed the nature of international relations and thus made impossible the outbreak of hegemonic war, a transformation of human consciousness itself would have to take place. Humankind would have to be willing to subordinate all other values and goals to the preservation of peace. To insure mutual survival, it would need to reject the anarchy of international relations and submit itself to the Leviathan of Thomas Hobbes. Little evidence exists to suggest that any nation is close to making this choice. Certainly in this world of unprecedented armaments of all types, no state is behaving as if nuclear weapons had changed its overall set of national priorities.

One cannot even rule out the possibility of a great or hegemonic war in the nuclear age. The theory of hegemonic war does

---

24 Hans J. Morgenthau in idem, Sidney Hook, H. Stuart Hughes, and Charles P. Snow, "Western Values and Total War," Commentary, XXXII (1961), 280.
25 Robert Jervis, The Illogic of American Nuclear Strategy (Ithaca, 1984), 19–46.

not argue that statesmen "will" a great war; the great wars of history were seldom predicted, and their course has never been foreseen. As Thucydides argued in his discussion of the role of accident in war, once it has begun, war unleashes forces that are totally unanticipated by the protagonists. In the nuclear age there is no guarantee that a minor conflict between the superpowers or their allies will not set in motion untoward developments over which they would soon lose control. In brief, the fact that nuclear war would wreak unprecedented devastation on mankind has not prevented the world's nuclear powers from preparing for such a war, perhaps thereby making it more likely.

What nuclear weapons have accomplished is to elevate the avoidance of a total war to the highest level of foreign policy and the central concern of statesmen. Yet this goal, as important as it surely is, has joined, not supplanted, other values and interests for which societies in the past have been willing to fight. All of the nuclear states seek to avoid nuclear war at the same time that they are attempting to safeguard more traditional interests. The result has been, for the superpowers at least, the creation of a new basis of international order. In contrast to the balance-of-power system of early modern Europe, the Pax Britannica of the nineteenth century, or the ill-fated collective security system associated with the League of Nations, order in the nuclear age has been built on the foundation of mutual deterrence.

The long-term stability of this nuclear order is of crucial importance, and the threat to its existence over time certainly cannot be disregarded. Each superpower fears that the other might achieve a significant technological breakthrough and seek to exploit it. How else can one explain the hopes and anxieties raised by the Strategic Defense Initiative? In addition, with the proliferation of nuclear weapons to more and more states, there is a growing danger that these weapons might fall into the hands of desperate states or terrorist groups. The nuclear order is a function of deliberate policies and not, as some argue, an existential condition.

Historically, nations have consciously decided to go to war, but they have seldom, if ever, knowingly begun hegemonic wars. Statesmen try to make rational or cost/benefit calculations concerning their efforts to achieve national objectives, and it seems unlikely that any statesman would view the eventual gains from the great wars of history as commensurate with the eventual costs of those wars. It cannot be overstressed that, once a war, however limited, begins, it can release powerful forces unforeseen by the instigators of the war. The results of the Peloponnesian War, which was to devastate classical Greece, were not anticipated by the great powers of the day. Nor were the effects of World War I, which ended the primacy of Europe over other civilizations, anticipated by European statesmen. In both cases, the war was triggered by the belief of each protagonist that it had no alternative but to fight while the advantage was still on its side. In neither case did the protagonists fight the war that they had wanted or expected.

The advent of nuclear weapons has not altered this fundamental condition. A nation still might start a war for fear that its relative strength will diminish with time, and an accident still might precipitate unprecedented devastation. It is not inconceivable that some state, perhaps an overpowered Israel, a frightened South Africa, or a declining superpower, might one day become so desperate that it resorts to nuclear blackmail in order to forestall its enemies. As in war itself, an accident during such a confrontation could unleash powerful and uncontrollable forces totally unanticipated by the protagonists. Although the potential violence and destructiveness of war have been changed by the advent of nuclear arms, there is unfortunately little to suggest that human nature has also been transformed.

CONCLUSION   One can hope that the fear of nuclear holocaust has chastened statesmen. Perhaps they have come to appreciate that a nuclear order based on mutual deterrence should be their highest priority. But against this expectation one must set the long history of human foibles and mankind's seeming inability to sustain peace for very long. Only time will tell whether the theory of hegemonic war holds true in the nuclear age. In the meanwhile, avoidance of a nuclear war has become imperative.

Kenneth N. Waltz

The Origins of War in Neorealist Theory   Like

most historians, many students of international politics have been skeptical about the possibility of creating a theory that might help one to understand and explain the international events that interest us. Thus Morgenthau, foremost among traditional realists, was fond of repeating Blaise Pascal's remark that "the history of the world would have been different had Cleopatra's nose been a bit shorter" and then asking "How do you systemize that?"[1] His appreciation of the role of the accidental and the occurrence of the unexpected in politics dampened his theoretical ambition.

The response of neorealists is that, although difficulties abound, some of the obstacles that seem most daunting lie in misapprehensions about theory. Theory obviously cannot explain the accidental or account for unexpected events; it deals in regularities and repetitions and is possible only if these can be identified. A further difficulty is found in the failure of realists to conceive of international politics as a distinct domain about which theories can be fashioned. Morgenthau, for example, insisted on "the autonomy of politics," but he failed to apply the concept to international politics. A theory is a depiction of the organization of a domain and of the connections among its parts. A theory indicates that some factors are more important than others and specifies relations among them. In reality, everything is related to everything else, and one domain cannot be separated from others. But theory isolates one realm from all others in order to deal with it intellectually. By defining the structure of international political

Kenneth N. Waltz is Ford Professor of Political Science at the University of California, Berkeley. He is the author of *The Spread of Nuclear Weapons* (London, 1981). He is currently the President of the American Political Science Association.

The author thanks David Schleicher, who was most helpful in the completion of this article.

1 Hans J. Morgenthau, "International Relations: Quantitative and Qualitative Approaches," in Norman D. Palmer (ed.), *A Design for International Relations Research: Scope, Theory, Methods, and Relevance* (Philadelphia, 1970), 78.

systems, neorealism establishes the autonomy of international politics and thus makes a theory about it possible.[2]

In developing a theory of international politics, neorealism retains the main tenets of *realpolitik*, but means and ends are viewed differently, as are causes and effects. Morgenthau, for example, thought of the "rational" statesman as ever striving to accumulate more and more power. He viewed power as an end in itself. Although he acknowledged that nations at times act out of considerations other than power, Morgenthau insisted that, when they do so, their actions are not "of a political nature."[3] In contrast, neorealism sees power as a possibly useful means, with states running risks if they have either too little or too much of it. Excessive weakness may invite an attack that greater strength would have dissuaded an adversary from launching. Excessive strength may prompt other states to increase their arms and pool their efforts against the dominant state. Because power is a possibly useful means, sensible statesmen try to have an appropriate amount of it. In crucial situations, however, the ultimate concern of states is not for power but for security. This revision is an important one.

An even more important revision is found in a shift of causal relations. The infinite materials of any realm can be organized in endlessly different ways. Realism thinks of causes as moving in only one direction, from the interactions of individuals and states to the outcomes that their acts and interactions produce. Morgenthau recognized that, when there is competition for scarce goods and no one to serve as arbiter, a struggle for power will ensue among the competitors and that consequently the struggle for power can be explained without reference to the evil born in men. The struggle for power arises simply because men want things, not because of the evil in their desires. He labeled man's desire for scarce goods as one of the two roots of conflict, but, even while discussing it, he seemed to pull toward the "other root

2 Morgenthau, *Politics among Nations* (New York, 1973; 5th ed.), 11. Ludwig Boltzman (trans. Rudolf Weingartner), "Theories as Representations," excerpted in Arthur Danto and Sidney Morgenbesser (eds.), *Philosophy of Science* (Cleveland, 1960), 245–252. Neorealism is sometimes dubbed structural realism. I use the terms interchangeably and, throughout this article, refer to my own formulation of neorealist theory. See Waltz, *Theory of International Politics* (Reading, Mass., 1979); Robert Keohane (ed.), *Neorealism and its Critics* (New York, 1986).

3 Morgenthau, *Politics among Nations*, 27.

of conflict and concomitant evil"—"the *animus dominandi*, the desire for power." He often considered that man's drive for power is more basic than the chance conditions under which struggles for power occur. This attitude is seen in his statement that "in a world where power counts, no nation pursuing a rational policy has a choice between renouncing and wanting power; *and, if it could*, the lust for power for the individual's sake would still confront us with its less spectacular yet no less pressing moral defects."[4]

Students of international politics have typically inferred outcomes from salient attributes of the actors producing them. Thus Marxists, like liberals, have linked the outbreak of war or the prevalence of peace to the internal qualities of states. Governmental forms, economic systems, social institutions, political ideologies—these are but a few examples of where the causes of war have been found. Yet, although causes are specifically assigned, we know that states with widely divergent economic institutions, social customs, and political ideologies have all fought wars. More striking still, many different sorts of organizations fight wars, whether those organizations be tribes, petty principalities, empires, nations, or street gangs. If an identified condition seems to have caused a given war, one must wonder why wars occur repeatedly even though their causes vary. Variations in the characteristics of the states are not linked directly to the outcomes that their behaviors produce, nor are variations in their patterns of interaction. Many historians, for example, have claimed that World War I was caused by the interaction of two opposed and closely balanced coalitions. But then many have claimed that World War II was caused by the failure of some states to combine forces in an effort to right an imbalance of power created by an existing alliance.

Neorealism contends that international politics can be understood only if the effects of structure are added to the unit-level explanations of traditional realism. By emphasizing how structures affect actions and outcomes, neorealism rejects the assumption that man's innate lust for power constitutes a sufficient cause of war in the absence of any other. It reconceives the causal link between interacting units and international outcomes. According

---

4 *Idem, Scientific Man vs. Power Politics* (Chicago, 1946), 192, 200. Italics added.

to the logic of international politics, one must believe that some causes of international outcomes are the result of interactions at the unit level, and, since variations in presumed causes do not correspond very closely to variations in observed outcomes, one must also assume that others are located at the structural level. Causes at the level of units interact with those at the level of structure, and, because they do so, explanation at the unit level alone is bound to be misleading. If an approach allows the consideration of both unit-level and structural-level causes, then it can cope with both the changes and the continuities that occur in a system.

Structural realism presents a systemic portrait of international politics depicting component units according to the manner of their arrangement. For the purpose of developing a theory, states are cast as unitary actors wanting at least to survive, and are taken to be the system's constituent units. The essential structural quality of the system is anarchy—the absence of a central monopoly of legitimate force. Changes of structure and hence of system occur with variations in the number of great powers. The range of expected outcomes is inferred from the assumed motivation of the units and the structure of the system in which they act.

A systems theory of international politics deals with forces at the international, and not at the national, level. With both systems-level and unit-level forces in play, how can one construct a theory of international politics without simultaneously constructing a theory of foreign policy? An international-political theory does not imply or require a theory of foreign policy any more than a market theory implies or requires a theory of the firm. Systems theories, whether political or economic, are theories that explain how the organization of a realm acts as a constraining and disposing force on the interacting units within it. Such theories tell us about the forces to which the units are subjected. From them, we can draw some inferences about the expected behavior and fate of the units: namely, how they will have to compete with and adjust to one another if they are to survive and flourish. To the extent that the dynamics of a system limit the freedom of its units, their behavior and the outcomes of their behavior become predictable. How do we expect firms to respond to differently structured markets, and states to differently structured international-political systems? These theoretical questions require us to take firms as firms, and states as states, without paying attention to differences among them. The questions are then answered by reference to the placement of the units in their system and not by reference to the internal qualities of the units. Systems theories explain why different units behave similarly and, despite their variations, produce outcomes that fall within expected ranges. Conversely, theories at the unit level tell us why different units behave differently despite their similar placement in a system. A theory about foreign policy is a theory at the national level. It leads to expectations about the responses that dissimilar polities will make to external pressures. A theory of international politics bears on the foreign policies of nations although it claims to explain only certain aspects of them. It can tell us what international conditions national policies have to cope with.

From the vantage point of neorealist theory, competition and conflict among states stem directly from the twin facts of life under conditions of anarchy: States in an anarchic order must provide for their own security, and threats or seeming threats to their security abound. Preoccupation with identifying dangers and counteracting them become a way of life. Relations remain tense; the actors are usually suspicious and often hostile even though by nature they may not be given to suspicion and hostility. Individually, states may only be doing what they can to bolster their security. Their individual intentions aside, collectively their actions yield arms races and alliances. The uneasy state of affairs is exacerbated by the familiar "security dilemma," wherein measures that enhance one state's security typically diminish that of others.[5] In an anarchic domain, the source of one's own comfort is the source of another's worry. Hence a state that is amassing instruments of war, even for its own defensive, is cast by others as a threat requiring response. The response itself then serves to confirm the first state's belief that it had reason to worry. Similarly an alliance that in the interest of defense moves to increase cohesion among its members and add to its ranks inadvertently imperils an opposing alliance and provokes countermeasures.

Some states may hunger for power for power's sake. Neorealist theory, however, shows that it is not necessary to assume

[5] See John H. Herz, "Idealist Internationalism and the Security Dilemma," *World Politics*, II (1950), 157–180.

an innate lust for power in order to account for the sometimes fierce competition that marks the international arena. In an anarchic domain, a state of war exists if all parties lust for power. But so too will a state of war exist if all states seek only to ensure their own safety.

Although neorealist theory does not explain why particular wars are fought, it does explain war's dismal recurrence through the millennia. Neorealists point not to the ambitions or the intrigues that punctuate the outbreak of individual conflicts but instead to the existing structure within which events, whether by design or accident, can precipitate open clashes of arms. The origins of hot wars lie in cold wars, and the origins of cold wars are found in the anarchic ordering of the international arena.

The recurrence of war is explained by the structure of the international system. Theorists explain what historians know: War is normal. Any given war is explained not by looking at the structure of the international-political system but by looking at the particularities within it: the situations, the characters, and the interactions of states. Although particular explanations are found at the unit level, general explanations are also needed. Wars vary in frequency, and in other ways as well. A central question for a structural theory is this: How do changes of the system affect the expected frequency of war?

KEEPING WARS COLD: THE STRUCTURAL LEVEL   In an anarchic realm, peace is fragile. The prolongation of peace requires that potentially destabilizing developments elicit the interest and the calculated response of some or all of the system's principal actors. In the anarchy of states, the price of inattention or miscalculation is often paid in blood. An important issue for a structural theory to address is whether destabilizing conditions and events are managed better in multipolar or bipolar systems.

In a system of, say, five great powers, the politics of power turns on the diplomacy by which alliances are made, maintained, and disrupted. Flexibility of alignment means both that the country one is wooing may prefer another suitor and that one's present alliance partner may defect. Flexibility of alignment limits a state's options because, ideally, its strategy must please potential allies and satisfy present partners. Alliances are made by states that have some but not all of their interests in common. The common interest is ordinarily a negative one: fear of other states. Divergence comes when positive interests are at issue. In alliances among near equals, strategies are always the product of compromise since the interests of allies and their notions of how to secure them are never identical.

If competing blocs are seen to be closely balanced, and if competition turns on important matters, then to let one's side down risks one's own destruction. In a moment of crisis the weaker or the more adventurous party is likely to determine its side's policy. Its partners can afford neither to let the weaker member be defeated nor to advertise their disunity by failing to back a venture even while deploring its risks.

The prelude to World War I provides striking examples of such a situation. The approximate equality of partners in both the Triple Alliance and Triple Entente made them closely interdependent. This interdependence, combined with the keen competition between the two camps, meant that, although any country could commit its associates, no one country on either side could exercise control. If Austria-Hungary marched, Germany had to follow; the dissolution of the Austro-Hungarian Empire would have left Germany alone in the middle of Europe. If France marched, Russia had to follow; a German victory over France would be a defeat for Russia. And so the vicious circle continued. Because the defeat or the defection of a major ally would have shaken the balance, each state was constrained to adjust its strategy and the use of its forces to the aims and fears of its partners.

In alliances among equals, the defection of one member threatens the security of the others. In alliances among unequals, the contributions of the lesser members are at once wanted and of relatively small importance. In alliances among unequals, alliance leaders need worry little about the faithfulness of their followers, who usually have little choice anyway. Contrast the situation in 1914 with that of the United States and Britain and France in 1956. The United States could dissociate itself from the Suez adventure of its two principal allies and subject one of them to heavy financial pressure. Like Austria-Hungary in 1914, Britain and France tried to commit or at least immobilize their ally by presenting a fait accompli. Enjoying a position of predominance, the United States could continue to focus its attention on the major adversary while disciplining its two allies. Opposing Britain and France endangered neither the United States nor the alliance because the security of Britain and France depended much more heavily on us than our security depended on them. The ability of the United States, and the inability of Germany, to pay a price measured in intra-alliance terms is striking.

In balance-of-power politics old style, flexibility of alignment led to rigidity of strategy or the limitation of freedom of decision. In balance-of-power politics new style, the obverse is true: Rigidity of alignment in a two-power world results in more flexibility of strategy and greater freedom of decision. In a multipolar world, roughly equal parties engaged in cooperative endeavors must look for the common denominator of their policies. They risk finding the lowest one and easily end up in the worst of all possible worlds. In a bipolar world, alliance leaders can design strategies primarily to advance their own interests and to cope with their main adversary and less to satisfy their own allies.

Neither the United States nor the Soviet Union has to seek the approval of other states, but each has to cope with the other. In the great-power politics of a multipolar world, who is a danger to whom and who can be expected to deal with threats and problems are matters of uncertainty. In the great-power politics of a bipolar world, who is a danger to whom is never in doubt. Any event in the world that involves the fortunes of either of the great powers automatically elicits the interest of the other. President Harry S. Truman, at the time of the Korean invasion, could not very well echo Neville Chamberlain's words in the Czechoslovakian crisis by claiming that the Americans knew nothing about the Koreans, a people living far away in the east of Asia. We had to know about them or quickly find out.

In a two-power competition, a loss for one is easily taken to be a gain for the other. As a result, the powers in a bipolar world promptly respond to unsettling events. In a multipolar world, dangers are diffused, responsibilities unclear, and definitions of vital interests easily obscured. Where a number of states are in balance, the skillful foreign policy of a forward power is designed to gain an advantage without antagonizing other states and frightening them into united action. At times in modern Europe, the benefits of possible gains have seemed to outweigh the risks of likely losses. Statesmen have hoped to push an issue to the limit without causing all of the potential opponents to unite. When there are several possible enemies, unity of action among them is difficult to achieve. National leaders could therefore think—or desperately hope, as did Theobald von Bethmann Hollweg and Adolf Hitler before two world wars—that a united opposition would not form.

If interests and ambitions conflict, the absence of crises is more worrisome than their presence. Crises are produced by the determination of a state to resist a change that another state tries to make. As the leaders in a bipolar system, the United States and the Soviet Union are disposed to do the resisting, for in important matters they cannot hope that their allies will do it for them. Political action in the postwar world has reflected this condition. Communist guerrillas operating in Greece prompted the Truman Doctrine. The tightening of Soviet control over the states of Eastern Europe led to the Marshall Plan and the Atlantic Defense Treaty, and these in turn gave rise to the Cominform and the Warsaw Pact. The plan to create a West German government produced the Berlin blockade. During the past four decades, our responses have been geared to the Soviet Union's actions, and theirs to ours.

Miscalculation by some or all of the great powers is a source of danger in a multipolar world; overreaction by either or both of the great powers is a source of danger in a bipolar world. Which is worse: miscalculation or overreaction? Miscalculation is the greater evil because it is more likely to permit an unfolding of events that finally threatens the status quo and brings the powers to war. Overreaction is the lesser evil because at worst it costs only money for unnecessary arms and possibly the fighting of limited wars. The dynamics of a bipolar system, moreover, provide a measure of correction. In a world in which two states united in their mutual antagonism overshadow any others, the benefits of a calculated response stand out most clearly, and the sanctions against irresponsible behavior achieve their greatest force. Thus two states, isolationist by tradition, untutored in the ways of international politics, and famed for impulsive behavior, have shown themselves—not always and everywhere, but always in crucial cases—to be wary, alert, cautious, flexible, and forbearing.

Moreover, the economies of the great powers in a bipolar world are less interdependent than those of the great powers of a multipolar one. The size of great powers tends to increase as their numbers fall, and the larger a state is, the greater the variety of its resources. States of continental size do proportionately less of their business abroad than, for example, Britain, France, and Germany did in their heydays. Never before in modern history have the great powers depended so little on the outside world, and been so uninvolved in one another's economic affairs, as the United States and the Soviet Union have been since the war. The separation of their interests reduces the occasions for dispute and permits them, if they wish, to leave each other alone even though each defines its security interests largely in terms of the other.

Interdependence of parties, diffusion of dangers, confusion of responses: These are the characteristics of great-power politics in a multipolar world. Self-dependence of parties, clarity of dangers, certainty about who has to face them: These are the characteristics of great-power politics in a bipolar world.

KEEPING WARS COLD: THE UNIT LEVEL   A major reason for the prolongation of the postwar peace is the destruction of the old multipolar world in World War II and its replacement by a bipolar one. In a bipolar world, we expect competition to be keen, yet manageable. But to believe that bipolarity alone accounts for the "long peace" between the United States and the Soviet Union is difficult. Given the depth and extent of the distrust felt by both parties, one may easily believe that one or another of the crises that they have experienced would, in earlier times, have drawn them into war. For a fuller explanation of why that did not happen, we must look to that other great force for peace: nuclear weapons.

States continue to coexist in an anarchic order. Self-help is the principle of action in such an order, and the most important way in which states must help themselves is by providing for their own security. Therefore, in weighing the chances of peace, the first questions to ask are questions about the ends for which states use force and about the strategies and weapons they employ. The chances of peace rise if states can achieve their most important ends without actively using force. War becomes less likely as the costs of war rise in relation to the possible gains. Realist theory, old and new alike, draws attention to the crucial role of military technology and strategy among the forces that fix the fate of states and their systems.

Nuclear weapons dissuade states from going to war much more surely than conventional weapons do. In a conventional world, states can believe both that they may win and that, should they lose, the price of defeat will be bearable, although World Wars I and II called the latter belief into question even before atomic bombs were dropped. If the United States and the Soviet Union were now armed only with conventional weapons, the lessons of those wars would be clearly remembered, especially by the Soviet Union, which suffered more in war than the United States. Had the atom never been split, those two nations would still have much to fear from each other. Armed with increasingly destructive conventional weapons, they would be constrained to strive earnestly to avoid war. Yet, in a conventional world, even sad and strong lessons like those of the two world wars have proved exceedingly difficult for states to learn. Throughout modern history, one great power or another has looked as though it might become dangerously strong: for example, France under Louis XIV and Napoleon Bonaparte, and Germany under Wilhelm II and Hitler. In each case, an opposing coalition formed and turned the expansive state back. The lessons of history would seem to be clear: In international politics, success leads to failure. The excessive accumulation of power by one state or coalition of states elicits the opposition of others. The leaders of expansionist states have nevertheless been able to persuade themselves that skillful diplomacy and clever strategy would enable them to transcend the normal processes of balance-of-power politics.

The experience of World War II, bipolarity, and the increased destructiveness of conventional weapons would make World War III more difficult to start than earlier wars were; and the presence of nuclear weapons dramatically increases that difficulty. Nuclear weapons reverse or negate many of the conventional causes of war. Wars can be fought in the face of nuclear weapons, but the higher the stakes and the closer a country comes to winning them, the more surely that country invites retaliation and risks its own destruction. The accumulation of significant power through conquest, even if only conventional weapons are used, is no longer possible in the world of nuclear powers. Those individuals who believe that the Soviet Union's leaders are so bent on world domination that they may be willing to run catastrophic risks for problematic gains fail to understand how governments behave. Do we expect to lose one city or two? Two cities or ten? When these are the pertinent questions, political leaders stop thinking about running risks and start worrying about how to avoid them.

Deterrence is more easily achieved than most military strategists would have us believe. In a conventional world, a country can sensibly attack if it believes that success is probable. In a nuclear world, a country cannot sensibly attack unless it believes that success is assured. A nation will be deterred from attacking even if it believes that there is only a possibility that its adversary will retaliate. Uncertainty of response, not certainty, is required for deterrence because, if retaliation occurs, one risks losing all. As Clausewitz wrote: If war approaches the absolute, it becomes imperative "not to take the first step without thinking what may be the last."[6]

Nuclear weapons make the implications even of victory too horrible to contemplate. The problem that the nuclear powers must solve is how to perpetuate peace when it is not possible to eliminate all of the causes of war. The structure of international politics has not been transformed; it remains anarchic in form. Nuclear states continue to compete militarily. With each state striving to ensure its own security, war remains constantly possible. In the anarchy of states, improving the means of defense and deterrence relative to the means of offense increases the chances of peace. Weapons and strategies that make defense and deterrence easier, and offensive strikes harder to mount, decrease the likelihood of war.[7]

Although the possibility of war remains, the probability of a war involving states with nuclear weapons has been drastically reduced. Over the centuries great powers have fought more wars than minor states, and the frequency of war has correlated more closely with a structural characteristic—their international standing—than with unit-level attributes. Yet, because of a change in military technology, a change at the unit level, waging war has

6 Karl von Clausewitz (ed. Anatol Rapaport; trans. J. J. Graham), *On War* (Hammondsworth, 1968), V, 374.
7 See Malcolm W. Hoag, "On Stability in Deterrent Races," in Morton A. Kaplan (ed.), *The Revolution in World Politics* (New York, 1962), 388–410; Robert Jervis, "Cooperation under the Security Dilemma," *World Politics*, XXX (1978), 167–214.

increasingly become the privilege of poor and weak states. Nuclear weapons have banished war from the center of international politics. A unit-level change has dramatically reduced a structural effect.

The probability of major war among states having nuclear weapons approaches zero. But the "real war" may, as James claimed, lie in the preparations for waging it. The logic of a deterrent strategy, if it is followed, also circumscribes the causes of "real wars."[8] In a conventional world, the structure of international politics encourages states to arm competitively. In a nuclear world, deterrent strategies offer the possibility of dampening the competition. Conventional weapons are relative. With conventionl weapons, competing countries must constantly compare their strengths. How secure a country is depends on how it compares to others in the quantity and quality of its weaponry, the suitability of its strategy, the resilience of its society and economy, and the skill of its leaders.

Nuclear weapons are not relative but absolute weapons.[9] They make it possible for a state to limit the size of its strategic forces so long as other states are unable to achieve disarming first-strike capabilities by improving their forces. If no state can launch a disarming attack with high confidence, comparing the size of strategic forces becomes irrelevant. For deterrence, one asks how much is enough, and enough is defined as a second-strike capability. This interpretation does not imply that a deterrent force can deter everything, but rather that, beyond a certain level, additional forces provide no additional security for one party and pose no additional threat to others. The two principal powers in the system have long had second-strike forces, with neither able to launch a disarming strike against the other. That both nevertheless continue to pile weapon upon unneeded weapon is a puzzle whose solution can be found only within the United States and the Soviet Union.

WARS, HOT AND COLD   Wars, hot and cold, originate in the structure of the international political system. Most Americans

8 William James, "The Moral Equivalent of War," in Leon Bramson and George W. Goethals (eds.), War: Studies from Psychology, Sociology, and Anthropology (New York, 1968; rev. ed.), 23.
9 Cf. Bernard Brodie, The Absolute Weapon: Atomic Power and World Order (New York, 1946), 75–76.

blame the Soviet Union for creating the Cold War, by the actions that follow necessarily from the nature of its society and government. Revisionist historians, attacking the dominant view, assign blame to the United States. Some American error, or sinister interest, or faulty assumption about Soviet aims, they argue, is what started the Cold War. Either way, the main point is lost. In a bipolar world, each of the two great powers is bound to focus its fears on the other, to distrust its motives, and to impute offensive intentions to defensive measures. The proper question is what, not who, started the Cold War. Although its content and virulence vary as unit-level forces change and interact, the Cold War continues. It is firmly rooted in the structure of postwar international politics, and will last as long as that structure endures.

In any closely competitive system, it may seem that one is either paranoid or a loser. The many Americans who ascribe paranoia to the Soviet Union are saying little about its political elite and much about the international-political system. Yet, in the presence of nuclear weapons, the Cold War has not become a hot one, a raging war among major states. Constraints on fighting big wars have bound the major nuclear states into a system of uneasy peace. Hot wars originate in the structure of international politics. So does the Cold War, with its temperature kept low by the presence of nuclear weapons.

The Contribution of Expected Utility Theory to the Study of International Conflict

The study of international conflict has languished without appreciable evidence of scientific progress for more than two millennia. Diplomatic and military history found in the Old Testament and in the writings by such classical authors as Thucydides or Kautilya, and of such more modern authors as Clausewitz, Creasy, Richardson, and Morgenthau indicate that good foundations have been laid and give hope that progress can be made. A common theme runs throughout the classics of international relations. That theme is the self-interested pursuit of gain by national leaders on their own behalf and on behalf of their nations. This is also the theme of research concerned with exchanges in markets. In this article I apply a version of that self-interested perspective—expected utility theory—to the study of international conflict.[1]

EXPECTED UTILITY THEORY   Expected utility theory originated as an explanation of microeconomic behavior. Although the subject of some controversy, expected utility theory is widely recognized as being at the core of contemporary microeconomics. The essence of the theory is that:

(1) Individual decision-makers order alternatives in terms of their preferences;

Bruce Bueno de Mesquita is Senior Fellow at the Hoover Institution, Stanford University. He is the author of *The War Trap* (New Haven, 1981).

The author expresses his gratitude to William T. Bluhm, Bruce Jacobs, and William H. Riker for their many helpful comments and to the University of Rochester and the Hoover Institution at Stanford University for support in the completion of this article.

1 See Thucydides (trans. Rex Warner), *The Peloponnesian War* (New York, 1980); Kautilya (trans. R. Shamasastry), *Arthasastra* (Mysore, 1961); Karl von Clausewitz (eds. and trans., Michael Howard and Peter Paret), *On War* (Princeton, 1976); Edward Creasy, *The Fifteen Decisive Battles of the World: From Marathon to Waterloo* (London, 1870; 7th ed.); Lewis F. Richardson, *Arms and Insecurity* (Chicago, 1960); Hans J. Morgenthau, *Politics among Nations* (New York, 1973).

(2) The order of preferences is transitive so that if A is preferred to B and B p C (where p is to be read as "is preferred to") then A p C;

(3) Individuals know the intensity of their preferences, with that intensity of preference being known as utility;

(4) Individuals consider alternative means of achieving desirable ends in terms of the product of the probability of achieving alternative outcomes and the utility associated with those outcomes; and

(5) Decision-makers, being rational, always select the strategy that yields the highest *expected* utility.[2]

Recently, there have been several attempts to apply expected utility reasoning to such aspects of international conflict as deterrence and war termination. Additionally, several colleagues and I are trying to construct a general theory of conflict using an expected utility approach. It remains to be seen how successful that endeavor will be.[3]

EXPECTED UTILITY MODELING   I review here the basic structure of decisions as seen from the expected utility perspective. Consider a choice between a sure thing (which I denote O_2 for outcome 2) and a risky lottery. I posit three outcomes, O_1, O_2, and

2 Two examples of prominent critiques of classical expected utility theory include Amos Tversky and Daniel Kahneman, "The Framing of Decisions and the Psychology of Choice," *Science*, CCXI (1981), 453–458; Kahneman and Tversky, "The Psychology of Preference," *Scientific American*, CCXLVI, 160–173. The classic description of this theory is found in John von Neumann and Oskar Morgenstern, *Theory of Games and Economic Behavior* (Princeton, 1947).

3 Three examples of an expected utility approach in international relations are Bueno de Mesquita, *The War Trap* (New Haven, 1981); Robert Gilpin, *War and Change in International Politics* (New York, 1981); Dagobert Brito and Michael Intriligator, "Conflict, War, and Redistribution, *American Political Science Review*, LXXIX (1985), 943–957. Expected utility analyses of deterrence include Bruce Russett, "The Calculus of Deterrence," *Journal of Conflict Resolution*, VII (1963), 97–109; Daniel Ellsberg, "The Crude Analysis of Strategic Choices," in John Mueller (ed.), *Approaches to Measurement in International Relations: A Non-Evangelical Survey* (New York, 1969), 288–294; Jacek Kugler, "Terror Without Deterrence: Reassessing the Role of Nuclear Weapons," *Journal of Conflict Resolution*, XXVIII (1984), 470–506; Paul Huth and Russett, "What Makes Deterrence Work: Cases from 1900 to 1980," *World Politics*, XXXVI (1984), 496–526; Walter Petersen, "Deterrence and Compellence: A Critical Assessment of Conventional Wisdom," *International Studies Quarterly*, XXX (1986), 269–294. An application to the study of war termination is Donald Wittman, "How a War Ends: A Rational Model Approach," *Journal of Conflict Resolution*, XXIII (1979), 743–763.

O_3, such that O_1 p O_2 p O_3. This is equivalent to saying outcome 1 is valued more highly than outcome 2 and that outcome 2 is valued more highly than outcome 3. Using notation as a short-hand we can say then that $U(O_1) > U(O_2) > U(O_3)$ where U denotes utility. Let the probability of attaining O_1 be P and let the probability of attaining O_3 be $1-P$. A decision-maker chooses between O_2 for sure or a strategy that has some chance (P) of resulting in the most desirable outcome (O_1) and some chance $(1-P)$ of resulting in the least desirable outcome (O_3). The option to pursue O_1 at the risk of ending up with outcome 3 is called a lottery. In a lottery there are two or more possible outcomes, each of which will occur with some probability, such that *the sum of the probabilities must be 1.0.* An expected utility maximizing decision-maker selects the risky lottery between O_1 and O_3 over the sure outcome O_2 if the anticipated return from the gamble is believed to be larger than the assured value of achieving outcome 2. The strategic decision to gamble on attaining O_1 can be represented with the following notation:[4]

[1] $$PU(O_1) + (1\text{-}P)U(O_3) > U(O_2).$$

By the same expected utility logic, the decision-maker selects the sure outcome (O_2) if:

[2] $$PU(O_1) + (1-P)U(O_3) < U(O_2).$$

and is indifferent between the alternatives if:

[3] $$PU(O_1) + (1-P)U(O_3) = U(O_2).$$

   I do not suggest that decision-makers *consciously* make the calculations of the expected utility model. Rather, I argue that leaders act *as if* they do. Such calculations sometimes lead to unintended—and undesirable—consequences. This observation, which motivates much formal analysis, is one of the essential elements bonding rational choice analysis to historical and contemporary investigations of war. As I will draw out seemingly important, unexpected principles from a rational choice theory of

---

4 I have not made explicit the terms for costs to keep the presentation as simple as possible. These expressions may be thought of in the context of equal expected costs across strategies or else, again for simplicity, costs may be thought of as endogenous to the calculations.

war, let me begin by noting instances of surprising historical events that apparently follow from rational choices.

An example of expected utility reasoning is found in Maier's analysis of World War I. He asks why this war, "that seemed so inconclusive and so costly lasted so long. Was it merely a savage nationalism or an unwillingness to lose face that impeded settlement? Or does it not make more sense to assume that for those in charge some compelling logic was at stake, that it was a 'rational' war . . . that the anticipated costs of quitting the conflict outweighed the disadvantages of remaining engaged."[5] Maier argues, contrary to many historians, that the Schlieffen plan did not make war inevitable. He bases his analysis on a careful assessment of lotteries (or wagers, as he calls them).

Maier gives us a succinct description of a series of choices, each rational *given what was known to the decision-makers at the time*, and yet each leading to horrendous consequences. Why, for instance, did negotiation fail for so long? The Germans were reluctant to negotiate because they held significant gains which they were confident of sustaining over the short term. The allies were unwilling to settle because they believed that their losses could be reversed in the long run. Thus, each side calculated its chances for success and failure and the value associated with these alternatives. Both the allies and the Germans apparently believed that the time was not right for negotiations. Maier's evaluation is an informal expected utility analysis. The virtue that formalism might bring to this elegant assessment is to focus on the logically precise relationships among the key variables.

STANDARDS FOR EVALUATING SCIENTIFIC PROGRESS   The remainder of this article focuses on a general explication of how the expected utility approach establishes insights and how it provides a foundation for accurate forecasting and for policy formation. My goal is to show that an expected utility approach offers a more comprehensive explanation of generalizable results than do its available alternatives. I also show that it encompasses other perspectives, while yielding important generalizations and significant benefits as a precise tool for forecasting and case study analysis.

5 Charles Maier, "Wargames: 1914–1919," *Journal of Interdisciplinary History*, XVIII (1988), 822–823.

I make substantial claims for the efficacy of a deductive, axiomatic approach to the study of international conflict. However, there are important limitations of such an approach and, significant complementarities between mathematical models of conflict and less formal but often more subtle and more detailed studies of particular events. Formal models are not intended to illuminate the rich details and texture of events. Rather, they are designed to specify a simplified, ordered view of reality that reveals internally consistent and externally useful general principles. In doing so, formal models sacrifice details for breadth; specificity for generality. But, when combined with expert knowledge, a powerful synergy results in which the level of insight is often greater than can be gleaned from expert judgment or from formal models alone. In several years of close collaboration with area specialists I have found that expected utility analyses informed by expert knowledge and interpreted with the expert's eye for nuance yield results beyond those of the modeler's interpretation, and also beyond those of the area expert working without the model's structure and logical rigor.

Important limitations of any decision-maker-oriented perspective arise out of the difficulties of attributing policies to specific leaders. If, as is usually done, we speak of *national* policy, we must be conscious of the assumptions made regarding the aggregation of preferences. Policies are often the product of discussion and compromise among competing elites. Groups of individuals, each behaving in an individually rational way, may produce policies that are contrary to the interests of many, and even possibly all. This outcome occurs because cycles yielding intransitive social orderings are possible if issues are multidimensional or if utilities are not single peaked. The well-known Condorcet paradox draws our attention critically to any endeavor that assumes collective rationality. Such behaviors as bluffing in the face of war may be explicable on strategic grounds, but they may also be the consequence of cyclical preferences among competing elites or bureaucracies. These problems are not insurmountable, but they do remind us of the limitations inherent in applying rational choice theories to collective action.[6]

---

6 For treatments of this problem in an international context, see Bueno de Mesquita, *War Trap*; *idem*, David Newman, and Alvin Rabushka, *Forecasting Political Events* (New Haven, 1985).

The main objectives behind theory construction are the identification of lawlike statements and the attainment of scientific progress. An interesting feature of most standards of scientific progress is that they require evidence from many events, rather than from a single case history. Virtually all widely used means of evaluating the gains from scientific inquiries focus attention on the implications that follow from the *preponderance* of evidence. This is as true of studies rooted in the methodology that leads to the accumulation of many case histories as it is of those with methodologies that encourage statistical significance testing. The standard for measuring scientific progress that I use is that suggested by Lakatos: one theory is superior to another if it encompasses the corroborated empirical content of the rival theory and some more.[7]

THEORIES OF POWER, ALLIANCES, AND WAR   Two prominent "rival" views of war emanate from balance of power and from power preponderance theories. These perspectives lead to alternative hypotheses about the factors leading to war (or peace) and the motives underlying the selection of allies. For instance, balance of power theorists hypothesize that a balance of power tends to produce peace and an imbalance tends to produce war; that alliances tend to be nonideological, power-seeking, and short-lived arrangements. Power preponderance theorists claim that a balance of power tends to produce war and an imbalance tends to produce peace; and that alliances tend to be long-lived, ideological arrangements.[8]

These propositions seem incompatible. Yet, an expected utility theory of conflict choices provides the foundation for deducing the conditions under which each of these propositions is true. This is a bold claim. My burden is to demonstrate that this claim is supportable in the face of Lakatos' criteria for assessing scientific progress.

7   Imre Lakatos, *The Methodology of Scientific Research Programmes* (London, 1978), 32.
8   For examples of the balance of power perspective, see Edward Gulick, *Europe's Classical Balance of Power* (Ithaca, 1955); Morgenthau, *Politics among Nations* (New York, 1973); Waltz, *Theory of International Politics* (Reading, Mass., 1979). Examples of preponderance theory include Kenneth Organski, *World Politics* (New York, 1968); George Modelski, *Principles of World Politics* (New York, 1972); Organski and Kugler, *The War Ledger* (Chicago, 1980); Gilpin, *War and Change*; Robert Keohane, *After Hegemony* (Princeton, 1984).

EXPECTED UTILITY, POWER, AND WAR   Assume that decision-makers calculate the expected utility associated with challenging and not challenging a putative adversary. For those in a threatening situation, assume the probability that they will escalate their effort to achieve their objectives increases as a strictly monotonic function of their expected utility. The more they believe they stand to gain, the more likely they are to use force in pursuit of their objectives. Then the functional form of the probability of escalation by nations i and j is as in Figure 1[9].

We may now define the probability of various types of conflict in accordance with the probability that i, j, or both choose the strategy of escalation over the strategy of negotiation. Let:

Fig. 1   The Probability of Conflict Escalation

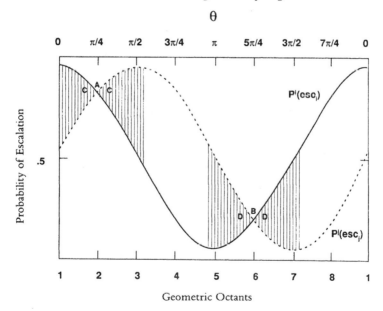

The Relative Advantage of Competing Nations

(i) $P(War) = P^i(Esc_i) * P^j(Esc_j)$

(ii) $P(Intervention) = [p^i(Esc_i) * (1-p^j(Esc_j))] + [p^j(Esc_j) * (1-P^i(Esc_i))]$

(iii) $P(Peace) = [1-p^i(Esc_i)] * [1-p^j(Esc_j)]$

(iv) $P(Violence) = 1 - P(Peace) = P(War) + P(Intervention)$

Definition (i) says that the probability of war [P(War)] is equal to the product of the probability that i escalates its threat against j [$p^i(Esc_i)$] and j escalates its threat against i [$p^j(Esc_j)$]. The other definitions are analogous. It is evident from Figure 1 that two points exist in which expectations about the consequences of challenging an adversary (and its coalition of supporters) is balanced. From definition (i) we see that the probability of war is relatively high at the point marked A on Figure 1 because the probability of using force is high for both nation i and nation j. At the point marked B, the probability of war is lower. Balance of power theorists do not differentiate between two scenarios under which the balance has different implications. Areas C and D represent situations of imbalanced expectations in which one adversary expects far more than the other from a conflict. In one such situation (area C) the probability of war is high. In the other (area D), the probability of war is low.

Points A and B depict two power transitions in which one hegemon is surpassed by another. These two transitions are accompanied by a high and a low probability of war respectively. The empirical attention to those supporting a balance of power perspective seems focused on situations typified by point B or area C. Power preponderance theorists draw attention to situations characterized by point A or area D, but fail to note such circumstances as point B or area C in which balanced expectations lead to peace. Balance of power theories overlook conditions under which balance implies war (point A) or imbalance implies peace (area D). The expected utility framework makes these distinctions, thereby differentiating between situations when preponderance or balance encourages peace or war.

A critical aspect of Figure 1 is that it distinguishes situations with high or low risks of war as a function of the expectations of gains by adversaries. Most realist theorists mistakenly assume that if both sides have the same expectations, each side's probability of victory is .5, thereby confusing subjective and objective probabilities of victory. Of course, i may believe its prospects of victory are high at the same time that j's expectations are high (e.g., point A in Figure 1) or both i and j may believe that their prospects for victory are low (e.g., point B).[10]

Debates over how the distribution of power affects the prospects for peace persist largely because of two limitations of realist theories. One common shortcoming of power-centered perspectives is the conviction that understanding power alone is sufficient to comprehend relations among nations. As one observer astutely notes:

> It is dangerous to put in a key position a concept which is merely instrumental. Power is a means toward any of a large number of ends (including power itself). The quality and quantity of power used by men are determined by men's purposes. . . . The "realist" theory neglects all the factors that influence or define purposes. . . . The . . . beliefs and values, which account in great measure for the nation's goals and for the statesmen's motivations are either left out or brushed aside.[11]

Focusing on power alone is not enough. The expected utility approach takes power into account by estimating probabilities of success and failure, while taking values and purposes into account by estimating utilities.

A second limitation of many power-based theories is rooted in misunderstandings about the relationship between system structure and international conflict. Theories about the balance of power and war, or about bipolarity and peace, for instance, are not primarily theories about structural determinants of conflict. The assumptions underlying such theories are generally about how people respond to uncertainty and to risks. What makes these theories appear systemic is the tendency to assume that everyone responds to risks or to uncertainty in the same way.

10 The power transition theory is discussed in Organski, *World Politics* (New York, 1958), 299–338; Organski and Kugler, *War Ledger*, 13–63. Its relationship to theories of hegemony is discussed in Organski and Kugler, "Hegemony and War," paper prepared for presentation at the International Studies Association meeting (1986). A. Geoffrey Blainey, *The Causes of War* (New York, 1973), 35–67, has an interesting discussion on the expectations of victory of belligerents.
11 Stanley Hoffmann, *Contemporary Theory in International Relations* (Englewood Cliffs, 1960), 31.

According to many balance of power theorists, for instance, the incentive to wage war is diminished by the belief that the chances for success are only fifty-fifty. This is analogous to the statement that decision-makers facing the choice of waging war behave as if they are risk averse. Conversely, many preponderance theorists seem to subscribe to the belief that war is most likely when opposed forces are roughly equal, implying that decision-makers are somewhat risk acceptant. Assumptions of uniform willingness to take risks are very restrictive and inconsistent with even casual observation. Expected utility theory allows for the possibility that decision-makers vary in their willingness to take chances, with that willingness described by the curvature of each decision-maker's utility function. Unlike most power-centered theories, expected utility theory does not assume that decision-makers share a common orientation toward taking risks. In expected utility theory, risk-taking propensities may vary. Consequently, the expected utility approach demonstrates that the distribution of power—independent of utilities—has no direct theoretical bearing on the likelihood of war. That power by itself does not determine the likelihood of war is easily shown by recognizing that expected utility is always the product of the probability of alternative outcomes and the utility associated with those outcomes.[12]

Assume that the probability of success in war is a function of power, as is asserted by virtually all *Realpolitik* theorists. The expected utility theory reveals deductively that rational national leader i can initiate a war if and only if:

$$[4] \qquad P_s^i \geq 1 - [U_s^i - E^i\,(U_{nc})] \,/\, [S_j(U_s^i - U_f^i)]$$

where P_s refers to i's probability of success, U_s and U_f refer to the utility of success and failure respectively, and $E^i(U_{nc})$ refers to i's expected utility from not challenging the putative opponent. Expression [4] indicates just how small a chance of success a decision-maker is willing to live with before deciding not to challenge a putative adversary. This "law" of conflict decision-making reveals that rational actors can choose to wage war even

---

12 For further discussion about the relationships between power, utility, and decisions to wage war, see Seif Hussein, "Modeling War and Peace," *American Political Science Review*, LXXXI (1987), 221–227.

when their subjective (or real) prospects of victory are very small if they care enough about the issues in question.[13]

Rothenberg offers a profound example of this principle at work. He notes that Napoleon's

> reliance on force as the primary tool of foreign policy eventually put him at odds with Charles Maurice de Tallyrand, his foreign minister, who from 1807 on realized that his master was overextended and vainly tried to persuade him to end the conflict and stabilize the European state system. . . . Even as late as the fall of 1813, both Britain and Austria, concerned about possible Russian and Prussian aggrandizement, were prepared to make a compromise peace, leaving Napoleon on his throne and France with the frontiers of 1792. But the emperor refused to make any substantial concessions, and in the end he lost all.

Napoleon valued his policy objectives so highly that he was willing to risk everything. That this policy was rational follows directly from equation [4] and from Rothenberg's argument that Napoleon's "actions were precisely calculated. . . . Napoleon always had excellent strategic intelligence and made war deliberately."[14] Apparently the emperor attached so much value to his objectives that he was willing, in the end, to tolerate a very small chance of success rather than accept a compromise.

A similar example of the tendency for decision-makers to pursue intensely held objectives even when their prospects of success are slim is found in the decisions leading to the outbreak of World War I. Williamson, for instance, observes that "nationalism and ethnic arrogance should never be underestimated. The powerful, emotive forces of prestige and survival press statesmen to take chances that ostensibly rational actors might not take." Regrettably, he confuses taking chances (being highly risk-acceptant) with irrationality. As expression [4] shows, intensely held utilities ("nationalism and ethnic arrogance should never be underestimated") raise the willingness of rational decision-makers to take risks. Here, then, we have an example of how the formalism

13 Bueno de Mesquita, "The War Trap Revisited," *American Political Science Review*, LXXIX (1985), 157–176.
14 Gunther E. Rothenberg, "The Origins, Causes, and Extension of the Wars of the French Revolution and Napoleon," *Journal of Interdisciplinary History*, XVIII (1988), 790.

of expected utility theory can help us make logical sense of what otherwise seems like bizarre behavior.[15]

For any probability of success (and, therefore, for any level of relative power), there is a possible set of utility values such that waging war is preferred to not waging war *or* such that the opposite is true. Power by itself is neither necessary nor sufficient for a rational, *realist* leader to choose war over peace, despite the arguments of *realist* theorists to the contrary. This claim is self-evident from an expected utility perspective. This simple insight helps make sense of many seemingly anomalous behaviors by forcing the analyst to look at the situation, not with hindsight, but through the decision-maker's eyes.

Despite logical inadequacies in theories that link power directly to the likelihood of war initiation, such perspectives persist. Yet even a simple empirical test shows the superiority, in a Lakatosian sense, of expected utility theory over, for example, Kissinger's balance of power theory. According to Kissinger, "throughout history the political influence of nations has been roughly correlative to their military power. . . . In the final reckoning weakness has invariably tempted aggression and impotence brings abdication of policy in its train. . . . The balance of power . . . has in fact been the precondition of peace." As is true for so many balance of power theorists, Kissinger stipulates that war initiators are more powerful than their adversaries.[16]

Expected utility theory does not impose this restriction, but rather requires that the gains expected by initiators are larger than their expected losses. As equation [4] shows, this result may be true even when the probability of success is very low, provided the value attached to success is sufficiently large. Using all wars as defined by Singer and Small, I tested the relative merits of these two propositions. The balance of power proposition does well, with twenty-five of thirty-seven wars being consistent with Kissinger's hypothesis. The expected utility rule proves significantly superior, with thirty-one of thirty-seven wars consistent with its expectations. Given the prospects of human error and the limitations of data, it is expected that neither fits perfectly. The strength of the expected utility result is sufficiently greater than

15 Samuel R. Williamson, Jr., "The Origins of the World War I," *ibid.*, 817.
16 Henry Kissinger, *White House Years* (Boston, 1979), 195.

the support for the balance of power rule that the difference would have occurred by chance fewer times than one in a hundred.[17]

EXPECTED UTILITY, POWER, AND ALLIANCES   The alliance hypotheses of the seemingly contradictory power theories are subsets of expected utility theory. Consider the argument by Organski and Kugler:

> Most of the time alliances are simply not a realistic method of preventing threatening changes in the distribution of world power, given the skewness of relations between the great and the lesser nations, and also among the half-dozen great powers themselves. . . . It is clear that, if the intervals separating the nations in question are as large as we suggest, more probable alliances could affect only the size of the intervals between the strata, but could not alter the fundamental ranking of the great powers dominating the international system.[18]

This hypothesis stands in sharp contrast to Morgenthau's argument:

> It is true that the princes allowed themselves to be guided by the balance of power in order to further their own interests. By doing so, it was inevitable that they would change sides, desert old alliances, and form new ones whenever it seemed to them that the balance of power had been disturbed and that a realignment of forces was needed to restore it.[19]

The key difference in assumptions about alliances can be formalized. Let C_i be the power of the most powerful nation or alliance of nations. Let C_j be the power of i's rival. Let C_k be the power of a third nation or coalition of nations. Organski and Kugler's argument that alliances are ineffectual in wars among the most powerful states is logically equivalent to:

$$C_i - C_j > C_k. \text{ Therefore } C_j + C_k < C_i.$$

Given that C_i dominates the combined forces of j and k, alliances are more likely to be motivated by considerations of ideology or

17 J. David Singer and Melvin Small, *The Wages of War* (New York, 1972).
18 Organski and Kugler, *War Ledger*, 25.
19 Morgenthau, *Politics*, 197.

world view than by power, making them long-term arrangements. Morgenthau and others, however, maintain that:

$$C_i - C_j \leq C_k. \text{ Therefore } C_j + C_k \geq C_i.$$

Given this view, power considerations, not ideology, become the
major factor influencing the formation of alliances, making them
short-lived, nonideological arrangements of convenience.

An expected utility view of third-party choices to align with
side i or side j encompasses the generalizations of both balance of
power and power preponderance theorists. Assume that the
choice to join i, join j, or remain nonaligned is determined by
expected utility maximizing criteria. Further, assume that the
more k expects to gain from helping a nation at war, the larger
the commitment k is willing to make in pursuit of those gains.
Figure 2 depicts the decision problem confronting third party k.

According to the model in Figure 2, k's choice between
joining side i or j depends on the probability of i winning given
help from k (P_{ik}), the probability of i losing even though k helps
i ($1 - P_{ik}$), the probability of j winning (i losing) given that k helps
j (P_{jk}), the probability of j losing (i winning) even though k helps

Fig. 2 Third-Party Decision Problem

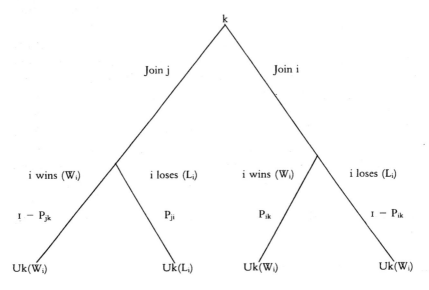

j $(1-P_{jk})$, and the utility k attaches to the two possible outcomes. Let the utility to k of i winning $= U(W_i)$ and let the utility to k of i losing and j winning $= U(L_i)$. Then, k's expected utility for joining i or j equals:

[5]
$$E(U)_k = [P_{ik}U^k(W_i) + (1-P_{ik})U^k(L_i)]$$
$$- [(1-P_{jk})U^k(W_i) + P_{jk}U^k(L_i)].$$

The terms inside the first set of brackets in equation [5] delineate k's expectations if it joins side i. The terms inside the second set of brackets delineate k's expectations if it selects the strategy of joining side j. By subtracting these two expressions we see if joining i, joining j, or remaining out of the conflict is k's preferred strategy. If equation [5] is positive, k expects more utility from joining i than j and so k is predicted to join i. If [5] is negative, k is predicted to join j, and if the expression equals zero, then k is indifferent between i and j and so abstains from the dispute.

The concepts of equation [5] can be seen at work in the decision of Istvan Tisza, the Magyar premier, in July 1914, to endorse military action against Serbia. Williamson reports that when the Common Ministerial Council met on July 7 to review the situation, "the Magyar premier persisted in opposing military action but, by the end of the lengthy session, his resistance had weakened. Tisza then appealed to Franz Joseph, only to find that his sovereign was *strongly committed to action* [italics added]. In his efforts to sway Tisza, [Leopold von] Berchtold stressed Germany's support for action and, possibly more important, warned of Rumania's probable defection from the alliance" if action were not taken against Serbia. In this passage we see, first, Tisza's utilities shifting as he learns of Franz Joseph's commitment. Then we see a shift in his estimate of the probability of success as he learns of Germany's commitment and the risk of losing Rumania's aid if action does not come swiftly. Thus, his decision to endorse the use of force follows from new information about the magnitude of preferences for such action and the magnitude of the probability of success.[20]

20 Williamson, "Origins," 808.

The terms in equation [5] may be rearranged by factoring to yield:

$$[6] \qquad E(U)_k = [P_{ik} + P_{jk} - 1]\, [U^k(W_i) - U^k(L_i)].$$

Equation [6] helps make clear that k, not surprisingly, always joins the side that it prefers. Since $[P_{ik} + P_{jk} - 1]$ can only be greater than or equal to zero, the sign of expression [6] is determined by the relative magnitude of the utilities of k for victory by i or j. How much effort k makes depends both on the intensity of k's preferences and on k's power. The value of Tisza's decision, for instance, was magnified by the shift in his own intensity of commitment as he came to understand Franz Joseph's determination. To see this principle analytically, assume no nation enters a conflict with the expectation of harming the side it chooses to join so that:

$$P_{ik} \ge P_{ib};\ P_{jk} \ge P_{jb} = (1 - P_{ib})$$

where P_{ib} and P_{jb} are the respective probabilities of i and j winning a *strictly bilateral* dispute (as estimated by k).

Once P_{ib} and P_{jb} (which together equal 1.0, and represent the probabilities when i and j act alone) are subtracted (as dictated by equation [6]), all that remains is k's contribution to the probability of the outcome. This result can be seen by adding an operational assumption. Let $P_{ik} = (C_i + C_k) / (C_i + C_k + C_j)$, where, as before, C refers to the capabilities or power of the subscripted actor. Similarly, let $P_{jk} = (C_j + C_k) / (C_i + C_j + C_k)$. Then:

$$[7] \quad (P_{ik} + P_{jk} - 1) = \frac{C_i + C_k}{C_i + C_j + C_k} + \frac{C_j + C_k}{C_i + C_j + C_k} - \frac{C_i + C_j + C_k}{C_i + C_j + C_k}$$

$$= \frac{C_k}{C_i + C_j + C_k}.$$

Under the power transition condition stipulated above and with the assumption that effort increases monotonically with expected utility, we see that C_k in [7] is small compared to C_i and C_j. Therefore, holding utilities constant, k's expected utility must approach zero for a finite value of $(U(W_i) - U(L_i))$ relative to the conditions stipulated for the balance of power (where C_k is *relatively* large). Given monotonicity of effort with expected utility,

[6] and [7] reveal that alliances are less important when third parties are weak compared to initial belligerents and are more important when third parties are relatively strong. Thus, the balance of power and power transition hypotheses are not incompatible at all. Rather, they are each special cases of behavior predicted by the expected utility approach. Each of these theories is subsumed under the expected utility framework.

Expected utility theory satisfies Lakatos' criteria with respect to many balance of power and power preponderance hypotheses about the likelihood of war and about the efficaciousness of alliances. It explains the facts accounted for by each, but excluded by the other. In this way, it has excess empirical content over either. Consider, for instance, the differences in empirical results between an expected utility explanation of third-party decisions to join one side or the other in an ongoing war and the results reported by Siverson and King using essentially the same data, but a more power-oriented theoretical perspective. Table 1 contains results for the Siverson and King test; Table 2 contains Altfeld and Bueno de Mesquita's expected utility test.[21]

These two tables reveal that the expected utility model better fits the historical record, yielding a two-thirds reduction in error as compared to Siverson and King's one-third reduction in error. Additionally, the Altfeld and Bueno de Mesquita test explains not only whether nations would participate in ongoing wars (the

Table 1 War Participation Predictions Based on the Siverson and King Model

		Predicted War Participant?	
		No	Yes
Actual War Participant?	No	211	12
	Yes	32	35

SOURCE: Randolph Siverson and Joel King, "Attributes of National Alliance Membership and War Participation, 1815–1965," *American Journal of Political Science,* XXIV (1980), Table 4.

21 Altfeld and Bueno de Mesquita, "Choosing Sides," 106; Siverson and King, "Attributes of National Alliance Membership," 1–15.

Table 2 War Participation Predictions Based on the Altfeld and Bueno de Mesquita Model

		Predicted War Participant?	
		No	Yes
	No	104	4
Actual War Participant?			
	Yes	9	27

SOURCE: Michael Altfeld and Bueno de Mesquita, "Choosing Sides in Wars," *International Studies Quarterly,* XXIII (1979), Table 2b.

dependent variable for Siverson and King), but also explains which side each third party would join. Even using crude data, thirty-party choices seem consistent with expected utility maximizing behavior. Sixteen of the eighteen nations predicted to join the weaker side in an ongoing war actually did so. Ten of thirteen predicted to join the stronger side also did so, suggesting that the theory was very powerful at discriminating who would join, which side they would join, and who would stay out of the fight (104 of 108 predicted to stay out of the war did stay out).

As a final observation on expected utility theory and third-party alignment behavior, note that other theoretical results can also be derived from equation [6]. For instance, equation [6] contains an explanation of why major powers are more likely to participate as third parties in wars than are minor powers; and why major powers are likely to participate in wars, such as the Vietnam war, where they do not have vital interests at risk. Thus, expected utility theory provides a vehicle for making consistent the seemingly incompatible propositions of the balance of power and power preponderance theories, does better at accounting for third-party alignment decisions than do rival theories, and offers additional empirically supported deductions about major and minor power behavior. Although some argue that a separate theory of major power war is required, much of the evidence from research using expected utility theory suggests that major power choices can be explained in the same way as minor power choices. They differ primarily in the magnitudes of their respective values on the utility and probability terms.[22]

22 The case for a separate theory of major power war is made in Modelski and Patrick

CONFLICT AND EXPECTED UTILITY THEORY | 71

SURPRISING RESULTS FROM EXPECTED UTILITY THEORY   Power-based theories have been an important bedrock for explanations of war and peace decisions and for alliance formation choices. A large and closely related body of theory has grown up around the question of deterrence. Expected utility theory has also proven to be a useful tool for explaining the successes and failures of efforts to deter conventional or nuclear war. Huth and Russett, testing a number of deterrence hypotheses, note that their best fitting result gives insignificantly different predictions from my expected utility formulation. Other, seemingly anomalous, behaviors are consistent with the expected utility perspective of conflict decision-making. For instance, allies are shown to be substantially more likely to wage war (but not severe wars) against one another than are enemies. The potential advantages of nonalignment for a weak nation engaged in a dispute with a stronger adversary that has allies have been demonstrated, while at the same time I have shown that nonalignment can be a liability for a weak nation if the same adversary does not have allies to help it. Conditions under which nuclear proliferation decreases the threat of war have been identified, while some circumstances under which arms control exacerbates the risks of conflict have also been isolated. Others have shown that behavior that complies with or deviates from standard norms within international treaty organizations can be predicted using expected utility theory. That approach has also proven useful in predicting escalatory behavior in conflicts and in explaining alliance formation behavior in the face of threats.[23]

Morgan, "Understanding Global War," *Journal of Conflict Resolution*, XXIX (1985), 391–418; Organski and Kugler, *War Ledger*. See also William Moul, "A Catch to The War Trap," *International Interactions*, XIII (1987), 171–176; Bueno de Mesquita, "A Catch to Moul's Catch, Or Why Great Powers Act as Expected Utility Maximizers," *ibid.*, 177–181.

23 On conflict and alignment, see Bueno de Mesquita, *War Trap*. For the relationship between alliance cohesion and expected utility shifts, see Bruce Berkowitz, "Realignment in International Treaty Organizations," *International Studies Quarterly*, XXVII (1983), 77–96; Altfeld and Won Paik, "Realignment in ITOs: A Closer Look," *International Studies Quarterly*, XXX (1986), 107–114. Analyses of escalation include Bueno de Mesquita, "War Trap Revisited"; Bueno de Mesquita and Lalman, "Reason and War"; Petersen, "Deterrence and Compliance." On the linkage to alliance formation, see Altfeld, "The Decision to Ally: A Theory and Test," *Western Political Quarterly*, XXXVII (1984), 523–544; Newman, "Security and Alliances: A Theoretical Study of Alliance Formation," unpub. ms. (1985). For applications of this perspective to nuclear proliferation, see Bueno de Mesquita and William Riker, "Assessing the Merits of Selective Nuclear Proliferation," *Journal of Conflict Resolution*, XXVI (1982), 283–306; Intriligator and Dagobert Brito, "Nuclear

A particularly important set of results shows that rational conflict initiation and escalation decisions are consistent with decision-maker misperceptions. They are shown to have systematic, predictable effects on the likelihood of war. These results call into question arguments that place misperceptions outside the realm of rational behavior.[24] Lalman and I have shown the circumstances under which rational decision-makers engage in actions for which the perceived probability of war is low, when in fact the likelihood of war is high. And we have shown the conditions under which nations engage in policies that they think are highly risky, when the actual likelihood of war is low.

To illustrate the ability of the expected utility approach to incorporate misperceptions into a rational-choice perspective refer back to definition (i) which states that:

(i) $P(\text{War}) = P^i(\text{Esc}_i) * P^j(\text{Esc}_j)$.

Define the probability of war *as perceived by i and as perceived by j* as:

(ia) $P^i(\text{War}) = P^i(\text{Esc}_i) * P^i(\text{Esc}_j)$
(ib) $P^j(\text{War}) = P^j(\text{Esc}_i) * P^j(\text{Esc}_j)$.

Definition (i) states that the probability of war is a function of i's probability of escalating a dispute and j's probability of escalating the same dispute. Definition (ia) stipulates that i's perception of the probability of war is a function of i's probability of escalating the conflict and i's estimate of j's probability of escalating the dispute. The perception of j is derived analogously. Suppose i believes that the relevant probabilities equal .6 and .9, whereas j believes that they equal .8 and .6. Then, i perceives the probability of war to be .54 and j believes it to be .48, with each viewing the opponent as the more hostile party. The actual probability of war is .36, substantially lower than they thought. Suppose i thought that the probabilities were .9 and .6 respectively, whereas j

Proliferation and the Probability of War," *Public Choice*, XXXVII (1981), 247–260; Berkowitz, "Proliferation, Deterrence, and the Likelihood of Nuclear War," *Journal of Conflict Resolution*, XXIX (1985), 112–136.

24 Bueno de Mesquita, "War Trap Revisited," and Bueno de Mesquita and Lalman, "Reason and War," place misperceptions within the rational choice context. For another point of view, see Robert Jervis, *Perception and Misperception in International Politics* (Princeton, 1976).

thought that they were .6 and .9. Each anticipates a .54 chance of war. Yet, the actual likelihood in this case is .81. Finally, suppose i perceives the probabilities of escalation as .6 and .7 respectively, whereas j perceives them to be .9 and .8. Then i perceives the situation to have a probability of war equal to .42; j perceives it to be .72. In actuality, the probability of war rests in between, with a value of .48.

These examples illustrate the ability of the expected utility formulation to incorporate perceptual variation in a rational choice framework and to use those perceptions to account for decisions resulting in losing efforts. They help lend formal structure to Creasy's important observation that "we thus learn not to judge of the wisdom of measures too exclusively by the results. We learn to apply the juster standard of seeing what the circumstances and the probabilities were that surrounded a statesman or a general at the time he decided on his plan."[25]

POLICY FORECASTING, INSTABILITY, AND EXPECTED UTILITY THEORY
A difficult test for any social science theory is its ability to forecast future events. Explaining events after the fact is the empirical basis for theory testing, but predicting events before they happen dispels suspicions that "the theory was made to fit the data" or that the theory is no more than a tautology. Real-time forecasting is a test to which theories are rarely subjected. An expected utility approach is particularly difficult to test predictively because hard data do not exist for many of its variables, especially the utility terms. Tests of the theory must therefore depend either on proxy indicators of utilities or on implications from the theory that do not require the direct observation of utilities. I have used both methods in the context of current international and intranational conflict and policy formation. I turn now to the value of the theory as a tool for forecasting policy decisions.

The key problem in applying the expected utility approach to forecasting policy formation around the world, and the degree of contentiousness surrounding policy decisions, is that there are no pre-existing data readily used to approximate probabilities or utilities. As a forecasting tool, the expected utility model focuses

25 Creasy, *Fifteen Decisive Battles*, preface to the first edition, xiii.

on competition among groups (both within and across national boundaries). In particular, the model requires:

(a) the specification of the relative power (political, economic, military, or otherwise) of each relevant group;
(b) the enumeration of specific policy issues that are indicative of the questions that one wishes to answer (e.g., what will happen to civil liberties in Hong Kong after the People's Republic of China regains sovereignty; what restructuring of debt will the Mexican government negotiate with its creditors; how stable will the new government be in the Philippines?);
(c) each group's preferred policy outcome on the issue(s) in question; and
(d) the degree of importance or salience each group attaches to the policy under discussion.

Here we have an opportunity to combine the greatest strengths of abstract theory and of detailed expert knowledge on particular situations or places. Data for forecasting purposes are developed in close consultation with area experts. They identify the groups, issues, and other variables required by the model (policy preferences held by each group on each issue; the relative power controlled by each group; and the salience, or level of importance, each group attributes to each issue).

Experts are not asked for their personal judgments about outcomes or about the contentiousness of the political situation. The model, not a Delphi technique, is used to answer these questions. The model also is used to estimate each group's willingness to take risks, and to specify what kind of conflictual relationship (if any) is likely to emerge between each pair of groups. Each group's perceptions about what it can do and about what it believes others can or will do are also derived using only the data specified above. Indeed, the model allows the analyst to look at the world "as if" through the eyes of each group leader. The methodology is explained in great detail elsewhere. The key here is that the model adds considerable information (of the sort that many students of international political economy view as essential) beyond that provided by the experts. Indeed, the model-based forecasts often differ from those of the very experts who provided the input information. When the experts and the model differ, the model's predictions of outcomes and strategies prove to be more accurate than the experts.[26]

The expected utility model has proven to be a flexible and reliable forecasting tool. Included among its successful applications are forecasts of such diverse events as:

(1) the ascent of Yuri Andropov as successor to Leonid Brezhnev before most analysts viewed him as a serious contender;[27]

(2) the resolution of Italian deficit policy, and the attendant fall of the Italian government, in 1982;[28]

(3) the successful prediction of election results for El Salvador in 1981 and again later;

(4) the shift in Iran of Hasheimi Rafsanjani from his hardline stand of promoting a military solution to the Iran-Iraq war to his stance in favor of economic sanctions and a less bellicose resolution of the dispute as well as a prediction of movement in Iran toward more free market policies in response to pressures from the Bazaaris;[29] and

(5) the eruption of a dispute between Chen Yun of the ideological faction of China's Communist Party and Deng Xiao Ping on the issue of free market reforms.[30]

This illustrative sampling of forecasts highlights the ability of the model to predict policy formation and political conflict accurately within democratic and authoritarian regimes, and in domestic, international, or mixed situations; to deal with socialist and capitalist settings for decision-making; and to cope with policy decisions in virtually every type of economic, social, cultural, and

26 See Bueno de Mesquita, Newman, and Rabushka, *Forecasting*. For a discussion of the importance of linking issue-specific and non-state actor decisions to state-level choices in bringing the study of international conflict and international political economy into closer harmony, see Keohane, "The Study of International Regimes and the Classical Tradition in International Relations," paper presented to the annual meetings of the American Political Science Association (1986).

27 Bueno de Mesquita, "Conflict Forecasting Project: Iran and Soviet Union Analysis, April 1982," report to the Defense Advanced Research Projects Agency.

28 Douglas Beck and Bueno de Mesquita, "Forecasting Policy Decisions: An Expected Utility Approach," in Stephen Andriole (ed.), *Corporate Crisis Management* (New York, 1985), 103–122.

29 Bueno de Mesquita, "Forecasting Policy Decisions: An Expected Utility Approach to Post-Khomeini Iran," *PS*, XVII (1984), 226–236.

30 Bueno de Mesquita, Newman, and Rabushka, *Forecasting*, 149–150.

political setting. As such, it is evidence of the potential benefits to be gained from exploring expected utility theory as a paradigm for understanding political conflict.

The search for knowledge is a quest for accurate description, explanation, and prediction. The fundamental quality of science is that we cannot know if one or another explanation is truly correct. But, agreement should be possible on the consistency between competing explanations and the evidence. The predictive power of rival theories is not a matter of taste; it is a matter of empirical record. The application of conventional views of evidence lends strong support to claims for the merits of an expected utility approach. Many of the main streams of international relations research have been shown to fall within the purview of expected utility theory. Perspectives that before appeared incompatible were shown to be special cases of expected utility conditions. Events that seemed like anomalies have been shown to be consistent with more mundane events when viewed from an expected utility perspective. A high percentage (around 90 percent) of policy forecasts and strategic scenarios, including many counterintuitive ones, have been borne out. The evidence for an expected utility view of decision-making about international conflict is too strong to be dismissed.

The Origins of War:
Explanation of Non-rational Causality

Jack S. Levy

Domestic Politics and War

It is difficult to read both the theoretical literature in political science on the causes of war and historians' case studies of the origins of particular wars without being struck by the difference in their respective evaluations of the importance of domestic political factors. Whereas historians devote considerable attention to these variables, most political scientists minimize their importance. Domestic political variables are not included in any of the leading theories of the causes of war; instead, they appear only in a number of isolated hypotheses and in some empirical studies that are generally atheoretical and noncumulative. This gap is troubling and suggests that political scientists and historians who study war have learned little from each other. A greater recognition of the role of domestic factors by political scientists would increase the explanatory power of their theories and provide more useful conceptual frameworks for the historical analysis of individual wars.

This study takes a first step toward bridging this gap by examining some of the disparate theoretical literature on domestic politics and war. It examines the relationship between national attributes and war behavior, the relative likelihood of democratic and non-democratic regimes going to war, Marxist and liberal theories regarding the impact of economic structure, the influence of nationalism and public opinion, and the scapegoat hypothesis. First, however, this article takes a closer look at the different treatment of domestic sources of war by political scientists and historians.

Jack S. Levy is Associate Professor of Political Science at the University of Minnesota. He is the author of *War in the Modern Great Power System, 1495–1975* (Lexington, Ky., 1983).

Research for this article has been supported by the Stanford Center for International Security and Arms Control, by the Carnegie Corporation, and by a Social Science Research Council/MacArthur Foundation fellowship in international peace and security. The views expressed here do not necessarily represent those of the Center, the Council, or either foundation. The author would like to thank Alexander George, Kimberly Marten, Steven Weber, Mark Cioc, and Chris Gacek for their helpful comments.

DOMESTIC POLITICS AND WAR IN POLITICAL SCIENCE AND HISTORY
Traditionally, most political science research on war has followed
the "realist" paradigm and has focused on the structure of the
international system and the strategic interaction between states
as the primary determinants of international conflict. In the last
fifteen years there has been increasing interest in the role of bu-
reaucratic-political and psychological variables in the processes
leading to war, particularly in the literature on crisis decision-
making. Although economic theories of imperialism and war have
been developed by Marxist-Leninists, political scientists have generally minimized the direct impact of economic variables on the
processes leading to war. Recently there has been increased attention to the role of economic factors, although the focus has been
primarily on the effect of economic change on the differential
rates of national growth and the resulting changes in the international distribution of military power.

There has been far less emphasis on domestic politics and
other societal-level causes of war. One can find numerous hypotheses regarding the impact of a particular variable on the
outbreak of war, but these hypotheses are rarely integrated into
more comprehensive theories. Unlike variables at other levels of
analysis, it is difficult to find anyone, other than a few Kantians,
suggesting that domestic political factors are the most important
causes of war. Even the most notable recent attempts to construct
theories of war that incorporate explanatory variables from several
levels of analysis—including those by Choucri and North, Snyder
and Diesing, and Bueno de Mesquita—generally ignore the role
of domestic political variables altogether.[1] This pattern is not
surprising given a similar tendency in the general theoretical literature on foreign policy decision-making. Allison's paradigms
include a "rational model" which focuses on systemic and external
factors and two models of the operation of governmental politics
and processes. Steinbrunner and Jervis have added a cognitive

---

1 Nazli Choucri and Robert North, *Nations in Conflict* (San Francisco, 1975); Glenn H.
Snyder and Paul Diesing, *Conflict Among Nations* (Princeton, 1977); Bruce Bueno de
Mesquita, *The War Trap* (New Haven, 1981). One important exception is Lebow, who
examines the phenomenon of deterrence failure. He argues that the domestic political
interests of political elites often lead them to defy their adversary's deterrence threats and
initiate hostile actions, even when those threats are credible and backed by adequate
military strength. See Richard Ned Lebow, *Between Peace and War* (Baltimore, 1981).

model, but no one has constructed a comparable model based on domestic politics. This pattern is also reflected in several general surveys of the literature on the causes of war. Other than a brief mention of the in-group/out-group hypothesis and more extended discussions of Marxist-Leninist theories, societal-level sources of war are basically ignored.[2]

This neglect of societal variables by political scientists attempting to construct theories of the causes of war contrasts sharply with recent trends among historians in their studies of the causes of individual wars. The Rankean concept of the *Primat der Aussenpolitik* (primacy of foreign policy) and of the influence of the foreign relations of states on their internal structures and processes, which once dominated continental historiography, is no longer in ascendance. The traditional focus of diplomatic historians on the strategic interaction between rival states through the study of official diplomatic files has given way to a much greater recognition of the role of internal social, economic, and political determinants of foreign policy. Some historians have argued that the pendulum has swung too far. Craig, for example, has deplored the relative neglect of political and diplomatic history and the tendency of historians studying foreign policy to assert a *Primat der Innenpolitik*.[3]

One clear manifestation of this trend toward an increasing focus on the internal determinants of policy is the historiography on World War I, which has been influenced by the work of Kehr and Mayer, and particularly by that of Fischer. Fischer's methodological emphasis on the importance of socioeconomic variables is as important as his substantive emphasis on German responsibility for the war. Kaiser has concluded that "a far-reaching consensus now agrees that German foreign policy after 1897 must

2 Graham T. Allison, *The Essence of Decision* (Boston, 1971); John Steinbrunner, *The Cybernetic Theory of Decision* (Princeton, 1974); Robert Jervis, *Perception and Misperception in International Politics* (Princeton, 1976). For some general surveys of the literature on the causes of war, see Bernard Brodie, *War and Politics* (New York, 1973); Dina A. Zinnes, "Why War? Evidence on the Outbreak of International Conflict," in Ted Robert Gurr (ed.), *Handbook of Political Conflict* (New York, 1980), 331–360; Bueno de Mesquita, "Theories of International Conflict: An Analysis and An Appraisal," in *ibid.*, 361–398.
3 Gordon A. Craig, "Political and Diplomatic History," in Felix Gilbert and Stéphen R. Graubard (eds.), *Historical Studies Today* (New York, 1971), 356–371. For a more general survey of some of these recent trends in the historical literature, see Georg G. Iggers, *New Directions in European Historiography* (Middletown, Conn., 1984; rev. ed.).

be understood as a response to the internal threat of socialism and democracy." This emphasis on the domestic causes of the war is not confined to Germany. Joll argues that the foreign policy of Austria-Hungary was "wholly the product of its internal problems," and that in both France and Russia domestic and foreign policy were so inextricably intermixed that primacy cannot be given to one over the other. Some scholars have emphasized the domestic sources of British social imperialism of the late nineteenth century, and others have argued that Britain's critical failure to give a commitment to France prior to July 1914 was due to cabinet and parliamentary politics.[4]

The importance of internal factors in the processes leading to war is also evident in the other historical cases included in this volume. As Gutmann notes, nearly all treatments of the Thirty Years' War trace its origins to the civil war within the Holy Roman Empire over religion and the internal power of the emperor. Similarly, the French Revolutionary Wars engulfing all of Europe were intimately linked to the social, economic, and political forces within France that led to the revolution and to the dynamics which sustained it. As Chandler argues, internal party politics in France were particularly important in that many internal factions supported war but for different and often conflicting reasons. The socioeconomic forces contributing to the rise of the National Socialist movement and to Hitler's coming to power were key factors in German expansionist policy and the causes of World War II. Some have argued that domestic political constraints shaping British appeasement policy contributed to that war by undermining deterrence.[5]

---

4 Eckart Kehr (ed. Hans-Ulrich Wehler), *Der Primat der Innenpolitik* (Berlin, 1965); Arno J. Mayer, "Internal Causes and Purposes of War in Europe, 1870–1956: A Research Assignment," *Journal of Modern History*, XLI (1969), 291–303; Fritz Fischer, *War of Illusions* (New York, 1975); David E. Kaiser, "Germany and the Origins of the First World War," *Journal of Modern History*, LV (1983), 443. On the role of domestic politics in other states in contributing to the war, see James Joll, *The Origins of the First World War* (New York, 1984), 92–122; Michael R. Gordon, "Domestic Conflict and the Origins of the First World War: The British and German Cases," *Journal of Modern History*, XLVI (1974), 191–226; Samuel R. Williamson, Jr., "The Origins of World War I," *Journal of Interdisciplinary History*, XVIII (1988), 795–818; Joseph A. Schumpeter, *Imperialism and Social Classes* (Oxford, 1951); Bernard Semmel, *Imperialism and Social Reform* (Cambridge, Mass., 1960).
5 Myron P. Gutmann, "The Origins of the Thirty Years War," *Journal of Interdisciplinary History*, XVIII (1988), 749–770; and David G. Chandler, "The Origins of the Napoleonic Wars," unpub. ms. (1986); T. C. W. Blanning, *The Origins of the French Revolutionary Wars*

Although most of the leading theories of the causes of war in the political science literature minimize the importance of domestic political variables, one can find individual hypotheses that link these variables to war. Although these hypotheses are not integrated into a larger theoretical system, it is useful to examine some of them here.

NATIONAL ATTRIBUTES AND WAR   Although international war is a widespread phenomenon, the frequencies of war involvement for different states are not equal, which suggests that the attributes of states may constitute important variables contributing to war. It is sometimes asserted that certain political cultures, ideologies, or religions are more warlike than others, but this proposition finds little support from the quantitative empirical literature. Studies by Richardson, Rummel, Haas, and others have found essentially no relationship between national attributes and foreign conflict behavior.[6]

These and other scholars hence look for explanations for war not in the characteristics of individual states but in the *differences* between states. One common view is that national differences in religion, language, and other characteristics contribute to war, whereas similarities along these dimensions facilitate peace. Nef argues that a "common universe of customs and beliefs" is the "true basis for international peace." Some balance of power theorists, who emphasize the role of power distributions in determining behavior and outcomes, have also suggested that a common in-

(New York, 1986). For a review of the literature on the domestic sources of German expansion and of British appeasement, see Jeffrey L. Hughes, "The Origins of World War II in Europe: British Deterrence Failure and German Expansionism," *Journal of Interdisciplinary History*, XVIII (1988), 851–891.

6   For the variation in war behavior among states, see Quincy Wright, *A Study of War* (Chicago, 1965; 2nd ed.), Tables 31–42; J. David Singer and Melvin Small, *The Wages of War, 1815–1965* (New York, 1972), 257–287. On the disproportionate incidence of great power war behavior, see Levy, *War in the Modern Great Power System, 1495–1975* (Lexington, Ky., 1983). Lewis F. Richardson, *Statistics of Deadly Quarrels* (Chicago, 1960), 168–183, 211–246; Rudolph Rummel, "National Attributes and Foreign Conflict Behavior," in Singer (ed.), *Quantitative International Politics* (New York, 1968), 187–214; Michael Haas, "Societal Approaches to the Study of War," *Journal of Peace Research*, IV (1965), 307–323; Raymond Tanter, "Dimensions of Conflict Behavior within and between Nations, 1958–1960," *Journal of Conflict Resolution*, X (1966), 41–64; Wright, *War*, 828–829. It is difficult to generalize from these studies, however, because many of them follow Rummel and are limited to the 1955–1960 period.

tellectual and moral framework is a precondition for stability and peace. There have been some attempts to test these hypotheses empirically. Although many of the results are contradictory, the bulk of the evidence points to positive but weak relationships between societal differences and the incidence of war.[7]

The implications of these findings are unclear, however, for the absence of a well-defined theoretical framework guiding these studies precludes a meaningful interpretation of the observed empirical associations. There needs to be greater specification of the types of states and conditions under which these empirical relationships are valid. There also needs to be far more theoretical attention to the causal mechanisms by which these factors are translated into decisions for war. For example, do these differences generate conflicting interests which lead to war by creating expectations of gains from war, or do they generate misleading images of the adversary which contribute to war through misperceptions of adversary intentions or capabilities?

DEMOCRACY AND WAR   Although earlier studies found no consistent relationship between type of regime and war behavior, there has recently been renewed interest in the Kantian proposition that democracies are inherently peaceful and that non-democratic regimes are more warlike. Kant's basic argument is that in a republican regime (characterized by a constitutional, representative government and separation of powers) the citizens rule, and "those who would have to decide to undergo all the deprivations of war will very much hesitate to start such an evil game." Decision-makers in non-democratic states are more likely to engage in war, even "for the most trivial reasons" because they do not themselves directly suffer its human consequences and because

7 On the importance of a common cultural or moral framework, see John Nef, *War and Human Progress* (Cambridge, Mass., 1950), 257–258; Hans J. Morgenthau, *Politics Among Nations* (New York, 1967; 4th ed.), 208–215; Edward Vose Gulick, *Europe's Classical Balance of Power* (New York, 1955), 19–24. For quantitative empirical work on this question, see Wright, *War*, 1240–1260; Haas, "Communication Factors in Decision Making," *Peace Research Society (International) Papers*, XII (1969), 65–86; Richardson, *Deadly Quarrels*, 211–246; Rummel, "Dimensions of Dyadic War, 1820–1952," *Journal of Conflict Resolution*, XI (1967), 176–183; Francis A. Beer, *Peace Against War* (San Francisco, 1981), 169. Beer estimates that political, linguistic, and religious differences together account for about 20% of the variance in foreign conflict.

they are not constrained by a system of checks and balances or electoral accountability.[8]

Many who accept the basic Kantian argument concede that, once aroused, democracies adopt a crusading spirit and often fight particularly destructive wars. Democratic polities transform conflicts of interests into moral crusades, demand nothing less than total victory and unconditional surrender, and engage in "liberal interventionism" to promote their own vision of the morally proper international order. Thus Churchill asserted in 1901 that "democracy is more vindictive than Cabinets. The wars of peoples will be more terrible than those of kings." Lippmann reflected the paradox of democracy and foreign policy when he argued that public opinion has forced governments "to be too late with too little, or too long with too much, too pacifist in peace and too bellicose in war, too neutralist or appeasing in negotiation or too transient."[9]

There are other characteristics of decision-making in democratic states which may affect their tendency to become involved in wars, although the linkages to war are not always made explicit. Many have argued that the democratic decision-making process is flawed with respect to the conduct of foreign policy. In a well-known remark, de Tocqueville concluded that "foreign politics demand scarcely any of those qualities which are peculiar to a democracy; they require, on the contrary, the perfect use of almost all those in which it is deficient." Morgenthau emphasizes the importance of a democratic government securing popular approval for its policies, but argues that "the conditions under which popular support can be obtained for a foreign policy are not necessarily identical with the conditions under which a foreign policy can be successfully pursued." Similarly, Kennan argues that public and congressional involvement are "congenital deficiencies" with respect to the effective conduct of foreign policy. More specifically, the factors that are said to be necessary for the effec-

8 Immanuel Kant, "Eternal Peace," in Carl J. Frederich (ed.), *The Philosophy of Kant* (New York, 1949), 430–476; Kenneth N. Waltz, *Man, the State, and War* (New York, 1954), 80–123; idem, "Kant, Liberalism, and War," *American Political Science Review*, LVI (1962), 331–340; Michael W. Doyle, "Kant, Liberal Legacies, and Foreign Affairs: Part I," *Philosophy and Public Affairs*, XII (1983), 205–235.
9 Winston Churchill, speech in the House of Commons (May 13, 1901), in Martin Gilbert (ed.), *Churchill* (Englewood Cliffs, 1967), 21–22; Walter Lippmann, *The Public Philosophy* (Boston, 1955), 20.

tive conduct of foreign policy in a hostile world but are unchar-
acteristic of democracies include coherence, long-range planning
and continuity, flexibility, dispatch, and secrecy. Waltz, however,
disputes the argument that authoritarian states have decisive advantages in international security affairs, and suggests that the
impact of internal politics on foreign policy may be even greater
in authoritarian states than in democracies.[10]

Even if it were true that liberal democratic regimes are less
inclined to *initiate* foreign wars, it would not automatically follow
that they are less likely to become *involved* in international wars.[11]
A reduced willingness to prepare for war or to resort to the threat
or use of force may under some conditions make war more likely
by undermining deterrence. Thus Wright and many others have
argued that democracies are ill-adapted to the successful use of
threats and force as instruments of foreign policy and often fail
to preserve peace by balancing power. Many balance of power
theorists argue more generally that the stability of the international system, and hence a low likelihood of major war, depends
in part on the freedom of decision-makers to pursue realpolitik
without internal constraints. Democratic public opinion impedes
the formation of alliances with ideologically hostile states and the
sudden shifts in alignments that may be necessary for the maintenance of a proper balance of military power in the system or,
more generally, the military commitments that may be necessary
for the purposes of deterrence. Public demands for an open foreign policy process also preclude the secrecy that is often necessary, realists argue, for delicate negotiations with an adversary.
Many have argued, for example, that a definitive British commitment to France before 1914 would probably have been sufficient to deter Germany from its aggressive policies and hence
would have avoided a continental war, but that British public
opinion precluded such a commitment. It has also been argued
that public opinion in Britain was the primary reason for British
diplomatic and military passivity during the enormous shifts in

10   Alexis de Tocqueville, *Democracy in America* (New York, 1975), I, 234–235; Morgenthau, *Politics*, 241; George Kennan, *The Cloud of Danger (Boston, 1977), 3–4;* Waltz, *Foreign
Policy and Democratic Politics* (Boston, 1967), 308–311.
11   I use the concepts of war involvement or participation to refer to behavior in which
no distinction is made as to who initiates the war.

the European balance of power between 1864 and 1875 which created the disequilibrium that undermined stability.[12]

The debate regarding the relative likelihood of democratic and non-democratic regimes going to war has been conducted at the empirical as well as the theoretical level. Most analyses have confirmed the findings of a 1976 study by Small and Singer that there have been no significant differences between democratic or non-democratic states in terms of the proportional frequency of their war involvement or the severity of their wars. Democratic states may be slightly less inclined to initiate wars than non-democratic states, but the evidence is not conclusive. The debate has been rekindled by Rummel's study which suggests that libertarian states are more peaceful, but Rummel's conclusions have been challenged on the grounds that they are due almost entirely to biases in his empirical indicators and the excessively narrow and unrepresentative temporal domain of most of his analyses.[13]

The evidence is conclusive that democratic states have been involved, proportionately, in as many wars as non-democratic states. There is one aspect of the military behavior of democratic states, however, that is clearly distinguished from that of non-democratic states: liberal or democratic states do not fight each other. This observation was first emphasized by Babst in 1972 and reconfirmed in most of the subsequent studies surveyed earlier. The number of wars between democracies during the past two centuries ranges from zero to less than a handful depending

12 On domestic politics and the balance of power, see Wright, *War*, 842–848; Inis L. Claude, Jr., *Power and International Relations* (New York, 1962), 40–93; Morgenthau, *Politics*, 141–144. On public opinion and the British non-commitment in 1914 and earlier, see Mayer, "Internal Causes," 298–299; Gordon, "Domestic Conflict," 195–198. On British passivity during the rise of Prussia, see Paul Kennedy, *The Realities behind Diplomacy* (London, 1981), 74–139; R. W. Seton-Watson, *Britain in Europe, 1789–1914* (Cambridge, 1955), 466–504.

13 Small and Singer, "The War-Proneness of Democratic Regimes, 1816–1965," *Jerusalem Journal of International Relations*, I (1976), 50–69; Rummel, "The Relationship between National Attributes and Foreign Policy Behavior," in Singer, *International Politics*, 187–214; Rummel, "Libertarianism and International Violence," *Journal of Conflict Resolution*, XXVII (1983), 27–71. On the question of war initiation, Small and Singer, "War-Proneness," 64–66, find no difference between democratic and non-democratic states, whereas Chan finds a small but non-statistically significant tendency for democratic states to initiate proportionately fewer wars. Steve Chan, "Mirror, Mirror on the Wall . . . Are the Freer Countries More Pacific?" *Journal of Conflict Resolution*, XXVIII (1984), 617–648. See Chan for a critique of Rummel.

on precisely how democracy is defined, but these are marginal deviations from a robust finding generated by rigorous and systematic empirical investigations. Moreover, in general wars involving all or nearly all of the great powers, democratic states have never fought on opposite sides. This absence of war between democracies comes as close as anything we have to an empirical law in international relations.[14]

Although a number of plausible explanations for the absence of war between democracies have been proposed, none has been rigorously and systematically tested. One reasonable conclusion, however, is that purely structural explanations, which do not differentiate between states on the basis of their internal characteristics, cannot account for the observed behavioral differences between democratic and non-democratic states. The answer probably lies in variables internal to the states.[15]

ECONOMIC STRUCTURE   The most comprehensive of all societal-level approaches to international conflict is Marxist-Leninist theory, which focuses on economic structure as the key independent variable. The basic argument is that the inequitable distribution of wealth in capitalist societies generates overproduction, inadequate domestic investment opportunities, and generally stagnant economies. These effects lead to expansionist and imperialist policies abroad; competition between capitalist enterprises for access to markets, investment opportunities, and raw materials; and ultimately to wars between capitalist states. Capitalist economic systems also generate war economies and high levels of military spending as replacement markets to absorb excess capital, which can lead to war through arms races, international tensions, and a conflict spiral. Capitalist states may also initiate wars against so-

14 Although there is some variation in the definitions of democratic or liberal political systems in this literature, most definitions are comparable to that of Small and Singer in "War-Proneness," 55: "bourgeois democracies" involve 1) regular elections and the free participation of opposition parties, 2) at least 10% of the adult population being able to vote for 3) a parliament that either controlled or shared parity with the executive branch. In this article I do not distinguish between liberal and democratic regimes. Dean Babst, "A Force for Peace," *Industrial Research* (April 1972), 55–58. For possible exceptions, see Small and Singer, "War-Proneness," 19; Rummel, "Libertarianism," 42; Doyle, "Liberal Legacies, 1," 209–217.

15 For alternative explanations of this phenomenon see Small and Singer, "War-Proneness," 67; Doyle, "Kant, Liberal Legacies, and Foreign Affairs, Part II," *Philosophy and Public Affairs*, XII (1983), 323–353.

cialist states in a desperate attempt to prevent the further deterioration of their own positions.[16]

There are numerous critiques of the theoretical coherence and historical validity of the Marxist-Leninist theory of imperialism; a few points will suffice here. First, even if one were to accept the link between capitalism and imperialism, the theoretical linkages between imperialism and war, particularly interstate war, have never been convincingly demonstrated. It is equally plausible that imperialist expansion, particularly in an era of an open colonial frontier, reduces the likelihood of major war by diverting great power competition from the core of the system into the periphery, where their vital interests are much less likely to conflict and where compromise solutions are more feasible. Kautsky suggested that imperialist competition would lead to "ultra-imperialism," the cooperation among capitalist states for the joint exploitation of the periphery. Second, on the empirical level, if we assume a strong association between liberal democratic political systems and capitalist economic systems, Marxist-Leninist theory makes two predictions that are directly contradicted by the observed empirical relationships between liberal democracy and war. The predicted wars between liberal capitalist states have not been commonplace, and capitalist states have not been disproportionately war prone or more likely to initiate wars than other states in the international system.[17]

Liberal theory also explains international war largely in terms of the structure of economic relationships, but reaches the opposite conclusions from Marxist-Leninists. The Manchester liberals argued strongly that free trade promotes economic efficiency and prosperity, which in turn promotes peace. Any interference with the operation of the market mechanism, such as constraints

16 Vladimir Ilyich Lenin, *Imperialism* (New York, 1939); John A. Hobson, *Imperialism* (London, 1954).

17 These particular arguments regarding the empirical inaccuracy of Marxist-Leninist theory depend on the assertion that liberal democratic political systems have historically tended to coincide with capitalist economic systems. For critiques of the Marxist-Leninist theory, see Lionel Robbins, *The Economic Causes of War* (London, 1939), 19–59; Waltz, *Theory of International Politics* (Reading, Mass., 1979), 18–37. On the safety valve hypothesis, see Morgenthau, *Politics*, 340–343; T. Clifton Morgan and Levy, "The Structure of the International System and the Relationship between the Frequency and Seriousness of War," in Margaret P. Karns (ed.), *Persistent Patterns and Emergent Structures in a Waning Century* (New York, 1986), 75–98. Karl Kautsky, "Ultra-imperialism," *New Left Review*, LIX (1970), 41–46.

on trade, reduces profits and increases conflict. Veblen, Schumpeter, and others emphasized the radical opposition of the industrial spirit and the military spirit. They argued that imperialism and war only squander the riches generated by industrial capitalism and are contrary to the interests of the masses as well as the bourgeoisie. Liberal states have material incentives to avoid hostile policies that might lead others to break their established economic ties. Moreover, in relationships between liberal states, difficult questions of production, distribution, price, and other aspects of trade and finance are resolved through impersonal market forces, and interstate conflicts over these issues are minimized. Economic relations between centralized economies, however, tend to be determined by considerations of power rather than by the market, and this politicization of economic conflicts introduces additional tensions into interstate relations.[18]

NATIONALISM AND PUBLIC OPINION   For Kant, Bentham, and most liberals, public opinion is inherently peaceful, and it is widely believed that when wars occur it is because political leaders force war on an unwilling public. There appear to be numerous examples, however, of precisely the opposite: of a hawkish public pressuring political elites into war, or into adopting more hardline policies than they would otherwise prefer. Some examples include the United States in the War of 1812, both the United States and Spain in the Spanish-American War, and Britain and possibly France in the Crimean War. With respect to the Spanish-American War, for example, May writes that, because of domestic politics, President William McKinley "led his country unhesitatingly toward a war which he did not want for a cause in which he did not believe."[19]

18 For surveys of liberal theories of war, see A. Geoffrey Blainey, *The Causes of War* (New York, 1973), 18–32; Edmund Silberner (trans. Alexander H. Krappe) *The Problem of War in Nineteenth Century Economic Thought* (Princeton, 1946); Barry Buzan, "Economic Structure and International Security: The Limits of the Liberal Case," *International Organization*, XXXVIII (1984), 597–624. On the relationship between industrialism, capitalism, democracy, and peace, see Thorstein Veblen, *Imperial Germany and the Industrial Revolution* (Ann Arbor, 1966); Schumpeter, *Imperialism*; Raymond Aron, *War and Industrial Society* (London, 1958). On the politicization of international economic relations between states with centralized economies, see *idem, War*; Benjamin J. Cohen, *The Question of Imperialism* (New York, 1973).
19 Jeremy Bentham (ed. John Bowring), *The Works of Jeremy Bentham* (Edinburgh, 1843), II–IV. On public opinion, party politics, and the origins of the War of 1812, see Roger

Peoples in both democratic and non-democratic states are often highly enthusiastic at the beginning of wars, although this support may decline rapidly if the war becomes prolonged and costly. In American politics popular support for a president invariably increases immediately after the use of force, regardless of the wisdom or success of that military action. This pattern has been explained by the tendency of the public to rally around the flag, the president, and the party, and ultimately by the phenomenon of modern nationalism.[20]

Nationalism has created the sense of a common interest in the nation, a concept of the national interest as the highest value, and an intense commitment to the well-being of the state. This commitment is strengthened by national myths regarding the omniscience and omnipotence of the nation and the congruence of one's national morality with a supranational ethic. Such myths and doctrines can be used by elites to advance their own view of the national interest or their own political interests, but, once created, these myths and doctrines take on a life of their own. Assertive national policies and even war can be psychologically functional for individuals by increasing their sense of power and control over an oppressive environment and by reinforcing the tendency of some individuals to seek their identity and fulfillment through the state. Thus Proudhon wrote that war had acquired the status of religion: "For the masses, the real Christ is Alexander, Caesar, Charlemagne, Napoleon." Thus nationalism can generate a hardline public opinion which imposes major constraints on statesmen who recognize the limits of power and who would prefer to act with more prudence in their interactions with other states. In Morgenthau's words, "compromise, the virtue of the old diplomacy, becomes the treason of the new." Thus statesmen are sometimes pressured by a jingoistic public to pursue bellicose

---

Brown, *The Republic in Peril* (New York, 1964). On the Spanish-American War, see Richard Hofstadter, *The Age of Reform* (New York, 1955); Ernest May, *Imperial Democracy* (New York, 1961). On Britain and the Crimean War, see Olive Anderson, *A Liberal State at War* (London, 1967).

20 The support of presidential actions by the American public is analyzed by John E. Mueller, *War, Presidents and Public Opinion* (New York, 1973). For some recent empirical work which qualifies the rally-around-the-flag hypotheses, see Richard Stoll, "The Guns of November," *Journal of Conflict Resolution*, XXVII (1984), 231–246; Charles W. Ostrom, Jr., and Brian L. Job, "The President and the Political Use of Force," *American Political Science Review*, LXXX (1986), 541–566.

policies for which the risk of war far outweighs the interests at stake and to forego compromises which are in the best interests of all.[21]

Public opinion is not always hawkish, and there are numerous examples of public opinion constraining decision-makers from taking more hardline policies. Although it would be useful to know whether public opinion is usually more hawkish or more dovish, there are other questions that are probably more important. One concerns the conditions under which public opinion prefers more belligerent policies and the conditions under which it prefers more conciliatory policies. Another concerns the particular kinds of military actions that the public is likely to support (for example, the quick and massive use of force as opposed to gradual and limited actions). An even more basic question is the extent to which public preferences influence state decisions relating to war and peace. These are complex questions, particularly because of the diversity of political systems and historical circumstances over which we want to generalize. In addition, political elites are not only constrained by public opinion, but they can also actively manipulate public opinion for their own purposes. The nature of this reciprocal relationship between political elites and the mass public is poorly understood. The complexity of the relationship between public opinion and foreign policy decision-making is undoubtedly one of the reasons for the absence of a theory of public opinion and war.

THE SCAPEGOAT HYPOTHESIS   The tendency of peoples in a wide range of circumstances to support assertive national policies which appear to enhance the power and prestige of the state may lead decision-makers, under certain conditions, to embark on aggressive foreign policies and sometimes even war as a means of increasing or maintaining their domestic support. This old idea is often referred to as the scapegoat or diversionary theory of war, for political elites can use a foreign war to divert popular attention from internal social, economic, and political problems.[22]

21 John Breuilly, *Nationalism and the State* (Chicago, 1985); Erich Fromm, *Escape from Freedom* (New York, 1941); Pierre-Joseph Proudhon, *La Guerre et la paix* (Paris, 1861), quoted in Nef, *War*, 405; Morgenthau, *Politics*, 532–550.
22 A different theoretical question, which is not discussed here, concerns the symbiotic relationship between domestic politics and external war in the processes involved in the

Theoretically, the scapegoat theory is based on the in-group/ out-group hypothesis in sociology. Simmel, in the first systematic treatment of the subject, argued that conflict with an out-group increases the cohesion and political centralization of the in-group, and generalized to international relations: "war with the outside is sometimes the last chance for a state ridden with inner antagonisms to overcome these antagonisms, or else to break up definitely." Coser modified many of Simmel's propositions. He argues that the cohesion of the in-group will be increased only if there already exists some minimal level of internal cohesion and only if it is generally perceived that the external threat menaces the group as a whole and not just some part of it. Otherwise, external conflict will lead to internal conflict and disintegration rather than cohesion. Coser is the most widely cited authority on the in-group/out-group hypothesis, but this important qualification is not always recognized.[23]

There has been a great deal of empirical research on the in-group/out-group hypothesis by psychologists, anthropologists, sociologists, and political scientists. This literature has been thoroughly reviewed elsewhere, and a brief summary of the political science literature will suffice. Numerous quantitative studies, which simply correlate a variety of indicators of the internal and foreign conflict behavior of states, have generally agreed that there exists no relationship between the two. However, some studies which attempt to control for other variables (such as type of regime) have found positive but weak relationships between internal and external conflict.[24]

Some comparative historical studies have found, contrary to the large-N correlational studies, a much stronger relationship between internal instability and external war. Rosecrance con-

---

development of the modern state. See Charles Tilly, "War Making and State Making as Organized Crime," in Peter B. Evans, Dietrich Rueschemeyer, and Theda Skocpol (eds.), *Bringing the State Back In* (Cambridge, 1985), 169–191; Tilly (ed.), *The Formation of National States in Western Europe* (Princeton, 1975).

23 Georg Simmel (trans. Kurt H. Wolff), *Conflict* (Glencoe, Ill., 1955), 93; Lewis Coser, *The Functions of Social Conflict* (Glencoe, Ill., 1956).

24 See Rummel, "The Dimensions of Conflict Behavior within and between Nations," *General Systems Yearbook*, VIII (1963), 1–50; Tanter, "Dimensions of Conflict"; Jonathan Wilkenfeld, (ed.), *Conflict Behavior and Linkage Politics* (New York, 1973), 148–190. For more detailed reviews of this literature, see Arthur A. Stein, "Conflict and Cohesion," *Journal of Conflict Resolution*, XX (1976), 143–172; Michael Stohl, "The Nexus of Civil and International Conflict," in Gurr (ed.), *Handbook*; Zinnes, "Why War?" 341–344.

cludes that the primary determinant of international stability and peace in the European system from 1740 to 1960 was internal stability and the resulting security of elites, whereas domestic instability and elite insecurity were associated with war. Rosecrance argues, contrary to some of the quantitative correlational studies, that this relationship holds regardless of the political structure or ideology of the regime. In addition, there have been numerous historical case studies suggesting that a major cause of individual wars was the motivation of political leaders to solve their internal problems through a diplomatic or military victory abroad.[25]

The arguments by Kehr, Mayer, and others that the aggressive policies of Germany and other powers in 1914 were driven by the hope that they would help maintain a precarious domestic status quo against the forces of democracy and socialism have already been mentioned, and there are numerous other cases. Michon adopts a scapegoat interpretation of French policy in 1792: "War was willed solely to act as a diversion from the social problems. . . . [War] would give the government dictatorial powers and would allow it to eliminate its detested enemies. For these groups the war was a grand maneuver of domestic politics." Many trace the origins of the Russo-Japanese War to the motivation articulated by the Russian minister of the interior: "What this country needs is a short victorious war to stem the tide of revolution." Hitler also used an aggressive foreign policy to consolidate his internal political position (although this was probably not the primary cause of the war), and similar motivations have been widely attributed to the Argentine junta in their 1982 attempt to seize the Falkland (Malvinas) Islands from Britain. Thus the quantitative empirical research bearing on the scapegoat hypothesis contradicts much of the historical literature, and it is not clear which (if either) is correct.[26]

Although the quantitative studies of the relationships between domestic and foreign conflict are beset by numerous methodological problems, the conceptual problems are even more se-

25 Richard Rosecrance, *Action and Reaction in World Politics* (Boston, 1963).
26 On the 1914 case, see the sources in n. 4. Georges Michon is quoted by Blanning, *French Revolutionary Wars*, 71. William L. Langer, "The Origin of the Russo-Japanese War," in *idem, Explorations in Crises* (Cambridge, Mass., 1969), 3–45; Max Hastings and Simon Jenkins, *The Battle for the Falklands* (New York, 1983).

rious.[27] These studies have not been based on or guided by theory, but instead have been driven too much by method and (after Rummel) by data availability. They have focused on the question of whether there exists an empirical association between internal and external conflict without regard for the causal processes which might produce such a result. Their strictly correlational methodology fails to distinguish processes in which internal conflict generates external conflict from those in which external conflict generates internal conflict.[28]

The first of these processes can be further subdivided. Conflict within state A may tempt A's leaders to resort to the use of force externally for diversionary purposes, as suggested by the scapegoat hypothesis. Alternatively, conflict within state A may tempt state B to intervene, either to exploit a temporary military advantage created by the impact of A's turmoil on its military strength, or to attempt to influence the outcome of the struggle for power in A. It is possible that both of these processes may be operative. Conflict within A may generate weaknesses which provide an opportunity for B to attack, which in turn provides the political leadership of A with a real external threat which can be exploited for its own domestic political purposes. This external threat can be particularly useful for revolutionary regimes, as suggested by the cases of France in 1792, Russia in 1918, and Iran in 1980.[29]

Another weakness of empirical studies of the in-group/out-group hypothesis is their failure to identify the conditions under

27 One serious flaw in the research design of these quantitative studies is the 1955–1960 period upon which most of them are based. This is not only too narrow a temporal domain but also coincides with a period which is relatively peaceful and entirely unrepresentative of "normal" international political behavior, and thus restricts the generalizability of the findings. For an excellent methodological critique, see Joseph M. Scolnick, Jr., "An Appraisal of Studies of the Linkages between Domestic and International Conflict," *Comparative Political Studies*, VI (1974), 485–509.

28 External war often results in an increase in the government's extraction of resources from society to fund the war effort, which under certain conditions generates resistance from key elites or masses. War may also weaken the government's repressive capacity and encourage its internal enemies to rebel. See Tilly, "Reflections on the History of European State-making," in idem, *Formation*, 74.

29 Blainey, *Causes of War*, 68–86, argues that external attacks to exploit internal weaknesses have historically been more common than diversionary actions, but this claim is an unresolved empirical question. The possibility of a revolutionary regime responding to an externally initiated attack in a way that helps consolidate its own political power was emphasized to me by Joseph Nye.

which the proposition is likely to hold. The resulting correlational analyses over a universe of cases have a minimum of scientific controls and may be masking stronger relationships that hold in more restricted circumstances. Although many of these empirical studies refer to Coser, they generally neglect his qualification that if the level of pre-existing internal conflict is too high, foreign conflict will increase rather than decrease internal conflict. If this is true, the point at which the relationship reverses must be specified before the hypothesis can be tested. External constraints are also important. A diplomatic defeat usually (but not always) intensifies internal political divisions, and therefore a state's relative power position may be an important factor affecting scapegoating. The rate of change in military power may also have an impact. Decision-makers faced with a decline in military strength as well as internal divisions may be particularly willing to gamble on a war that might solve their external and internal problems simultaneously, and thus be driven to war by the interaction of scapegoat and preventive motivations. Fischer and others argue that these were the two primary motivations leading Germany to precipitate a war in 1914. Lebow's work suggests that this phenomenon may be more general. In fact, internal conflict—and the social and economic problems that often generate it—may sometimes be an important cause of national decline.[30]

For these and other reasons, the international relations literature on the in-group/out-group conflict serves as a classic example of the futility of rigorous empirical research that is not guided by adequate theorizing. As Stohl argues, "The continuing lack of theoretical foundation has worked against the cumulation of evidence" producing instead only "isolated bits of information." One reason, in this author's opinion, for the atheoretical nature of much of the research by political scientists on the relationship between domestic and foreign conflict is the failure to give much attention to work in other disciplines. These researchers have accepted Coser's basic hypothesis without considering its qualifications, and have not utilized the literature in psychology, anthropology, and sociology regarding some of the other conditions affecting the relationship between in-group and out-

30 Fischer, War, 398; Lebow, Between Peace and War; Levy, "Declining Power and the Preventive Motivation for War," World Politics, XL (1987), 82–107.

group conflict. Historical research on this question is also useful, not just for analysis of individual cases which demonstrate the importance of scapegoating, but also for more theoretically oriented efforts to generalize about these relationships.[31]

Mayer's work on the internal causes of war is a good example of historical analysis which provides a richer theoretical development of the scapegoat hypothesis than can generally be found in the political science literature.[32] Mayer argues, with Coser, that the impact of external war on internal cohesion depends on preexisting levels of internal unity, and also on the outcome of the war: victory strengthens the internal political position of those who advocate and direct the war, whereas defeat reduces their power and increases that of the opposition. Political decision-makers recognize these dangers and, Mayer suggests, refrain from external diversionary actions if internal tensions are sufficiently acute or if the risks of defeat are too great. He hypothesizes that internal politics have the greatest impact on foreign policy, whether by providing incentives or disincentives for war, in revolutionary and prerevolutionary times and under conditions of internal instability rather than in times of domestic and international peace. Internal crises create a siege mentality among conservatives and an effort to maintain their privileged political, social, and economic positions through the diversionary use of force against external enemies. Mayer applies his framework to a number of cases beginning with the French Revolution and concludes that the primary cause of internal crises and foreign wars was "over-reaction to over-perceived revolutionary dangers rather than any calibrated and hazardous resistance to enormous and imminent insurgencies."[33]

31 Stohl, "Civil and International Conflict," 326–329. For a more extensive analysis of the scapegoat hypothesis, see Levy, "The Diversionary Theory of War," in Manus I. Midlarsky (ed.), *Handbook of War Studies*, forthcoming.

32 It is revealing that Mayer's work is rarely cited in political science research on the relationship between internal and external conflict. One exception is Michael G. Fry and Arthur N. Gilbert, "A Historian and Linkage Politics," *International Studies Quarterly*, XXVI (1982), 425–444.

33 Mayer, "Internal Causes of War"; *idem*, "Internal Crises and War since 1870," in Charles L. Bertrand (ed.), *Revolutionary Situations in Europe, 1917–1922: Germany, Italy, Austria-Hungary* (Montréal, 1977); Mayer, "Domestic Causes of the First World War," in Leonard Krieger and Fritz Stern (eds.), *The Responsibility of Power* (New York, 1967), 286–300. Note that Mayer's conclusion does not appear to be fully consistent with his

Mayer may go too far in always assuming the existence of a relatively homogeneous upper class which attempts to hold onto the reins of power through the diversionary use of force abroad. A more pluralistic political model, in which one faction may seek a foreign confrontation to advance its own interests in the intra-elite competition for power, may be more plausible. Lebow suggests such a hypothesis. He argues that the attempts to expand Russian influence in Korea prior to the Russo-Japanese War were the result of deliberate efforts of the Bezobrazov faction to undermine the political influence of Sergei Witte, the minister of finance. Alternatively, each of several internal factions may believe that war or warlike policies would advance its own bureaucratic or domestic political objectives. A good example is revolutionary France, where nearly all of the major factions (save the extreme radicals) sought war but for different reasons.[34]

It is also possible for a decision for imperialism or war to emerge from an internal coalition-building process without it being the leading preference of any single political faction. Snyder has constructed a theory which emphasizes divisions in the elite, the lack of a compelling interest for external expansion in any one group, and the processes of logrolling and compromise that lead to internal harmony and imperial overcommitment. The German coalition of iron and rye in the late 1800s would be one example, and the British coalition of liberals and conservatives supporting social imperialism during the same period would be another.[35]

A major theme of this article is the gap between historians and political scientists in their evaluations of the relative importance of domestic political variables in the processes leading to war. The political science literature on the relationship between the domestic and foreign conflict behavior of states is a particularly striking example of this discrepancy. The lack of any support for such a relationship in the quantitative empirical literature contrasts sharply with the case studies of individual wars by historians,

argument that political elites' awareness of the risks of external diversionary actions under conditions of low internal cohesion deters them from undertaking such actions.

34 Lebow, "Deterrence Deadlock: Is There a Way Out?" in Jervis, Lebow, and Stein (eds.), *Psychology and Deterrence*, 180–202. On the French case, see Blanning, *French Revolutionary Wars*.

35 Jack Snyder, *Myths of Empire: Domestic Politics and Strategic Ideology*, unpub. ms.

with historical studies by political scientists, and with the theoretical literature in political science. These discrepancies, in conjunction with the methodological limitations of the quantitative studies, lead to the tentative conclusion that the relationship between internal conflict and the foreign conflict behavior of states is more substantial than implied by the quantitative empirical literature in political science.

The primary explanation for the lack of evidence for such a relationship is the absence of a well-developed theoretical framework guiding the empirical studies. One reason for this theoretical impoverishment is exceedingly narrow disciplinary boundaries and the failure of political scientists to appreciate the potentially rich sources of theoretical insights in other fields. Although political scientists often acknowledge the potential utility of historical literature for testing their own theoretical generalizations, they underestimate its utility as a source of theoretical propositions. The literature relating to the scapegoat hypothesis is an excellent example of Bueno de Mesquita's argument that "too often we do not bring as much rigor to our theorizing as we do to our data analysis," but it also illustrates the multiple sources of important theoretical insights that might aid in the task of theoretical development.[36]

36 Bueno de Mesquita, "Theories," 396.

Robert Jervis

War and Misperception   War has so many causes—in part
because there are so many kinds of wars—and misperception has
so many effects—again in part because there are so many kinds
of misperceptions—that it is not possible to draw any definitive
conclusions about the impact of misperception on war.[1] But we
can address some conceptual and methodological problems, note
several patterns, and try to see how misperceptions might lead to
World War III. In this article, I use the term misperception
broadly, to include inaccurate inferences, miscalculations of consequences, and misjudgments about how others will react to one's
policies.

Although war can occur even when both sides see each other
accurately, misperception often plays a large role. Particularly
interesting are judgments and misjudgments of another state's
intentions. Both overestimates and underestimates of hostility
have led to war in the past, and much of the current debate about
policy toward the Soviet Union revolves around different judgments about how that country would respond to American policies that were either firm or conciliatory. Since statesmen know
that a war between the United States and the Soviet Union would
be incredibly destructive, however, it is hard to see how errors
of judgment, even errors like those that have led to past wars,
could have the same effect today. But perceptual dynamics could
cause statesmen to see policies as safe when they actually were
very dangerous or, in the final stages of deep conflict, to see war
as inevitable and therefore to see striking first as the only way to
limit destruction.

POSSIBLE AREAS OF MISPERCEPTION   Although this article will
concentrate on misperceptions of intentions of potential adversar-

Robert Jervis is Professor of Political Science and member of the Institute of War and
Peace Studies at Columbia University. He is the author of *The Illogic of American Nuclear
Strategy* (Ithaca, 1984).

[1] For a good typology of wars caused by misperception, see George H. Quester, "Six
Causes of War," *Jerusalem Journal of International Relations*, VI (1982), 1–23.

ies, many other objects can be misperceived as well. Capabilities of course can be misperceived; indeed, as Blainey stresses, excessive military optimism is frequently associated with the outbreak of war.[2] Military optimism is especially dangerous when coupled with political and diplomatic pessimism. A country is especially likely to strike if it feels that, although it can win a war immediately, the chances of a favorable diplomatic settlement are slight and the military situation is likely to deteriorate. Furthermore, these estimates, which are logically independent, may be psychologically linked. Pessimism about current diplomatic and long-run military prospects may lead statesmen to exaggerate the possibility of current military victory as a way of convincing themselves that there is, in fact, a solution to what otherwise would be an intolerable dilemma.

Less remarked on is the fact that the anticipated consequences of events may also be incorrect. For example, America's avowed motive for fighting in Vietnam was not the direct goal of saving that country, but rather the need to forestall the expected repercussions of defeat. What it feared was a "domino effect" leading to a great increase in Communist influence in Southeast Asia and the perception that the United States lacked the resolve to protect its interests elsewhere in the world. In retrospect, it seems clear that neither of these possibilities materialized. This case is not unique; states are prone to fight when they believe that "bandwagoning" rather than "balancing" dynamics are at work—that is, when they believe that relatively small losses or gains will set off a self-perpetuating cycle. In fact, such beliefs are often incorrect. Although countries will sometimes side with a state which is gaining power, especially if they are small and can do little to counteract such a menace, the strength and resilience of balancing incentives are often underestimated by the leading powers. Statesmen are rarely fatalistic; they usually resist the growth of dominant powers.[3] A striking feature of the Cold War is how little

2 For a discussion of the concept of intentions in international politics, see Jervis, *Perception and Misperception in International Politics* (Princeton, 1976), 48–57. For a discussion of the meaning of that concept in general, see Gertrude E. M. Anscombe, *Intention* (Ithaca, 1969); Ernest May, "Conclusions: Capabilities and Proclivities," in *idem* (ed.), *Knowing One's Enemies* (Princeton, 1984), 503. A. Geoffrey Blainey, *The Causes of War* (New York, 1973).
3 See Arnold Wolfers, *Discord and Collaboration* (Baltimore, 1962), 122–24; Kenneth Waltz, *Theory of International Politics* (Reading, Mass., 1979); Stephen Walt, "Alliance

each side has suffered when it has had to make what it perceived as costly and dangerous retreats.

At times we may need to distinguish between misperceptions of a state's predispositions—that is, its motives and goals—and misperceptions of the realities faced by the state. Either can lead to incorrect predictions, and, after the fact, it is often difficult to determine which kind of error was made. When the unexpected behavior is undesired, decision-makers usually think that they have misread the other state's motives, not the situation it faced.[4] Likewise, scholars generally focus on misjudgments of intentions rather than misjudgments of situations. We, too, shall follow this pattern, although it would be very useful to explore the proposition that incorrect explanations and predictions concerning other states' behaviors are caused more often by misperceptions concerning their situations than by misperceptions about their predispositions.

WAR WITHOUT MISPERCEPTION   It has often been argued that, by definition, the proposition is true that every war involves at least one serious misperception. If every war has a loser, it would seem to stand to reason that the defeated state made serious miscalculations when it decided to fight. But, whereas empirical investigations reveal that decisions to go to war are riddled with misperceptions, it is not correct that such a proposition follows by definition.

A country could rationally go to war even though it was certain it would lose. First, the country could value fighting itself, either as an ultimate goal or as a means for improving man and society. Second, faced with the choice of giving up territory to a stronger rival or losing it through a war, the state might choose war because of considerations of honor, domestic politics, or international reputation. Honor is self-explanatory, although, like the extreme form of Social Darwinism alluded to earlier, it sounds strange to modern ears. Domestic politics, however, are likely to remain with us and may have been responsible for at least some

Formation and the Balance of World Power," *International Security*, IX (1985), 3–43; *idem, The Origins of Alliances* (Ithaca, 1987).
4 For a good review, see Edward Jones, "How Do People Perceive the Causes of Behavior?" *American Scientist*, LXIV (1976), 300–305. For an analysis of related phenomena in international politics, see Jervis, *Perception and Misperception*, 343–354.

modern wars. It is a commonplace that leaders may seek "a quick and victorious war" in order to unify the country (this sentiment is supposed to have been voiced by Vyacheslav Plehve, the Russian minister of the interior on the eve of the Russo-Japanese War), but statesmen might also think that a short, unsuccessful war might serve the same function.

Although examples seem rare, international considerations could also lead a statesman to fight a war he knows he will lose. The object would be to impress third countries. Such a decision might appear particularly perverse because a loss would seem to show that the country is weak. But more important than the display of its lack of military capability could be the display of its resolve, if not foolhardiness. Other nations which had quarrels with the state might infer that it is willing to fight even when its position is weak, and such an inference might strengthen the state's bargaining position.[5]

Only rarely can statesmen be certain of a war's outcome, and once we take the probabilistic nature of judgments into consideration, it is even more clear that one can have wars without misperception. A state may believe that the chances of victory are small and yet rationally decide to fight if the gains of victory are large and the costs of losing are not much greater than those of making the concessions necessary to avoid war.

Although a state could start a war that it had little prospect of winning solely because of the attractions of victory, psychology and politics both conspire to make it much more likely that states go to war because of their gloomy prognostications of what will happen if they do not fight. Psychologically, losses hurt more than gains gratify. Both domestic and international politics produce a similar effect. Public opinion and partisan opposition is more easily turned against a government which seems to be sac-

---

5 This concept is similar to the economist's notion of the "chain store paradox." It applies in cases in which the state can prevail in the conflict, but only at a cost which exceeds the immediate gains. The reason for fighting in this case is again to impress other potential challengers, and the analogy is the behavior of a large chain store toward small stores which challenge it by cutting prices. The chain store can respond by cutting prices even more, thus losing money but succeeding in driving the competitor out of business. The point of taking such action is to discourage other challengers, but the paradox is that in each particular case the chain store loses money and the tactic will be effective only if others believe it will be repeated. See Reinhard Selten, "The Chain Store Paradox," *Theory and Decision*, IX (1978), 127–159.

rificing existing values than one which is not expanding the country's influence rapidly enough. Analyses of international politics reinforce these pressures. Statesmen are generally slower to believe that the domino effect will work for them than against them. They realize that other states will often respond to their gains by attempting to block further advances; by contrast, they also believe that any loss of their influence will lead to a further erosion of their power.

Because a state which finds the status quo intolerable or thinks it can be preserved only by fighting can be driven to act despite an unfavorable assessment of the balance of forces, it is neither surprising nor evidence of misperception that those who start wars often lose them. For example, Austria and Germany attacked in 1914 largely because they believed that the status quo was unstable and that the tide of events was moving against them. As Sagan shows, the Japanese made a similar calculation in 1941.[6] Although they overestimated the chance of victory because they incorrectly believed that the United States would be willing to fight—and lose—a limited war, the expectation of victory was not a necessary condition for their decision to strike. According to their values, giving up domination of China—which would have been required in order to avoid war—was tantamount to sacrificing their national survival. Victory, furthermore, would have placed them in the first rank of nations and preserved their domestic values. The incentives were somewhat similar in 1904, when they attacked Russia even though "the Emperor's most trusted advisers expressed no confidence as to the outcome of the war. . . . The army calculated that Japan had a fifty-fifty chance to win a war. The Navy expected that half its forces would be lost, but it hoped the enemy's naval forces would be annihilated with the remaining half."[7] Fighting was justified in light of Japan's deteriorating military position combined with the possibility of increasing its influence over its neighbors.

METHODOLOGICAL PROBLEMS   The most obvious way to determine the influence of misperception on war would be to employ

6 Scott D. Sagan, "The Origins of the Pacific War," *Journal of Interdisciplinary History*, XVIII (1988), 893–922.
7 Shumpei Okamoto, *The Japanese Oligarchy and the Russo-Japanese War* (New York, 1970), 101.

the comparative method and contrast the effects of accurate and inaccurate perceptions. But several methodological problems stand in the way. First is the question of whether perceptions should be judged in terms of outcomes or processes—that is, whether we should compare them to what was later revealed to have been reality or whether we should ask how reasonable were the statesmen's inferences, given the information available at the time. The two criteria call for different kinds of evidence and often yield different conclusions.[8] People are often right for the wrong reasons and, conversely, good analyses may produce answers which later will be shown to have been incorrect. Shortly after Adolf Hitler took power, Robert Vansittart, the permanent undersecretary of the British Foreign Office, concluded that the Germans would increase their military power as rapidly as possible in order to overturn the status quo. In criticizing military officials, who generally disagreed with him, he said: "Prophecy is largely a matter of insight. I do not think the Service Departments have enough. On the other hand they might say I have too much. The answer is that I knew the Germans better."[9] His image of Hitler was quite accurate, but it is not clear that he reached it by better reasoning or supported it with more evidence than did those who held a different view.

A second difficulty is that historians and political scientists are drawn to the study of conflict more often than to the analysis of peaceful interactions. As a result, we know little about the degree to which harmonious relationships are characterized by accurate perceptions. I suspect, however, that they are the product of routinized and highly constrained patterns of interaction more often than the result of accurate perceptions.

A third problem lies in determining whether perceptions were accurate, which involves two subproblems. First, it is often difficult to determine what a statesman's—let alone a country's—perceptions are. We usually have to tease the person's views out of confused and conflicting evidence and try to separate his true beliefs from those he merely wants others to believe he holds.

8 Processes which seem highly rational may yield less accurate perceptions than those which are more intuitive. See Kenneth Hammond, "A Theoretically Based Review of Theory and Research in Judgment and Decision Making," unpub. ms. (Boulder, 1986).
9 Quoted in Donald Watt, "British Intelligence and the Coming of the Second World War in Europe," in May (ed.), *Knowing One's Enemies*, 268.

Indeed, in some cases the person initially may not have well-defined perceptions but may develop them to conform to the actions he has taken.[10] Second, even greater difficulties arise when the perceptions are compared with "reality." The true state of the military balance can be determined only by war; states' intentions may be impossible to determine, even after the fact and with all the relevant records open for inspection.

Our ability to determine whether statesmen's assessments are accurate is further reduced by the probabilistic nature of these assessments. Statesmen often believe that a given image is the one most likely to be correct or that a given outcome is the one most likely to occur. But the validity of such judgments is extremely hard to determine unless we have a large number of cases. If someone thinks that something will happen nine out of ten times, the fact that it does not happen once does not mean that the judgment was wrong. Thus if a statesman thinks that another country probably is aggressive and we later can establish that it was not, we cannot be sure that his probabilistic judgment was incorrect.[11]

MISPERCEPTIONS AND THE ORIGINS OF WORLD WARS I AND II   Tracing the impact of beliefs and perceptions in any given case might seem easy compared to the problems just presented. But it is not, although even a brief list of the misperceptions preceding the major conflicts of this century is impressive. Before World War I, all of the participants thought that the war would be short. They also seem to have been optimistic about its outcome, but there is conflicting evidence. (For example, both Edward Grey and Theobald von Bethmann Hollweg made well-known gloomy predictions, but it is unclear whether these statements accurately reflected their considered judgments. In addition, quantitative analysis of the available internal memoranda indicates pessimism,

10   Daryl Bem, "Self-Perception Theory," in Leonard Berkowitz (ed.), *Advances in Experimental Social Psychology* (New York, 1972), VI, 1–62. For an application to foreign policy, see Deborah Larson, *The Origins of Containment* (Princeton, 1985).
11   In politics, not only are situations rarely repeated, but the meaning of probabilistic judgments is not entirely clear. Are these statements merely indications of the degree to which the person feels he lacks important facts or an understanding of significant relationships? Or do they reflect the belief that politics is inherently uncertain and that, if somehow the same situation was repeated in all its details, behavior might be different on different occasions?

although there are problems concerning the methodology employed.[12])

May argues that the analyses of the intentions of the adversaries during this period were more accurate than the analyses of their capabilities, but even the former were questionable.[13] Some of the judgments of July 1914 were proven incorrect—for example, the German expectation that Britain would remain neutral and Germany's grander hopes of keeping France and even Russia out of the war. Furthermore, the broader assumptions underlying the diplomacy of the period may also have been in error. Most important on the German side was not an image of a particular country as the enemy, but its basic belief that the ensuing events would lead to either "world power or decline." For the members of the Triple Entente, and particularly Great Britain, the central question was German intentions, so brilliantly debated in Eyre Crowe's memorandum and Thomas Sanderson's rebuttal to it. We still cannot be sure whether the answer which guided British policy was correct.[14]

The list of misperceptions preceding World War II is also impressive. Capabilities again were misjudged, although not as badly as in the previous era.[15] Few people expected the blitzkrieg to bring France down; the power of strategic bombardment was greatly overestimated; the British exaggerated the vulnerability of the German economy, partly because they thought that it was stretched taut at the start of the war. Judgments of intention were even less accurate. The appeasers completely misread Hitler; the anti-appeasers failed to see that he could not be stopped without a war. For his part, Hitler underestimated his adversaries' determination. During the summer of 1939 he doubted whether Britain would fight and, in the spring of 1940, expected her to make peace.[16]

12 See Ole Holsti, Robert North, and Richard Brody, "Perception and Action in the 1914 Crisis," in J. David Singer (ed.), *Quantitative International Politics* (New York, 1968), 123–158.

13 May, "Conclusions," 504. For a more detailed discussion of May's argument, see Jervis, "Intelligence and Foreign Policy," *International Security*, XI (1986/87), 141–61.

14 This continuing debate also underlies the difficulty of determining when perceptions are misperceptions. Indeed, when we contemplate the task of avoiding World War III, it is disheartening to note that we cannot even be sure how the participants could have avoided World War I.

15 See May (ed.), *Knowing One's Enemies*, 237–301, 504–519.

16 This belief may not have been as foolish as it appears in retrospect. While France was

It might also be noted that in both cases the combatants paid insufficient attention to and made incorrect judgments about the behavior of neutrals. To a large extent, World War I was decided by the American entry and World War II by the involvement of the Soviet Union and the United States.[17] But we cannot generalize from these two examples to say that states are prone to make optimistic estimates concerning the role of neutrals; it may be equally true that pessimistic judgments may lead states to remain at peace, and we would have no way of determining the validity of such assessments.

DID THE MISPERCEPTIONS MATTER?   But did these misperceptions cause the wars? Which if any of them, had they been corrected, would have led to a peaceful outcome? In attempting to respond to such questions, we should keep in mind that they are hypothetical and so do not permit conclusive answers. As Stein has noted, not all misperceptions have significant consequences.[18]

If Britain and France had understood Hitler, they would have fought much earlier, when the balance was in their favor and victory could have been relatively quick and easy. (Managing the postwar world might have been difficult, however, especially if others—including the Germans—held a more benign image of Hitler.) If Hitler had understood his adversaries, the situation would have been much more dangerous since he might have devised tactics that would have allowed him to fight on more favorable terms. But on either of these assumptions, war still would have been inevitable; both sides preferred to fight rather than make the concessions that would have been necessary to maintain peace.[19]

---

falling, the British Cabinet spent two days debating whether to open talks with Germany. See Philip M. H. Bell, *A Certain Eventuality* (Farnborough, Eng., 1974), 31–54; Martin Gilbert, *Winston Churchill, VI: Finest Hour, 1939–1941* (London, 1983), 402–425. Given the situation Britain faced, seeking peace might have been reasonable. See David Reynolds, "Churchill and the British 'Decision' to Fight on in 1940: Right Policy, Wrong Reason," in Richard Langhorne (ed.), *Diplomacy and Intelligence during the Second World War* (Cambridge, 1985), 147–67.

17   The role of states which are not involved in the first stages of combat is stressed by Blainey, *Causes of War*, 57–67, 228–242; Bruce Bueno de Mesquita, *The War Trap* (New Haven, 1981).

18   Arthur Stein, "When Misperception Matters," *World Politics*, XXXIV (1982), 505–526.

19   Oddly enough, almost the only view of Hitler which indicates that he could have

The case of 1914 is not as clear. I suspect that the misperceptions of intentions in July, although fascinating, were not crucial. The Germans probably would have gone to war even if they had known that they would have had to fight all of the members of the Triple Entente. The British misjudgment of Germany—if it were a misjudgment—was more consequential, but even on this point the counterfactual question is hard to answer. Even if Germany did not seek domination, the combination of her great power, restlessness, and paranoia made her a menace. Perhaps a British policy based on a different image of Germany might have successfully appeased the Germans—to use the term in the older sense—but Britain could not have afforded to see Germany win another war in Europe, no matter what goals it sought.

Capabilities were badly misjudged, but even a correct appreciation of the power of the defense might not have changed the outcome of the July crisis. The "crisis instability" created by the belief that whoever struck first would gain a major advantage made the war hard to avoid once the crisis was severe, but may not have been either a necessary or a sufficient condition for the outbreak of the fighting. The Germans' belief that time was not on their side and that a quick victory would soon be beyond their reach was linked in part to the mistaken belief in the power of the offensive, but was not entirely driven by it. Thus, a preventive war might have occurred in the absence of the pressures for preemption.

Had the participants realized not only that the first offensive would not end the war, but also that the fighting would last for four punishing years, they might well have held back. Had they known what the war would bring, the kaiser, the emperor, and the czar presumably might have bluffed or sought a limited war, but they would have preferred making concessions to joining a general struggle. The same was probably true for the leaders of Britain and France, and certainly would have been true had they known the long-term consequences of the war. In at least one sense, then, World War I was caused by misperception.

---

been deterred is that of Taylor, who paints a picture of the German leader as an opportunist, inadvertently misled by the acquiescence of Western statesmen (Alan J. P. Taylor, *The Origins of the Second World War* [New York, 1961]).

MODELS OF CONFLICT   Two possible misperceptions of an adversary are largely the opposites of each other, and each is linked to an important argument about the causes of conflict. On the one hand, wars can occur if aggressors underestimate the willingness of status quo powers to fight (the World War II model); on the other hand, wars can also result if two states exaggerate each other's hostility when their differences are in fact bridgeable (the spiral or World War I model). These models only approximate the cases that inspired them. As noted earlier, World War II would have occurred even without this perceptual error, and the judgments of intentions before 1914 may have been generally accurate and, even if they were not, may not have been necessary for the conflict to have erupted. Nevertheless, the models are useful for summarizing two important sets of dynamics.

The World War II model in large part underlies deterrence theory. The main danger which is foreseen is that of an aggressive state which underestimates the resolve of the status quo powers. The latter may inadvertently encourage this misperception by errors of their own—for example, they may underestimate the aggressor's hostility and propose compromises that are taken as evidence of weakness. In the spiral model, by contrast, the danger is that each side will incorrectly see the other as a menace to its vital interests and will inadvertently encourage this belief by relying on threats to prevent war, thereby neglecting the pursuit of agreement and conciliation.

As I have stated elsewhere, the heated argument between the proponents of the two models is not so much a dispute between two rival theories as it is a dispute about the states' intentions.[20] The nature of the difference of opinion then points up both the importance and the difficulty of determining what states' motives and goals are, what costs and risks they are willing to run in order to expand, and the likely way in which they will respond to threats and conciliation. Determining others' intentions is so difficult that states have resorted to an approach that, were it suggested by an academic, would be seen as an example of how out of touch scholars are with international realities. On several occasions, states directly ask their adversaries what it is they want.

20 Jervis, *Perception and Misperception*, 58–113.

The British frequently discussed directing such an inquiry to Hitler, and the United States did so to Joseph Stalin shortly after the end of World War II. Statesmen might be disabused of their misperceptions if they could listen in on their adversary's deliberations. Thus in his analysis of the Eastern crisis of 1887/88, Seton-Watson argues that Benjamin Disraeli's government greatly exaggerated the Russian ambitions, and points out that "it is difficult to believe that even the most confirmed Russophobe in the British Cabinet of those days could have failed to be reassured if it had been possible for him to [read the czar's telegrams to his ambassador in London]."[21] But of course were such access possible, it could be used for deception, and the information would therefore not be credible.

It is clear that states can either underestimate or overestimate the aggressiveness of their adversaries and that either error can lead to war. Although one issue raised by these twin dangers is not central to our discussion here, it is so important that it should at least be noted. If the uncertainty about others' intentions cannot be eliminated, states should design policies that will not fail disastrously even if they are based on incorrect assumptions. States should try to construct a policy of deterrence which will not set off spirals of hostility if existing political differences are in fact bridgeable; the policy should also be designed to conciliate without running the risk that the other side, if it is aggressive, will be emboldened to attack. Such a policy requires the state to combine firmness, threats, and an apparent willingness to fight with reassurances, promises, and a credible willingness to consider the other side's interests. But the task is difficult, and neither decision-makers nor academics have fully come to grips with it.[22]

21 Robert W. Seton-Watson, *Disraeli, Gladstone, and the Eastern Question* (New York, 1972), 127, 192. It is interesting to note that during and after World War II the Soviet Union did have high-level spies who had good access to American thinking. The more recent penetrations of the American Embassy in Moscow may have duplicated this feat. The results may not have been entirely deleterious—both the United States and the Soviet Union may gain if the latter has convincing evidence that the former is driven by defensive motivations.

22 For a further discussion, see Jervis, *Perception and Misperception*, 109–113; idem, "Deterrence Theory Revisited," *World Politics*, XXXI (1979), 289–324; Richard Ned Lebow, "The Deterrence Deadlock: Is There a Way Out?" in Jervis, Lebow, and Janice Stein, *Psychology and Deterrence* (Baltimore, 1985), 180–202; Alexander George, David Hall, and William Simons, *Coercive Diplomacy* (Boston, 1971), 100–103, 238–244; George and Rich-

The existence of a spiral process does not prove the applicability of the spiral model, for increasing tension, hostility, and violence can be a reflection of the underlying conflict, not a cause of it. For example, conflict between the United States and Japan increased steadily throughout the 1930s, culminating in the American oil embargo in 1941 and the Japanese attack on Pearl Harbor four months later. Misperceptions were common, but the spiral model should not be used to explain these events because the escalating exchange of threats and actions largely revealed rather than created the incompatibility of goals. Japan preferred to risk defeat rather than forego dominance of China; the United States preferred to fight rather than see Japan reach its goal.

Blainey advances similar arguments in his rebuttal of Higonnet's views on the origins of the Seven Years' War. Higonnet claims that "no one wanted to fight this war. It would never have occurred if, in their sincere efforts to resolve it, the French and English governments had not inadvertently magnified its insignificant original cause into a wide conflict."[23] Hostilities escalated as Britain and France attempted to counteract (and surpass) each other's moves. They became increasingly suspicious of their adversary's motives, and felt that the stakes were higher than originally had been believed. The cycle of action and threat perception eventually led both sides to believe that they had to fight a major war in order to protect themselves. Blainey's rebuttal is simple: what was at stake from the beginning was "mastery in North America." The initial moves were at a low level of violence because each side, having underestimated the other's willingness to fight, thought it was possible to prevail quickly and cheaply.[24] Resolving such differences would require detailed research and responses to a number of hypothetical questions. But it should be kept in mind that the existence of increasing and reciprocal hostility does not always mean that the participants have come to overestimate the extent to which the other threatens its vital interests.

---

ard Smoke, *Deterrence in American Foreign Policy* (New York, 1974), 588–613; Glenn Snyder and Paul Diesing, *Conflict among Nations* (Princeton, 1977), 489–493.

23 Patrice Louis-René Higonnet, "The Origins of the Seven Years' War," *Journal of Modern History*, XL (1968), 57–58. See also Smoke, *War* (Cambridge, Mass., 1977), 195–236.

24 Blainey, *Causes of War*, 133–134.

Furthermore, even if the initial conflict of interest does not justify a war and it is the process of conflict itself which generates the impulse to fight, misperception may not be the crucial factor. The very fact that states contest an issue raises the stakes because influence and reputation are involved. To retreat after having expended prestige and treasure, if not blood, is psychologically more painful than retreating at the start; it is also more likely to have much stronger domestic and international repercussions.[25] The dilemmas which are created were outlined in 1953 by the American intelligence community in a paper which tried to estimate how the Russians and Chinese would react to various forms of American military pressure designed to produce an armistice in Korea:

> If prior to the onset of any UN/U.S. military course of action, the Communists recognized that they were faced with a clear choice between making the concessions necessary to reach an armistice, or accepting the likelihood that UN/U.S. military operations would endanger the security of the Manchurian and Soviet borders, destroy the Manchurian industrial complex, or destroy the Chinese Communist armed forces, the Communists would probably agree to an armistice. However, it would be extremely difficult to present them with a clear choice of alternatives before such action was begun. Moreover, once such UN/U.S. action was begun, Communist power and prestige would become further involved, thereby greatly increasing the difficulties of making the choice between agreeing to [an] armistice or continuing the war.[26]

ASSESSING HOSTILE INTENT   On balance, it seems that states are more likely to overestimate the hostility of others than to underestimate it. States are prone to exaggerate the reasonableness of their own positions and the hostile intent of others; indeed, the former process feeds the latter. Statesmen, wanting to think well of themselves and their decisions, often fail to appreciate others' perspectives, and so greatly underestimate the extent to which their actions can be seen as threats.

25 One of the psychological mechanisms at work is cognitive dissonance. In order to justify the effort they are expending to reach a goal, people exaggerate its value.
26 Department of State, *Foreign Relations of the United States, 1952–54. XV: Korea* (Washington, D.C., 1984), Pt. I, 888.

When their intentions are peaceful, statesmen think that others will understand their motives and therefore will not be threatened by the measures that they are taking in their own self-defense. Richard Perle, former assistant secretary of defense, once said that if we are in doubt about Soviet intentions, we should build up our arms. He explained that if the Russians are aggressive, the buildup will be needed, and, if they are not, the only consequence will be wasted money. Similarly, when United States troops were moving toward the Yalu River, Secretary of State Dean Acheson said that there was no danger that the Chinese would intervene in an effort to defend themselves because they understood that we were not a threat to them. Exceptions, such as the British belief in the 1930s that German hostility was based largely on fear of encirclement and the Israeli view before the 1973 war that Egypt feared attack, are rare.[27] (The British and the Israeli perceptions were partly generated by the lessons they derived from their previous wars.)

This bias also operates in retrospect, when states interpret the other side's behavior after the fact. Thus American leaders, believing that China had no reason to be alarmed by the movement of troops toward the Yalu, assumed the only explanation for Chinese intervention in the Korean War was its unremitting hostility to the United States. India, although clearly seeing the Chinese point of view in 1950, saw the Chinese attack on her in 1962 as unprovoked, and so concluded that future cooperation was impossible. Similarly, although all Westerners, even those who could empathize with the Soviet Union, understand how the invasion of Afghanistan called up a strong reaction, Soviet leaders apparently did not and instead saw the Western response as "part of a hostile design that would have led to the same actions under any circumstances."[28]

27 Daniel Yergin, "'Scoop' Jackson Goes for Broke," *Atlantic Monthly*, CCXXIII (1974), 82. Perle, then an aide to Sen. Henry Jackson, is describing the latter's views, but what he says seems to apply to his own beliefs as well. Acheson's views are presented in John Spanier, *The Truman-MacArthur Controversy and the Korean War* (New York, 1965), 97; Allen Whiting, *China Crosses the Yalu* (Stanford, 1968), 151. (Similar examples are discussed in Jervis, *Perception and Misperception*, 67–76.) The case of Israel in 1973 is analyzed in Janice Stein, "Calculation, Miscalculation, and Conventional Deterrence. II. The View from Jerusalem," in Jervis, Lebow, and Stein, *Psychology and Deterrence*, 60–88. See also Richard Betts, *Surprise Attack* (Washington, D.C., 1982).
28 Raymond Garthoff, *Detente and Confrontation* (Washington, D.C., 1985), 1076.

This problem is compounded by a second and better known bias—states tend to infer threatening motives from actions that a disinterested observer would record as at least partly cooperative. John Foster Dulles' view of Nikita Khrushchev's arms cuts in the mid-1950s is one such example and President Ronald Reagan's view of most Soviet arms proposals may be another.[29]

These two biases often operate simultaneously, with the result that both sides are likely to believe that they are cooperating and that others are responding with hostility. For example, when Leonid Brezhnev visited President Richard Nixon in San Clemente during 1973 and argued that the status quo in the Middle East was unacceptable, and when Andrei Gromyko later said that "the fire of war [in the Mid-East] could break out onto the surface at any time," they may well have thought that they were fulfilling their obligations under the Basic Principles Agreement to consult in the event of a threat to peace. The Americans, however, felt that the Soviets were making threats in the spring and violating the spirit of detente by not giving warning in the fall.[30]

People also tend to overperceive hostility because they pay closest attention to dramatic events. Threatening acts often achieve high visibility because they consist of instances like crises, occupation of foreign territory, and the deployment of new weapons. Cooperative actions, by contrast, often call less attention to themselves because they are not dramatic and can even be viewed as nonevents. Thus Larson notes how few inferences American statesmen drew from the Soviet's willingness to sign the Austrian State Treaty of 1955.[31] Similarly, their withdrawal of troops from Finland after World War II made little impact, and over the past

---

29 See the classic essay by Holsti, "Cognitive Dynamics and Images of the Enemy: Dulles and Russia," in David Finlay, Holsti, and Richard Fagen, *Enemies in Politics* (Chicago, 1967), 25–96. Michael Sullivan, *International Relations: Theories and Evidence* (Englewood Cliffs, N.J., 1976), 45–46, questions the links between Dulles' beliefs and American behavior.

30 Gromyko is quoted in Galia Golan, *Yom Kippur and After* (London, 1977), 68. The treatment of the 1973 war is a good litmus test for one's views on detente: compare, for example, the discussions in Harry Gelman, *The Brezhnev Politburo and the Decline of Detente* (Ithaca, 1984), 135–139, 152–156; Garthoff, *Detente and Confrontation*; George, *Managing U.S.-Soviet Rivalry* (Boulder, 1983), 139–154.

31 Larson, "Crisis Prevention and the Austrian State Treaty," *International Organization*, XXXXI (1987), 27–60.

few years few decision-makers or analysts have commented on the fact that the Soviets have *not* engaged in a strategic buildup.

MISPERCEPTION AND THE ORIGINS OF WORLD WAR III   Misperception could prove to be an underlying cause of World War III through either the overestimation or the underestimation of hostile intent. If the Soviet Union is highly aggressive—or if its subjective security requirements can be met only by making the West insecure—then war could result through a Soviet underestimation of American resolve. If the Soviet Union is driven primarily by apprehension that could be reduced by conciliation, then war could result through a spiral of threat-induced tensions and unwarranted fears. But, although it is easy to see how either of these misperceptions could increase conflict, it is hard to see how a nuclear war could start under current technology when both sides know how costly such a clash would be. To analyze this topic, concentrating on the role of misperception, we first examine the dynamics of the game of chicken and then discuss the psychological aspects of crisis stability and preemption.

Misperception, Commitment, and Change   In a situation that is similar to the game of chicken (that is, any outcome, including surrender, would be better than war), war should not occur as long as both sides are even minimally rational and maintain control over their own behavior.[32] Both sides may bluster and bluff, but it will make no sense for either of them to initiate all-out conflict. Each side will try to stand firm and so make the other back down; the most obvious danger would result from the mistaken belief that the other will retreat and that it is therefore safe to stand firm.

But if both sides maintain control, war can occur only if either or both sides become irrevocably committed to acting on their misperception. In other words, so long as either state retains its freedom of action, war can be avoided because that state can back down at the last minute. But commitment can inhibit this

32 In fact, statesmen realize that large-scale conflict can result from confrontations even if they do not desire it. They then both fear and employ what Schelling calls "threats that leave something to chance" (Thomas Schelling, *Strategy of Conflict* [Cambridge, Mass., 1960], 187–203). Under current circumstances, control may be hard to maintain in a crisis if the decision-makers delegate the authority to fire nuclear weapons to local commanders.

flexibility, and that, of course is its purpose. Standard bargaining logic shows that if one side persuades the other that it is committed to standing firm, the other will have no choice but to retreat.[33] What is of concern here is that this way of seeking to avoid war can make it more likely.

Whether a commitment—and indeed any message—is perceived as intended (or perceived at all) depends not only on its clarity and plausibility, but also on how it fits with the recipient's cognitiye predispositions. Messages which are inconsistent with a person's beliefs about international politics and other actors are not likely to be perceived the way the sender intended. For example, shortly before the Spanish-American War President William McKinley issued what he thought was a strong warning to Spain to make major concessions over Cuba or face American military intervention. But the Spanish were worried primarily not about an American declaration of war, but about American aid for the Cuban rebels, and so they scanned the president's speech with this problem in mind. They therefore focused on sections of the speech that McKinley regarded as relatively unimportant and passed quickly over the paragraphs that he thought were vital.[34]

Furthermore, the state sending the message of commitment is likely to assume that it has been received. Thus one reason the United States was taken by surprise when the Soviet Union put missiles into Cuba was that it had assumed that the Soviets understood that such action was unacceptable. Statesmen, like people in their everyday lives, find it difficult to realize that their own intentions, which seem clear to them, can be obscure to others. The problem is magnified because the belief that the message has been received and understood as it was intended will predispose the state to interpret ambiguous information as indicating that the other side does indeed understand its commitment.

Psychological Commitment and Misperception   Misperception can lead to war not only through mistaken beliefs about the

---

33   *Ibid.*, 119–161.
34   May, *Imperial Democracy* (New York, 1961), 161. For an extended discussion of this problem, see Jervis, *Perception and Misperception*, 203–216; *idem*, "Deterrence Theory Revisited," 305–310. For a discussion of this problem in the context of the limited use of nuclear weapons, see Schelling, "The Role of War Games and Exercises," in Ashton Carter, John Steinbruner, and Charles Zraket (eds.), *Nuclear Operations and Command and Control* (Washington, D.C., 1987), 426–444.

impact of the state's policy of commitment on others, but also through the impact of commitment on the state. We should not forget the older definition of the term commitment, which is more psychological than tactical. People and states become committed to policies not only by staking their bargaining reputations on them, but by coming to believe that their policies are morally justified and politically necessary. For example, the process of deciding that a piece of territory warrants a major international dispute and the effort that is involved in acting on this policy can lead a person to see the territory as even more valuable than he had originally thought. Furthermore, other members of the elite and the general public may become aroused, with the result that a post-commitment retreat will not only feel more costly to the statesman; it may actually be more costly in terms of its effect on his domestic power.

Commitment can also create misperceptions. As the decision-maker comes to see his policy as necessary, he is likely to believe that the policy can succeed, even if such a conclusion requires the distortion of information about what others will do. He is likely to come to believe that his threats will be credible and effective and that his opponents will ultimately cooperate and permit him to reach his objectives. Facing sharp value trade-offs is painful; no statesman wants to acknowledge that he may have to abandon an important foreign policy goal in order to avoid war or that he may have to engage in a bloody struggle if he is to reach his foreign policy goals. Of course, he will not embark on the policy in the first place if he thinks that the other will fight. Quite often, the commitment develops incrementally, without a careful and disinterested analysis of how others are likely to react. When commitments develop in this way, decision-makers can find themselves supporting untenable policies that others can and will challenge. The result could be war because the state behaves more recklessly than the chicken context would warrant.[35]

35 The literature on these perceptual processes, which are a subcategory of what are known as "motivated biases" because of the important role played by affect, is large. The best starting place is Irving Janis and Leon Mann, *Decision Making* (New York, 1977). For applications to international politics, see Richard Cottam, *Foreign Policy Motivation* (Pittsburgh, 1977); Lebow, *Between Peace and War* (Baltimore, 1981); Jervis, "Foreign Policy Decision-Making: Recent Developments," *Political Psychology*, II (1980), 86–101; *idem*, Lebow, and Stein, *Psychology and Deterrence*. For earlier versions of the argument, see Holsti, North, and Brody, "Perception and Action," 123–158; Snyder, *Deterrence and*

The Ultimate Self-Fulfilling Prophecy   Even if the processes of commitment can entrap statesmen, it is hard to see how World War III could occur unless one or both sides concluded that it was inevitable in the near future. As long as both sides expect that all-out war will result in unlimited damage, they will prefer peace to war. But if either thinks that peace cannot be maintained, the choice is not between maintaining peace—even at a significant cost in terms of other values—and going to war, but between striking first or being struck first. Even under these circumstances, attacking would make sense only if the former alternative is preferable to the latter. Since strategic weapons themselves are relatively invulnerable, scholars, until recently, have believed that there were few incentives to strike first. But they are now aware of the vulnerability of command, control, and communication (C^3) systems which could lead decision-makers to believe that striking first would be at least marginally, and perhaps significantly, better than receiving the first blow.[36] Preemption would be advantageous, thereby creating what is called crisis instability.

Crisis instability is a large topic, and here it is addressed only in terms of the potential role of misperception.[37] First, perceptions create their own reality. Determinations about the inevitability of war are not objective, but instead are based on each side's per-

Defense (Princeton, 1961), 26–27. For a rebuttal to some points, see Sagan, "Origins of the Pacific War," 893–922. John Orme, "Deterrence Failures: A Second Look," *International Security*, XI (1987), 96–124. For further discussion of the tendency to avoid trade-offs, see Jervis, *Perception and Misperception*. Quester points to the strategic value of commitment in making the other side retreat (Quester, "Crisis and the Unexpected," *Journal of Interdisciplinary History*, XVIII [1988], 701–719.). He is correct, but such behavior can still lead to war if the other side does not gauge the situation accurately.

36 For further discussion of situations that could lead to World War III, see Warner Schilling et al., *American Arms and a Changing Europe* (New York, 1973), 172–174, and George, "Problems of Crisis Management and Crisis Avoidance in U.S.-Soviet Relations," unpub. paper (Oslo, 1985). C^3 is discussed by Desmond Ball, *Can Nuclear War Be Controlled?* (London, 1981); Paul Bracken, *The Command and Control of Nuclear Forces* (New Haven, 1983); Bruce Blair, *Strategic Command and Control* (Washington, D.C., 1985); Carter, Steinbruner, and Zraket (eds.), *Nuclear Operations*. The resulting dangers are analyzed in Graham Allison, Albert Carnesale, and Joseph Nye (eds.), *Hawks, Doves, and Owls* (New York, 1985). The fundamental argument about "the reciprocal fear of surprise attack" was developed by Schelling in *Strategy of Conflict*, 207–229.

37 For further discussion of some of the arguments being made here, see Jervis, *The Illogic of American Nuclear Strategy* (Ithaca, 1984); Lebow, *Nuclear Crisis Management* (Ithaca, 1987); Jervis, "Psychological Aspects of Crisis Instability," in idem, *The Implications of the Nuclear Revolution* (forthcoming); idem, *The Symbolic Nature of Nuclear Politics* (Urbana, 1987).

ceptions of what the other will do, which in turn is influenced by what each side thinks its adversary thinks that it is going to do. To maintain the peace, a state would have to convince the adversary that it will not start a war and that it does not believe the other will either. This interaction would take place within the context of a crisis of unprecedented severity, probably involving military alerts, if not the limited use of force.

We know very little about how states in such circumstances would think about the problem, judge the adversary's behavior, try to reassure the adversary, and decide whether these reassurances had been believed. But however these analyses are carried out, they will constitute, not just describe, reality; the question of whether war is inevitable cannot be answered apart from the participants' beliefs about it.

War itself would provide an objective answer to the question of whether there would be a significant advantage to striking first. But even here beliefs would play a role—the military doctrine adopted by a state and its beliefs about the other side's doctrine would strongly influence a decision to strike first. On the one hand, the incentives to strike first would remain slight so long as each side believed that the war would be unlimited, or, if controlled, would concentrate on attacks against cities. On the other hand, if each side believed that it was crucial to deny the other any military advantage, first-strike incentives would be greater because attacks against weapons and C^3 systems might cripple the other's ability to fight a counterforce war, even if they could not destroy the other's second-strike capability.

The uncertainties here, and in other judgments of the advantages of striking first, are enormous. Furthermore, they cannot be resolved without war. Thus statesmen's perceptions will involve both guesswork and intuition. In such circumstances, many factors could lead to an exaggeration of the benefits of taking the offensive.[38] Military organizations generally seek to take the initiative; statesmen rarely believe that allowing the other to move

38 For a discussion of the operation of such factors in previous cases, see Jack Snyder, *The Ideology of the Offensive* (Ithaca, 1984); Barry Posen, *The Sources of Military Doctrine* (Ithaca, 1984). See also Sagan, "1914 Revisited: Allies, Offense, and Instability," *International Security*, XI (1986), 151–176, and the exchange between Sagan and Jack Snyder, "The Origins of Offense and the Consequences of Counterforce," in *International Security*, XI (1986/87), 187–198.

first is beneficial; and the belief that war is inevitable could lead decision-makers to minimize psychological pain by concluding that striking first held out a significant chance of limiting damage.

If war is believed to be very likely but not inevitable, launching a first strike would be an incredible gamble. As noted at the start of this article, such gambles can be rational, but, even when they are not, psychological factors can lead people to take them. Although most people are risk-averse for gains, they are risk-acceptant for losses.[39] For example, given the choice between a 100 percent chance of winning $10 and a 20 percent chance of winning $55, most people will choose the former. But if the choice is between the certainty of losing $10 and a 20 percent chance of losing $55, they will gamble and opt for the latter. In order to increase the chance of avoiding any loss at all, people are willing to accept the danger of an even greater sacrifice. Such behavior is consistent with the tendency for people to be influenced by "sunk costs" which rationally should be disregarded and to continue to pursue losing ventures in the hope of recovering their initial investment when they would be better off simply cutting their losses.

This psychology of choice has several implications concerning crisis stability. First, because the status quo forms people's point of reference, they are willing to take unusual risks to recoup recent losses. Although a setback might be minor when compared to the total value of a person's holdings, he will see his new status in terms of where he was shortly before and therefore may risk an even greater loss in the hope of reestablishing his position. In a crisis, then, a decision-maker who had suffered a significant, but limited, loss might risk world war if he thought such a war held out the possibility of reversing the recent defeat. Where fully rational analysis would lead a person to cut his losses, the use of the status quo as the benchmark against which other results are measured could lead the statesman to persevere even at high risk. The danger would be especially great if both sides were to feel

39 This discussion is drawn from Daniel Kahneman and Amos Tversky, "Prospect Theory: An Analysis of Decision Under Risk," *Econometrica*, LVII (1979), 263–291; Tversky and Kahneman, "The Framing of Decisions and the Psychology of Choice," *Science*, CCXI (1981), 453–458; Kahneman and Tversky, "Choices, Values, and Frames," *American Psychologist*, XXXIX (1984), 341–350; Tversky and Kahneman, "Rational Choice and the Framing of Decisions," *Journal of Business*, LIX (1986), S251–S278.

that they were losing, which could easily happen because they probably would have different perspectives and use different baselines. Indeed, if the Russians consider the status quo to be constant movement in their favor, they might be prone to take high risks when the United States thought that it was maintaining the status quo. Furthermore, it could prove dangerous to follow a strategy of making gains by fait accompli.[40] Unless the state which has been victimized quickly adjusts to and accepts the new situation, it may be willing to run unusually high risks to regain its previous position. The other side, expecting the first to be "rational," will in turn be taken by surprise by this resistance, with obvious possibilities for increased conflict.

A second consequence is that if a statesman thinks that war—and therefore enormous loss—is almost certain if he does not strike and that attacking provides a small chance of escaping unscathed, he may decide to strike even though a standard probability-utility calculus would call for restraint. Focusing on the losses that will certainly occur if his state is attacked can lead a decision-maker to pursue any course of action that holds out any possibility of no casualties at all. Similar and more likely are the dynamics which could operate in less severe crises, such as the expectation of a hostile coup in an important third-world country or the limited use of force by the adversary in a disputed area. Under such circumstances, the state might take actions which entailed an irrationally high chance of escalation and destruction in order to avoid the certain loss entailed by acquiescing.[41] With his attention riveted on the deterioration which will occur unless he acts strongly to reverse a situation, a statesman may accept the risk of even greater loss, thereby making these crises more dangerous.

The response can also be influenced by how the decision is framed. Although a powerful aversion to losses could lead a decision-maker to strike when the alternatives are posed as they were in the previous example, it also could lead him to hold back. For instance, he might choose restraint if he thought that striking first, although preferable to striking second, would lead to certain

40 See George and Smoke, *Deterrence*, 536–540.
41 States may try to gain the bargaining advantages that come from seeming to be irrational, as Quester reminds us ("Crises and the Unexpected," 703–706).

retaliation whereas not striking would offer some chance—even if small—of avoiding a war, although he risked much higher casualties if the other side attacked. If a decision-maker takes as his baseline not the existing situation, but the casualties that would be suffered in a war, his choice between the same alternatives might be different. He would then judge the policies according to lives that might be saved, not lost, with the result that he would choose a course of action that he believed would certainly save some lives rather than choose another that might save more, but might not save any. The obvious danger is that a first strike which would significantly reduce the other side's strategic forces would meet the former criterion whereas restraint could not provide the certainty of saving any lives and so would not seem as attractive as standard utility maximization theory implies.

But the picture is not one of unrelieved gloom. First, situations as bleak as those we are positing are extremely rare and probably will never occur. The Cuban missile crisis was probably as close as we have come to the brink of war, and even then President John F. Kennedy rated the chance of war at no more than 50 percent, and he seems to have been referring to the chances or armed conflict, not nuclear war. So American, and presumably Soviet, officials were far from believing that war was inevitable.

Second, the propensity for people to avoid value trade-offs can help to preserve peace. To face the choice between starting World War III and running a very high risk that the other side will strike first would be terribly painful, and decision-makers might avoid it by downplaying the latter danger. Of course to say that a decision-maker will try not to perceive the need for such a sharp value trade-off does not tell us which consideration will guide him, but some evidence indicates that the dominating value may be the one which is most salient and to which the person was committed even before the possibility of conflict with another central value arose. Thus the very fact that decision-makers constantly reiterate the need to avoid war and rarely talk about the need to strike first if war becomes inevitable may contribute to restraint.

Finally, although exaggerating the danger of crisis instability would make a severe confrontation more dangerous than it would otherwise be, it also would serve the useful function of keeping states far from the brink of war. If decision-makers believed that crises could be controlled and manipulated, they would be less inhibited about creating them. The misperception may be useful: fear, even unjustified fear, may make the world a little more tranquil.

CONCLUSION   The methodological problems noted earlier make it impossible to draw firm generalizations about the relationships between war and misperception, but we tentatively offer a number of propositions. First, although war can occur in the absence of misperception, in fact misperception almost always accompanies it. To say that statesmen's beliefs about both capabilities and intentions are usually badly flawed is not to say that they are foolish. Rather, errors are inevitable in light of the difficulty of assessing technological and organizational capabilities, the obstacles to inferring others' intentions correctly, the limitations on people's abilities to process information, and the need to avoid excessively painful choices.

Second, to say that misperceptions are common is not to specify their content. Statesmen can either overestimate or underestimate the other side's capabilities and its hostility. Wars are especially likely to occur when a state simultaneously underestimates an adversary's strength and exaggerates its hostility. In many cases, however, estimates of capabilities are the product of a policy, not the foundation on which it is built. Policy commitments can influence evaluations as well as be driven by them. Others' hostility can also be overestimated or underestimated and, although exceptions abound, the former error seems more common than the latter. Similarly, more often than falling into the trap of incorrectly believing that other statesmen are just like themselves, decision-makers frequently fail to empathize with the adversary. That is, they tend to pay insufficient attention to constraints and pressures faced by their opponent, including those generated by the decision-maker's own state.

Third, objective analyses of the international system which are so popular among political scientists are not likely to provide a complete explanation for the outbreak of most wars. To historians who are accustomed to explanations which rely heavily on reconstructing the world as the statesmen saw it, this reality will not come as a surprise. But I would also argue that such reconstructions can both build and utilize generalizations about how people perceive information. Although some perceptions are random and idiosyncratic, many others are not. We know that decision-makers, like people in their everyday lives, are strongly driven by the beliefs that they hold, the lessons that they have learned from history, and the hope of being able to avoid painful choices.

Even if these generalizations are correct, any single case can be an exception. World War III, if it occurs, might not fit the dominant pattern. But, given the overwhelming destruction which both sides would expect such a war to bring, it seems hard to see how such a confict could erupt in the absence of misperception. It would be particularly dangerous if either the United States or the Soviet Union or both believed that war was inevitable and that striking first was significantly preferable to allowing the other side to strike first. Since a number of psychological processes could lead people to overestimate these factors, it is particularly important for statesmen to realize the ways in which common perceptual processes can lead to conclusions that are not only incorrect, but also extremely dangerous.

George H. Quester

Crises and the Unexpected
"A war nobody wanted" goes to the heart of a pathological puzzle that energizes our analyses of crises. Where nobody's interest is served, are we not required to lament and condemn all of the decision-making and policy processes that are involved? "War serves the interests of no one" has been a staple of many a sermon and commentary in the past; it is today an even more persuasive and plausible synopsis during any crisis that forces us to contemplate what modern weapons can do.[1]

Thus, we will not treat a "crisis" simply as an enhanced likelihood of war, for this definition may be both too narrow and too broad.[2] It may be too narrow in that it excludes the analogous family tensions and other human encounters where the worst each side can inflict on the other is far less than war, but where much of the same game of mutual risk-taking is at work. It may be too broad (even though much of popular usage might include all risks of war as crises) in that it draws in cases where no contest of wills is in place, and where neither side is betting its position on estimates of the other side's resolve. For example, if India loses its patience with the Portuguese and, minimizing costs all around in the process, tells its military to seize Goa, is the enhanced likelihood of war immediately prior to the seizure really a part of what we need to analyze in this article? Where war is *not* a mutual

George H. Quester is Professor of Government and Politics at the University of Maryland. He is the author of *The Future of Nuclear Deterrence* (Lexington, Mass., 1986).

1 For a book-length analysis developing such arguments about situations where war is a major setback for both sides, see Ralph K. White, *Nobody Wanted War* (Garden City, 1968).
2 Richard Ned Lebow, in *Between Peace and War* (Baltimore, 1981), identifies three distinct notions of crisis as enhanced risk of war. Two of these will concern us less here: the situation where one side (having already concluded that a decision for war is appropriate to its national interests) is simply laying the groundwork for justifying a war to world opinion or its own domestic opinion; and the situation where one side does not necessarily want war, but badly wants some political goal to which its adversary is very much opposed, and hence becomes progressively resigned to a war, as the inescapable price of its political aspirations.

disaster, all of politics and our sensations about politics take on a different form.

For my analysis, I concentrate instead on cases where war *is* a mutual disaster rather than an expeditious solution. These are crises where each side knows that a mutually unwanted result may emerge, but where each is also reluctant to eliminate this risk because such efforts would grant too many concessions to the other side.

This sense of crisis is often compared to the game of "chicken," where American teenagers drive automobiles toward each other, risking a collision.[3] Each driver could eliminate the risk by veering to one side, but this move would grant a victory to the other side in the contest of resolve. A typical workers' strike also has much of the same logic, since the implicit threat is that the firm being struck will be so damaged in the competitive marketplace that neither labor nor management will ever be well off again.

There are important parallels also between a crisis, as defined by the fear of an outbreak of war, and the logic of a war already underway, a war being prolonged as a contest of endurance. Fighters on each side of wars of attrition and guerrilla wars often know that they would be better off surrendering, but, knowing that the other side would also be better off surrendering, each side persists simply on the bet and hope that the other will be the first to throw in the towel. The prolongation of World War I, once it had been launched, was a prime example of this strategy, as was the Vietnam War.

The differences between a crisis and a war of attrition stem mainly from how the mutual threat is phrased. In a war already underway, the damage being inflicted on each side increases incrementally every day, as each side wonders when the other will eventually be willing to concede. Where such a war is not yet underway, but where instead each side faces an increased risk of such war, each side is threatened with a sudden increase in suffering, countered by the possibility that there will be no suffering at all if the crisis is somehow resolved.[4]

3 See Glenn H. Snyder, "'Prisoner's Dilemma' and 'Chicken' Models in International Relations," *International Studies Quarterly*, XV (1971), 66–103.
4 See Thomas C. Schelling, *Arms and Influence* (New Haven, 1966).

Ongoing wars are also burdened by the ever-looming prospect that there will be an escalation to higher levels of hostility. Yet some of the prolonged wars in the present nuclear age have pulled remarkably away from threats of further escalation, as each side instead bets on the likelihood that the damage already being inflicted will force its adversary to surrender.[5] Crisis stability was not so much in question during the Vietnam War, but each side's endurance was very much in question.

THE IMPACT OF RATIONALITY   Does such a crisis atmosphere increase the chances of unexpected and unanticipated outcomes? Do crises bring out the irrational in man, amid various kinds of folly? For at least two very different reasons, the answer would have to be "of course"; but it is important to distinguish these reasons and to separate our analyses of them.

Decision-making in a crisis can deteriorate simply because the sheer enormity of the risks and the extreme pressures on the decision-makers produce a degree of nervousness that makes simple tasks difficult. It is not always the case that stress makes for less effective decision-making; but it certainly is plausible that extreme stress could have such an effect. Degradations of decision quality are easy to lament, and the decisions reached in such an environment must certainly have the burden of proof directed against them.

Mistakes can thus be made, by either of the parties, on a long list of questions, including which side had the military capability to win the war (the Russo-Japanese War); how much destruction could a war cause (the Iran-Iraq War); what demands and attitudes the opposing side had; and to what degree the adversary received the messages being sent (the Korean War, or the Falklands War).

One could image some mistakes or losses of rationality which would actually lead to peace instead of war, but most irrationalities would rather make war more likely. War is a loss for both sides; hence wars are mistakes.

The more tragic point, however, is that crises do not only produce wars because of simple error. At one remove of analysis, at a higher stage of rational calculation of national interest, op-

5   The patterns of limited war since 1945 are discussed in Morton H. Halperin, *Limited War in the Nuclear Age* (New York, 1963).

posing parties may in fact elect to impose error on themselves in an attempt to win the game of chicken.

A different syndrome thus stems from the very logic of what a crisis or an endurance contest is all about, for here we at last encounter a form of "rationality of irrationality." Each side would be better off surrendering than prolonging the agony, and each would surely be better off surrendering than letting the crisis become a global war. Yet each side would also do well if it could seem to be indifferent to such disasters. If one side thought that his opponent would never choose to surrender, he would have no choice but to surrender. If one side "irrationally" pretends to be unaware of an impending collision in a game of chicken, or pretends to be unafraid of such a collison, then the other side will need to swerve to avoid this disaster, and the steadfast side will collect the gains of the contest.

It is thus rational, in terms of our country's long-term interests, for our governmental leaders to seem to be irrational during the immediate short-term period; and one way to seem to be irrational during the immediate crisis period is to become so in fact.

In the first instance, we dealt with reductions of rationality and imperfections of assessment, which the affected parties would have wished to avoid. In the latter case, however, we encountered deviations from rationality which the affected party might have imposed upon himself, because the very logic of the contest delivered better returns to the side which was less "sensible," and more stubborn or determined.

To achieve what we want in such contests, we must blind ourselves to some of the consequences that we might suffer should our strategy fail. To achieve what we desire and anticipate, we must expose ourselves to a greater variety of the unanticipated. To win against a side which increases the range of uncertainty, we must ourselves expand the uncertainties. A president, therefore, who has played a cowboy on television, and has self-punishingly fired an entire generation of air traffic controllers "on principle," may thus do better in a crisis than a president who has always radiated calm and has never shown signs of anger.

It is easy to describe a contest between two such "principled" opponents as the height of folly, for each side expects the other to give up first, and one of the contenders must surely be wrong.

But which one? The crucial errors pertain precisely to whether the other side is making errors and is thus more likely to persist in the mutually destructive contest. The calculations here fold back on themselves in a way that can produce self-confirming or self-denying propositions. Who is going to be the outside expert who will determine which of the two sides is the more likely to submit in order to end a crisis? And would not the advice itself of such an analyst be self-verifying, if both the contenders could hear his judgment?

By contrast, it is safer to be critical of wars caused by a simple mistake whereby each side mis-estimates the comparative military capablities. If the military commanders on each side (for example, the Italians and Greeks in 1941) expect to win in a war, one side has to be in error, and presumably has not done its analyses carefully enough. An outside analyst here might be able to offer the most valuable advice on how the war would go, perhaps thereby sparing both prospective winners and prospective losers the human and economic costs of actually going through with a battle.[6] The calculations that are crucial pertain mainly to the counterforce aspects of weaponry—whether our navy can sink their navy before their navy sinks ours—and much less to any mutual anxieties about the countervalue costs of war—the human burdens imposed on each side if a war is initiated or prolonged. We must therefore be much more sympathetic to failures to anticipate consequences in crises or in contests of resolve, than in wars which are simply contests of military capabilities.

Is it thus reasonable to charge that overconfidence besets all military decision-making? In some sense there must be a net of overconfidence across the two sides in any war, indeed in any dispute which wastes the total resources and utility available to both sides. In terms of the simple measuring of capabilities, one of the sides must overestimate its capabilities if both expect to win. (Either the Egyptians were right about victory in 1967, or the Israelis were.) In terms of a contest of endurance, if both expect to be the last to quit, one of the sides must overrate its own resolve, or overrate the credibility and visibility of its own

---

6 On pathologies of analysis of military capabilities, see Janice Gross Stein, "Calculation, Miscalculation and Conventional Deterrence: The View From Cairo," in Robert Jervis, Lebow, and Stein, *Psychology and Deterrence* (Baltimore, 1985), 34–59.

commitments to the other side (Washington vs. Hanoi in the Vietnam War).[7]

Of the two kinds of military conflict, however, the contest of wills is much the more self-confirming. Troops in combat sometimes fight better because they believe in themselves. (How else could a smaller number of British troops defeat a larger number of Argentines?) But the largest part of the outcome of counterforce-exchange battles is determined by the quality of weapons and the basic efficiency of the weapons' operators. By contrast, the outcome of an endurance contest depends only partially on any objective factors, such as who has the larger reserves of oil or manpower, and much more on what we are guessing about the other side's endurance, and what we are guessing about the other side's guesses about our endurance, and so on.

CRISIS DYNAMICS   The basic game theory matrix illustrating an ordinary endurance contest war is that shown here.[8] Each side is immediately better off if it surrenders. But each side is immensely better off if the other side surrenders. Hoping for the very best payoff, each side for the moment persists in accepting its worst payoff. Each side indeed prefers to be the second to be agreeable, ahead of any simultaneous commitment to peace.

	Settle Conflict		War	
Settle Conflict		4		5
	4		3	
War		3		1
	5		1	

The parallel matrix for a crisis is different only in that each side for the moment is not worse off for sticking to its guns (which have not yet begun firing). Each side, however, senses a pervading risk that the entire system may soon be worse off

7 Tendencies toward overconfidence or wishful thinking are discussed in Jervis, *Perception and Misperception in International Relations* (Princeton, 1976), passim.
8 For a useful introduction to the applications of game theory matrices, see Anatol Rapaport, *Two-Person Game Theory: The Essential Ideas* (Ann Arbor, 1973).

should the crisis be maintained by ongoing resolve on both sides. Again each side is better off if the other has to do all the work of resolving the crisis.

	Settle	Stick to Guns
Settle	4 4	5 3
Stick to Guns	3 5	4 ↙ 1 ↗ 1 4

Yet if each side knows that the other prefers peace to war, we may have a paradox at the very outset of a crisis. We base our model on a raised expectation of warfare, but such a change in expectations begs an explanation as to *why* anyone should fear a war if the crisis does not terminate. If each side is worse off in war, and the other side can see this result, does it not take all the essential risk out of the crisis situation?

One can uncover several ways of bringing anxiety back into a crisis. First, there is the elementary uncertainty of what the other side will do, and what the other side thinks we will do. It is still possible that the other side does not mind the crisis, and would not mind a war. As already noted, it is also possible that either side will make a mistake.

Second, more concretely, we could append a different matrix to our first matrix, positing some kind of transition, once a crisis has lasted a certain length of time, or once a large number of political decisions had become dependent on who wins this contest of resolve. At this crucial turning point, each side might feel itself better off attacking than waiting to be attacked, and might feel it appropriate to attack in any event.

If "chicken" thus changes to "prisoners' dilemma" after a crisis has persisted for a certain length of time, the mere prospect of the dilemma may then (as in 1914) be sufficient to activate the "chicken" contest of a crisis.

One side, or both, might prefer to attack after a time (this being the prospect hanging over both the sides, as neither at the outset wishes to get into a prisoners' dilemma situation and a horrible war), because too many of the political issues being

	Peace (Stick to Guns)	War (Use Guns)
Peace (Stick to Guns)	4 ... 4	2 ↙ o ... 3 ↗ 5
War (Use Guns)	2 ↗ o ... 3 ↙ 5	1 ... 1

disputed will now depend on how the crisis is settled. As a crisis is prolonged over time, it may collect more and more political variables that have been opened up for dispute and rearrangement, thus worsening the price of giving in when the other side has not given in. (All of this maturation of the crisis is shown in the changes in the lower left and upper right boxes, changes which convert "chicken" into "prisoners' dilemma.")

Our intuitive perceptions of a crisis thus necessarily include contradictory elements. For the early stages, each side is inclined to be patient as it waits for the other side to give in first in face of the mutual fear of what might occur if the crisis is not resolved. For the end stages of the crisis, however, each side may be rendered impatient, lunging to attack in fear that the other side is about to attack. We are in an almost dialectical process here, as the prospect that supports a mutual contest of waiting at the outset is that of a mutual inability to wait at later stages.

The earlier stages of a crisis are thus a contest of mutual countervailing efforts. As in other contests of a war of attrition, for example in a guerrilla war exchange, each side counts upon the human disutility felt on the other side. Unlike a war of attrition or a guerrilla war, however, the crisis imposes a disutility of prospect, that is, the prospect of an initiation of warfare where the world is still at peace—the prospect of an escalation to levels of destruction which have not yet been experienced. By contrast, the later stages of the crisis are a contest of counterforce efforts, as each side is plunged into shooting by the prospect of how well it will do on the first strike, as compared with how well it will do if it waits to strike second.

What we have more trouble isolating is the exact location and shape of a discontinuity in calculations—the turning point of an abrupt shift in preferences in which each side chooses between waiting and striking instead of quitting and waiting. The situation where each side is inclined to strike, because each side expects the other to strike, is viewed from both sides' advance perspective as a disaster. Because both sides see it as a disaster for both sides, however, and guess that the adversary sees it that way as well, the initial waiting contest evolves into what we call a crisis.

Does a crisis thus emerge because each side underrates the hostility and the stubbornness of the other, or because there is an overrating of hostility and combativeness? The answer is unfortunately again a complicated "both," with differing attributions of motivation applying in stages.[9]

For the opening round, each side is betting that the other will be more inclined to back off. The adversary has to want to avoid war, just as we do, and, it is hoped, more than we do, so we should stick to our principles and not make concessions. For the later round, should the crisis run on too long, the other side might instead elect to lunge out at us; and our prudent calculations would then tell us to anticipate his hostility and combativeness. As one draws close to prisoners' dilemma, one exaggerates adversary hostility, rather than wishfully understating it.

POLITICAL PREREQUISITES FOR CRISES   What are the necessary background ingredients that make crises possible? I offer a relatively parsimonious model, considering as few as two variables: the degree of active political conflict between the separate parties; and the degree to which the military systems at their disposal favor taking the offensive.

For a crisis to emerge in almost any sense, we assume that the parties disagree substantially about some of the political and social arrangements of this world. What is pleasant and appropriate for one side is distasteful to the other. In some periods of time, moreover, such arrangements are frozen into a status quo; neither side can do much to change them. At other critical periods, however, these arrangements are more capable of being changed, depending on the interplay of the actions of the interested parties,

9 Arguments about the paradoxes for the causes, and avoidance, of war are elaborated in Quester, "War and Peace: Necessary and Sufficient Conditions," in Robert O. Matthews, Arthur G. Rubinoff, and Stein (eds.), *International Conflict and Conflict Management* (Scarborough, Ontario, 1984), 44–54.

with each side ready to threaten war if the other does not give up its contrary preferences.

The beginning of any historical crisis is thus often dated by a change in what people anticipate politically; that is, by the unsettling of what had previously been settled, by an opening up of old questions, by an activation of a new set of challenges, and by an enhancement of what is at stake and what is unceretain.

At stake is the combination of what is immediately subject to change *and* what are the longer-term implications and precedents that are affected by such a change. One or both of the sides may stake out assertive inferences from whatever has just happened. This could activate a crisis, as each side becomes ensnared in a contest of wills. An example would be the Franco-German crisis over Morocco in 1905.[10] Or perhaps some new kind of event has occurred which activates the commitments of the two sides in ways that neither had foreseen. Examples here might include the assassination of Archduke Ferdinand in 1914, or the destruction of the *U.S.S. Maine* in 1898.

The likelihood of war could be perceived as having risen simply because of changes in this first variable, namely that much larger slices of political and social life suddenly have come to depend on the settlement of the crisis. Each side suddenly has much more at stake, and each knows that the other has much more at stake. Each side understands that the other will be tempted to hold out for a longer time in the endurance contest; each knows that the other is more prepared to run risks of war. The price of failing to run such risks would be to accept far greater setbacks.

A situation where opposing parties do not just have conflicting interests, but have mortgaged larger portions of the future by declarations that are incompatible constitutes a crisis. If the kaiser declares at Tangier that Morocco will not be allowed to fall under French rule, and the French have meanwhile declared that they intend to impose a kind of reform on Morocco that amounts to French rule, each side then risks losing face, the image of resolve, and portions of the political future in places far removed from Morocco, if it does not get its way.

Crises amount to comparisons of the future with the present. The present can always be improved instantly by a concession,

10 See Ima C. Barlow, *The Agadir Crisis* (Chapel Hill, 1940).

but the future might then be worsened, as the other side will have proven its resolve (for example, over the Sudetenland).[11] The future which one laments may close in rapidly enough if an aggressor is emboldened to impose new tensions during a new crisis.

Those who advocate toughness in a crisis sometimes seek to simplify choice by arguing that the adversary will *always* come back to demand more if concessions are made. Therefore there is no gain in choosing the present over the future, since the bully will be emboldened for the immediate future. If this result were truly so, crises would cease to be crises, for no one would then be persuaded that a concession could end the fighting or the threat of fighing.

In reality, it is entirely plausible, just as it is inherently un-certain, that either side to a crisis, by making a concession, can terminate the threat of war for months or years. The trade-offs then become much more difficult to judge. Just how much of the future are we giving up when we choose to be conciliatory? Is it too much? Is it needlessly too much, since the other side would have provided its own concessions within a day or two? In ad-dition to caring objectively about the human arrangements that are in dispute in a crisis, we also care relatively about being effective bargainers. We feel that we owe it to our people and to our allies to strike as good a deal as possible—to eke out as much as we can by the scale of values that we are supporting.

Having a great deal of the political future at stake makes for a tense situation; it is critical and it imposes a price in terms of the clarity and wisdom of the decisions taken.

MILITARY PREREQUISITES   There is a second set of background assumptions for a crisis, from which we can note the following three possibilities.

> a case where neither side gains by attacking militarily, with each side's military commanders perhaps wishing that the other would be so foolish as to attack;
> a case where each side gains militarily by attacking, as compared with being attacked, but where the human costs of war are still

11   On Hitler's confrontation with the democracies, see Keith Middlemas, *Diplomacy of Illusion* (London, 1972).

normally large enough to outweigh the military gains that can be won in warfare;

a case where each side gains militarily by attacking, and indeed can gain so much that this precludes or blots out the human costs of a war.

Since the advent of nuclear weapons, the last case has become considerably less credible but has not yet been totally dismissed. It is what is sometimes labelled "splendid first strike," a counter-force attack capable of precluding most of the adversary's second-strike countervalue retaliation against an aggressor's population. In the pre-nuclear age, there would have been many more wars that in this way seemed profitable. The same may hold true for some limited wars where each side withholds its nuclear weapons.

The first case is one which should delight any seeker after peace, because it suggests that wars will not break out even when two political regimes are supremely hostile to each other. For me to attack you would simply be to play into your hands and to allow more of the political future of the globe to be dictated according to your whims. For you to attack me would simply be to play into my hands. So the forces in being simply sit waiting (and almost praying) for attacks which never come.

The second case might strike us, lamentably, as the most normal. It is very much the setting required to bring crisis diplomacy into play. Here there is no magic panacea to taking the offensive, for victories in warfare will at least be costly, and most probably will also still be a little uncertain; but the emergence of any uncertainties and vulnerablities on the political front may lead either side to turn to military forces, and/or to fear that the other side is about to make such a move, since striking first will indeed provide military advantages.

The crisis of 1914 after the assassination of the Archduke Ferdinand and the ensuing outbreak of World War I can plausibly be blamed on the groundforce mobilization schemes of all the major powers. They offered great advantages to first strikes across borders.

In crisis situations, we must assume that each side has a significant, but not infinite, distaste for the destruction that it will suffer in a war. We must assume that each sees some moderate, but not overwhelming, advantages in attacking first (as compared with attacking second) if war is to break out anyway. (If the reverse were to be surely and reliably true, it might blessedly be very difficult, if not impossible, to commence fighting in any crisis situation. Each side would always be better off if the other struck first.)

We repeatedly confront the offensive or defensive implications of types of weaponry, translating these classifications into distinctions of whether such weapons render the political situation stable or unstable (stable or unstable in the sense of crisis stability).[12] Weapons might be truly labelled defensive if they reward the side that is attacked and impose greater military disadvantages on the side that is taking the initiative to attack, thus making war less likely overall, and thus rendering situations in general, and crisis situations in particular, more stable. Weapons should instead be labelled as offensive when they reward the side that is attacking, imposing higher losses on the side that sat waiting for an attack, thus making war more likely in general, and making relations less stable.

One can hardly be too vehement in endorsing the kinds of weapons that are stabilizing—that reward the defense instead of the offense. As noted, at the extreme they might eliminate the very sense of crisis. If no one ever could wish to strike first, what would be the looming threat to activate the crisis syndrome? Short of this blissful state, weapons which favor the defense, in terms of military outcomes, discourage any "shooting first and asking question later," and instead encourage a more leisurely and calm contemplation of the options.

We may not so easily be able to control the occasions when portions of the political status quo are opened up to outside influence and to antithetical pressures for change. Archdukes sometimes are assassinated unexpectedly, and other opportunities/ threats of political revolution are also difficult to anticipate.

We might have greater success with efforts to alter our other significant background variable: whether the military technologies of the world are loaded toward the offense or the defense, loaded toward offering military or human rewards to whoever strikes first, or instead rewarding whoever is patient enough to let the

---

12 On the distinction between the offensive and defensive in weapons, see Jervis, "Co-operation under the Security Dilemma," *World Politics*, XXX (1978), 167–214.

other side strike the first blow. Yet we also can expect only partial and limited successes because military technology advances swiftly. If we could be sure that anti-tank guided missiles would blunt any tank attacks in the late 1980s, can we be sure that they will remain dominant in the 1990s?[13] Or might not some new weapons come along to restore advantage to the tank?

As long as major political conflicts continue to break out— political conflicts where either or both sides want to affect the outcome by applications of military force—and as long as there can be no guarantee that whoever initiates the use of military force will not thereby win an advantage over his opponent, we will be burdened by the possiblity of a crisis.

THE TRADEOFF WITH OTHER RISKS   By the very nature of crises, we tend to dread them. A contest of wills, whereby one side must back off to avoid a mutual disaster, is always unpredictable. Our worst fear, for purposes of clarity of modeling, has pertained to a strike "out of the blue," where neither side had been making particularly great demands on the other.

This situation is not quite a model of prisoners' dilemma, but rather of one-sided advantage in taking the miltary offensive. The Soviets in this view are better off attacking us regardless of what we do. We are better off attacking the Soviets if we know that Moscow is committed to war, but otherwise we would prefer to remain at peace.

Similarly, and significant for later American perceptions of international power struggles, the confrontation between the United States and Japan in 1941 was indeed a crisis in that the United States was imposing trade cutoffs on Japan, with a view

	Peace	War
Peace	3 _____ 3	2 _____ 0
War	0 _____ 4	1 _____ 1

13   The prospects for anti-tank weapons are discussed in John J. Mearsheimer, "Why the Soviets Can't Win Quickly in Central Europe," *International Security*, VII (1982), 3–39.

to forcing Tokyo to withdraw from China. But it also saw Washington underestimating, rather than overestimating, the likelihood of escalation to war. The threat of an attack on American soil as at Pearl Harbor was not the cause of crisis anxiety in Washington in the fall of 1941; in retrospect, Americans wish there had been more anxiety about such a possibility.

Memories of Pearl Habor can also cause anxieties about surprise attacks where the other side has no such plans. Related to the above model, but also as yet without any element of crisis reasoning, is a situation where the Soviets have no surprise attack intentions, but where, because of the inherent secrecy of the Soviet decision-making process, they are wrongly suspected of planning such an attack. Misleading signals on radar scopes and early warning sysems might thus trigger a foolish counter-attack by the United States (or the entire pattern of misunderstanding could be activated in reverse), producing a somewhat different version of "a war nobody wanted."

The cause of war would occur when each side overrates the hostility of the other. If each side could be shown how much the other hates war, if myths about the other side's resolution, stubbornness, and fanaticism could be dispelled, then the risk of war would abate. The paradox for those who seek peace is that different assumptions about the opponent, indeed exactly the opposite assumptions, are at work rather than the assumptions that initiate a crisis. In a crisis, each side may overrate the other's reasonableness and peacefulness; in the case of "mirror-image misunderstanding"—of "reciprocal fear of surprise attack"—each may underrate the other side's reasonableness and commitment to peace.[14]

	Peace		War	
Peace		3		2 ("4")
	3		0	
War		0		1
	("4") 2		1	

[14] On the non-crisis worry about "mirror-image misunderstanding," see Rapaport, *Fights, Games, and Debates* (Ann Arbor, 1960), Pt. I, 15–103.

To counter such mistaken presumptions, systems for mutual verification and observation are essential. Just as it is easier to avoid mutual arms races where there are verification systems for disarmament agreements, it is easier to avoid wars where nature or man has interposed warning arrangements to reassure against attack.

Mistaken apprehensions of an adversary's "bolt out of the blue" attacks are a serious concern, but they are not at all what we have been considering here as a crisis. Perhaps we should thus note simply that we must worry about other risks besides crises.

Yet, there are some complicated linkages between our fears of surprise attacks and our aversion to crises. If we are too alert in preparing for an enemy's attack, we may provoke a crisis, with all of the tensions and risks that it entails. If we are averse to the tensions and risks of a crisis, we may conversely blot out any advance warnings that we have been given of an enemy's plans for a surprise attack, and hence may still be vulnerable to such an attack.

One can thus lay out a different step-by-step progression, illustrating another set of fears: one side through an entire sequence refuses to let a crisis occur. This is the situation which Betts and others have painted as the most worrisome: an attack which would not be totally unanticipated, but which would be launched after our side had avoided mobilizing its reserves because of our fear of provoking a crisis and our fear of overreacting to hostile signs and thereby confirming them. Might we one day embolden an adversary to be aggresive simply out of our aversion to the tensions inherent in a confrontation of wills? Might we move into a zone where the other side could gain militarily by attacking, precisely because we had been overly concerned about keeping him from having to fear our attack?[15]

Wars can occur because one side prefers war to peace just as much as because either side prefers a war in which it is attacking to a war in which it is being attacked. A maximum effort to avoid "a war nobody wanted" can set up too attractive a possibility of "a war one side wanted."

As outlined by Betts, Whaley, Erickson, and many others, this was basically the syndrome in May and June of 1941, as the

15   Richard K. Betts, *Surprise Attack* (Washington, 1982).

reports and evidence that Germany was planning to attack the U.S.S.R. were interpreted by Stalin as merely the early signs of a crisis—a crisis which could be terminated or even headed off if Hitler were only given enough concessions. Stalin feared that Hitler might attack if a crisis were launched—if a mutual contest of wills were to be allowed to develop where too much would suddenly be at stake. Just as with earlier efforts by the Western Allies to affect the German calculations, in the Munich crisis—which was resolved by giving Hitler the Sudetenland border strip with Czechoslovakia—Stalin attempted appeasement at a time when the term "appeasement" was not yet so generally regarded as discredited.[16]

The evil being avoided was not just a crisis, for it amounts more generally to the possibility that the other side may be so dissatisfied with the status quo as to be ready to go to war. A part of what was being averted was the simple tensions of unknown proclivities to war, the waiting game where each side increases the risks of warfare as the waiting is prolonged.

A straightforward way to deal with the problems of crises is preemptively to concede the issues that will be at stake. The obvious difficulty with such a policy is that it can embolden one's adversaries to increase their demands (as they conclude that the other side's fear of war is much greater than their own), and/or that such appeasement can massively increase one's adversaries' ability to fight a war (thus perhaps bringing the costs of war down to acceptable levels).

The fear of a surprise attack and our fear of what can happen in a crisis confront us with one more foreign policy dilemma. Each threatens our national interest; but sometimes either can be reduced only by increasing the other. Part of the reason we do not wish crises to be prolonged is that one side or the other may be tempted or stampeded into striking first. But we do not wish to give up so much, in terminating or avoiding crises, that we tempt our adversary into another kind of first strike.

If one compares what have been put forward most often as hypothetical scenarios for a nuclear war since 1945, with the closest call the world has had with such a war being the Cuban

16 Barton Whaley, *Codeword Barbarossa* (Cambridge, Mass., 1973); John Erickson, *The Road to Stalingrad* (New York, 1975).

missile crisis, one faces a paradox. Most of our concerns have been the results of deep suspicions and fears of a surprise attack, where one side launched a splendid first strike during a window of opportunity (a window of vulnerability for the victim), thereby preventing all possible second-strike retaliation against the aggressor's cities by the victim, or where the second side itself struck first because it had (perhaps mistakenly) anticipated such an attack.

In the Cuban missile crisis, the war would have stemmed instead from our crisis syndrome, rather than from any anticipation of surprise attack. Nuclear war could have broken out in 1962 because President Kennedy underestimated Soviet hostility and the chances that the Soviets would stick by the positions that they had staked out in Cuba. First Secretary Khrushchev, rather than remaining in constant fear of American bellicosity and attack, had originally concluded that the United States would not object to the deployment of Soviet medium-range missiles to within firing-range of the United States.

It is too easy to lament crises, and to complain about the tensions and mispredictions that occur in a crisis atmosphere. It is too easy to complain about the ways in which nations encounter the unexpected, achieving the opposite of what they intended, when they are embroiled in contests of resolve. Crises and contests of resolve may simply be inevitable, in that nations periodically find it necessary to risk such situations as part of serving their own national interests. To do the maximum to avoid a crisis would be to imitate the behavior of Stalin facing Hitler in 1941, or the politically worse fate of sovereign units which have been lost to memory because they gave up so much to avoid crisis confrontations.

The "threat that leaves something to chance" is a perfect example of the burden of possibly unexpected outcomes with which we have been wrestling, but a threat which may also explain why the NATO countries have not been absorbed into the Soviet bloc. We call it crisis tension when we compare these situations with a more secure peace; but we call it deterrence when we compare these situations with wars or with blatant aggressions. In what sense was there a crisis in Korea before Kim Il-sung launched his aggression in 1950? Would it not have been better to have had more of a crisis, to have given Stalin and Kim warnings that such aggression would not be tolerated? There was similarly no superpower crisis about the future of Afghanistan in the winter of 1978, with the Soviets perhaps drawing mistaken signals about the impact of their intervention on the future of detente with the West.[17]

We do not thereby have to shrug our shoulders at the tensions of a crisis, resigning ourselves to their occurrence. For all the reasons noted, we cannot look forward to these punctuation marks of world history, for they produced a World War I and might one day produce a World War III. Yet, we have only a limited control over the background factors that bring crises into being. What cannot be cured must be endured. The mature crisis of a confrontation of wills looks more pathological and more irrational than it truly is. What makes sense in dealing with a friendly neighbor may not make sense in dealing with an aggressive neighbor. In the latter case, the threat of mutual disaster, even in effect the threat of mutual suicide, may have to be harnessed and applied.

17 See Schelling, *Strategy of Conflict* (Cambridge, Mass., 1960), 187–204.

Lessons and Analogies
from Early Major Wars

John F. Guilmartin, Jr.

Ideology and Conflict: The Wars of the Ottoman Empire, 1453–1606

This analysis of the wars of the Ottoman Empire between the mid-fifteenth and early seventeenth centuries tests the proposition that we can enhance our understanding of the origins of war by study of the past. Embedded within the analysis, and integral to it, is a critical examination of the application of historical analogy to current issues of war and peace and of the role which theory plays in the process. The article grew out of the author's observation that contemporary Americans and western Europeans tend to view war as a formally recognized state of conflict between sovereign nations, sharply delineated from peace and prosecuted by major field, naval, and air operations. Two primary English-language dictionary definitions, separated by nearly a half century, reflect both this theory of war and the historical experience of eighteenth-century Europe from which it was drawn:

a state of usually open and declared armed hostile conflict between political units (as states or nations) (cannot exist between two countries unless each of them has its own government).

Webster's Third New International Dictionary
(Springfield, Mass., 1981)

a contest between nations or states (international war) or between parties in the same state (civil war), carried on by force of arms for various purposes, as to settle disputes about territorial possessions,

John F. Guilmartin, Jr., is Associate Professor of History at Ohio State University. He is the author of *Gunpowder and Galleys: Changing Technology and Mediterranean Warfare at Sea in the Sixteenth Century* (Cambridge, 1974).

I am grateful to Andrew C. Hess of the Fletcher School of Law and Diplomacy, Tufts University, for serving as a sounding board and, particularly, for his careful critique of my interpretations of Ottoman history. Special acknowledgement is due to Norman Itzkowitz of Princeton University, in whose seminars many of the ideas advanced here first took root. Finally, my conviction that scholars have slighted the role of guerrilla and positional operations in war was reinforced by my experience in teaching the history of warfare and technology at Rice University during 1983–1986. My understanding of the issues involved was sharpened by active interchange with my students there.

to maintain rights that have been interfered with, to resist opres-
sion, to avenge injuries, to conquer territory to extend dominion,
etc.

Webster's Monarch Dictionary (Chicago, 1916)

The prevailing Western view holds that the natural pattern
of human affairs consists of prolonged periods of peace inter-
spersed with brief, intensive wars. War is a departure from the
norm and is fought in pursuit of clear-cut and limited objectives,
typically the seizure of territory, the overthrow of a regime, or
economic advantage. Wars end when one side defeats the armed
forces of the other in battle and peace is restored by treaty. In
fact, this view of war is anomalous. Far more common in the
broad sweep of history are prolonged conflicts where the transition from peace to war is blurred, where guerrilla and positional
operations are more important to the outcome than field or naval
campaigns of limited duration, and where objectives tend to be
total.[1] This type of conflict—the term war is frequently inadequate—tends to end only with the elimination or cultural absorption of the losers. Examples of this kind of war are manifold:
especially relevant are the Reconquista, the 700-year struggle by
which Spanish Christians achieved unchallenged dominance over
the Iberian peninsula, and the analogous process by which Turco-
Muslim warriors conquered Anatolia for Islam.

There is persuasive evidence that the widely shared western
theory of war and its prevalence results in distortions when it is
applied to conflicts which do not fit the assumptions upon which
it is based. The inability of the news media of the United States
to grasp the importance or nature of the Persian Gulf war between
Iraq and Iran is a case in point; early assessments that neither side
could endure a long war—the conflict began in 1980—have been
replaced for the most part by silence. The difficulties experienced
by the news media, government, and military services of the

1 For the division of war into field, positional, and guerrilla warfare and the nature of
battle, see John Keegan, "Command Performances," *New York Review of Books* (January
20, 1983); *idem, The Face of Battle* (New York, 1976), 15–22. For the distinction between
naval warfare and guerrilla warfare at sea, see Guilmartin, *Gunpowder and Galleys: Changing
Technology and Mediterranean Warfare at Sea in the Sixteenth Century* (Cambridge, 1974),
22–23.

United States in coming to grips with the realities of transnational terrorism provide another example. The huge volume of media coverage given in 1982 to the South Atlantic war between Argentina and Great Britain is yet another case in point. This coverage, wildly out of proportion to the scale of forces engaged or the issues involved, cannot be explained away by some presumed fascination on the part of the American public for all things British.[2] The comfortable way in which the conflict fit the prevailing Western theory of war was surely a major factor.

It is plain that historical analogy plays a major role in shaping theories of war and peace. Any scholarly analysis of the causes and prevention of war must, at bottom, be based on historical analogy. If the data upon which the analysis is based are not explicitly historical, then the implicit assumptions concerning human behavior upon which the data were selected and analyzed must be historical, for war and peace are human phenomena and all of our information concerning human behavior is, in a broad sense, historical. This proposition, with which both Karl von Clausewitz and Sigmund Freud would have agreed, in no way degrades the role of theory in amplifying and deepening our understanding of human behavior. To the contrary, sound theory (theory that is both testable and analytically useful) is essential to the understanding of any facet of human behavior. The more complex the phenomenon under consideration—and war and peace are among the most complex—the more essential is the role of theory in its study. We therefore use historical analogy in one way or another and logic and experience alike suggest that analogies are most likely to be drawn from events that are historically recent and culturally familiar. We must explicitly recognize this reality and come to grips with the problems which it presents. The uncritical use of analogy is a serious impediment to under-

2 Until November 1986, when the involvement of members of President Ronald Reagan's administration became known, coverage of the Persian Gulf war by U.S. print and electronic media was relatively limited, especially in light of the economic, political, and, especially, religious issues that are at stake. (Note that the above text concerning the Persian Gulf war was drafted in October 1986, before the Iranian arms sales revelations.) By contrast, the South Atlantic War of 1982 was surely the most overreported conflict in history. See Guilmartin, "The South Atlantic War: Lessons and Analytical Guideposts. A Military Historian's Perspective," in James Brown and William P. Snyder (eds.), *The Regionalization of Warfare: The Falkland/Malvinas Islands, Lebanon, and the Iran-Iraq Conflict* (New Brunswick, N.J., 1985), 55–75, esp. 57 n. 10.

standing, and the uncritical (and frequently unconscious) application of analogies from the immediate past is surely first on the list of potentially lethal abuses of history. This abuse of historical analogy is readily observed in the tendency of soldiers and statesmen to "fight the last war."

The value of examining alternative analogies is therefore evident; the question is, which ones? The Ottoman Empire's wars between 1453 and 1606 are an attractive candidate for a number of reasons: Close enough to the present to be reasonably familiar politically and technologically, they are not as strange to our sensitivities as those of the medieval or classical past. As today, warfare prosecuted by economically developed and technologically advanced nations tended toward ideologically inspired mass conflict. World affairs were at times dominated by the struggle between the Habsburg and Ottoman empires and their proxies, a struggle which spanned much of the globe.[3] Moreover, guerrilla and positional warfare were far more important relative to field warfare than in the eighteenth and nineteenth centuries. Yet, political and operational factors so contrast with those of the present that we are unlikely unconsciously to incorporate present motivations and causal relationships into our analysis. The unfamiliarity of Ottoman institutions offers particular advantages. Terms such as "crusader" and "the nobility" are attitudinally loaded in ways that "ghazi" and "timar holders" are not, and we can approach the latter without preconceptions. At the same time, the Ottoman culture is comprehensible to us because it was at least as European as it was Eastern. In short, the issues then are both similar enough to those of today to bear comparison without an excess of intrusive interpolation and distinctive enough that we are unlikely to mistake the one for the other.

This article focuses on the Ottoman wars against Christendom, although conflict between the Ottomans and their Muslim opponents was necessarily also considered. The study is further restricted to the years between the capture of Constantinople, 29 May 1453, and the Treaty of Zsitva-Torok, concluded on 11 November 1606. This period is of particular interest because it

3 Andrew C. Hess, in "The Ottoman Conquest of Egypt (1517) and the Beginning of the Sixteenth Century World War," *International Journal of Middle Eastern Studies*, IV (1973), 55–76, termed the struggle the sixteenth century world war, attesting to its striking similarity to twentieth-century conflict.

encompasses the greatest and most rapid expansion of the Ottoman Empire.

CONCEPTS OF WAR   Any analysis of the causes of war must begin with an examination of the opposing sides' concepts of armed conflict. Here we are struck by a marked dissymmetry. The European theories of war and peace, codified early in the seventeenth century by Hugo Grotius, a Dutch jurist, are sufficiently familiar to require little explanation (See *The Law of War and Peace* [1625]). The same cannot be said for Ottoman concepts of war. Derived from pre-Islamic Arab and Turco-Mongol traditions, they were articulated in a rhetoric based on the Koran and elaborated in the *sharia,* the holy law of Islam. Islamic concepts of war and peace did not clash with pre-Islamic Arab and Turkic ideas, but served to legitimize them in religious terms. The Ottoman word for war was the Arabic term *harb*; it meant either fighting or a state of war between two groups, a meaning derived from pre-Islamic Arabic usage.[4] The lack of a recognized central authority in pre-Islamic Arabia combined with a semi-nomadic lifestyle to make war the basis for normal relationships among groups. The lack of natural frontiers and barriers in the desert reinforced the importance of war and raiding; peace existed by exception. Finally, the Turco-Mongol ideal of world empire meshed with concepts of war derived from the pre-Islamic Arabian past and was easily accommodated by the vocabulary of the sharia.

Islam, by prohibiting Muslims from shedding the blood of another Muslim, turned pre-Islamic concepts of war outward against the enemies of the faith. Only one kind of war was recognized as lawful, the jihad, or holy war, conducted to expand the domain of Islam. A collective obligation of the community of the faithful, jihad served to expand the rule of Islamic law, which is to say the domain of justice. A permanent state of war was considered to exist between the Islamic state, the *darülîslam* (the house of Islam, the abode of those who submit to the will of God) and the rest of the world, the *darülharb*. The use of the

4 Majjid Khadduri, "HARB, war; i.—Legal Aspect," *The Encyclopaedia of Islam, New Edition* (London, 1971), III, 180–181. Nineteenth-century Ottoman usage defined *harb* as "a war; battle; fight; combat." See *New Redhouse Turkish-English Dictionary* (Istanbul, 1968).

term darülharb, literally the house of war, to describe the non-Islamic world is a cogent illustration of Ottoman ideas concerning war with Christendom. So is the use of the term *harbi* to describe a Christian who was not a subject of the Ottoman Empire.[5]

In practice, there were two kinds of war. The first was the war of imperial campaigns, formally legitimized by the Ottoman state's chief religious authority, the sheikh ul-Islam, and justified in terms of the sharia. The second was the perpetual war of raid and counter-raid along the borders of the Ottoman Empire and its Christian neighbors. This type of conflict was called ghazi warfare, from the term *ghaza,* a raid; it was the concrete manifestation of the unceasing obligation of the faithful to expand the boundaries of the darülîslam.[6] Ghazi was an honored title and the legitimacy of the Osmanli regime derived largely from Ottoman success as ghazis. The closest equivalent Christian concept is the crusade, but crusades were efforts of limited duration mounted in pursuit of discrete and clearly specified objectives, usually geographical. The traditional numbering of crusades is indicative; the concept of a first, second, or seventy-fifth ghaza would have been inconceivable to a ghazi for the ghaza was unending. Although crusades are associated with major field battles or brief sieges, ghazi warfare was a matter of incessant raids, skirmishes, and prolonged blockades.

The emphasis placed on ghazi warfare by the Osmanli state was unusual even by Islamic standards. This emphasis, a function of the absorption of large numbers of semi-Islamized Turks and Mongols, reduced the importance of the jihad. Although the practice of formally proclaiming the jihad to justify war for a specific purpose was common in most Islamic states, the Ottomans rarely went to the trouble. With a stolid, matter-of-fact self-confidence, matched in the west only by the Iberians, they considered themselves always justified—and always at war. Finally, ghazi war paid off; the populace in areas brought under control by ghazis tended to become Muslim whereas that in areas conquered by imperial campaigns tended to remain Christian.

---

5 *Harbi,* literally "pertaining to war," meaning inhabitants of the darülharb, retained the meaning of Christian foreigner into the nineteenth century. (*Ibid.,* 450.)

6 Khadduri, "HARB"; Norman Itzkowitz, *Ottoman Empire and Islamic Tradition* (New York, 1972), 6.

Some of the Christian military groups along the frontiers with Islam approached war in much the same way as the ghazi; the Knights of St. John and Habsburg Croatian Grenzers are prominent examples, and the generalization might be expanded to include Spanish and Portuguese fighting men.[7] These individuals viewed war in terms much like the ghazis, but, unlike the ghazis, they functioned outside the mainstream of their culture. The concept of perpetual war to defend the faith and expand its boundaries was inherently compatible with the Ottoman world view; it was not, however, consonant with the outlook of their Christian enemies.

INSTITUTIONAL BACKGROUND   It is axiomatic that the causes of wars cannot be understood without an appreciation of the institutional context within which they were conceived and waged. Ottoman institutions require our attention, for they are far less familiar than their Christian equivalents.[8] The effect of royal succession by male primogeniture as a causal factor in the wars of Christian Europe, for example, is commonly appreciated, whereas the impact of the Ottoman succession on the timing and nature of the empire's wars is not. Although the influence of feudal dues and obligations as a factor in the wars of Western Europe is generally well understoood, knowledge of the corresponding Ottoman institution of timar is restricted to specialists.

Our lack of familiarity with the Ottoman institutional context is emphasized by the eight-point Ottoman formula of statecraft given in Figure 1. Normally inscribed in a circle so that the end of the last injunction ran into the beginning of the first, it implied an unending chain of causation in the functioning of the

---

7   Based first in Rhodes and, after their expulsion in 1522 by Suleiman I (the Magnificent), then in Malta, the Knights of St. John carried on unceasing maritime campaigns against Muslim shores and commerce. Grenzers were border tribesmen armed by the Habsburg state and granted exemption from certain taxes, in return for their military services. See Gunther E. Rothenberg, *The Austrian Military Border in Croatia, 1522–1747* (Urbana, 1960).

8   Much of the following discussion of institutional factors, operational and technological considerations, and the wars themselves is based on an unpublished chronology of Ottoman affairs compiled by the author. The chronology depicts the major wars and internal rebellions of western Eurasia, 1375-1923, along with the incumbency of Ottoman sultans, grand viziers, and other key officials plotted in reference to a common timeline. The principal source of Ottoman institutional and chronological data was Ismail Hami Danishmend, *Izahi Osmanli Tarini Kronoljisi* (Istanbul, 1948), a four-volume biographical dictionary and chronology of the incumbency of major Ottoman offices.

Fig. 1 The Ottoman Circle of Equity

1. There can be no royal authority without the military.
2. There can be no military without wealth.
3. The *reaya* [the peasantry, literally cattle] produce the wealth.
4. The sultan keeps the *reaya* by making justice reign.
5. Justice requires harmony in the world.
6. The world is a garden; its walls are the state.
7. The state's prop is the religious law.
8. There is no support for the religous law without royal authority.

SOURCE: Itzkowitz, *Ottoman Empire*, 88.

Islamic state. The strangeness of this formulation to individuals who are attuned to Judeo-Christian traditions highlights the differences between the institutional factors which shaped Ottoman conduct and those prevailing in the Christian West.

One of the most important distinctions was the overtly Sunni nature of the religious and institutional character of the Ottoman Empire, a factor which ensured conflict with Shii Islam. The friction between Shii and Sunni stemmed from a deep-seated religious tension within Islam, which expressed itself in fundamental disagreement over who should rule the community of the faithful and how.[9] It affected the Ottoman state in two principal ways: First, Shii influence was strong among the Turcoman tribesmen of eastern Anatolia, due partly to the general tendency of the heterodox to migrate toward the frontiers, a tendency hardly unique to Ottoman society. The problem was exacerbated by the emphasis on martyrdom in Shii doctrine, an emphasis which meshed with the ghazi ethic and the strong undercurrent of ascetic mysticism in the religious beliefs of the Muslim Turcoman tribesmen of the border regions. Second, although Shii Islam was a minority faith elsewhere, Twelver Shii Islam was dominant in Persia. These two factors in combination effectively guaranteed conflict between the Persian Safavids and the Ottomans.[10]

9 To the two original articles of the Muslim faith, "I believe in God the One" and "I believe in the revelation of the Kur'an which is uncreated from all eternity," Shii Islam added a third: "I believe that the Imam especially chosen by God as the bearer of a part of the divine being is the leader to salvation." See "Shi'a," in Hamilton A. R. Gibbs and J. H. Karmer (eds.), *Shorter Encyclopaedia of Islam* (New York, 1965), 575.
10 The principal Shii sects are identified with the number of imams which they recognize as legitimate, in this case twelve.

The social structure of the Ottoman state is a necessary start-ing point for addressing changes in the institutional context within which it waged war. Although the hierarchial ordering of the structure remained essentially constant during the period of our concern, its articulation changed markedly. This transformation, which affected the Ottoman ability and proclivity to make war, can be traced through five institutions: the royal succession; the sultanate; *ghulam,* or royal slaves; the standing, salaried *kapi kulu* army; and timar, a system of land tenure based on non-hereditary, feudatory grants.

The Sultan's importance as a leader and symbol of legitimacy made the mechanics of succession critical to dynastic success. The Ottoman theory of succession, derived from Arab-Muslim and Turco-Mongol traditions, gave an equal claim to all males in the royal line, and the death of a sultan signaled a battle to the death among the claimants. Although sultans normally could control their sons, any Osmanli male apart from the sultan himself rep-resented a potential threat to unity, a problem which Mehmed II addressed by legitimizing royal fratricide. At first, this practice ensured unity and selected out weak sultans. The early, ghazi sultans spent much of their lives on campaign and had few off-spring. Princes, too, served as governors and military command-ers, and only the strong survived to adulthood. As a result, contests for succession were short, decisive, and relatively non-disruptive.[11]

But, as the Ottoman state grew powerful and secure, the succession was corrupted by harem politics and power brokering. Originally, court factions formed around princes on the basis of policy differences rather than narrowly construed self-interest. When expansion ceased, sultans spent more time at home and had

11 When Murad I was killed by a Serbian knight on the field of Kossovo, 10 June 1389, Bayezid and his brother Ya'cub were summoned to the spot from their posts commanding the wings of the Ottoman army and fought to the death while the battle was in progress. Although this traditional account may be apocryphal in part, it accurately reflects Ottoman attitudes.

Even though royal cousins and uncles were not a factor in the period under discussion, they had been a source of instability and disruption in earlier times, and the lesson was remembered. During the years under consideration, the system broke down only once, in 1481 following Mehmed II's death. Defeated by his brother Bayezid, prince Jem sought refuge with the Mamluk sultanate of Egypt, returned to re-assert his claim, and was defeated a second time and fled to the Knights of St. John of Rhodes. Jem's survival as an alternate locus of dynastic loyalty severely constrained Bayezid II's strategic options.

more offspring; the number of princes became unmanageable, and they were confined to the imperial household to limit intrigue. Succession brokering began in the princes' infancy, and princely factions coalesced around issues of influence and income. Finally, princes ceased to be the leaders of factions and became their tools, and succession came to be controlled by royal mothers and grandmothers.[12]

These changes were accompanied by a realignment in the discharge of the sultan's authority. Until the latter part of Suleiman I's reign, grand viziers were chiefs of staff to strong sultans who personally made major policy decisions. In old age, Suleiman I turned over his day-to-day responsibilities to his grand viziers, who increasingly acted in his place. His successors retained this custom, and grand viziers came to run the government and lead the imperial army. The extended vizierate of Sokollu Mehmed Pasha (1565–1579), encompassing the last year and a half of Suleiman's reign, all of Selim II's, and the first half decade of Murad III's, is indicative.

Change also occurred in the pivotal institution of *ghulam,* or royal slaves, originally Christian boys who were enslaved in youth and converted to Islam.[13] Sharia law placed few constraints on the sultan in dealing with ghulams, as opposed to free Muslims, and the institution magnified his authority. Since ghulams were personal slaves of the sultan, not fully subject to the commands of his subordinates, there was a premium on strong imperial leadership, a factor magnified by the importance of ghulam to the army.

The backbone of the army consisted of full-time professionals known as *kapi kulus,* a Turkish term applied to any royal slave supported by government emoluments. Originally synonymous with ghulam, the term kapi kulu was also loosely applied to the

12 The period during which the leadership of the empire was determined by imperial wives and mothers is known in Ottoman history as the Sultanate of the Women. It reached its apex toward the end of the period with which we are concerned here.

13 Ghulam was based on the fact that although sharia law forbade the enslavement of Muslims, the conversion of a slave to Islam did not require maumission. The manpower for ghulam was provided by young boys taken from among the empire's Christian populace by *devshirme,* the child-tax. The bulk of devshirme recruits became janissaries or sipahis of the imperial guard; however, exceptional candidates were carefully educated and groomed for higher posts. Ghulams rose to the highest offices and formed the backbone of imperial administration in the Ottoman heyday.

entire standing army and came to mean salaried. The kapi kulu army was organized into five corps: the janissaries, the salaried sipahis (armored horse archers) of the sultan's household, the bombardiers or siege gunners, the sappers, and the cart artillery. Of these, the janissaries and sipahis, the largest and most important, were at first entirely ghulam. The kapi kulus were joined on campaign by sipahis supported by timar land grants and by volunteer irregular light cavalry and infantry who served for booty and imperial reward. Although non-ghulam soldiers provided the bulk of the army's manpower, the kapi kulu enforced the sultan's orders and kept in check the influence of provincial notables, descendants of the ghazis who had conquered the land on which they lived. This scheme remained politically viable so long as it was militarily effective.

The decline of ghulam can be traced through the fortunes of the janissaries, the sultan's elite shock infantry. Originally they were forbidden to marry and lived in barracks, their energies absorbed by frequent campaigning. When campaigning slackened—in part because of the janissaries' inability to defeat western infantry in the open field—procreative desires manifested themselves, and Suleiman I allowed them to marry. Selim II allowed janissaries to enroll their sons in the corps, undermining the sultans' authority over the corps and eventually swelling it to unmanageable proportions. Similar factors affected the salaried sipahis, and decay manifested itself in a janissary revolt in 1589 and sipahi revolts in 1592 and 1603.[14]

Timar, the Ottoman system of non-hereditary land grants given in return for military service, usually as an armored horse archer, underwent parallel decay. Timar grants were normally organized from territory seized from the darülharb, where there was no conflicting Muslim title. A timar's income was established by imperial survey and the land assigned to a holder who used the revenues for his maintenance and upkeep. Resident holders had a personal stake in local order and justice, and, so long as most timars were allotted to fighting men, the system worked well. But timars could also be used to produce income for the

14 The janissaries traditionally revolted on the accession of a new sultan and demanded payment of a donative, but these revolts were more symbolic than real. Those listed above occurred in mid-reign and entailed serious combat; the sipahi revolt in 1603, for example, had to be suppressed by the janissaries.

imperial treasury or to support court officials. Inflation, the increasing cost of warfare, and the failure to replenish the treasury with conquered booty all intensified pressure to convert timar grants to tax farms. At the same time, the shifting emphasis in land warfare from field operations, the horse-archers' forte, to positional warfare, dominated by artillery and infantry armed with firearms, further undermined the position of the timariot sipahi. In the first place, he represented revenue lost to the imperial treasury; in the second, his military services were no longer as valuable; finally, inflation increased his expenses without expanding his revenues, and many small timar holders were forced off the land. The recruitment of salaried firearms-armed infantry in the rural areas exacerbated the problem. Unlike the timariots, these men lived in barracks and, when their salaries were not met, they turned to banditry, often joined by dispossessed timariots.

These developments were cumulative. The number of timariot sipahis declined steadily; rural order decayed as timar lands fell to absentee landlords and tax farmers, and, in a vicious spiral, declining prosperity reduced tax revenues further still.[15] These trends culminated in the 1590s with the return of large numbers of firearms-armed soldiers to the rural areas in the wake of unsuccessful campaigns. The deterioration of rural order produced the Jalali revolts, which began on a large scale in the late 1590s and were not brought under control until 1611.

OPERATIONAL AND TECHNOLOGICAL CONSIDERATIONS   Just as the causes of wars cannot be understood outside of the cultural and institutional context within which they were conceived and waged, war itself cannot be understood outside of the operational and technological context within which it is fought. A study of war which ignores the mechanics of combat makes no more sense than a study of commerce which ignores cash payment or a study

15 Halil Inalcik, "The Heyday and Decline of the Ottoman Empire," in P. M. Holt, Ann K. S. Lambton, and Bernard Lewis (eds.), *The Cambridge History of Islam* (Cambridge, 1970) (hereafter CHI), I, 344-349. The inflationary impact of precious metals imported from America by the Spanish exacerbated these trends and an Austrian peasant revolt of 1594-1597 suggests that the Ottoman difficulties were partly due to European-wide economic trends. The structure of the Ottoman state made the social and political impact of inflation particularly destructive.

of fertility which ignores sex.[16] Between the middle of the fifteenth century and the first decades of the seventeenth century, the technology of war changed with unprecedented rapidity, significantly altering the manner in which economic and social resources could be applied to achieve political ends by military means.[17] The rate and nature of change differed significantly from nation to nation and had a major impact on the effectiveness of Ottoman forces.

The erroneous image of technological stasis which pervades all too many historical treatments of early modern war stems in part from an excessively narrow definition of technology and in part from a failure to view war from the viewpoint of the combatant.[18] Suffice it to say that a veteran of Mehmed II's campaigns of the 1460s would have been astonished by the formations, weaponry and discipline of the Christian infantry which opposed Suleiman I's army at Vienna in 1529. More dramatically, the Ottoman bombardiers who planned and executed the destruction of Venetian fortresses in the Morea during Bayezid II's lightning campaign of 1499-1502 would have been confounded by the Venetian fortifications of Corfu in 1537.

Among the most basic operational factors influencing the military and dynastic viability of the Ottoman Empire were the limits of expansion imposed by geography and climate. On land,

16 According to Clausewitz, "In war, there is only one [means]. Combat." (See Clausewitz [eds. and trans., Michael Howard and Peter Paret], On War [Princeton, 1976], I, 95). He went on to say, as paraphrased above, that "The decision by arms is for all major and minor operations in war what cash payment is in commerce" (ibid., 97).

17 For summary treatment of the changes, see Charles W. C. Oman, A History of the Art of War in the Sixteenth Century (London, 1937); Christopher Duffy, Siege Warfare: The Fortress in the Early Modern World, 1494-1660 (London, 1979); Simon Pepper and Nicholas Adams, Firearms and Fortifications: Military Architecture and Siege Warfare in Sixteenth-Century Siena (Chicago, 1986).

18 My working definition of technology is: 1. the application of knowledge to achieve a physical effect by means of an object, artifact, or thing. 2. the object, artifact, or thing itself. 3. the knowledge required to create, produce, employ, maintain, and logistically support the object, artifact, or thing.

The qualification "to achieve a physical effect" distinguishes technology from art, the application of knowledge to achieve an aesthetic effect. The term object was included in recognition of the fact that technology can involve the application of naturally occurring tools or materials; the use of suitably shaped rocks to open nuts or shellfish is a technology, as is the breeding and use of livestock for food or transportation. The term thing was included since physical effects may be induced by means such as sound waves and electronic emissions which do not involve concrete objects.

these were determined by the length of the campaigning season and the fact that kapi kulu troops could be effectively commanded only by the sultan. Since the sultan was needed in Constantinople for the administration of the government, campaigns began there. Since the movement of large forces in winter was not feasible for an army dependent upon animal transport, land campaigns began in the spring. They had to be concluded by the onset of winter to prevent the wastage and economic dislocation which would result from holding an army in winter quarters (in particular, timar holders had to be home by winter to manage their lands). These factors imposed a limit on how far an Ottoman army could penetrate into the Balkans. In practical terms, Vienna marked that limit; and, once Vienna was reached, there was little benefit to further campaigning since all of the land within reach of the sultan's armies was already in Muslim hands and thus unavailable for incorporation into the timar system.

Similar factors operated at sea where the campaign season was dictated by the winter storms which ran from mid-October through mid-March. The war galley was the dominant Mediterranean warship, and low-lying galleys were notoriously unseaworthy except in the calm spring and summer months. Strategic reach could be extended by wintering over at a friendly port in the western Mediterranean (since the Kapudan Pasha commanded the fleet, the sultan's presence was not required). Fleets wintered over in the western Mediterranean on occasion, but it was expensive and entailed the same problems of economic dislocation which limited the campaigning of Ottoman field armies. In addition, developments in naval technology during the last half of the sixteenth century increased the cost of warfare at sea and reduced the strategic radius of galley fleets. In the 1550s, squadrons based in Constantinople campaigned as far west as the Balearic islands; by 1565, Malta was the effective limit, and, after the recapture of Tunis from the Spanish in 1574, imperial squadrons rarely entered the western Mediterranean.

In the years immediately preceding Mehmed II's capture of Constantinople, the Ottomans capitalized on a number of technological advantages by virtue of their superior organization and powers of taxation. In particular, the Ottoman ability to cast large siege bombards yielded a decisive superiority in siegecraft. This advantage was not overcome until the 1520s and 1530s when

Italian engineers began to construct fortifications with sunken profiles and bastioned traces. In terms of manpower and munitions, these fortifications, if not immune to Ottoman methods, proved prohibitively costly to overcome. In the meantime, Christian fortifications were at risk.[19]

In 1512, when Selim I ascended the throne, the Ottoman field army was probably superior to any other in the world. The Ottoman advantage stemmed from the excellence of the kapi kulu troops, the tactical skills of ghazi warriors who had become timar holders, the superiority of the Osmanli state in levying and raising taxes, and on the quickness with which the Ottomans embraced firearms. Superior logistical organization and planning played a major role as did excellent camp discipline, which was in part a product of the Koranic prohibition on the consumption of alcohol (a point which Western observers were quick to note).

The Ottoman field array consisted of a barricaded center defended by the janissaries and the cart artillery, flanked by two wings of armored horse archers that were formed from the timar holders of Europe and Anatolia respectively, and a reserve of kapi kulu sipahis, normally positioned near the imperial standard behind the center of the line.[20] The front of the army was covered by a screen of irregular light cavalry and infantry. Although these arrangements seem relatively crude by the standards of late sixteenth century Europe, they had no equal until the mid-1520s, when interactive developments in positional, field, and guerrilla warfare began to work to the disadvantage of the Ottomans. Western advances in military engineering placed the reduction of even relatively minor fortifications beyond the means of local ghazi leaders. Conversely, Western advances in siegecraft placed the strongholds of the ghazis themselves at risk. Ghazi warfare

19 V. J. Parry, "Warfare," CHI, II, 824-850, esp. 839-840. The largest Ottoman siege bombards threw balls of cut granite or marble weighing 1,000 pounds and more. The high curtain walls of medieval fortifications were horribly vulnerable to these cannon, as demonstrated by the Ottoman victories over Venetian fortresses in the Morea in 1499-1502. The cannon could be moved for extended distances only by ship, but the Ottomans overcame the problem on land by casting them on site, a capability reflecting the excellence of Ottoman logistical organization.

20 The janissaries and the cart artillery were largely responsible for the Ottoman advantage in field operations. The cart artillery employed light cannon fired from atop small supply carts; these were chained together in a barricade from behind which the janissaries fought, forming the center of the Ottoman line. The janissaries adopted individual firearms as early as the mid-fifteenth century.

remained a viable means of expanding the boundaries of the darülîslam, by land or by sea, but ghazis needed forward bases and such bases could be seized only by an imperial force with its sappers and siege train, to which seasonal limits applied.

The advances in fortress design and the proliferation of well-sited, well-gunned fortifications in strategic regions worked on balance against the Ottomans; the problem was exacerbated in the Balkans by a decline in the effectiveness of Ottoman field armies relative to those of the Austrian Habsburgs. By the 1530s, Spanish and German infantry had learned to fight in balanced formations that combined firearms with weapons of shock combat, notably the pike, an eighteen- to twenty-foot-long spear. Good infantry using these tactics could deliver crushing shock action and repel cavalry charges with ease; the combination posed tactical problems which the Ottomans never solved.[21] The institutional decline of the kapi kulu army coincided with these developments.

The Ottomans' disadvantage in the field was never so severe that it could not be redressed by surprise, numbers or the effective use of terrain, but these occurrences were exceptional. Between the battle of Mohacs in 1526 and Kerestres in 1596 there was no major clash of the Ottoman and Christian field armies in the Balkans. Whether the absence of field battles was due to an implicit Ottoman awareness of tactical vulnerability, the geographical limits on Ottoman expansion, Habsburg preoccupation with more pressing problems elsewhere, or—most likely—a combination of all of these factors, we cannot say. It is clear, however, that Ottoman field and naval forces had lost their edge.

In guerrilla (which is to say ghazi) warfare, the issues were not so clear-cut. On land, the balance seems to have gone against the Ottomans toward the middle of the sixteenth century, but this shift was as much for cultural and political reasons as for technical and tactical ones. Although their expansive powers were curtailed, the ghazi bands of the frontiers continued to gain occasional victories into the seventeenth century. In the Mediterranean, the North African sea ghazis and their Turkish compatriots

---

21 The janissaries were skilled in positional warfare and retained their status as elite shock troops well into the seventeenth century, but they never learned to wield pikes and repel cavalry charges in the open field.

remained a menace to Christian coasts and commerce well into the seventeenth century.

ANALYSIS   From the capture of Constantinople in 1453 to the Treaty of Zsitva-Torok in 1606, the Ottoman state was, to all practical intents and purposes, continuously at war. The Ottomans were a military class and war was integral to the functioning of their state. Even an abbreviated narrative is beyond the scope of this article, but our interest is in causation, and the wars of the Ottomans can be summarized in this regard in a two-part structural and chronological typology.[22] Structurally, the wars of the Ottoman Empire fell into the following categories according to opponent, objective, and justification:

War against Christian states to expand and defend the darüîslam   These conflicts occurred first within the periphery of the empire in an effort to absorb the remnants of the Byzantine domains in Greece and Anatolia and then along an expanding perimeter which eventually encompassed the Balkans from the Adriatic to the Danube and Dniester, the shores of the Black Sea, and much of the Mediterranean basin including the North African coast as far west as Morocco. Ottoman strategic interests encompassed concern for threatened Muslim populations in Spain, India, Arabia and the Crimea. These concerns prompted clashes with the Portuguese in Arabia, the Yemen, and the Coromandel coast early in the sixteenth century; they also led to conflict with Muscovy on the Ukrainian steppes and with the Portuguese in Morocco. In the mid-1500s, Ottoman forces entered Italy and penetrated deep into the western Mediterranean in response to these impulses.

War against Shii states to protect the integrity of the realm   These conflicts, prosecuted against the Persian Safavids and their predecessors, were legitimized in terms of the defense of religious

---

22 The most comprehensive single narrative of the wars of the Ottoman Empire is in Inalcik, "Ottoman Heyday and Decline"; *idem*, "The Rise of the Ottoman Empire," CHI, 295–323. Itzkowitz, *Ottoman Empire*, is the best brief treatment and incorporates a valuable strategic analysis. Hess combines insightful narrative with analysis of underlying cultural issues in *The Forgotten Frontier: A History of the Sixteenth-Century Ibero-African Frontier* (Chicago, 1978); "The Battle of Lepanto and its Place in Mediterranean History," *Past & Present*, 57 (1972), 53–73; and "The Ottoman Conquest of Egypt," 55–76.

orthodoxy, but in fact revolved around concern over Shii-inspired unrest in eastern Anatolia. These concerns prompted Selim I to invade Persia in 1514 and led to the incorporation of southern Mesopotamia into the Ottoman Empire during the reign of Suleiman I.

War against rival Sunni states   The Ottomans were least comfortable with conflict in this category, but did not shirk from it when their interests were involved; the absorption of the Mamluk sultanate under Selim I during 1516/17 is the most significant example. The Ottomans justified conflict against Sunni opponents with arguments couched in terms of the need to prevent interference with Ottoman ghazi activities.

War against internal rebellion and rival dynasties   Conflict in this category stemmed from the traditional independence of the various ghazi dynasties of eastern Anatolia, overlapped Ottoman concerns with the Shii threat in the border regions and frequently merged with internal rebellions such as the Jalali revolts. The Ottoman goal was to maintain their legitimacy as the leader of the ghazis and to secure their vital interests in the geographical heart of their domains as a base for expansion at the expense of the darülharb.

Internal dynastic struggle   Conflict in this category rarely rose to the level of open violence, let alone full-scale war, but when it did the consequences were momentous. The potential for intra-dynastic conflict was always present, and many otherwise obscure turns in Ottoman policy are explainable in terms of the need to avoid straining the body politic in ways which might lead to internal war. The most important conflict in this category was the inconclusive struggle for the succession following the death of Mehmed II in 1481.

The chronological categorization reflects the importance of leadership at the top. The strong, early sultans assumed power with mature strategic agendas, and their policies bore the mark of their personalities. Later sultans were unwilling or unable to implement strategic agendas in a forceful manner, and their personalities were hidden by the institutions which had assumed much of their power. The wars of Murad III, Mehmed III and Ahmed I may be viewed as a unit. The breakdown is as follows:

Mehmed II (1452-1481)   Mehmed pursued a frenetic policy of expansion through a combination of ghazi war and imperial campaigns; his method seems to have revolved around use of the imperial siege train to reduce hostile strong points, turning them into ghazi bases. Mehmed's wars, at least overtly, encompassed all of the structural categories with the sole exception of intra-dynastic conflict.[23] He consolidated the Ottoman hold on Anatolia, defeating the remnant Greek Empire of Trebizond and suppressing the Karamanids; he brought much of Greece within the darülîslam, fighting Venice in the process; he expelled the Genoese from the Black Sea; he absorbed Serbia while fighting an extended war with Hungary; he suppressed an Albanian revolt and laid siege to the stronghold of the Knights of St. John on Rhodes in 1481, albeit unsuccessfully. Shortly before his death, he ordered an expeditionary force into southern Italy, seizing the formerly Byzantine city of Otranto. This victory was, in retrospect, the high point of the Osmanli threat to Christendom, for Italy was not capable of resisting Ottoman arms at that time. Mehmed's policies imposed severe strains on the empire and his policies of taxation were particularly resented; oposition to these policies was reflected in those of his successor.

Bayezid II (1481-1512)   The faction which supported Bayezid in his contested succession was opposed to the fiscal and political measures taken by Mehmed II to support his expansive policies. Bayezid, constrained by the survival of his brother Jem after the failure of his attempt to seize the throne, was unable to proceed agressively in the west, but he did establish his reputation as a ghazi—a politically essential task—through wars of expansion in Moldavia. He fought a desultory war with the Mamluks in Syria in 1485-1491 and, after Jem's death, launched a short, successful war against Venice in 1499-1502, using superior siegecraft to reduce the major fortifications along the Greek coast.

Selim I (1512-1520)   The accession of Selim I marked a return to the policies of Mehmed II, although the emphasis was on field operations, which was appropriate given the superiority of the

23 Although internal stresses were great, Grand Vizier Chandarli Halil Pasha opposed Mehmed II's attack on Constantinople, and his removal and execution following the capture of the city show just how close to the surface they lay.

Ottoman field army. Where Mehmed II had used his siege train to support the ghazis, Selim I was arguably the most successful field general of his age. He suppressed Shii-inspired instability in eastern Anatolia, launched a successful Persian campaign against Shah Isma'il, and then turned against the Mamluks, whom he defeated in decisive field actions at Merj Dabik and Ridaniyeh.[24] The first of these battles gained him Syria; the second brought down the Mamluk sultanate. Caliph al-Mutawakkil fell into his hands at Merj Dabik; the capture of the caliph and the assumption of custody of the holy cities of Mecca and Medina from the Mamluks brought the Ottomans immense prestige. Shortly after Ridaniyeh Selim's support of Mamluk resistance to the Portuguese bore fruit in a major defensive victory off Jidda, the port of Mecca.

Suleiman I (1520-1566) The wars of Suleiman's long reign encompassed all of our functional categories but the last; it was during his reign that the empire reached its geographical limits and that the Ottoman field army lost its superiority. Suleiman campaigned actively in the northern Balkans, captured Rhodes, fought an endless war against the Spanish Habsburgs in the Mediterranean, defeated a combined Venetian-Habsburg fleet at Prevesa, pursued active campaigns of expansion in Armenia and the Yemen, fought the Portuguese in India and Arabia, and extended Ottoman control into southern Mesopotamia. Suleiman is best known for his retreat from Vienna in 1529. Between his destruction of the Hungarian monarchy at Mohacs in 1526 and his retreat from Vienna, the armies of Christendom took the measure of the Ottomans in both field and positional warfare. Suleiman, in implicit recognition of the altered military balance, made the Sublime Porte a player in European diplomacy, maintaining an anti-Habsburg alliance with France.

Selim II (1566-1575) Selim II's sultanate was transitional strategically, operationally, and dynastically. His reign differed in character from those of the strong sultans who preceded him (he never exercised effective command in the field) and the weak

24 There is evidence that Selim's battle plan at Chaldiran was driven by concern for Shii-inspired defections within the Ottoman ranks, clear evidence of the seriousness of the Shii challenge to Ottoman legitimacy. See Inalcik, "Rise of the Ottoman Empire," 315.

sultans who followed. Whatever Selim's personal leadership abilities—his sobriquet, "the Sot," is as likely an indication of opposition to his policies as an accurate assessment of his character—he pursued an aggressive military policy which showed real strategic insight and was not without success. If the Ottoman fleet was defeated at Lepanto in 1571, the Christian victory was, in a sense, an empty one, for the Turks had already conquered Cyprus just as they had seized Chios from Genoa in 1566. Ottoman forces successfully opposed the Portuguese in the east and, in the Mediterranean, gave nothing to the Spanish after Lepanto. The high point of Ottoman military ambitions was the Don-Volga canal project, undertaken to turn the Caspian into an Ottoman lake. Launched in 1569, the project's strategic ends exceeded the operational means available; after a brief siege of Astrakhan, it collapsed.

Murad III (1575-95), Mehmed III (1595-1604) and Ahmed I (1604-1618)   With the passing of Selim II, the empire entered a period of decline as the debilitating effect of changes in the succession became manifest. A final victory in the west came on 4 August 1578 when Ottoman proxies crushed an attempt to install a Portuguese candidate on the throne of Morocco. In 1587, the ascent to the Persian throne of Shah Abbas, an able and aggressive Safavid prince, forecast a further Ottoman-Safavid war in 1602-1618, during which the Ottomans lost Tabriz, Azerbaijan, and Georgia. The Austrian Habsburgs responded by discontinuing the payment of tribute to the Ottomans in 1591, leading to the so-called Long War between the Ottomans and an Austrian coalition. The war was a protracted conflict of economic and social attrition, an affair of sieges and raids punctuated by occasional major field engagements; it coincided with the Jalali revolts and the decline of the sipahi timar holders, dramatic symptoms of a major internal Ottoman crisis. The Long War marked the end of the Ottoman Empire as an expansive power.

CONCLUSION   The causes of war between the Ottomans and their Christian enemies in the sixteenth century are self-evident only on the most superficial plane. Although the tradition causal hypotheses—religion, economics, and culture—enhance our understanding of the whens and hows, they tell us little about the underlying whys. Class is even less helpful; understanding the means of production and its relationship to the creation and use of military force is essential to any causal analysis, but class interest in Marxist terms provides few insights into Ottoman behavior. Geographical analysis provides powerful analytical tools for understanding the way in which the wars of the Ottoman Empire developed; indeed, geographical knowledge is essential to explaining the ebb and flow of campaigns and understanding the relationship between economics and military power, but geography tells us little about underlying causation. The skills of the military historian, applied to operational and technological considerations, yield similar insights concerning the timing of wars and the realism, or lack thereof, of political designs and strategic formulations, factors which clearly bear on any causal explanation. Clausewitzian analysis provides essential insights into the relationships between the ends and the means in war which any causal analysis must consider, but Clausewitz accepted the reality of war as a given in human affairs, and his theory tells us little about its underlying causes. Methodologies developed by political scientists offer prospects for refining our understanding of the operation of all of these factors; expected utility theory, in particular, has considerable promise for deepening our understanding of the rationale of decisions concerning war and peace. Finally, the concept of macroparasitism offers a conceptual framework within which to organize the historical data and apply the insights gained from consideration of the causal mechanisms listed previously.[25]

Religion, which was a causal mechanism in the Ottoman wars, is of limited value in explaining underlying motivation. Ottoman military ventures in the Balkans attracted considerable Christian support and Christian auxiliary troops were routinely employed on the frontiers; mercenary Greek Christian oarsmen powered Ottoman galleys and timars were awarded to Christians.[26] Roman Catholic Hungarians fought as Ottoman allies

25 See Bruce Bueno de Mesquita, "The Contribution of Expected Utility Theory to the Study of International Conflict," *Journal of Interdisciplinary History*, *XVIII* (1988), 629–652; William McNeill, *The Pursuit of Power: Technology, Armed Force and Society Since A.D. 1000* (Chicago, 1982).
26 Guilmartin, *Gunpowder and Galleys*, 112; Oman, *A History of the Art of War in the Middle Ages* (New York, 1924), II, 354.

against their coreligionists during Suleiman I's incursions.[27] The Ottomans took their responsibilities as ghazis seriously, just as the Spanish and Portuguese regarded their obligation to pursue the war against the infidel as a sacred duty. The perpetual Spanish anger with the Venetians over their willingness to come to terms with the Turks was no doubt religious in origin as well as justification. Religious impulses may not have been the principal force behind Portugal's eastward expansion, but they were a major factor.[28]

Religion was a causal factor in the wars of the Ottomans, but we cannot be certain to what degree it acted in its own right rather than simply as a means of legitimizing preexisting conflicts. Although the wars of the Ottoman Empire cannot be understood without understanding the religious factors involved, their influence must be examined within the total cultural, economic, social, and political context, not in isolation.

Similarly, straightforward economic explanation provides no generally useful hypotheses. Granted, fiscal concerns were high on any responsible Ottoman agenda and the fiscal integrity of the realm was dependent upon expansion, but the extent to which the connection was appreciated at the time is very much in question. There is little evidence that internal support for military expansion stemmed from any perceived need for new timar land as an economic palliative. A better case for economic motivation can be made for the Venetians, who saw profit as justification in war and whose warlike fervor against the Turks was visibly modulated by Ottoman control over the spice routes. Likewise, the behavior of the Genoese within the Spanish alliance was clearly shaped by commercial self-interest. But both Venetians and Genoese were good Catholics and saw special merit in fighting the infidel. The term Holy Alliance was not applied lightly to the union which the Venetians, the Spanish Habsburgs, and the Papacy formed against the Turks in 1537 and 1570, and if the Vene-

27 Inalcik, "Heyday and Decline," 324–326; Guilmartin, *Gunpowder and Galleys,* 256, n. 3. In an even stranger tangle of divided loyalties, the Italian Roman Catholic city state of Ragusa, a dependency of the Porte, routinely contracted warships out to the Spanish crown. Ragusan ships sailed with the Invincible Armada of 1588 and at one point early in the seventeenth century formed the core of the Spanish West Indies fleet.
28 Guilmartin, *Gunpowder and Galleys,* 7–10. The impulse behind the Portuguese expedition which came to grief off Jidda in 1517 was plainly more than commercial.

tians left the alliance as soon as victory gave them room to negotiate or defeat made it imperative, they fought as hard as their
coreligionists.

McNeill's concept of macroparasitism provides a useful lens
through which to view causal hypotheses. He compares the relationship between society and the microparasites which carry
human disease to the relationship between society and economically nonproductive military groups. He terms these military
groups macroparasites, "men who, by specializing in violence,
are able to secure a living without themselves producing the food
and other commodities they consume."[29] The concept of a symbiotic relationship between the host society and its means of
defense and aggression leads to a number of useful perceptions.
Plainly, a macroparasitic class must attach itself to the means of
production if it is to survive; equally plainly, dramatic differences
in the means of production will produce sharp differences in
perceived macroparasitic self-interest. The Aztec warrior elite's
fatal incomprehension of the motivation of Hernando Cortes'
conquerors, although puzzling when viewed from the standpoint
of objective class interests, is readily understandable in these
terms. If we are dealing with competing societies which operate
at about the same level of technological and economic advancement, as is the case here, the differences are more subtle.[30] In such
situations, the stress point is not the means of production, but
the nature of the social relationships by which the macroparasitic
class exploits the producers. The question is not how much the
macroparasite exploits the host, but how.

A number of variables above and beyond straightforward
economic and technological considerations determine both the
nature of the symbiosis and the military strength of the macroparasite. Clearly, the military elite that exploits its host populace
most efficiently has the advantage; equally clearly, the willing
cooperation of the populace promotes efficiency and cultural and

29 McNeill, *Pursuit of Power*, vii.
30 My concept of a level of technological and economic advancement is analogous to
the concept of modernization advanced by Marion J. Levy, Jr., *Modernization and the
Structure of Societies*, (Princeton, 1966), and was in part inspired by it. While arguing that
modernization cannot be precisely defined, Levy identified the degree to which a society
has replaced animate with inanimate sources of energy as a meaningful measure of its level
of social advancement.

religious factors have a direct bearing on the process.[31] Both logic and the historical record support the proposition that states in which macroparasitic classes employ markedly different tactics of exploitation are more likely to come into conflict than those in which military elites support themselves and justify their existence in similar fashion. The rationale behind this observation is similar to that employed by political scientists explaining the relative absence of armed conflict among liberal democracies in the modern world.[32]

As the historical data show, there were fundamental differences between the Ottomans and their Christian opponents in the nature of their respective macroparasitic relationships. The character of seigneurial rights in Christian feudal Europe and the manner in which the land-owning elite exercised its authority over the servile agricultural classes differed sharply from equivalent relationships within the Ottoman system. At the most basic level, the difference was attributable to the non-hereditary nature of the authority of local Ottoman officials. A deeper underlying consideration was a contrasting attitude toward boundaries. To the Christian states of Western Europe, the acquisition of land was an end in itself; to the Ottomans, the individual parcel of land was less important. Where Christians saw the conquest of provinces and the fall of kingdoms, Ottomans saw the advance or retreat of a continuously moving zone of ghazi warfare which formed the boundaries of the darülislam. These differences in outlook, rooted in the landholding traditions of the Greco-Roman past on the one hand and in nomadic Arab and Turco-Mongol traditions on the other, combined with differences in the nature of macroparasitic relationships to ensure armed conflict.

The Christian peasantry in the frontier zones appreciated that falling under Ottoman control represented something less than catastrophe. Where newly acquired territories were incorporated into the empire, no hereditary rights to the land were recognized

---

31 Religious legitimacy, for example, can make palatable exactions which would otherwise be resented and resisted. Similarly, a predictable, consistent, and smoothly functioning system of justice fosters legitimacy. The whole societal mechanism must be considered as a unit (note the applicability of the Ottoman circle of equity to this observation).

32 Michael W. Doyle, "Liberalism and International Relations," unpub. paper presented at the conference on The Origin and Prevention of Major Wars (Durham, N.H., 1986).

beyond the peasant's traditional right to his dwelling and an allotment of soil to till. Manorial rights were abolished and title to the land passed to the state and responsibility for governance was reallocated under timar grants. In a crude sense, the feudal lord was simply replaced by the timar holder, but, from the peasants' viewpoint, the difference was enormous. Most important, the existing structure of taxes in kind, labor obligations, and corvée service were replaced by the monetary head tax imposed on non-Muslims and a fixed tax called plow dues.[33] These differences constituted a real threat to the Christian military elites of the border regions and formed the underlying causes of the ghazi warfare of the fourteenth, fifteenth, and early sixteenth centuries. Similarly, the subsequent decay of the timar system, and the deterioration in justice and order which accompanied it, produced a gross convergence in macroparasitic relationships and played a major role in reducing the proclivity to war between the Ottomans and their Christian enemies.

These observations support the most basic conclusion of all, that the roots of war lie deep within the social fabric. This observation is most evident where there are sharp cultural and religious differences between the contending parties. A second conclusion is that these underlying social factors are more evident and more important in sustained guerrilla and positional wars. It follows as a corollary that analyses which focus on field or naval operations in the classic sense are apt to miss these causal factors. This corollary is true in the first instance because an analysis which begins by searching for major decisive campaigns may overlook entire wars which were thoroughly decisive, despite the absence of "decisive" battles. It is true in the second instance because short wars decided by field and naval operations tend to involve noncombatant populations at a more superficial level, although the aerial bombardment of civilian populations has begun to engage civilians more directly. The very episodic drama which characterizes brief wars of the traditional kind distances them from their underlying social causes.

Underlying social causation is most likely to manifest itself in a sustained war of economic and cultural attrition. The sixteenth-century struggle between the Ottoman Empire and its

---

33 Inalcik, "The Emergence of the Ottomans," CHI, I, 286–287.

Christian opponents is an excellent example of such a conflict, particularly in its early stages. It is also true that the causes of war cannot be assessed in any meaningful way without considering the operational context within which they were conceived, fought, and concluded. This reality is particularly true of sustained positional and guerrilla war, where standards of competence for the leaders are higher and where causal calculations are correspondingly more realistic.[34] The ends cannot be cleanly separated from the means at any level, and changes in the technology of war have a significant bearing not only on the way in which wars are fought, but on their causes. Shifts in the balance between field, positional, and guerrilla warfare, shifts caused largely by changes in technology, play an important role in determining the nature of the line between war and peace and the clarity with which it can be discerned.

Our exercise in alternative analogy suggests that the distinctions commonly drawn in contemporary Western rhetoric between major and minor wars, and between peace and war, are artificial because they are based on the anomalous experience of the recent past and because the inherent bias of Western historiography toward major wars, big battles, and field and naval operations interferes with our ability to understand war and its causes.

34 Such wars, because they last longer, give national military and political leaders more operational experience and expertise; in addition they are more apt to involve deep-seated social motivations, thus placing a higher perceived premium on capable leadership. Ironically, wars in which this kind of positional and guerrilla operations have great significance, have a low historical profile. Expected utility theory could be used to test this hypothesis.

Myron P. Gutmann

The Origins of the Thirty Years' War

Among the major wars of modern European history, the Thirty Years' War stands out not only for its duration but also for its striking impact on the international system in which it took place. Before 1618, the Spanish Habsburgs were the central power in a Europe where religious differences were crucial. The war and its Franco-Spanish extension ended in 1659. By that time, France and other nations had increased their power, and religion played a much less important role in defining alliances. Moreover, Europe's center had moved east, as Russia, Prussia, and the Austrian Habsburgs became more powerful.

The war's origins are well known. Conflict in the Holy Roman Empire, especially in the Habsburg lands, over religion and over the power of the emperor provoked a civil war in Bohemia in 1618. The Bohemian war both resurrected and created a network of alliances which caused the conflict to continue into the 1620s. The opportunities offered by the disruption in Germany led the Danes to invade in 1625, and the Swedes and French to intervene in the 1630s, which continued the war by bringing in fresh combatants. The result was a conflict that could not be controlled by the Bohemians and the emperor, who had begun it. They were not allowed to extricate themselves until they had completely exhausted themselves and everyone else; as fitting compensation, the Bohemians and the emperor were important losers.

Most histories of the war explain its origins in a straightforward way. The imperial civil war was the real starting point, and the continuation of the war was the result of the opportunistic schemes of the Dutch under Maurice of Nassau, Denmark under Christian IV, Sweden under Gustavus Adolphus, and France un-

Myron P. Gutmann is Associate Professor of History at the University of Texas, Austin. He is the author of *Toward the Modern Economy: Early Industry in Europe, 1500–1800* (New York, 1988).

The author thanks Theodore K. Rabb, Geoffrey Parker, and James Boyden for their critical readings of this paper.

der Cardinal Armand de Richelieu. All that need be explained is why the initial conflict started, and why the opportunists chose to act. This explanatory scheme is followed by virtually every author writing on the war, including those with a strictly nation-alistic perspective as well as those who proclaim a more open and international point of view. Parker's remarkable book, *The Thirty Years' War,* uses this approach, enlivened with a thoroughly in-ternational flavor. So do all the other well-known authors who have written on the war. The reason for the near unanimity is not hard to explain: this way of looking at the war makes sense, especially if one is writing a (necessarily) long narrative history of the war. Too much explanatory comment would make an already complicated narrative break down.[1]

My goal is to emphasize the war's origins. Although the history of the war has been an active field of study recently, there have not been many discussions of why it took place. The war was a product of problems which arose from patterns of conflict and the nature of the leaders who controlled the governments of the time. It grew out of a number of deep-seated and well estab-lished domestic and international conflicts which were old by 1618, and to which we must give equal weight. These conflicts represented differences between the recognized loci of power in Europe, and the national and international realities which would have placed that power elsewhere.

These conflicts, which had arisen by the second half of the sixteenth century, might have been resolved during the first two decades of the seventeenth century. For a number of reasons, no leader or state was willing or able to force their resolution. This resolution might have been accomplished by a single state, or a group of states, demonstrating the existence of new patterns of

---

1 Geoffrey Parker, *The Thirty Years' War* (London, 1984). Attributing this work exclu-sively to Parker does a disservice to both Parker and others. Parker wrote nearly half the book, and brought together and edited the work of nine other specialists. The book is thorough and up to date, and yet reads like the work of a single author. For discussions of other authors who have written about the war, see Parker's bibliography. My article is an interpretive study based on secondary sources, and not an introduction to a new work based on original research. The notes refer to the works I have consulted in preparing this paper, especially where they will give the reader an idea of how to pursue the question further. They do not constitute a complete bibliography, which is impossible in a work of this scale.

power. Such a demonstration, for example by the Spanish against the Dutch or French, by one of the Scandinavian powers against the others or against the Holy Roman Empire, or by the Protestants or Catholics in the empire, might have removed just enough of the tension to prevent the explosion in the Habsburg monarchy from engulfing much of Europe for thirty years or more. Thus, the failure to resolve even some of the disputes before 1618 helped make the eventual war very serious. Leaders who could settle the developing conflicts were in short supply, either because of weakness or timidity.

Uncontrolled before 1618, these conflicts were transformed between 1618 and 1635 from disagreements, grudges, and fears to open war. Although the conflict within the Habsburg Empire broke into war first, it was not necessarily more important than the others. The fact that the war involved so many parties and lasted so long clearly demonstrates the depth of the conflict. What we need to explain is not only why the war started, but why it could not be ended sooner, especially given the emperor's victories in the 1620s. Only these deep and broad conflicts help us understand exactly why so many parties entered and why the war was so difficult to end. The treaties which settled the war recognized a new international system and a new German reality. It is not necessary to argue here that the gap between official power and reality required a war, but such an argument could be made. What is required is the realization that the conflicts existed, that they required resolution, and that the diplomatic system of that age (as of most others) was unlikely, short of war, to recognize the emergence of new power relationships.

The conclusions drawn here have their foundations partly in the way that historians and social scientists explain revolutions, and partly in the way that political scientists explain the origins of wars. A chronology of events is used to explain the origins of the Thirty Years' War in much the same way that it would be used to explain the origins of a revolution. The conflicts between states are the long-term preconditions of war; the processes which converted them to war, the medium-term precipitants; and the actual events that start the war, the short-term triggers. Johnson originally devised this terminology in 1964, but it is well known from Stone's 1970 essay, "The English Revolution." Another theoretical starting point comes from the "theory of hegemonic war," which Gilpin attributes to Thucydides. Because of its generality, it is more appropriate than Bueno de Mesquita's "expected utility theory," which demands that we measure with some precision the thinking of major actors. The theory of hegemonic war helps us to see and measure the importance of changes in the distribution of power in an international system. When a powerful state loses its position, and when a less powerful state gains, the hegemonic formulation tells us that we should expect war. It does not tell us which side will be the aggressor, nor does it tell us which side (if either) will win. As discussed later, many of the causes of the Thirty Years' War can be attributed to the changing balance of power, and to the changing perceptions of the balance of power. The hegemonic theory of war helps us to understand those factors. Nonetheless, the behavior of individual policymakers is important, because this article attributes much of the cause of the Thirty Years' War to the behavior of two generations of leaders—those in power in the first two decades of the seventeenth century, and those in power later.[2]

WHAT WAS THE THIRTY YEARS' WAR ABOUT? The Thirty Years' War was a complicated event, part civil war and part international war. It was divided into phases fought by different belligerents, each element having its own causes. The war began as a conflict in central Europe between the Catholic Habsburg emperor and his Bohemian subjects over religion and imperial power. This Bohemian civil war quickly escalated as German princes lined up along sectarian lines to support one side or the other. What was then an imperial civil war became linked to other, wider, conflicts, which extended it to other parts of Europe and prolonged it. The first extension came in 1621, when the Twelve-Year Truce between the Dutch and the Spanish in the war for Dutch Independence (The Eighty Years' War) ended. The Dutch were unwilling to extend the peace; the Spanish feared the economic impact of

2 Lawrence Stone, "The English Revolution," in Robert Forster and Jack P. Greene (eds.), *Preconditions of Revolution in Early Modern Europe* (Baltimore, 1970), 55–108. Stone included a revised version of this paper and his "Theories of Revolution," in *idem, The Causes of the English Revolution* (New York, 1972), 3–25. He attributes his theoretical position to Chalmers Johnson, *Revolution and the Social System* (Stanford, 1964). Robert Gilpin, "The Theory of Hegemonic War," *Journal of Interdisciplinary History*, XXVIII (1988), 591–613; Bruce Bueno de Mesquita, "The Contribution of Expected Utility Theory to the Study of International Conflict," *ibid.*, 629–652.

Dutch power on their colonies, and needed but little encouragement from their Austrian cousins to continue it as a means to dilute Protestant strength. By the early 1620s there was a two-front war, one in central Europe and one in the Low Countries, linked by conflict in the Rhineland.[3]

In the 1620s, the war was extended to northern Germany and the Baltic by the entry into the war of Denmark (in 1625), and later Sweden (in 1630). Although Christian IV of Denmark was not able to stay the course of this long war, Sweden was, even after the death of Gustavus Adolphus in 1632. Sweden remained an important participant throughout the war, and an important party to the treaties which ended it in 1648. In the late 1620s, France entered the war, fighting Spain from 1628 to 1631 in the Third Mantuan War, and continuously from 1635, when its policy escalated from financial support of the Dutch and the Swedes to an open declaration of war against the Habsburgs.

We might describe the Thirty Years' War as not one but three wars, with six or more principal parties. First there was the imperial civil war, a conflict about religion and imperial authority, which was ended by the Peace of Prague in 1635. Then there was the western war, involving Spain against the Netherlands and France, which was the continuation of sixteenth-century conflicts. Finally, there was the Baltic war, fought mostly in Germany, between Denmark first, and then Sweden, on one side, and the emperor and his allies on the other. This war concerned the growing power of the Baltic states, especially Sweden. Because most of the fighting during these three wars took place in Germany, the main elements became thoroughly intertwined, and the armies constantly rushed across the continent to help out allies in one of the other theaters. Although these three wars are not easily distinguishable, they give us a starting point by telling us where to look for the conflicts which led to the Thirty Years' War.

3 Parker, *Thirty Years' War*, is the best recent book in English on the war. There have been many others, which are cited in his bibliography. An invaluable overview of Germany is found in Moriz Ritter, *Deutsche Geschichte im Zeitalter des Gegenreformation und des dreissigjährigen Krieges, 1555–1648* (Stuttgart, 1889), 3 v. For the participation of various states, see Table 5 in Parker, *Thirty Years' War*, 155. Helmut G. Koenigsberger presents the best brief explanation of every participant's motivation. See "The European Civil War," in idem, *The Habsburgs and Europe, 1516–1660* (Ithaca, 1971), 219–285.

PRECONDITIONS: EUROPEAN CONFLICT BEFORE 1600   The war's preconditions can be divided into three broad areas of civil conflict, one within the empire, one in western Europe, and a third involving the Baltic states and their role in German affairs. These conflicts interacted with underlying dynastic structures and religious disagreements. They were not new in the early seventeenth century, but they became increasingly immediate under the pressure of the political and diplomatic behavior of various European states, especially the Habsburgs. The conflict over imperial power and religion was the first to erupt into war, but it should not be given precedence. The other conflicts, in western and northern Europe, and between Protestants and Catholics, need to be seen as equally significant.

The East: Reformation, Counter-Reformation, and Imperial Authority   The war began with the defenestration of Prague and the civil war in Bohemia. These episodes are well known and hardly demand repetition here. Likewise, the causes of the defenestration and the war which followed are easy to ascertain. The political and religious development of the Habsburg lands in central and eastern Europe ran counter to general European trends during the second half of the sixteenth century. Maximilian II and Rudolf II permitted the Protestant churches in their monarchical territories to increase in strength. Simultaneously, the nobility and towns in these lands gained political power. This rise of competing groups was especially marked in Bohemia and Hungary, which had monarchies in which the election of the king was usually accompanied by royal concessions.

As happened so often in the late sixteenth century, these developments in the Habsburg monarchy contradicted other trends. The rise of Protestantism contradicted the fundamental principles of the 1555 Peace of Augsburg, which stated that a prince could determine the religion of his subjects. The rise of political power in the hands of the estates contradicted the long-term tendency for the monarchs of European states to gain power at the expense of their subjects. The alternative was the destruction of the state. By 1600, the Habsburgs were on the offensive both politically and religiously, limiting the power of their subjects and eliminating Protestants wherever possible. The events which led to Prague in 1618 were part of this process, which had accelerated after the deposition of Rudolf in 1611, and accelerated further with the accession of Ferdinand II later in the decade.[4]

Events in the empire outside the monarchical lands complicated Habsburg efforts to restore Catholicism and the political power of the monarchy. The Augsburg settlement had not stabilized the religious structure of Germany. Calvinism, unrecognized at Augsburg, grew, and territories continued to be converted from Catholic to Protestant. Individual German states, especially Saxony, Brandenburg, Bavaria, and the Palatinate, gained power just as the emperor became less powerful and imperial institutions more fragmented and paralyzed. No one was capable of enforcing the Augsburg settlement or even of defusing extremists. Catholic Bavaria was ambitious. So were the Calvinist Palatine electors. Neither side wanted to see the other expand. By the late sixteenth century, the Habsburgs and their subjects were increasingly at odds. The subjects expected continued and even increased liberties, and continued tolerance of religious practices, despite the monarch's disapproval. The Habsburgs firmly expected heretics to be eliminated and political dominance to be reestablished. These divergent expectations were certain to lead to a contest. The problem was made worse by the double Habsburg role as king and emperor. In the late seventeenth century, emperors became resigned to allowing their imperial role to recede toward the symbolic, as Germany became a patchwork of essentially independent states. In the sixteenth century, such an attitude was unthinkable. Yet the growing religious and political schisms in Germany created contradictions which were difficult to diminish short of a decisive war.

Western Europe: Spain vs. the Netherlands and Spain vs. France We need not look far to find the underlying contradictions between Spanish, French, and Dutch views of the political balance of western Europe. What may be most striking is a difference in attitudes. The main players in the central European war were hardly the best of friends, striving for a harmonious resolution of legitimate disagreements. Far from it. But, compared with the

4 Parker and his colleagues deal very effectively with these questions. See *Thirty Years' War*, esp. 2–24. For another excellent overview, see Robert J. W. Evans, *The Making of the Habsburg Monarchy, 1550–1700: An Interpretation* (Oxford, 1979).

positions of the western European players, they were harmonious. The basic characteristic of relationships in the west was hostility, coupled with deep suspicion, toward each other. The Dutch hated the Spanish and suspected the French, the French suspected both the others, and the Spanish hated the Dutch and French. The result was war.

The conflict between the Dutch and the Spanish arose in the 1560s. It was the result of the spread of Calvinism in the Low Countries and Spanish attempts to control territories where members of the local elite expected to be consulted, and expected their traditional liberties to be respected. Whereas the roughly parallel eastern conflict developed much more slowly and did not turn into war until 1618, in the Low Countries war came fifty years earlier. From 1568, war waxed and waned between Spain and its subjects in the Netherlands, all depending on the ability of the Dutch to gather international support, and of Spain to provide the resources necessary for a victory. By 1580, the Dutch had shown their ability to wage war against Spain. The Spanish gained the advantage in the 1580s, but failed to capitalize on their advantage with a treaty; the Dutch gained again in the 1590s. Philip II died in 1598, leaving the Netherlands under the rule of the "Archdukes" Isabella and Albert, his daughter and her husband. The war continued despite negotiations which began in 1606. Although Spain was willing to recognize the independence of the Netherlands, other Dutch demands prevented a treaty. They settled on a truce only in 1609.[5]

By the early seventeenth century, the conflict between Spain and France was one of the oldest in Europe. These two ruling houses were natural competitors both in western Europe and in Italy. In the fifteenth century, their conflict had turned to intermittent war in Italy, and, despite truces and treaties (some involving marriages between the two houses), warfare continued into the sixteenth century. The Reformation, the rise of Calvinism in France, and the instability and internal disruption which produced the Wars of Religion all added to the tension between the

---

5 Parker has written the best (and almost only) recent history of the Dutch Revolt to be published in English. See *The Dutch Revolt* (Ithaca, 1977). The classics are Henri Pirenne, *Histoire de Belgique* (Brussels, 1903), III; Peter Geyl, *The Revolt of the Netherlands* (London, 1932). On seventeenth-century Dutch-Spanish relations, see Jonathan I. Israel, *The Dutch Republic and the Hispanic World 1606–1661* (Oxford, 1982).

two states. Spain intervened repeatedly in the Wars of Religion, against the kings of France. Only Henry IV's conversion to Catholicism and the defeat of his domestic opponents, combined with the death of Philip II and the financial exhaustion of Spain, led to peace in 1598 at Vervins. But this peace was meaningless in the context of the long conflict which it failed to resolve. The kings of France and of Spain still competed for preeminence in western Europe and Italy. Henry IV had avoided defeat in the 1590s by driving Spain from his territory, but he had not attained victory. At the end of the sixteenth century, the conflict simmered but neither side was close to a decisive defeat of the other; only the growing power of France and the declining power of Spain in the seventeenth century would make French victory possible.

Northern Europe: the Battle for the Baltic   At stake in northern Europe was the control of the Baltic, and the players were Denmark, Sweden, Poland, and Russia. National governments in northern Europe were less well established than in the great states of western Europe, and control had shifted between Denmark and Sweden. Before the Lutheran Gustavus I of Sweden (1523–1560) brought independence, Sweden and Denmark were joined by the Union of Kalmar. The sixteenth century saw the beginning of a long Swedish quest for preeminence in the Baltic, which culminated in the seventeenth century. The immediate consequence of Swedish independence in the sixteenth century was Danish resentment. Troubles continued when, in 1587, Sigismund, Gustavus' Catholic grandson and heir apparent to the Swedish throne, had himself elected king of Poland. On the death of John III, the king of Sweden, his brother Charles led a Lutheran and aristocratic rebellion against the Polish-Swedish union of crowns under Sigismund, and eventually prevailed. He was crowned Charles IX in 1604, and was succeeded in 1611 by Gustavus Adolphus, his own son.[6]

The sixteenth-century Swedish victories did not end the Baltic conflict and leave Sweden in control. Denmark still controlled the Sound, through which all Baltic trade passed, and all the parties still had ambitions. In part these were grudges, like the Polish and Danish desire to best Sweden, if not to reconquer it. But all of the Baltic states sought to expand their power so that

6   Michael Roberts, *The Early Vasas: A History of Sweden, 1523–1611* (Cambridge, 1968).

they could control territory on both sides of the sea, in Scandinavia as well as in northern Germany. These states had prospered in the sixteenth century with the growth of trade through the Baltic and the growth of demand for the raw materials that they produced. They were not rich on the scale of France or Spain, but they had new resources which could be used for expansion. Their desire for expansion should be considered on the same scale as their desire for revenge; it was a force that developed in the sixteenth century and remained to be resolved in the seventeenth.

In northern Europe, as in western Europe and central Europe, by the end of the first decade of the seventeenth century, there was little warfare and little likelihood of escalation to a continent-wide conflagration. Yet the ambitions, grudges, and points of disagreement were deep, and almost sure to produce war again. Two critical factors brought the three areas of potential conflict together: religion and the role of the Habsburgs in the empire. Religion was the most important shared element in all of the regional conflicts. If temporary settlements were in place by 1600 in the battles between Spain and France and Poland and Sweden, and if settlements were possible between Spain and the Netherlands and in the Empire, these settlements were fragile. The place of Calvinism was still to be determined, and few participants in the religious struggle felt that a proper resolution to religious conflict had been reached. The papacy would advocate a hard-line religious position throughout the war, encouraging the Catholic side to continue fighting. Until at least 1635, the Pope's views were often respected. Moreover, religious ties crossed national and regional boundaries in ways that could sabotage any political understanding. We see this confusion of religious and political ties everywhere, including the peculiar role played by James I and Charles I, the Stuart kings of England. Allied by inclination to the Catholic side, and by marriage to the Protestant side through the Palatine elector, they repeatedly intervened diplomatically without ever contributing to resolution. In the end, they were a continuing force of disruption in the Protestant alliance since they wanted to be involved in any settlement.

The second factor that contributed to the integration of all three areas was the Habsburg role in the empire. In the western conflict, convergence came through the need for joint action that was felt at least occasionally by the Spanish and Austrian Habsburgs. Thus the Austrians might be recruited against the Dutch or French (although they had not been in the sixteenth century), which made those two states suspicious. In the northern conflict, the aspirations of the Danes and the Swedes for territory on the German mainland meant becoming involved with the Holy Roman Empire, and dealing with the Habsburgs there. Once the empire was embroiled in war, the Scandinavians' involvement on the German mainland turned from likelihood to certainty.

The old and deep-seated conflicts which existed in Europe at the beginning of the seventeenth century were crucial preconditions for the Thirty Years' War. It is difficult to state conclusively what was most dangerous about these conflicts: the ambitions of some of the parties or the fears of others; both operated. What is certain is that the existence of these conflicts was an inauspicious sign for the wars to come. They were especially dangerous because of the likelihood that the three regional conficts, centered around animosity toward Austria, Spain, and Sweden, might become linked. The connections came through continuing religious strife and the role of the Habsburgs as a seventeenth-century lightning rod that attracted opposition and thus war.

PRECIPITANTS TO A CONTINENT-WIDE WAR: EVENTS FROM 1598 TO 1618. The unsatisfactory Treaty of Vervins made by Philip II and Henry IV in 1598 was a fitting prelude to the next twenty years. Wars were ended or avoided because the parties were exhausted, or occupied by domestic problems, or saw no way to a truly victorious end to hostilities, but the underlying conflicts and the discrepancies in the power structures within Europe were not resolved. The failure to resolve these difficulties, through force if necessary, meant that no clear new structure of international power had been created. In the time of Emperor Charles V, Spain had been the greatest power in Europe. In the second half of the sixteenth century, under Philip II, Spain was still usually the dominant force. After 1600 the situation was not so clear, but there was as yet no alternative power capable of guaranteeing some degree of stability and preventing the conversion of a domestic problem, such as the one in Bohemia, into an almost endless, continent-wide war.

Spain's weakness in the early years of the seventeenth century is clear in its behavior toward the Dutch republic. Despite earlier

Spanish attempts to crush the Dutch, and Dutch attempts to drive Spain out of the Low Countries altogether, neither side could win. They eventually signed a twelve-year truce, negotiated by English and French mediators, beginning in 1609. The failure to reach a decisive peace left both sides restive. The Dutch continued their attacks on Spanish and Portuguese colonies, and kept the Scheldt River closed. Many Spaniards viewed the truce as a statement of international failure and felt that it had damaged trade as well. On the Dutch side, the fall of Johan von Oldenbarnevelt in 1618, and the strengthening of the war party under the leadership of Prince Maurice of Nassau, opened the way for Dutch ambitions on the European continent. They were willing to renew hostilities against the Spanish, and align themselves with other Protestant (and even some Catholic) powers against the Austrian Habsburgs.[7]

The tension between France and Spain was equally incapable of resolution. Hindsight tells us that France would replace Spain as the dominant power in Europe, but, even had that been visible after 1598, the continuing domestic difficulties faced by Henry IV and the sheer exhaustion of France after decades of civil war, limited his actions. Surely this conflict was the most important in Europe after 1600, and its settlement in 1659 demonstrated the victory of France. Yet its outcome was by no means clear in the first decade of the seventeenth century. Spain continued its efforts to harass Henry and bring a weaker—and more rigidly anti-Protestant—alternative to power. In the years after Vervins, Henry IV fought against Spain in whatever ways he could, encouraging the German and Dutch Protestants, even if he did not openly ally with them. The Cleves-Jülich succession crisis, which erupted in 1609/10, showed his intentions clearly. He would not willingly allow an increase in Habsburg power in a territory so near him, because it would open up too many avenues of invasion and close too many routes necessary for future French expansion. Therefore, he attempted to organize support around himself and began to build an army for invasion before he was assassinated in May 1610.[8]

---

7 Israel, *Dutch Republic*. For a succinct view of his position, see *idem*, "A Conflict of Empires: Spain and the Netherlands 1618–1648," *Past & Present*, 76 (1977), 34–74.
8 James M. Hayden, "Continuity in the France of Henry IV and Louis XIII: French

"There is a serious possibility that had he survived Ravaillac's knife, the Thirty Years' War would have begun in 1610 and not 1618." So writes Bonney, echoing a common view of the consequences of the invasion that Henry was planning at the time of his death. Although that outcome was surely possible, it is also likely that Henry's show of force might have diminished or at least focused the tensions which erupted later in the decade. In a footnote, Bonney adds "Of course, the war might not have lasted for thirty years with France involved at the outset." We must of course avoid glorifying Henri le Grand, but one clear characteristic of this decade is that those who might have displayed the power required to resolve disputes failed to do so. Had he lived, Henry might have succeeded.[9]

Henry's death left a regency government so weakened that a serious anti-Habsburg foreign policy was impossible. Conditions in France echo those in many countries in this period. One important reason so little was resolved before 1618 was that many on the anti-Habsburg side were inexperienced or lacked a strong position within the state. This weakness was apparent in France, in Sweden, where Gustavus Adolphus came to the throne in 1611, in the Palatinate, where Frederick IV died in 1610, and in the Netherlands, where Oldenbarnevelt's Remonstrant party was involved in a continuing battle for power. A lack of leadership was also evident among the Austrian Habsburgs themselves, as Rudolf's precarious health and sanity limited action despite the wishes of Matthias (his brother) and Ferdinand. After Henry's death, the only strong leaders available were Maximilian of Bavaria and perhaps Philip III of Spain.[10]

The inability to bring any problems to a clear conclusion before 1618 is nowhere more evident than in the empire. The history of the two decades of religious and political strife in the empire and the Habsburg lands leading up to 1618 is very long

---

Foreign Policy 1598–1615," *Journal of Modern History*, XXXXV (1973), 1–23. Roland Mousnier (trans. Joan Spencer), *The Assassination of Henry IV* (London, 1973), 116–138.

9 Richard Bonney, *The King's Debts: Finance and Politics in France 1589–1661* (Oxford, 1981), 69.

10 Jan den Tex, *Oldenbarnevelt* (Cambridge, 1973). Roberts, *Gustavus Adolphus: A History of Sweden, 1611–1632* (London, 1953). On Spanish policy, see P. Brightwell, "The Spanish Origins of the Thirty Years' War," *European Studies Review* IX (1979), 409–431; idem, "Spain and Bohemia: The Decision to Intervene, 1619," ibid, XII (1982), 117–141; idem, "Spain, Bohemia and Europe, 1619–1621," ibid., XII (1982), 371–399.

and complicated. What is important is the growing madness of Rudolf, and the gradual assumption of his powers by Matthias as a result of a family agreement. Matthias sought to reestablish Catholicism wherever possible, but this goal often conflicted with concessions he had to give to Protestant-dominated estates (as was the case in Bohemia) in order to take the throne. Nonetheless, the Habsburgs did attempt in the years after 1600 to reestablish Catholic worship. For example, Rudolf ordered Donauwörth, an Imperial Free City (one in which both Lutherans and Catholics were permitted to worship under the Augsburg settlement), to permit Catholic processions and gave Maximilian of Bavaria authority to use force. In late 1607 Maximilian occupied the city, a situation made worse when, in mid-1609, the emperor gave him the city as a pledge against his expenses.

The main consequence of the Donauwörth affair was heightened antagonism between German Protestants and Catholics. Many of the Protestants walked out of the Regensburg Diet in April 1608, leading to its dissolution. In May 1608, several Protestant princes made an agreement called the Protestant Union. They pledged mutual assistance in case of attack. A year later, a number of the Catholic states formed a parallel Catholic League. The sides were drawn, and these antagonists parried in the two crises over the succession in Cleves-Jülich, in 1609/10 and in 1614. The Protestant side never seemed as unified as the Catholics, especially as the years passed. But the drift toward conflict and away from resolution was very real, as the Protestants led by Frederick V, the young elector Palatine, and the Catholics led by Maximilian of Bavaria took ever more radical positions. Surely, nothing was going to be resolved in this period short of a major war.

It is always difficult to present an argument based on the absence of an event or the failure of something to happen. Opportunities existed in the years between 1598 and 1618 to resolve the conflicts which had grown up in the second half of the sixteenth century; no one took advantage of them. The absence of Henry IV after 1610 is probably the most dramatic factor. Despite his ambivalence about supporting the Protestants, Henry's desire to limit Habsburg avenues of invasion and keep open his paths of expansion would have pushed the German situation toward a resolution before 1618. We must avoid the mistake of making

France (or any other single nation, for that matter) the linchpin. The war was truly international, but reducing any of its main bases of conflict would have made it shorter and easier to end.[11]

Despite opportunities for resolution, none of the major conflicts which had grown up by 1598 were resolved twenty years later. The first two decades of the seventeenth century were crucial in establishing the conditions under which war would be fought. In central Europe, northern Europe, and western Europe, the ambitions, fears, and disagreements which would lead to war had not evaporated. The religious undercurrent which pushed regional disputes toward a continental war had in no significant way been reduced. When events triggered war in the empire, the ambitions of the actors and the antagonisms of the age prevented its speedy resolution. Before 1618, the kind of leadership which would have brought a solution was lacking. In the years that followed, new leaders emerged, and with their strength and ambition came war.

TRIGGERING AND FUELING THE WAR: EVENTS FROM 1618 TO 1635
The events which sparked the beginning of the Thirty Years' War in 1618 are known to almost everyone. In 1611 Matthias confirmed the Letter of Majesty and was crowned king of Bohemia; the estates seemed exceptionally powerful. By late 1617, matters were at a turning point. Ferdinand had been designated heir to the thrones of Bohemia and Hungary. He turned control over to a largely Catholic regency council with instructions to provoke the estates. They did so by restricting Protestant worship in two Bohemian towns. The Protestant-dominated estates met to protest these actions, only to be ordered twice to be dissolved. To vent their anger at the regents, on May 23 they entered the palace and threw two Catholic regents and their secretary out of the window.

The Catholic Habsburgs and the Protestant estates moved toward war, securing allies in the year following the defenestration. On the Protestant side the estates looked for assistance. By the summer of 1619 the estates were prepared to offer the throne to the Elector Frederick, in return for the intervention of the Evangelical Union. In August, they deposed Ferdinand and

11 Georges Pagès, *The Thirty Years War, 1618–1648* (New York, 1971; orig. ed. 1939). In his otherwise excellent book, Pagès makes France the linchpin.

elected Frederick in his place, at the same time that Ferdinand was elected emperor to succeed Matthias. Simultaneously, Bethlan Gabor was making progress against the Habsburg forces in Hungary. On the Catholic side, everything rested on Spain and the Papacy. The Pope sent a monthly subsidy beginning in mid-1618. Spain sent men and money to Vienna, in order to thwart the possibility of Protestant victories in Bohemia and Hungary. The Spanish decision encouraged the Catholic League, and it too contributed arms under the leadership of Maximilian of Bavaria. The decisive part of the war lasted little more than a year, culminating in the Battle of White Mountain in late 1620. The Protestant side never received the kind of international support it needed. No one was eager to support a state that had deposed a properly chosen king. The unwillingness of the Palatine elector's English relatives to aid him was particularly noticeable.[12]

The Protestants were defeated within eighteen months of the defenestration of Prague, yet the war lasted thirty years. The task which faced Ferdinand after the victory at White Mountain was to reach a settlement with his international opponents so that he could finally enforce the results of his victory in his own territories. To obtain a settlement with the Elector Frederick, Ferdinand had to settle the unresolved question of the Palatinate, which had been occupied by Bavarian and Spanish armies. Regrettably, in his anxiety to secure allies in 1619, Ferdinand had promised the territory of the Upper Palatinate and the electoral title to Maximilian. The conflicts of the late sixteenth and early seventeenth century arose out of imbalances of power and the placement of power in the "wrong" hands. For example, Ferdinand was dependent on Bavaria and thus unable to renege on the promise he made to Maximilian. In early 1623, the transfer was made, and the opportunity for a settlement evaporated. War continued, and modest Protestant armies under Count Ernest Mansfield kept the imperial army occupied.

The continuation of the war in the early 1602s must be linked to the end of the Twelve-Year Truce and the resumption of hostilities between Spain and the Netherlands in 1621. Neither

12 The confusing German politics of this period are described well by Parker, *Thirty Years' War*. There is more detail in Ritter, *Deutsche Geschichte*, II. For the Palatinate, Claus Peter Clasen, *The Palatinate in European History, 1555–1618* (Oxford, 1966; rev. ed.), and the German works cited by Parker, *Thirty Years' War*. On Spanish participation, John H. Elliott, *The Count-Duke of Olivares: The Statesmen in an Age of Decline* (Cambridge, 1986).

side was eager to continue the truce, and their failure to reach agreement on largely commercial and religious issues brought them to war again. This conflict had a significant impact on the German war, because the renewal of hostilities in the Low Countries drained Spanish resources from the commitment to Ferdinand. Moreover, although the Dutch were reluctant to intervene actively before 1621, for fear of prematurely reopening their war with Spain, they gave moderate support to Frederick and his allies after the end of the truce, in order to create diversions which would prevent the Habsburgs from uniting against them. The result, of course, was that neither side of the conflict, in western Europe or in central Europe, was easily resolved. The gradual emergence of an anti-Habsburg foreign policy in France in 1624, at first under the brief tenure of Charles, the marquis and duke of La Vieuville and then under Richelieu's first ministry, confirmed Ferdinand's inability to end the conflict that he had begun. The Franco-Dutch alliance was renewed, the treaty of Lyon with Venice was reactivated, and French armies entered the Grisons and Italy. Ferdinand again confronted too many enemies at a time when he could barely contain the pathetic German Protestants.

From one point of view, the Thirty Years' War lasted as long as it did because none of the participants could convert a military victory or a series of military victories into a diplomatic settlement. Sometimes, this inability of any participant to convert a victory was because defeats could not convince the defeated parties that they would lose at the next engagement, especially if they were being subsidized by others. At other times, it was because the settlements offered by the victors were so unpleasant that even continued war was preferable to peace. Both situations fueled the war in the 1620s. The Protestants were defeated again and again in major engagements, and yet persisted because they felt that the Catholic forces could not continue to be victorious, because they were receiving support from another party which temporarily gained by the continuation of the war, or because a new party entered the war directly or indirectly. The Dutch in 1621, the French in 1624, 1628, and 1635, the Danes in 1625, and the Swedes in 1630 each allowed the war to continue by defusing a Catholic—that is, imperial—victory.

The second cause of the war's continuation was the inability of the emperor to make a realistic peace proposal. In part this failure was caused by his underlying weakness, as demonstrated by the Palatinate question in the early 1620s. Had he been able to restore Frederick while penalizing the Elector in a meaningful way, that problem would have ended. Still more striking is his failure to convert the victory gained by Albrecht von Wallenstein in the later 1620s to a settlement. The Edict of Restitution, issued by Ferdinand in 1629, attempted to set the religious clock back to 1552, wiping out all of the Protestant gains made in the interim. Many Protestant leaders in the empire, shown the limits of their power in the late 1620s, would have been willing to resolve their differences with Ferdinand had it not been for his insistence on the Edict. The electors failed to reach agreement on anything beyond the removal of Wallenstein at the Convention of Regensburg in the summer of 1630, with the result that the empire was unable to stop Gustavus Adolphus.[13]

The emperor's religious intransigence stands out among the religious motivations in the war. Even Spain, which we often think of in terms of the determination of Philip II in the late sixteenth century, was willing to compromise with the Netherlands as early as 1609 (when the Dutch insisted only on toleration for Catholics in the republic), and with the German Protestants at Regensburg. The Spanish were willing to compromise on religion in pursuit of other political and dynastic goals. Only at Prague in 1635 did Ferdinand modify his religious and absolutist principles sufficiently to begin the process of unifying the empire against outsiders. By that time the cause of pacification in Germany was almost lost. The Swedes had become a permanent presence, despite the death of Gustavus, and Richelieu chose that moment for his entry into the war. Germany would be less the center of diplomacy and conflict than western Europe, but even after Prague it took a long time for hostilities to subside, for foreign troops to leave, and for civilian life to be restored. The war in the west continued, between France and the Netherlands (with other allies) on one side, and Spain and her allies on the other. This war had a different rhythm, because it was fought among almost evenly matched powers, and because everyone was

---

13 For this paragraph and the next, see Robert Bireley, *Religion and Politics in the Age of the Catholic Reformation: Emperor Ferdinand II, William Lamormaini, S.J., and the Formation of Imperial Policy* (Chapel Hill, 1981). On Gustavus' intentions, see Roberts, "The Political Objectives of Gustav Adolf in Germany, 1630–32," in *Essays in Swedish History* (Minneapolis, 1967), 82–110.

already in the war; no state was on the sidelines. The 1640s brought internal disruption in Spain and later in France and the Netherlands. As time and the battlefield eroded domestic resources and the momentum of war, pressures for peace grew, and the parallel conferences in Westphalia produced a peace in 1648.

ASSESSING THE ORIGINS OF THE THIRTY YEARS' WAR   Among its many accomplishments, the Westphalian peace had three dramatic results. First, it cemented the Peace of Prague and thereby settled the religious situation in the empire. War was not likely to erupt again over religious differences. The desire of the Papacy for a militant religious policy would henceforth be ignored. Second, it confirmed the inability of the emperor to direct the foreign policy of the empire, while confirming his very strong position in the monarchical lands. The combination of Habsburg strength in their monarchical lands with the international weakness of the empire made possible the growth of a strong Habsburg monarchy in eastern Europe, and left central Europe divided and less threatening to France. Finally, the peace settled the question of the relationship between Spain and the Netherlands, which permitted the Dutch state eventually to join the emerging anti-French alliance. A new balance of power, unthinkable in 1618, had emerged. It recognized the stability of the religious settlement of the Reformation, the movement of Habsburg concerns to the east, the rise of Brandenburg-Prussia and Sweden in northern Europe, and the emergence of France as the most powerful state in Europe.

In retrospect, the need for these changes should have been obvious in 1618, and the military action required to attain them should have been far more limited. But retrospect, of course, rarely works. The war began and continued because the discrepancies between actual power and interest and imagined power and interest were so great. The theory of hegemonic war can help us understand the events of 1618. At that time the limits of Habsburg power were by no means clear. The Habsburgs played the role of Sparta in Thucydides' drama, while the Athenians were played by the Protestants and by France. Spain seemed to be the most powerful state in Europe, and a strong Austrian Habsburg as emperor was a real danger to the rest of Europe. A war of religious conquest and conversion, begun as an effort to re-Catholicize Bohemia and moving across Europe, was not impossible, especially once Ferdinand formed an alliance with his Spanish cousin and the Catholic League of German princes. The weakened condition of France, under the rule of a regent, made the potential danger still greater.

The fear that a united Habsburg front would dominate Europe politically and religiously was the spark that triggered the war. We know with hindsight that much of what contributed to this fear was unwarranted. On the Habsburg side, we know that Spain was getting weaker, its royal leadership and financial situation were depleted, and its resolve to fight a religious war anywhere on the globe was diminished. It would not stand behind Ferdinand in central and eastern Europe at the expense of its other priorities in Italy, western Europe, and America. With Spain an uncertain ally, Ferdinand's military weakness and his rigid commitment to the Edict of Restitution further reduced the Habsburg's potential for victory. On the other side, the parties feared each other as much as or more than they feared the Habsburgs. France, although weakened by a minority, always threatened expansion. The potential for overall disruption held by the Scandinavian powers, Sweden and Denmark, offered a wild card not often seen in European wars. But the fundamental issue we must recognize is the underlying strength and resolve of the anti-Habsburg camp.

The theory of hegemonic war does not demand that vision be clear, that the old power be doddering, or that the new power be certain of victory. What it demands is that there be some perceived or unperceived change in the balance of power, which throws older patterns out of control. That was certainly the case in late sixteenth- and early seventeenth-century Europe, as the balance of religious, political, and economic power changed. The balance of power was not everything, however, and it is important that we remember that the Thirty Years' War was the result of issues besides the changing balance of power. The balance of power is mostly a function of states. The war was also a consequence of evolving leadership and personal action. These characteristics lead us to explanations which are more "historical" and less systematic and theoretical than the hegemony theory.

All of the explanations for the Habsburg failure to achieve victory point to the long-term causes of the war which were described earlier in this article. The conflicts which had developed by the end of the sixteenth century were not easily resolved. In western Europe, in the Baltic, and in the empire, antagonisms ran deep, over territorial and dynastic questions, as well as over religious issues. They were the result of serious discrepancies between the actual location of power and its nominal location, nowhere more visible than in the Protestant dominance of the Habsburg lands. These potentially separable sets of disputes were brought together by international links among Protestants and by the danger of a Habsburg alliance, especially if it had encircled France or the Dutch republic, or had controlled northern Germany. In the 1630s the threat of Habsburg gains prompted Swedish, then French involvement in the imperial war, but in the 1590s the potential for conflict was already palpable.

The remarkable characteristic of the period from 1598 to 1618 is the length of time in which such strong tensions existed without resolution. Although we might agree that the "time was not yet ripe" for a decision, there are other, better explanations. Among these, the shortage of strong leaders capable of action in the international arena is the most important. Under Rudolf and Matthias, the Austrian Habsburgs were weakened. Henry IV lacked the domestic peace required for any international adventure, at least until just before his assassination and probably even then.[14] After his death, the regent was not secure enough to pursue a vigorous foreign policy and her pro-Catholic sentiments made it unlikely that she would attack the empire. In the Netherlands and Spain, mature leaders were in place, at least until the elimination of Oldenbarnevelt, but that quarrel was partly resolved in 1609. Yet, even these men can hardly be described as strong. It can be argued that this whole generation of leaders had been so exhausted by the late sixteenth-century wars that they were unable to take action.

The events of 1618 and 1619 began to clarify the situation. Ferdinand of Styria, a convinced absolutist and a dogmatic Catholic, assumed the thrones of the Austrian Habsburgs, and the imperial title. He provoked the Protestants within his territories to rebellion, and they were supported by at least part of the international Protestant consortium. For once, when war was imminent, the Spanish were willing to give aid, and sent men

14 This argument is made by Hayden, "Continuity," 1–23.

and money to Ferdinand. The risk of excessive Habsburg power on the side of Catholicism existed then, even if France took the bait only much later.

If at one level the war was the result of weak leadership during the first two decades of the seventeenth century, at a deeper level it was the result of discrepancies between perceived and actual power. This situation has some parallels with the hegemonic model. If France and the Netherlands were the new hegemons seeking expansion, Spain was the old, and war would then be the result. In central and northern Europe, the question is more complex, but we can see the old concept of the empire as vulnerable, and the emergence of powers—the Habsburg monarchy, Bavaria, Prussia, and Sweden—which sought to expand. The hegemonic explanation of the causes of war demands an old power or an old system reacting to the threat of a new power. The hegemonic theory helps explain why many saw the Habsburgs as aggressors, as least at the outset of the war, and why they were so reluctant to compromise in order to reach a conclusion. The end of the war led inevitably to a new power formula in Europe, one in which the Habsburgs played a much smaller role.

Gunther E. Rothenberg

The Origins, Causes, and Extension of the Wars of the French Revolution and Napoleon

Social scientists, philosophers, and other scholars have advanced theories on the causes of war, but many historians have found these general theories to be of only limited utility. They hold that, although such theories may help to explain war per se, they cannot explain the causations of individual conflicts, especially when such generalization may actually be counterfactual, and are used merely to impose an arbitrary and artificial plan. Even so, historians, too, have addressed the problem of causation. Competition for power, a concept dating to Thucydides, has been especially attractive. As one modern formulation puts it, war is "simply the use of violence by states for the enforcement, the protection, or the extension of their political power."[1]

This formulation is workable because it embraces a wide range of causations, meeting many, if not all, of Brodie's criteria that theories of causation must be "eclectic and comprehensive." "The enforcement, the protection, or the extension" of power can be seen as not only encompassing the traditional view that war derives primarily from the primacy of external affairs, but also applying to the more recent emphasis on the role of economic interests, domestic pressure groups, and ideology. It also conforms to Clausewitz's dictum that war is but one particular kind of conflict between social groups, "a clash between major interests that is resolved by bloodshed," which "is the only way in which it differs from other conflicts." Within a well-established state system, the decision whether to initiate war, or to resist, is based on assessments regarding the respective power of the contestants.

Gunther E. Rothenberg is Professor of Military History at Purdue University. He is the author of *Napoleon's Great Adversaries: The Archduke Charles and the Austrian Army 1792–1814* (Bloomington, 1982).

1 Michael Howard, "Military Power and International Security," in J. Garnett (ed.), *Theories of Peace and Security* (London, 1970), 41. Cf. the very similar formulation by A. Geoffrey Blainey, *The Causes of War* (London, 1973), 149–150.

Sometimes, as Bueno de Mesquita has pointed out, a state may go to war expecting to lose, but will nevertheless do so because it perceives a loss as a better option than not fighting. Or, as in the case of World War I, the assessment of strength was mistaken, a theory advanced by Williamson. Finally, and again the case in World War I, the military leadership may opt for war because of its conception of honor, even though realizing that the war may well be lost.[2]

But even if the desire to protect, maintain, and extend power is accepted as a general theory, we still need particular rather than general explanations for the outbreak of specific wars. Here historians usually distinguish among origins, long-range causes (such as territorial disputes, economic rivalries, and national-psychological antipathies), short-term causes (that is, the specific events which bring these matters to the crisis point), and finally the particular circumstances, events which tip the balance and produce the decision, or provide the excuse, to initiate hostilities.

Accurately to determine the long- and short-range causes of the wars of the French Revolution and Napoleon is especially difficult. When in 1792 the French Legislative Assembly voted to declare war on Austria, it acted in the expectation of a short and victorious conflict. In the event, this primal Austro-French war expanded to embrace all of the European states and extended overseas to the West Indies and America, becoming incomparably the largest conflict in the history of the world until that time. Moreover, the almost continuous fighting between 1792 and 1815 was not one single conflict, but a great number of wars, insurrections, and revolts that differed in kind as well as in chronology. Even if only the wars between the major European powers are considered, they are divided into seven separate coalitions during which, at one point or the other, all of the states, except for Great Britain, were opponents or allies of the French, joining or leaving coalitions, and on occasion changing sides, under different circumstances and for differing reasons.

2 Bernard Brodie, *War and Politics* (New York, 1973), 339. Karl von Clausewitz (eds. and trans., Michael Howard and Peter Paret) *On War* (Princeton, 1976), 149. Bruce Bueno de Mesquita, "The Contribution of Expected Utility Theory to the Study of International Conflict," *Journal of Interdisciplinary History*, XVIII (1988), 629–652. Samuel R. Williamson, Jr., "The Origins of World War I," *ibid.*, 795–818.; Rothenberg, *The Army of Francis Joseph* (West Lafayette, 1976), 176–177.

If there is wide agreement that these wars can be considered a single historical episode, with a division between the revolutionary and the Napoleonic era, this view prevails because the major political and military developments provided continuity. Wars changed from the affairs of kings to the wars of nations. "The tremendous effects of the French Revolution abroad," Clausewitz observed, "were not caused so much by new military methods and concepts as by radical changes in policies and administration, by the new character of government, the altered conditions of the French people." As a result, the "people became a participant in war; instead of governments and armies as heretofore, the full weight of the nation was thrown into the balance."[3]

Once war became an affair of the nation its objectives and conduct altered radically. Instead of the limited advantages sought by limited means during the preceding era of dynastic war, the objective of the republican as well as imperial campaigns was to destroy the adversary's means and will to resist and to impose settlements that were so unreasonable that the loser repudiated them at the first opportunity. Moreover, even though the French armies sustained about as many defeats as they gained victories, their progress was striking enough to compel opponents to remodel their forces and, to a greater or lesser degree, their entire military systems. Throughout Europe, national resources were engaged to an unprecedented degree, making possible the initiation, continuation, renewal, and expansion of the conflicts.

The century before the revolution, often called the Enlightenment, had not been peaceful. Not counting revolts and colonial clashes, no fewer than sixteen wars were fought between various combinations of major and minor European powers between 1700 and 1790. The relative frequency of wars in an environment lacking many of the resources for conflict was possible because the wars of the European nations had evolved into formal affairs, pursued with limited means for limited objectives. The "enlightened monarchs," loosely conforming to an "expected utility principle," decided on war and peace by calculating their interests; the people normally were neither consulted nor expected to take up arms. Fighting was left to standing armies of long-service

3 Clausewitz, *On War*, 592, 609–610.

troops. They were set apart from society and commanded, especially in the higher grades, by an international noble cousinage. National antagonism was absent or muted, and, in Churchill's sonorous prose: "All was governed by strict rules of war, into which bad temper was not often permitted to enter."[4] Lacking ideological or national content and with limited manpower, supplies, and finances, operations were conducted under severe restraints. The objective was to secure a favorable negotiating position, not to destroy the enemy and dictate terms. Civilians, at least in theory, were spared, and one writer described these wars as "one of the loftiest achievements of the eighteenth century," the product of an "aristocratic and qualitative civilization" destroyed by the French Revolution.[5]

To be sure, not too much emphasis should be placed on the moderate nature of war in eighteenth-century Europe. As actually conducted, war involved bloody battles, extended hostilities, and, sometimes, conscripted troops. Commanders of the ancien régime could be as ruthless as their successors, and objectives were not always limited. The coalition against Frederick II in 1756, for instance, was intended to reduce Prussia to a minor state. In eastern Europe, where Austria and Russia still faced the Turks, wars, as Guilmartin has shown, continued with little regard for humanitarian considerations.[6]

Do these facts negate the traditional view of the century as one of limited war? Probably not; they modify it but leave the essentials intact. Wars were limited because of the caution of princes combined with the relatively undeveloped potential for intense mass warfare, including a restricted agricultural, financial, industrial, and manpower base. These restrictions disappeared, at least to a substantial degree, in the second half of the century. The shift in agriculture from subsistence to surplus farming provided food for an enormously increased population. Between 1701 and 1801 Europe's population grew from 118 to 187 million.

---

4 Winston S. Churchill, *Marlborough: His Life and Times* (New York, 1934), II, 38.
5 Guglielmo Ferrero, *Peace and War* (New York, 1933), 63–64.
6 Paret, "The Relationship between the Revolutionary War and European Military Thought and Practice in the Second Half of the Eighteenth Century," in Donald Higginbotham (ed.), *Reconsiderations on the Revolutionary War* (Westport, Conn., 1978), 146–148, 153–155. John F. Guilmartin, Jr., "Ideology and Conflict: The Wars of the Ottoman Empire," *Journal of Interdisciplinary History*, XVIII (1988), 721–747.

After Russia with 44 million, France, rising from 18 to 26 million by 1792, was the most populous country. The Habsburg Empire doubled in population from 9 to 18 million, roughly the same figure as Great Britain, and the population of all German states combined rose from 10 to 20 million. For the most part, this increase was absorbed into the agricultural economies of eastern and central Europe and the growing industries of western Europe, although it also was available for military service. This demographic shift was even more pronounced in more densely populated France where the increase could be only partially absorbed, the remainder constituting a volatile urban mass and manpower for the armies of the Revolution and Napoleon.[7]

The enlarged manpower base coincided with the early industrial revolution which had greatly increased the output of iron and entered the first stages of mass production, capable of supplying, albeit with some difficulties, arms and equipment for much expanded military establishments.[8] Financial means were provided by an expansion of overseas trade in France and Britain and by improved means of administration and taxation elsewhere. Since the end of the Seven Years' War (1756–1763), new methods had been devised for the command and control of larger armies, and their movement and supply. French reformers had divided field armies into self-contained "divisions" able to operate independently, and these formations became standard in the revolutionary armies, with multi-divisional "corps" becoming the strategic components of the Napoleonic Wars. Movement was aided by new all-weather roads connecting major centers of western and central Europe and by improvements in cartography, both developments of the second half of the eighteenth century. Coordinating large autonomous formations required more sophisticated staff work, and these techniques, too, were pioneered in France during the last decades before the Revolution. In short, although sometimes only in seminal form, in the late eighteenth century the objective factors making possible more intense and prolonged warfare had come into being.[9]

7 Marcel Reinhard and André Armengaud, *Histoire générale de la population mondiale* (Paris, 1961), 151–201.
8 William H. McNeill, *The Pursuit of Power* (Chicago, 1982), 144–146.
9 For a short review of these developments, see Rothenberg, *The Art of Warfare in the Age of Napoleon* (London, 1977), 11–30.

At the same time, the non-objective, ideological, base for mass-based, popular warfare appeared. Standing armies and their limited war, considered as expensive tools of absolutism and contrary to the "natural order," came under increased intellectual criticism, especially in France. Denis Diderot, Charles Louis de Secondat Montesquieu, François Voltaire, and Jean Jacques Rousseau, to mention a few, opposed standing armies. Voltaire called soldiers hired assassins, and Rousseau described them as a plague that was depopulating Europe and suppressing liberty. A citizen militia, he argued, was needed to secure society against tyranny.[10] Other critics charged that standing armies were inherently ineffective. The most famous advocate of this point of view was Jacques de Guibert, whose *Essai générale de tactique* (Brussels, 1772), claimed that standing armies made the people unwilling to fight and that, because such forces were costly and hard to replace, monarchs hesitated to risk them in battle or to engage in prolonged war. By contrast, he exalted the soldier-patriot and proclaimed that European hegemony would fall to whichever nation first created a truly national army, combining warlike virtues with a fixed scheme of conquest, living at the expense of its adversaries and having a "style of war-making different from that practised by all states nowadays."[11]

Guibert's vision, in stark contrast to prevailing practices, was influential. It was supported by men like Joseph Servan de Gerbey, minister of war in 1792, and Edmond-Louis Alexis Dubois-Crancé, a military man and legislator during the early revolution. It was partially implemented through the creation of a huge national guard in mid-1789. Ultimately, of course, a national citizen army came into existence when France introduced universal conscription in 1792/93. As Guibert had predicted, these mass armies, the "nation in arms," pursued war with greater energy and ruthlessness, and effectively introduced a style of combat moving toward unlimited warfare.[12]

---

10 Alfred Vagts, *A History of Militarism* (New York, 1937), 77–85; Emile G. Leonard, *L'armée et ses problèmes au XVIIIe siècle* (Paris, 1958), 143–144, 146–150.
11 For a discussion of Guibert's views, see Geoffrey Best, *War and Society in Revolutionary Europe, 1770–1870* (New York, 1986), 53–58; Spenser Wilkinson, *The French Army before Napoleon* (Oxford, 1915), 56–68.
12 Eugène Carrias, *La pensée militaire française* (Paris, 1960), 177–183; John F. C. Fuller, *The Conduct of War 1789–1961* (New Brunswick, N. J., 1961), 29, 39–41.

Although the components for a major war and a new style of warfare were in place in 1789, the international situation did not make an outbreak of war inevitable. To be sure, the relations between France and the other European states were marked by various degrees of rivalry, even hostility, but in the early stages of the Revolution there was no idea of a European crusade against France, and, initially, French foreign policy was looking toward peace and not war. The other great continental powers, Austria, Prussia, and Russia, all were preoccupied with internal affairs and mutually suspicious of each other over plans further to divide Poland. Austria, moreover, was involved in an indecisive war with the Turks, complicated by unrest in Hungary and Belgium, and Russia was fighting both the Turks and the Swedes. Great Britain, the traditional rival, was resolved on a policy of peace. It regarded all wars as inimical to trade and British financial interests. Initially, therefore, the internal problems in France, the single most powerful nation in Europe, were regarded as a diversion likely to guarantee the continued balance of power and peace.

During the early months of the revolution, French policy continued along established lines. For two and a half centuries hostility to the House of Habsburg had been constant, and the French alliance of 1756 had been but a temporary interruption. Already shaky by the 1770s, it now was marked by dislike and distrust, a feeling shared by wide sectors of the French and Austrian public. Still, neither side wanted, or expected, war, and Joseph II, the Habsburg emperor, even considered the initial phase of the revolution as a sign of desirable progress. As for Prussia, the early, moderate revolutionaries considered it a model state, although they entertained hopes of reviving the former alignment with that monarchy. On the Prussian side, Frederick William II entertained various schemes of aggrandizement, but these were not directed at France.

The most serious differences existed between France and Great Britain. They had been locked in to a "Second Hundred Years' War" since 1688. Its last round had ended in 1783, leaving Britain vengeful and France disappointed, but renewed conflict was not likely for the moment. Both countries had emerged from the wars with heavy financial burdens and faced domestic problems. Britain confronted both social and political unrest, including the perennial Irish problem, and the Whigs at least initially welcomed the Revolution. In France, public finances were in disarray, there was social unrest, and the armed forces already were showing signs of disaffection. Although France's ambitions, including the building of a large navy, and its annexationist intentions in the Low Countries, were the cause of some suspicion in London, for the moment France was unable to do much. in 1787, France had stood by when Prussian troops had put down a popular and Francophile revolt in the United Provinces and, in 1790, had given no support to a short-lived insurrection in Belgium (then the Austrian Netherlands). That same year, when the Nootka Sound incident brought Britain and Spain to the brink of war, France had refused to honor the Bourbon family alliance.

The impression that French power had collapsed, its government divided between a weak king and a factionalized National Assembly, its economy in shambles, and its armed forces disrupted by politics, was further strengthened by some remarkable and utopian policy statements. Convinced that the "victory of liberty over despotism" spelled an end to wars, the National Assembly resolved in May 1790 that the "French nation renounces the initiation of war for the purposes of conquest," and Victor Comte de Mirabeau, its most influential early leader, proclaimed in August that "the moment is not far off when liberty will acquit mankind of the crime of war." Finally, the French Constitution of September 1791 incorporated the renunciation of "war for the purpose of conquest" in Article 6.

By this time, the revolution had begun to clash with established European interests and was being perceived as a threat to the international order. For that matter, war for conquest and war for the consolidation of the revolution were held to be different affairs in Paris, although armed action, or at least the threat of such action, was considered in Vienna, Berlin, and other quarters. Although such considerations did not yet constitute a linear progression toward war, the probabilities had become much greater. Relations between France and the European courts further deteriorated during the winter of 1791/92. The long-range causes were being displaced by short-terms causes, and the overall trend was toward war. On 20 April 1792, the Legislative Assembly finally declared war against the "King of Hungary and Bohemia." It was, so the assembly declared, a "just defense of a free people against the unjust agression of a king."[13]

The question of responsibility for the outbreak of war has been and continues to be, debated. Some historians described it as an ideological conflict, a "war brought about by rival systems of political outlook."[14] Others place the blame on one political faction, the Girondins. "There was," Soboul wrote, "no question of any threat from the outside. . . . War was willed soley to divert from social problems."[15] Others had blamed external factors, Austrian and Prussian machinations, for war. As for Austria, however, neither Joseph II nor Leopold II, his successor after 1790, was eager to defend the royal prerogatives in France. Frederick William II of Prussia was more bellicose, but looked eastward, mobilizing in 1790 against Austria and in 1791 against Russia. The only ruler to contemplate armed intervention against France before the late summer of 1791 was the unstable Gustavus III of Sweden. He was cynically encouraged by Russia, which hoped for complications in the west in order to gain a free hand in Poland.[16]

Even so, tensions between Austria and France had begun to rise as early as 1790. As Holy Roman Emperor, Leopold II had been obliged to protest when the French National Assembly had abrogated the rights of certain German princes in the Alsace, arguing that all of the contracts between princes were void. And, although Leopold had little interest in princely rights, his decision to nullify the contracts seemed to threaten the entire international order. For their part, the French were annoyed at the cordial reception given to French émigrés by some small German courts, even though Leopold, worried about the Turkish War, the Prussian threat, and unrest in Belgium, refused to offer them any assistance. Given the near collapse of state finances, he wanted

13   T. C. W. Blanning, *The Origins of the French Revolutionary Wars* (London, 1986), 83– 113. This book provides by far the best and most comprehensive modern treatment of this complex subject.
14   Alan J. P. Taylor, *How Wars Begin* (London, 1970), 18. Cf. Blanning, *Origins*, 120– 121.
15   Albert Soboul, quoted in *ibid.*, 71.
16   *Ibid.*, 74–75, 78–79.

peace and stability. As soon as relations with Prussia had been mended, peace negotiations started with the Turks, and Belgium pacified in December 1790, he reduced his military establishment the following spring. At the same time, the French National Assembly, worried about the decline and reliability of the army, started an active program to augment its strength by forming volunteer battalions.[17]

In late June 1791, matters took a sharp turn for the worse. The French king felt that the Assembly was constantly whittling away at his prerogatives and was unwilling to accept a proposed constitution. Encouraged by Marie Antoinette, his wife and the sister of Leopold II, he made an unsuccessful attempt to escape and, after being returned to Paris, was suspended from his powers and placed under virtual arrest. Leopold felt constrained to issue an appeal to all of the crowned heads of Europe, calling for the restoration of the royal family's liberty. In August, he pursued this issue at a summit meeting with Frederick William II. In the "Declaration of Pillnitz," the two monarchs stated that restoration of the monarchy in France was in the common interest of all of the European powers. Although much has been made of this declaration, it was an empty gesture. No action was contemplated except by all of the states together, and, as Leopold recognized, "if England fails to support us, there is no case."[18] And England had no intention of getting involved. Prussia, to be sure, was willing to undertake a forward policy, but the emperor refused even to enter into preliminary talks on military cooperation; he informed the leaders of the émigrés that no armed action was contemplated and that no troop reinforcements would be sent to the Rhine.

The crisis, if crisis it was, ended in September when the king accepted the constitution. There was rejoicing in France, where public reaction seemed to certify that the revolution was over. Count Wenzelvon Kaunitz, the Austrian Chancellor, observed that "God ought to be thanked for the King of France having

17 Rothenberg, *Napoleon's Great Adversaries: The Archduke Charles and the Austrian Army 1792–1814* (London, 1982), 25; Jean-Paul Bertaud, *La Révolution armée: Les Soldats-citoyens et la Révolution Française* (Paris, 1979), 65–71.
18 Alfred R. von Vivenot, *Quellen zur Geschichte der deutschen Kaiserpolitik Oesterreichs während der französischen Revolution 1790–1801* (Vienna, 1879), I. 234–243, 255. Blanning, *Origins*, 88–89.

gotten everyone out of a tight situation," and, on hearing the news, Frederick William exclaimed "the peace of Europe is at last assured." Indeed, given the reception of the Constitution in France and abroad, and "given the guaranteed neutrality of England, the vacillations of Frederick William II, and the well known pacifist views of Leopold II, everything pointed to peace."[19]

But it was not to be. Designed to frighten France into halting the drift to the left rather than as a prelude to war, the Declaration of Pillnitz had alarmed the assembly and was presented in the press as a direct threat. Also, it provided ammunition for the war party in the new Legislative Assembly, which was faced by a multitude of domestic difficulties, including financial problems, a looming food shortage, and tremors of counterrevolution. Although the constitutional royalists, the Feuillants, still were the largest faction they were divided, allowing the Girondin minority, who were middle-class republicans aiming to destroy the monarchy, to dominate the deputies through their fiery oratory and by playing on fears of foreign aggression and internal treason. In their desire for war against Austria, the most popular target, they were joined by Feuillant groups, as well as some moderate royalists like Marie Paul Joseph Marquis de Lafayette. All of the groups and individuals, albeit for their own ends, saw a short and victorious war as the solution to their problems, pushing the revolution to the left, strengthening the king's position, acquiring more power, and diverting attention from the mounting social unrest in the country. In fact, by spring only extreme left wingers like Maximilien de Robespierre, fearing that the army was unprepared and that, whatever the outcome, the Revolution would be endangered, opposed war.

Throughout the winter of 1791/92 the Girondins promoted their bellicose policies. In a number of speeches, Jacques-Pierre Brissot, one of their leaders, outlined the reasons: to rally the people, to test the king's loyalty, and to purge Europe of despotism. "A people who have conquered liberty after ten centuries of slavery," he thundered, "need war . . . to cleanse liberty from the vices of despotism."[20] He had little trouble convincing the assem-

19 For Prussia, see also Otto Hintze, *Die Hohenzollern und ihr Werk* (Berlin, 1915), 417–418. Louis M. Thiers, *Histoire de la Révolution française* (Paris, 1846; 14th ed.), II, 17.
20 Gerhard Ritter, *The Sword and the Scepter* (Coral Gables, 1969), I, 43; Blanning, *Origins*, 100–101.

bly that France faced an immense foreign conspiracy, although, at the same time, he promised that victory was assured because the enemies were weak and divided. In December 1791, he persuaded the assembly to send an ultimatum to the electors of Trier and Mainz, demanding that they expel the small émigré forces, about 2,000 in all, from their territories. Brissot had hoped that refusal would lead to war and was disappointed when, under pressure from Leopold II, the two princes complied.

The affair stiffened resolution in Vienna where, on 17 January 1792, the Crown Council decided that Austria should insist on the restoration of princely privileges in the Alsace, the disbanding of the three French armies being concentrated along the eastern frontier, and the restoration of royal rights. Meanwhile in Paris, following a ten day debate, the Legislative Assembly forced Louis XVI to send an ultimatum to Leopold II, demanding formal assurances that he intended to keep the peace and would renounce all agreements aimed against France. If no satisfactory response was received by March 1, a state of war was deemed to exist, and the king was instructed to prepare the army for immediate offensive operations. This ultimatum meant war.[21]

In Vienna, realizing the mutual escalation, the emperor had concluded a formal alliance with Prussia, signed on February 7, and a few days later, somewhat late, Austria started to mobilize. Archduke Francis, then within days of assuming the throne, wrote to Archduke Charles, his younger brother who was residing in Brussels, that "with the French massing on your frontiers and the locals restive, you are indeed in a bad situation. However, we are getting ready for war. 6,000 men are already marching to Freiburg and 40,000, under Prince Hohenlohe, are preparing to come to your aid."[22] At this point, even though recruitment had not been an unqualified success, the French armies in the eastern regions numbered about 180,000.

War had now become almost inevitable, though both sides had underestimated their adversaries and were overconfident. In Austria and Prussia, senior soldiers believed that recent experience showed that revolutionary armies had low combat value. After all, in 1787 the Prussians had conquered the United Provinces in

21 Vivenot, *Quellen zur Geschichte*, I, 327–330; Blanning, *Origins*, 102–106.
22 Letter cited in H. Hertenberger and F. Wiltschek, *Erzherzog Karl* (Vienna, 1983), 30.

one month, and in 1790 the Austrians had subdued Belgium in two weeks. For their part, the French assumed that they were militarily superior. Revolutionary armies, large because all citizens were potential soldiers, would fight better than the hirelings of the despots. The war minister assured the assembly that the army was well supplied and there were expectations that the French would be supported by fellow revolutionaries throughout Europe. Finally, the Girondins thought that Austria would stand alone and that Britain would be neutral. As late as April 1792, their emissaries in Berlin attempted to enlist Prussian support against Austria. Clearly then, for all the ideological rhetoric of both sides, the ideological factor, if not totally absent, was not foremost in causing war.[23]

Although almost inevitable, the rush toward war could still have been halted. No shots had been fired, and no frontiers had been crossed. But events continued toward the final decision. On 1 March 1792, Leopold died and was succeeded by his more combative brother, Francis II. Even then, however, some leading Austrian statesmen and soldiers did not expect war. In fact, one day after the Legislative Assembly in Paris had voted for war, Archduke Charles reported from Brussels that "no one here considers war likely."[24]

In Paris, however, in March 1792, Louis XVI, partly to avoid pressures and to repair his reputation, which had been damaged by accusations that he was treacherously in contact with Austria, appointed a hawkish Girondin ministry. It was headed by Charles François Dumouriez, an opportunistic soldier who had gained rapid promotion since 1789 by associating himself at the right time with the dominant faction. As foreign minister, acting war minister, and putative field commander, he undertook to persuade the king to do the popular thing and declare war. Although Dumouriez believed that such a conflict would be won, he also schemed that, in case of defeat, he would blame the throne and assume office as dictator. For that matter, other Girondins also hoped that initial defeats would discredit the king, whom they then would overthrow in favor of a republic. Finally, the Feuil-

23 Leopold von Ranke, *Ursprung und Beginn der französischen Revolution* (Leipzig, 1879), 132–133. Blanning, *Origins*, 107–112.
24 Rothenberg, *Napoleon's Great Adversaries*, 13.

lants, and even the remaining royalists, who were grouped around the queen, favored war. They were convinced that, win or lose, the monarchy would profit. On 21 April 1792, amid almost universal approval, France declared war against Austria, still hoping to avoid conflict with Prussia and the other German states.

Although Prussia honored its alliance with Austria, this decision did not necessarily mean that hostilities would escalate into a general conflict of unprecedented intensity and dimensions. This escalation arose out of the dynamics of its opening phases. Power, rather than ideology, was the main issue.

On 28 April 1792, elements of the French army advanced into Belgium but were easily repelled. Further attacks brought similar results, and by the end of June the invasion had collapsed. Austrian troops, in turn, entered Flanders and besieged Lille. These setbacks, combined with economic distress, radical agitation, and a threatening manifesto by the Duke of Brunswick, who was commanding an Austro-Prussian army then assembling on the frontier, triggered a savage radical uprising in Paris on August 10, culminating in the massacre of the king's Swiss Guards and the suspension of the monarchy. Moreover, the Austro-Prussians were as ill-prepared as the French, and their uncoordinated and slow invasion was turned back at Valmy on 20 September 1792. On that day, the National Convention, a newly elected and radical assembly, met for the first time in Paris. The next day, it abolished the monarchy and proclaimed France a republic.

The fortunes of war turned as French forces invaded Belgium, occupied Nice and Savoy, and entered the Rhineland. Exultant, the Convention voted on November 19 to extend aid to revolutionaries everywhere, and, as a further gesture of defiance, it ordered the execution of the king in January 1793. Confident of victory and looking to extend its power, the Convention then threatened the United Provinces and, when England showed that such a threat would not be tolerated, on February 1 declared war on Britain, the United Provinces, and Spain. The revolution was challenging the entire European social and political order, not with ideas, but with its bayonets. This threat brought about the First Coalition, a rather unlikely alliance of Austria, Prussia, Sardinia, Naples, Spain, and the minor German states, with Britain, the United Provinces, and Portugal.[25]

At the same time, radical rule in Paris created opposition in the provinces as well as defections from the army. During the winter of 1792/93 most of the one-year volunteers mustered in 1791/92 had dispersed, and the former royal army was disorganized. During the spring and summer of 1793, there was a crisis. Beset by domestic problems, the new republic was invaded by converging hostile forces. But the allies were divided by differing military and political objectives, whereas in Paris a strong executive body, the Committee of Public Safety, soon controlled by the fanatic Robespierre, instituted a dictatorship, the "Terror," to enforce national unity and organization.

When voluntary enlistment failed to supply needed troops, the Committee decreed the levée en masse of 23 August 1793, which mobilized all national resources, human and material, and produced a broad-based conscript army, 700,000 strong, the next year. Weapons, equipment, and supplies were produced by a directed war economy, and supervision of the armies and their commanders was entrusted to political commissars. In this fashion, the first modern "nation in arms" emerged.[26]

But this phase was only temporary. As long as there was a clear threat, the French people were willing to give their support and to make the sacrifices needed to create the armies to check invasions, suppress revolts, and carry the revolution abroad. But after the victories of 1794 removed the immediate danger, Robespierre's ever more radical and repressive regime became intolerable and, in July 1794, Thermidor, he was overthrown by his own colleagues in the Convention. During the next seventeen months the Thermidorians, exploiting the earlier victories, completed the conquest of Belgium, occupied all of Holland, and, early in 1795, expelled the British from the continent. Before the year ended, Prussia, Spain, and a number of the small German states withdrew from the war, with only Austria, Great Britain, and, at the end of the year, Russia continuing the conflict.

---

25 Blanning, *Origins*, 135–142, 152–163.
26 Hoffman Nickerson, *The Armed Horde* (New York, 1942), 64–67; Rothenberg, *Art of Warfare*, 98–102, 109–114.

But peace remained impossible because the Convention, albeit more moderate at home, continued expansionist policies abroad. Belgium was annexed, Holland was turned into the Batavian republic, and there were moves to create "sister republics" in Italy. This apparent return to a policy of aggressively promoting revolution in Europe worried Lazare Carnot, who was in charge of overall strategic direction. He held that, although the European monarchs might accept the situation in the short run, ultimately, if French influence continued to expand, they would once again unite in a war France could not win. In August 1795, he resigned in protest from the Committee of Public Safety, although he returned to office when the Directory, a new, essentially centrist government, was formed later that year.

But the Directory also had no program for making peace. Basically lacking wide popular support, it had come to power only after a monarchist uprising in Paris in October, the "Thirteenth of Vendemiaire," was dispersed by a "whiff of grapeshot," marking the appearance of Napoleon Bonaparte on the national scene. From its inception until its overthrow by Napoleon in 1799, the Directory was constantly challenged by coups from both the right and the left and increasingly had to rely on the soldiers to maintain itself. Under these circumstances, it did not dare to end the wars. Two of the three directors believed that victory would deflect unrest in France and also satisfy the ambitions and avarice of the generals.

By 1795, a war ostensibly begun in defense of the revolution and France, and for the liberation of oppressed people, had turned into one of conquest and plunder. After their first victories, the French armies had moved onto foreign soil, where costs for their support devolved largely on the local populations and where officers and men found opportunities to enrich themselves. "Our expedition across the Rhine," one participant wrote early in 1793, was undertaken "entirely because of pecuniary considerations. . . . Our incursion into a rich and defenseless country was to obtain the money of which we were in such dire need."[27] Armies, of course, always had subsisted on enemy territory, levying contributions and profiting from loot, but during the Terror the practice had been systematized. In December 1793, Pierre Joseph

27 Best, *War and Society*, 92.

Cambon, the finance specialist for the Committee of Public Safety, told the Convention that, although France had brought liberty and equality to its neighbors, it has not recieved the support that it had a right to expect. The beneficiaries, he argued, should be made to pay for their liberation. The proposal was enthusiastically adopted, and, in the coming years occupied or "liberated" countries were exploited not only to feed French troops and enrich their commanders, but to subsidize the French economy by transfers of money and treasures. Also, the Directory feared renewed social unrest if the troops returned to France. The large armies had taken in the masses of unemployed young men who had served as the fighting power for the mobs of the early revolution. Especially under the Directory, "the mass of young men who had been unable to find satisfactory careers in civil occupations before the revolution were either successfully absorbed into the workforce [military production] at home or living as soldiers at the expense of neighboring peoples, or else more or less gloriously dead."[28]

Peace and demobilization, the Directory feared, would destabilize the country; it therefore never developed a realistic peace program, but continued its wars, not caring where its armies went, so long as they and their generals stayed abroad. Under these circumstances, even the peace with Austria signed in 1797 could not last. By 1798 there was another coalition, and opportunities to end the wars and create a lasting settlement had much diminished, largely because the aggressive and opportunistic policy of the Directory, hanging on to power, had made war the dominant theme in Europe. At this point, a military dictator seized power in France who would expand war even further.

In 1799, Napoleon ousted the Directory, centralizing all power in his hands; for the next fifteen years, the history of Europe was indeed the Napoleonic era. Although Napoleon inherited much from the revolution, including huge, conscripted armies, that were led by young, ambitious commanders accustomed to mobile, offensive, and ruthless warfare, it seems likely that without him history would have been different. For all of its military

28 Felix Bornarel, *Cambon et la Révolution française* (Paris, 1905), 98–100. McNeill, *Pursuit of Power*, 194, 199.

achievements, the revolution had not been uniformly successful, and France had achieved most of its victories against adversaries who had not committed their entire power. Indeed, by 1799 many of its conquests had been lost. And from all that we know of Napoleon's most competent peers and rivals up to that date, including Carnot, Louis Lazare, Hoche, Jean Victor Moreau, and André Masséna, it is likely that they would have been defeated as often as not in battle and that the eventual exhaustion of France would have brought an end to, or at least a marked reduction in, the effort to expand.[29]

Without Napoleon, it is probable that the Anglo-Austrian-Russian alliance, the Second Coalition, would have been stopped. By October 1799 the Russians had quarreled with their British and Austrian allies and removed their forces, and the Austrians were tired of war and unable to continue offensive operations.[30] It is likely that without Napoleon a negotiated settlement might have been achieved, with France, a republic, established as the most powerful country on the continent, and with the European state system left essentially intact.

But, under Napoleon, a man whose will for power was unlimited and for whom "moderation had no meaning," war continued and assumed a hegemonic character.[31] Although the revolution was expansive in character, its conquests had been confined to western Europe and parts of northern Italy and it had not established itself permanently in central and eastern Europe. Even though these advances threatened important British and Austrian interests, they were negotiable. Indeed, the Treaty of Luneville with Austria in 1801 and the Treaty of Amiens with Britain in 1802 might have provided the basis for a durable settlement. But Napoleon almost immediately violated the terms and by his actions indicated that he would not accept any balance of power.

Britain had agreed to peace in 1802 because the years of fighting, coupled with the defeat of Austria, had led Prime Minister Henry Addington to conclude that there was no further point

29 Paret, "Napoleon and the Revolution in War," in idem, (ed.), Makers of Modern Strategy (Princeton, 1986), 126.
30 Rothenberg, Napoleon's Great Adversaries, 64, 75–76.
31 George Lefebvre, cited in J. Friguglietti and E. Kennedy (eds.), The Shaping of Modern France (Toronto, 1972), 175.

in pursuing war. Britain faced unrest in Ireland as well as serious economic problems, including a vast national debt and an annual budget which had tripled in eight years. Even William Pitt (the Younger) was willing to support peace. In Austria, exhausted by war and in financial disarray, the Francophobe Baron Johann Amadeus Thugut had been replaced as chancellor by the pacific Count Johann Ludwig Cobenzl. Even Russia, now ruled by Czar Alexander I, a liberal-minded if unstable young man, was looking toward an accommodation with Napoleon. But it soon became clear that Napoleon was determined to dominate the continent. He restructured and enlarged his army and began a vast naval program; he virtually annexed the Batavian republic, converted northwestern Italy into a cluster of French departments, and showed a renewed interest in pushing French power into southern Germany. In the spring of 1803, war with Britain recommenced. While Napoleon's army was gathering for an invasion across the Channel, in Austria, Cobenzl, albeit opposed by the emperor and by Archduke Charles, who were engaged in reforming the Habsburg army, lobbied for a new alliance with Russia. In Russia, Czar Alexander turned against Napoleon following the wanton kidnapping and execution of Louis Antoine Henri, Duc d'Enghien, in March 1804. British diplomacy and gold helped to forge a new coalition, but Napoleon's actions provided the impetus.

Soon after the renewal of war with England, Napoleon lamented that he was compelled to fight on because "between the old monarchies and the young republic the spirit of hostilities must always exist." But the real causes of the continuing conflict, the Napoleonic wars, were to be found in his policies. As he confided in exile, his ultimate aim was "to reestablish the kingdom of Poland as a barrier against the Muscovite barbarians, divide Austria, establish client states in Italy, declare Hungary independent, break up Prussia, form independent republics in England and Ireland, control Egypt, drive the Turks out of Europe, and liberate the Balkan nations."[32] Such grandiose hegemonic objectives, the objectives of a man for whom war always was the central instrument of foreign policy, could not fail but to arouse determined opposition and enable Britain to form five other suc-

32 Felix Markham, *Napoleon* (London, 1963), 95; Armand de Caulaincourt (trans. H. Miles), *Memoirs of General de Caulaincourt, Duke of Vicenza* (London, 1935), I, 429.

cessive coalitions. "In his hands," Paret concluded, "all conflicts tended to be unlimited, because openly or by implication they threatened the continued independent existence of his antagonists."[33] And this reality led them to resist to the utmost, or if defeated and forced to sign peace treaties, to repudiate them at the first opportunity and to mobilize all resources until they finally overcame him with a strength similar to his own.

Napoleon caused or provoked almost all of his wars, although he started very few of them. He usually maneuvered his adversaries into making the first overt moves, thereby revealing their strength and main objectives. He would then strike back and destroy their forces in one major blow. His actions were precisely calculated. Although the war of 1792 had started in part because of mistaken assessments of the capabilities of the adversaries, and an excellent case can be made for the decision to occupy Spain in 1808/09, Napoleon always had excellent strategic intelligence and made war deliberately. His reliance on force as the primary tool of foreign policy eventually put him at odds with Charles Maurice de Talleyrand, his foreign minister, who from 1807 on realized that his master was overextended and vainly tried to persuade him to end the conflict and stabilize the European state system.[34]

In 1808, after the Treaty of Tilsit with Prussia and Russia, and, again in 1811, even the British, who were tired of war and faced with financial problems, would have been willing to accept a settlement with the French Empire, provided that Napoleon agreed to restore some degree of the balance of power. Even as late as the fall of 1813, both Britain and Austria, concerned about possible Russian and Prussian aggrandizement, were prepared to make a compromise peace, leaving Napoleon on his throne and France with the frontiers of 1792. But the emperor refused to make any substantial concessions, and in the end he lost all.

The origins, causes, and extension of the revolutionary and Napoleonic wars, the first of the major modern wars, have been the subject of considerable debate among historians. It remains an open question whether the origins and causes of these conflicts pertain specifically to the events of 1792/93, that is, the outbreak

33 Paret, "Napoleon," 129.
34 Ritter, *Sword and Scepter,* 46.

of war between France, Austria, and Great Britain, or whether they apply equally to the successive wars until the final overthrow of Napoleon in 1815. Also unresolved is whether the origins and causes were specific to these wars or whether they can be fitted into a general pattern of causality leading to the outbreak of armed conflict.

The answers suggested in this article indicate both continuity and change, factors applicable to a general pattern of causation as well as issues specific to these conflicts. The protection or extension of political power was the most significant systemic factor, a factor that encompasses both the pressure generated by external affairs and the long-standing rivalries among major states, as well as considerations of maintaining domestic control. It was the most important component in this series of conflicts, as it has been in armed conflict in general. At the same time, the conjunction of objective factors, such as the great rise in population and the increase in agricultural and industrial production, contributed to making the wars of the French Revolution and Napoleon more intense and prolonged. Finally, it can be argued that the expansionist surge of the revolution, and later the will to dominate Europe, led to wars in which the French, especially under Napoleon, often inflicted crushing defeats on their opponents, and then imposed peace treaties that were so unreasonable that they were little more than armed truces. The losers signed them under duress, with the intention of repudiating them at the first opportunity. These treaties, which led to fears that France's ultimate objective was the complete elimination of other states, formed part of the overall pattern that led to renewed wars.[35]

Other factors apply only to the French revolutionary wars or are less important than has been assumed in the past. In particular, there is the issue of ideology. Although some historians have characterized the revolutionary wars primarily as an ideological conflict that was "brought about by rival political systems," this explanation cannot withstand close scrutiny.[36] Ideological differences do create antagonisms, but they do not necessary lead to war. Although the Girondins preached revolutionary principles and talked about giving "fraternal assistance"

35 Ferrero, *Peace and War*, cited in Fuller, *Conduct of War*, 37.
36 Taylor, *How Wars Begin*, 18.

to revolutionaries everywhere, they also sought an alliance with Prussia in 1792, and their Jacobin successors utilized Prussian antagonism against Austria in securing its withdrawal from war in 1795. Although ideological considerations played a role in the renewed expansionist surge under the Directory, other factors, especially the desire to maintain internal stability, appear to have been paramount. As for the opponents of the French, dislike of revolutionary ideology and fear of internal subversion certainly played a role in creating the various, and frequently improbable, coalitions, but they were not the primary considerations and ideology alone could not maintain unity of purpose among the allies.

It is true that nationalism played a role both in mobilizing French resources and in promoting national solidarity against French domination, but throughout the wars Austria was unwilling to embrace this potentially disruptive ideology, Russia used these sentiments in 1812, and Prussia did so only reluctantly in 1813. The greatest outpouring of nationalism appeared during the course of the Spanish popular war against the French, but it was really old-fashioned xenophobia rather than an ideological nationalism. Overall, nationalism was used to mobilize support for war, but it was not a primary cause of war. The threat of Napoleonic domination forced his opponents to enlist the "participation of the people" in war, but they did so reluctantly.

There also is no evidence, except for the forlorn Polish rising of 1794 (an event of considerable concern to Austria, Prussia, and above all Russia), that states entered into war expecting to lose. On the contrary, it can be argued that the war of 1792 and the wars of the Second Coalition (1798–1802) and the Third Coalition (1805–1808) were undertaken because the allies grossly underestimated their opponent's power. To be sure, they thought that not fighting would lead to further damage to their interests, and possibly even endanger their very existence as independent states, but in every case they believed that their chances for success were substantial.

Finally, regarding the Napoleonic wars, this discussion has held that the will of an individual, rather than external or internal circumstances, led to these wars. The proof is circumstantial and derives in large part from a posthumous psychological assessment. But there is more. Napoleon's actions as well as his own words indicate an unlimited drive for power, provoking ever greater resistance and continued war. Throughout history, there have been other leaders whose actions directly provoked war (Louis XIV, Frederick II, Adolf Hitler, and Benito Mussolini come to mind), but it remains dubious whether a "great man" theory can be sustained as an explanation for many major and prolonged wars. Still, for the Napoleonic wars there is surprising agreement on the role of Napoleon and his policies.

In the end, no general theory of causation can be considered valid for the entire period of the French revolutionary and Napoleonic wars. These wars show both continuity and change, with the element of power remaining the single unifying theme. Power, applied more extensively and supported by wider popular participation than ever before, formed the new pattern of warfare. After Napoleon's defeat, the European powers tried to return to the limited military system of the pre-revolutionary era, but they could not. The military-political situation had changed for good, and, during the next century and a half, wars in which "the full weight of the nation was thrown into the balance" became the general pattern of conflict.[37]

37 Clausewitz, *On War*, 592.

Lessons and Analogies
from the World Wars

Samuel R. Williamson, Jr.

The Origins of World War I   World War I began in
eastern Europe. The war started when Serbia, Austria-Hungary,
Russia, and Germany decided that war or the risk of war was an
acceptable policy option. In the aftermath of the Balkan wars of
1912/13, the decision-makers in eastern Europe acted more asser-
tively and less cautiously. The Serbian government displayed little
willingness to negotiate with Vienna; in fact, some elements of
the Belgrade regime worked to challenge, by violent means if
necessary, Habsburg rule in Bosnia and Herzegovina. Austria-
Hungary, threatened anew by the Balkan problems, grew more
anxious about its declining position and became more enamored
of the recent successes of its militant diplomacy. Having encouraged the creation of the Balkan League and benefited from Serbia's
military triumphs, Russian policymakers displayed a new aggressiveness toward their Danubian neighbor. The German leadership, for its part, fretted more than ever about its relative position
in the European system and found the new Russian self-confidence troubling. Then came the Sarajevo assassinations on 28
June 1914 of Archduke Franz Ferdinand, heir to the Austrian
throne, and his wife Sophie. Within a month of these deaths,
Austria-Hungary and Serbia would be at war, followed by the
rest of Europe shortly thereafter.[1]

   Although the war began in eastern Europe, the events there
have received only modest attention from historians. This neglect
is not entirely surprising, given the Versailles "war guilt" clause
against Germany and subsequent efforts to defend or denounce

Samuel R. Williamson, Jr., is Professor of History and Provost of The University of
North Carolina at Chapel Hill. He is the author of The Origins of a Tragedy: July 1914
(Arlington Heights, Ill., 1981).
   The author is indebted to Scott Lackey, Jonathan Randel, and Russel Van Wyk for
research assistance.

1   The most perceptive recent study is James Joll, The Origins of the First World War (New
York, 1984). For a survey of the issues, see Williamson, The Origins of a Tragedy: July
1914 (Arlington Heights, Ill., 1981). See also Steven E. Miller (ed.), Military Strategy and
the Origins of the First World War: An International Security Reader (Princeton, 1985).

the war guilt accusations. The interwar documentary collections encouraged this emphasis on Germany and Anglo-German relations, as did post-1945 access to the Western archives. Since 1961 Fischer and the Hamburg school have clarified further the irresponsible nature of German policy before and during the July crisis. Yet most scholarship has eschewed a broader focus, such as that used by Fay and Albertini, concentrating instead on single countries or focusing almost exclusively on the west European origins of the war. Too much concentration on Berlin's role slights developments taking place in Austria-Hungary, Russia, Serbia, and the Balkan states in the months before July 1914.[2]

Recent articles, multi-volume background works, and new monographs by scholars on both sides of the Iron Curtain offer insights into the east European origins of the July crisis—the linkages between events there and the onset of the larger war. These new studies also help to illumine the motivations and behaviors of the decision-makers in Belgrade, St. Petersburg, Vienna, and Budapest.[3] In seeking to prevent a future major war,

2 Fritz Fischer's two major works are *Griff nach der Weltmacht* (Düsseldorf, 1961) and *Krieg der Illusionen* (Düsseldorf, 1969); both are available in translation. See also *idem, Juli 1914: Wir sind nicht hineingeschlittert: Das Staatsgeheimnis um die Riezler-Tagebücher: Eine Streitschrift* (Hamburg, 1983). Among his students, see Imanuel Geiss (ed.), *Julikrise und Kriegsausbruch 1914: Eine Dokumentensammlung* (Hannover, 1963–64), 2v, and his English selection of documents, *July 1914: The Outbreak of the First World War: Selected Documents* (New York, 1967). Sidney B. Fay, *The Origins of the World War* (New York, 1928), 2v; Luigi Albertini, *The Origins of the War of 1914* (London, 1952–57), 3v.
3 Published by the Austrian Academy of Sciences and edited by Adam Wandruszka and Peter Urbanitsch, the series on *Die Habsburgermonarchie, 1848–1918* has volumes on the economy, nationalities, administration, and religion; one on the army will appear soon. József Galántai, *Die Österreichisch-Ungarische Monarchie und der Weltkrieg* (Budapest, 1979); István Diószegi, *Hungarians in the Ballhausplatz: Studies on the Austro-Hungarian Common Foreign Policy* (Budapest, 1983). For a recent East German view, see Willibald Gutsche, *Sarajevo 1914: Vom Attentat zum Weltkrieg* (Berlin, 1984). For Western scholarship, see Francis Roy Bridge, *From Sadowa to Sarajevo: The Foreign Policy of Austria-Hungary, 1866–1918* (London, 1972); John D. Treadway, *The Falcon and the Eagle: Montenegro and Austria-Hungary* (West Lafayette, Ind., 1982); Norman Stone, *The Eastern Front, 1914–1917* (London, 1975); Richard Crampton, *The Hollow Detente: Anglo-German Relations in the Balkans, 1911–1914* (London, 1979). See also Williamson, "Vienna and July 1914: The Origins of the Great War Once More," in Peter Pastor and Williamson (eds.), *Essays on World War I: Origins and Prisoners of War* (New York, 1983), 9–36. E. Willis Brooks has brought the following recent Russian titles to my attention: Iurii Alekseevich Pisarev, *Velikie derzhavy i Balkany nakanune pervoi mirovoi voiny* [*The Great Powers and the Balkans on the Eve of the First World War*] (Moscow, 1985); Andreï Sergeevich Avetian, *Russko-germanskie diplomaticheskie otnosheniia nakanune pervoi mirovoi voiny, 1910–1914* [*Russo-German Diplomatic Relations on the Eve of the First World War, 1910–1914*] (Moscow, 1985).

the crisis of the summer of 1914 remains fundamental to an understanding of the issues of peace and war.

Historians often talk about the long-term origins of World War I —those physical, intellectual, emotional, and political activities that created parameters and left legacies that influenced the July crisis. Although these causes remain a central feature of all recent historical works, new research reveals an almost quantum alteration in our perception of the character and nature of the causes of the war. Recent studies—based upon rigorous archival research—make clear the dramatic changes that took place after 1911 in the relationships resulting from the alliances and ententes, military planning, imperial attitudes, nationalism, and confidence about the future of the governmental systems.

By 1912, the Triple Entente and Triple Alliance had been consolidated by the Bosnian crises of 1908–09 and the Moroccan tensions of 1911. Russia, Britain, and France formed, along with Russia's Serbian client, the Triple Entente; Austria-Hungary, Italy, and Germany comprised, with their secret ally King Carol of Rumania, the Triple Alliance. In the months before July 1914, these two groupings collided with each other on fundamental issues, although brief periods of cooperation and apparent détente existed.

From 1912 to the eve of the war, France and Russia worked to convert the Triple Entente into an alliance. Paris pressed London to confer with Russia about naval issues, while assiduously working to define their own military and naval arrangements with Britain. In the spring of 1914, Sir Edward Grey, the most insular of British foreign secretaries, and Winston Churchill, First Lord of the Admiralty, agreed to start negotiations with St. Petersburg. Almost immediately German intelligence learned of this development. When asked about such conversations, Grey denied that any were underway. Berlin thus found itself unable to trust Grey's assurances about these talks and could only speculate that Britain had also made military and naval arrangements with France.[4]

4 Zara Steiner, *Britain and the Origins of the First World War* (London, 1977); Francis Harry Hinsley (ed.), *British Foreign Policy under Sir Edward Grey* (Cambridge, 1977); Keith M. Wilson, *The Policy of the Entente: Essays on the Determinants of British Foreign Policy, 1904–1914* (Cambridge, 1985); Williamson, *The Politics of Grand Strategy: Britain and France*

228 | SAMUEL R. WILLIAMSON, JR.

During 1912 and 1913, the Franco-Russian alliance within the Triple Entente assumed new meaning. The French wanted immediate Russian pressure on Germany if war came and invested capital in railway construction that could be used to facilitate the movement of Russian troops. Raymond Poincaré, first as premier and then as president of France, brought new vigor to French diplomacy and spared no effort to strengthen the Paris-St. Petersburg connection. Despite socialist opposition, he even managed to secure passage of a three-year military service law that increased the number of French troops on active duty.[5]

Russo-Serbian relations had also grown closer in the years before Sarajevo. St. Petersburg had played mid-wife to the Balkan League, a pact signed in the spring of 1912 and directed against both the Ottoman Empire and the Habsburg monarchy. Vigorous Russian diplomatic support, along with shipments of military supplies during the Balkan wars, buttressed the ties. In the spring of 1914, Nikola Pašić, the Serbian premier, depended upon Russian support in his disputes with the Serbian military. Indeed, when Pašić resigned in June 1914, the Russians pressured King Peter I to restore him to the premiership.[6]

The leaders of the Triple Alliance were also active in the months following the Agadir crisis over Morocco. In late 1911 Berlin and Vienna backed Rome in its war with the Ottoman Empire over Tripoli. At the end of 1912, the partners renewed the alliance for another five years and reinstituted military and naval planning, though neither Berlin nor Vienna expected much

---

Prepare for War, 1904–1914 (Cambridge, Mass., 1969); Paul Halpern, *The Mediterranean Naval Situation, 1908–1914* (Cambridge, Mass., 1971). Bernt von Siebert, third secretary of the Russian embassy in London, was the source of Berlin's information; see Fischer, *Krieg*, 632–635.

5 John F. V. Keiger, *France and the Origins of the First World War* (London, 1983); Gerd Krumeich (trans. Marion Berghahn), *Armaments and Politics in France on the Eve of the First World War: The Introduction of Three-Year Conscription, 1913–1914* (Dover, N.H., 1984); Jack Snyder, *The Ideology of the Offensive: Military Decision Making and the Disasters of 1914* (Ithaca, 1984); Thomas Hayes Conner, "Parliament and the Making of Foreign Policy: France under the Third Republic, 1875–1914," unpub. Ph.D. diss. (Chapel Hill, 1983).

6 Vladimir Dedijer, *The Road to Sarajevo* (New York, 1966), 385–388; Barbara Jelavich, *History of the Balkans* (Cambridge, 1983), II, 106–112; Hans Übersberger, *Österreich zwischen Russland und Serbien* (Köln, 1958); Andrew Rossos, *Russia and the Balkans: Inter-Balkan Rivalries and Russian Foreign Policy, 1908–1914* (Toronto, 1981). Publication of the Serbian diplomatic documents, now in progress, will facilitate a study of Serbo-Russian relations before 1914.

support from their southern ally. Furthermore, the three partners maneuvered for position with each other over a potential division of Turkish Asia Minor, and a new issue—Albania and its future—emerged after the Balkan wars as a point of friction between Vienna and Rome.[7]

Vienna's problems were not confined to Italy. The Balkan wars had shaken Vienna's confidence about German support if a crisis arose. On three occasions the Habsburgs had nearly gone to war; in each instance the Germans had counseled caution and prudence. To be sure, Kaiser Wilhelm II talked boisterously of strong action, but the German political leadership spoke about negotiation. As a result, there was considerable apprehension in Vienna over Berlin's possible behavior in a crisis involving either Serbia or Russia or both.[8]

The major problem confronting the Austro-German allies was not their own relationship, but evidence that Bucharest would probably defect from the alliance. If King Carol opted out, Austria-Hungary faced a new and nearly intolerable strategic situation. Furthermore, Rumanian nationalism, stirred by the successes of the month-long second Balkan war, demanded changes in the status of the three million Rumanians living in Transylvania under Magyar domination. Budapest, however, offered virtually no concessions. Thus the Rumanian problem, like the Serbian issue, encompassed both a domestic and a diplomatic dimension. For Vienna, distinctions between *Aussenpolitik* and *Innenpolitik* simply did not exist. Foreign policy provided much of the raison d'être for the Habsburg state, but foreign affairs also furnished most of the threats to its future.[9]

---

7 Michael Behnen, *Rüstung—Bündnis—Sicherheit: Dreibund und informeller Imperialismus, 1900–1908* (Tübingen, 1985); Richard Bosworth, *Italy and the Approach of the First World War* (New York, 1983) and *Italy, the Least of the Great Powers* (Cambridge, 1979). On Habsburg concerns about Albania, see Ludwig Bittner and Übersberger (eds.), *Österreich-Ungarns Aussenpolitik von der bosnischen Krise 1908 bis zum Kriegsausbruch* (hereafter *Aussen*) (Vienna, 1930), VII, VIII; Bridge, "'*Tarde venientibus ossa*': Austro-Hungarian Colonial Aspirations in Asia Minor, 1913–14," *Middle Eastern Studies*, VI (1970), 319–330.

8 Fischer, *Krieg*, 289–323; Bridge, *Sadowa*, 360–368; Erwin Hölze, *Die Selbstentmachtung Europas* (Frankfurt am M., 1975), 269–278; Hugo Hantsch, *Leopold Graf Berchtold: Grandseigneur und Staatsmann* (Graz, 1963), II, 520–539.

9 Keith Hitchins, "The Nationality Problem in Hungary: István Tisza and the Rumanian National Party, 1906–1914," *Journal of Modern History*, LIII (1981), 619–651; Gheorghe Nicolae Căzan and Serban Rădulescu-Zoner, *România si Tripla Alianță, 1878–1914* (Bucharest, 1979).

In a desperate effort to rescue the situation, Vienna sent Ottokar Czernin, a confidant of Franz Ferdinand, as minister to Bucharest in late 1913. Czernin achieved nothing. Then in June the czar and czarina visited Constantsa in Rumania. During the trip Serge Sazonov, the Russian foreign minister, actually crossed into Transylvania in a defiant show of support for the Rumanians living in Austria-Hungary. These events thoroughly alarmed Vienna. More than ever, Foreign Minister Count Leopold Berchtold and his associates believed that Bucharest was lost to the alliance and that Russia was determined to cause problems at all costs.[10]

Russia also antagonized Germany and Austria-Hungary more directly. The Liman von Sanders affair, a Russo-German dispute over whether the German general would have actual command over Turkish troops in Constantinople, embroiled St. Petersburg and Berlin for weeks in late 1913. The crisis created genuine concern in Berlin and accelerated a series of studies by the German general staff of Russian mobilization plans. For the first time since March 1909, the two Baltic powers were in direct confrontation, and this time St. Petersburg, not Berlin, was the protagonist.[11]

Relations between St. Petersburg and Vienna were more fragile still. The Austrians held the Russians partly responsible for the Balkan wars. Vienna had difficulty forgetting St. Petersburg's tactic in the fall of 1912, when it kept an additional 1.2 million troops on duty to check any Habsburg move against Serbia. Vienna had responded by calling up 200,000 reservists, stationing many of them in Galicia. The border tensions led to bank runs and public unrest in the Habsburg provinces; the potential conflict also prompted passage of emergency legislation in Austria and Hungary in December 1912 in the event that war should come. Not until March 1913, after extensive negotiations, did the two powers begin to demobilize troops and tensions abate. But the residual perceptions of the incident were not so easily

10   Czernin to Berchtold, 22 June 1914, *Aussen*, VIII, no. 9902; also Czernin to Berchtold, 22 June 1914, Berchtold Archiv, no. 9, Haus-, Hof-, und Staatsarchiv, Vienna; Hantsch, *Berchtold*, II, 545–557.
11   Fischer, *Krieg*, 481–515; Stone, "Austria-Hungary," in Ernest R. May (ed.), *Knowing One's Enemies: Intelligence Assessment before the Two World Wars* (Princeton, 1984), 43–48; Holger Herwig, "Imperial Germany," *ibid.*, 86–92; William C. Fuller, Jr. "The Russian Empire," *ibid.*, 115–123.

altered, certainly not among the military leaders in either St. Petersburg or Vienna.[12]

Despite the growing tensions, there were moments of co-operation and concession. The rhetoric of Anglo-German relations was muted somewhat; the powers cooperated to keep the Balkan turmoil within bounds in the spring and summer of 1913. Austrians invested funds in a Russian armaments factory, and royal visits continued. Yet the clashes of 1911 and thereafter were not easily forgotten. The future of the Balkans and the Macedonian inheritance of the Ottoman Empire were significant issues. The Eastern Question and the fate of Ottoman holdings in the Balkans, the bane of British foreign secretaries in the nineteenth century, had now become a problem for all foreign ministers.[13]

No group of decision-makers recognized this new danger more quickly than the military commanders. Everywhere the doctrine of offensive warfare and the "short war illusion" prevailed. The French revamped their war plans after 1911 to conform to these doctrines. The Germans, British, and Austro-Hungarians further refined their offensive schemes in the belief that offensive warfare alone offered the possibility of quick success. No one probed the question of what would happen if success did not in fact come quickly at the start of a war. Sufficient intelligence information existed about the manpower pools and general intentions of the opposing powers; what remained uncertain was the location and timing of the deployment. Few realized that stalemate could also be the result of offensive operations. Nor were general staffs cognizant of their own differing conceptions of what mobilization actually meant for the other governments; for some it meant actual war and for others, the mere possibility of war. Questionable assumptions had now become dogma.[14]

12 Ernst Christian Helmreich, *The Diplomacy of the Balkan Wars, 1912–1913* (Cambridge, Mass., 1938), 157–164, 281–290; Williamson, "Military Dimensions of Habsburg-Romanov Relations during the Era of the Balkan Wars," in Béla K. Király and Dimitrie Djordevic (eds.), *East Central European Society and the Balkan Wars* (New York, 1987), 318–337.
13 Paul Kennedy, *The Rise of Anglo-German Antagonism, 1860–1914* (London, 1980); Steiner, *Britain*, 42–78. Cf. Volker R. Berghahn, *Germany and the Approach of War in 1914* (New York, 1973), 165–185; Fischer, *Krieg*, 613–635.
14 Snyder, *Ideology*; Joll, *Origins*, 58–91; Lancelot L. Farrar, Jr., *The Short War Illusion* (Santa Barbara, 1973); Stone, *Eastern*; Douglas Porch, *The March to the Marne: The French*

No generals faced greater problems than did the Habsburg commanders after 1912. To the south, Serbia, their most formidable foe, had fought well in the Balkan wars, had virtually doubled its territory and population base, and possessed seasoned military leaders. Rumania's probable defection added another border to defend, and Bulgaria's defeat in the second Balkan war reduced its ability to offset either Serbia or Rumania. Reports from Berlin were even more disturbing; the Russians were shortening their mobilization timetables by five to seven days. Each day gained by the Russians endangered the Schlieffen-Moltke plan, in turn putting a higher premium on a Habsburg assault against Russia. In May 1914 General Franz Conrad von Hötzendorf, chief of the Austro-Hungarian general staff, met Helmuth von Moltke, his German counterpart, to review the increased Russian threat. Conrad asked for more German troops in the east to protect Germany (and Austria-Hungary); Moltke pressed for more immediate Austro-Hungarian action against Russia with only secondary action against Serbia. The two generals failed to reach agreement. Conrad had always wanted to defeat the troublesome Serbians, yet he could not ignore the Russian threat. He never overcame this dilemma.[15]

After 1912 the European military and naval leaders grew less confident. Troop increases and the continuing naval race (though with less rhetoric) fueled fears, as did the sudden shifts of military fortune in the Balkans. Everywhere the military leaders warned their civilian superiors of the dangers of falling behind in the race for military supremacy. The militarization of attitudes and unspoken assumptions, even in Britain, grew more noticeable and pervasive. Militarism, despite occasional signs of pacificism, remained a dynamic factor.[16]

Army, 1871–1914 (Cambridge, 1981); Arthur J. Marder, *From the Dreadnought to Scapa Flow. I: The Road to War, 1904–14* (London, 1961); Gunther E. Rothenberg, *The Army of Francis Joseph* (West Lafayette, Ind., 1976); Richard Ned Lebow, *Between Peace and War: The Nature of International Crisis* (Baltimore, 1981); Kennedy (ed.), *The War Plans of the Great Powers, 1880–1914* (London, 1979); Williamson, *Politics.*
15 Conrad's memoirs are valuable. See his *Aus meiner Dienstzeit, 1906–1918* (Vienna, 1921–25), III, 665–675; Rothenberg, *Army,* 172–176; Stone, "Die Mobilmachung der österreichisch-ungarischen Armee 1914," *Militärgeschichtliche Mitteilungen,* XVI (1974), 67–95. See also Kurt Peball's edition of Conrad's private notes, *Private Aufzeichnungen: Erste Veröffentlichungen aus den Papieren des k.u.k. Generalstabs-Chef* (Vienna, 1977).
16 Joll, "1914: The Unspoken Assumptions," in Hannesjoachim Wilhelm Koch (ed.), *The Origins of the First World War: Great Power Rivalry and German War Aims* (New York,

Closely linked with militarism was another long-term cause of war: imperialism. It was reinforced by ideas of Social Darwinism and racism as well. After the second Moroccan crisis in the summer of 1911, imperialism became more a Balkan phenomenon and less an Asian or African one. As the Eastern Question flared anew, the dangers for Europe, in the context of the rigidity of both the alliance and the entente, increased exponentially.

Three examples illustrate the dangerous changes. First, in the autumn of 1911, the Russians renewed their pressure on the Straits issue. Second, the Italians were reluctant to return Ottoman territory in the Aegean which they seized in their war with Turkey in 1912. Indeed, Rome and Berlin actually plotted to carve out potential gains in Asia Minor. Third, Bosnia and Herzegovina represented a special part of the Ottoman legacy. Annexed by Vienna in 1908 after thirty years of de facto Habsburg administration, the two provinces were Habsburg imperial gains at Ottoman expense. Bosnia and Herzegovina now became the focus of South Slav agitation for greater Serbian and/or Yugoslavian unity. Franz Joseph had, however, no intention of relinquishing the two provinces which represented the only gains of his long reign. Vienna would protect its acquisitions just as the British, French, and Italians had protected their gains from the gradual breakup of the Ottoman Empire.[17]

Nationalism as a long-term cause of World War I has received sustained historical attention. Nationalism and a mixture of chauvinism and racism were prevalent in both Europe and North America. In Germany, Britain, Russia, and France, nationalism often served as a centripetal factor.[18]

By contrast, in the Habsburg monarchy nationalism had a disruptive function. In Rumania, the impact of nationalism was growing, and St. Petersburg encouraged intensive campaigns

1972), 307–328. On the peace movement in Germany, see Roger Chickering, *Imperial Germany and a World without War: The Peace Movement in German Society, 1892–1914* (Princeton, 1975).

17 Little has been written about the two provinces, but the following books are helpful: Peter F. Sugar, *Industrialization of Bosnia-Hercegovina, 1878–1918* (Seattle, 1963); Robert J. Donia, *Islam under the Double Eagle: The Muslims of Bosnia and Hercegovina, 1878–1914* (New York, 1981).

18 Keiger, *France*; Fischer, *Krieg*; Bosworth, *Italy and the Approach*; Steiner, *Britain*, treat the issue of nationalism. For Russian attitudes, see Dominic C. B. Lieven, *Russia and the Origins of the First World War* (New York, 1983).

among the Ruthenians in Galicia and Bukovina. Although pan-Slavic propaganda did not match the intensity of the challenge posed by the South Slav demands, Russia's subvention of pan-Slavism provided still one more reason for Vienna to distrust its northern neighbor.[19]

The Habsburgs' most dangerous threat from nationalism lay along its southern border. The victorious Balkan states stimulated a new self-confidence among the monarchy's South Slav citizens. Serbian and Croatian political leaders talked openly of greater Yugoslavian unity. In Croatia political violence intensified. The Balkan wars not only revolutionized the geographical situation; they also revived and accentuated feelings of South Slav unity.[20]

Vienna held Serbia directly (and the Russians less directly) responsible for much of the mounting friction. Their annoyance, indeed anger, had basis in fact. After the 1908–09 Bosnian crisis, Belgrade, in spite of commitments to the contrary, developed a propaganda machine to inculcate the ideals of Yugoslavian unity (under Serbian leadership) among the Slavs living in the Habsburg realms. Political cells like the Narodna Odbrana served as instruments for political activity.[21]

Far more dangerous, however, was a secret organization known as the Black Hand, a group of Serbian military and political figures sworn to a violent solution to the South Slav problem. Although Habsburg intelligence was aware of the Black Hand, it never fully appreciated the strength of its commitment to the use of violence. Among the members, none was more sinister than Dragutin Dimitrijević (known as Apis), who participated in the 1903 murder of King Alexander of the Obrenović dynasty. By 1912, Apis had become chief of Serbian military intelligence. Although it is unlikely that the exact details will ever be established, Apis played a major part in the plot against Franz Ferdinand. In his plans for the assassination, Apis and his associates exploited the nationalism of young students and the inability of

19 Two excellent recent studies are Raymond Pearson, *National Minorities in Eastern Europe, 1848–1945* (London, 1983); Wandruszka and Urbanitsch (eds.), *Die Völker des Reiches* (Vienna, 1980), 2v. See also Robert A. Kann and Zdenek V. David, *The Peoples of the Eastern Habsburg Lands, 1526–1918* (Seattle, 1984).

20 Jelavich, *History*, II, 79–112; Dedijer, *Road*, 160–284; Ivo Banac, *The National Question in Yugoslavia: Origins, History, Politics* (Ithaca, 1984).

21 Dedijer, *Road*, 261–284. See also Friedrich Würthle, *Die Spur führt nach Belgrad: Die Hintergründe des Dramas von Sarajevo 1914* (Vienna, 1975).

the Pašić government to control the Black Hand. Serbia's sponsorship of South Slav agitation inside the Habsburg monarchy posed threats of an immediate and practical nature for the Habsburg leadership. For Vienna, Serbia represented the twin issues of state security and state survival.

The decay in the effectiveness of the political structures of the Habsburg, Hohenzollern, and Romanov regimes is noted as a final long-term cause of the war. After 1911, demands for constitutional change in Prussia increased, the growth of the socialist party frightened the established elites, and Kaiser Wilhelm II's ineffectiveness were matters of public comment. Certainly Chancellor Theobald von Bethmann Hollweg and his associates feared for the future of the existing political order. Much the same could be said of Russia where the abortive revolt of 1905 had already revealed the weaknesses of the czar's regime.

The future of Austria-Hungary after the death of Franz Joseph, an octogenarian, was already a matter of international speculation. In Vienna and Budapest, linked by a common monarch, common army, and common foreign policy, the blows of the Balkan wars and the prospect of Franz Ferdinand as ruler worried many. Yet the archduke desperately wanted the dynasty to survive, and he thought a pro-Russian foreign policy would help him achieve that goal. A force for peace during the Balkan wars, Franz Ferdinand had supported Berchtold's policy of militant diplomacy, but not militant action, against Conrad, his own protégé. The archduke's death removed a force for peace and provided the pretext for decisions in Vienna that launched the third Balkan war. Within these parameters, the decisions during late June and early July 1914 are critical.[22]

22 On internal pressures and the causes of war, see Arno J. Mayer, *The Persistence of the Old Regime: Europe to the Great War* (New York, 1981), 275–329. See also Joll, *Origins*, 92–122. On Germany, see Fischer, *Krieg*, 289–323, 663–738; David Kaiser, "Germany and the Origins of the First World War," *Journal of Modern History*, LV (1983), 442–474; Konrad Jarausch, *The Enigmatic Chancellor: Bethmann Hollweg and the Hubris of Imperial Germany* (New Haven, 1973), 153–170. On Russia, see Lieven, *Russia*, 139–151. On Austria-Hungary, see the period piece, Henry Wickham Steed, *The Hapsburg Monarchy* (London, 1914, 2nd ed.); Arthur J. May, *The Hapsburg Monarchy, 1867–1914* (Cambridge, Mass., 1951); Joachim Remak, "The Healthy Invalid: How Doomed Was the Habsburg Empire?" *Journal of Modern History*, XLI (1969), 127–143; idem, "1914: The Origins of the Third Balkan War Reconsidered," *ibid.*, XLII (1971); Robert A. Kann, *Erzherzog Franz Ferdinand Studien* (Vienna, 1976), 15–25; Williamson, "Influence, Power, and the Policy Process: The Case of Franz Ferdinand," *The Historical Journal*, XVII (1974), 417–434.

Many historians have devoted their attention to the July crisis, and any analysis here risks injustice to the complexity of historical thought concerning the events of that summer. To facilitate a systematic examination of that period, this essay focuses upon a number of key decisions taken during July. Each decision, one can argue, led to the next, and in the absence of any one of them, the crisis might have been averted. One may quarrel with the choices or the emphasis, but most will agree that the decisions discussed here were important, possibly decisive, on the road to war.[23]

The first steps toward war began in Vienna. The deaths of Franz Ferdinand and his wife Sophie shocked Berchtold and the other civilian ministers who wanted action against Serbia. Strongly supporting this view were Conrad and General Alexander von Krobatin, the minister of war. They were joined from Sarajevo by General Oskar Potiorek, who exaggerated the post-Sarajevo unrest in Bosnia and Herzegovina to justify immediate military action against Belgrade. Put simply, Potiorek demanded that Vienna should go to war to protect the two provinces. Thus, in early July, well before Germany indicated strong support, Vienna planned retribution against Serbia. Only István Tisza, the Hungarian premier, disliked this prospect.[24]

With the conversion of Franz Joseph to a policy of retribution, Berchtold had the crucial support he needed within the Habsburg government. The emperor/king's decision stemmed in part from evidence of Belgrade's complicity in the murders, for police interrogations in Sarajevo had quickly established the conspiracy of Gavrilo Princip and his associates and the possible involvement of some members of the Serbian government. By July 3, Franz Joseph was talking of the need for action. For the next ten days, Tisza was his only senior adviser who remained unconvinced. But his reluctance to act should not obscure the fact

---

23 Joll, *Origins*, has the most current bibliography; Dwight E. Lee, *Europe's Crucial Years: The Diplomatic Background of World War I, 1902–1914* (Hanover, N.H., 1974); Leonard Charles Frederick Turner, *Origins of the First World War* (New York, 1970); Stephan Verosta, *Theorie und Realität von Bündnissen* (Vienna, 1971).

24 Conrad, *Aus meiner Dienstzeit*, IV, 13–36; Hantsch, *Berchtold*, II, 557–569; Leon von Bilinski, *Wspominienia i dokumenty, 1846–1922* [*Memoirs and Documents, 1846–1922*] (Warsaw, 1924), I, 274–278; Potiorek's reports from Sarajevo are found in part in *Aussen*, VIII. See also Potiorek's separate reports to the military leadership in Nachlass Potiorek, Kriegsarchiv, Vienna.

that the Habsburg civilian and military leadership wanted to punish Belgrade for the deaths at Sarajevo. No pressure from Berlin was required for Vienna to reach that decision.[25]

The second step in the July crisis was Berlin's decision to support Habsburg military action against Belgrade. Kaiser Wilhelm II genuinely grieved over the Sarajevo victims and wanted action against Serbia, as did Chancellor Bethmann Hollweg. Thus both men proved receptive to the Hoyos mission in which Vienna asked for assurances of German support and indicated its plan to take radical action against Serbia. On July 5 and 6 Berlin gave Vienna the backing it sought. In contrast to its earlier hesitations during the Balkan wars, this time Berlin supported Vienna's desire to act. Thus, by July 6 Berchtold had assurances from Berlin and, he hoped, a deterrent against possible Russian intervention.[26]

Why did the German leaders endorse Austro-Hungarian action against Serbia? Alliance loyalties, personal feelings, and Bethmann Hollweg's desire for an assertive German policy are among the traditional explanations. To these reasons have been added Germany's desire to intimidate the Triple Entente and to end Serbian affronts against its Habsburg ally. The German decision had many fateful consequences.

Vienna probably would not have gone to war without Berlin's assurances of support. However, the unilateral and provocative measures taken by Vienna during the Balkan wars, often with scant German knowledge, suggest that Berchtold and Conrad might well have staged some kind of military action (for example, a border incident or alleged bombardment of a Habsburg town) without a firm German guarantee. In any event, in

25 On the investigation in Sarajevo, see Würthle, *Spur*, and idem, *Dokumente zum Sarajevoprozess: Ein Quellenbericht* (Vienna, 1978). For one indication of Franz Joseph's thinking, see Heinrich von Tschirschky to Bethmann Hollweg, 2 July 1914, in Max Montgelas and Walther Schücking (eds.), *Outbreak of the World War: German Documents Collected by Karl Kautsky* (New York, 1924) (hereafter *Kautsky Documents*), no. 11; Kann, *Kaiser Franz Joseph und der Ausbruch des Weltkrieges* (Vienna, 1971). On Tisza see Galántai, *Weltkrieg*, 251–278; Gabor Vermes, *István Tisza: The Liberal Vision and Conservative Statecraft of a Magyar Nationalist* (New York, 1985), and Burián's diary entries for 7–14 July 1914, in István Diószegi, "Aussenminister Stephen Graf Burian: Biographie und Tagebuchstelle," *Annales: Universitatis Scientiarum Budapestinesis, Sectio Historica*, VIII (1966), 205–206.
26 Fischer, *Krieg*, 686–694; Fritz Fellner, "Die 'Mission Hoyos'," in Vasa Čubrilović (ed.), *Recueil des travaux aux assises scientifiques internationales: Les grandes puissances et la Serbie à la veille de la Première guerre mondiale* (Belgrade, 1976), IV, 387–418; Albertini, *Origins*, II, 133–150.

July 1914 Austria-Hungary wanted action against Serbia; the Germans certainly did not discourage it; and they soon found themselves pulled into the crisis.[27]

Even though Vienna had obtained Berlin's pledge of support against Serbia by July 6, more than two weeks elapsed before the ultimatum was presented to Belgrade on July 23. A major factor explaining this delay lies in the organization of the Habsburg military. Early in his tenure as chief of staff, Conrad instituted a policy of "harvest" leaves to appease the monarchy's agrarian interests. This policy allowed soldiers to go home to help in the fields and then return to their duty stations for the annual summer maneuvers. In the days after Sarajevo, sizable numbers of Habsburg soldiers were scattered over the empire on harvest leave. Cancellation of the leaves would have alerted Europe to the impending military action, disrupted farm production, and risked confusion concerning the railway's mobilization plans. Conrad therefore decided to let the current leaves run their normal course, but to cancel any new harvest leaves. As a result, most of those leaves already granted would end by July 21 or 22. Conrad's decision gave Berchtold the parameters for the timing of the July crisis.[28]

Another cause of delay involved convincing Tisza to permit military action against Serbia. When the Common Ministerial Council met on July 7, the Magyar premier initially persisted in opposing military action but, by the end of the lengthy session, his resistance had weakened. Tisza then appealed to Franz Joseph, only to find that his sovereign was strongly committed to action. In his efforts to sway Tisza, Berchtold stressed Germany's support for action and, possibly more important, warned of Rumania's probable defection from the alliance. The foreign minister apparently suggested that a failure to deal with Serbia would encourage Bucharest to press the Transylvania issue ever more insistently. Whatever the arguments, Berchtold convinced Tisza that intervention was required. On July 15, the Magyar leader met with

27 See Fritz Stern, "Bethmann Hollweg and the War: The Limits of Responsibility," in Leonard Krieger and Stern (eds.), *The Responsibility of Power* (Garden City, 1967), 271–307. Fay argued that Austria-Hungary pulled Berlin along (*Origins*, II, 198–223).

28 General Staff memorandum, "Vorbereitende Massnahmen," n.d, but seen by Conrad on 6 July 1914, Generalstab: Operations Buro, faszikel 43, Kriegsarchiv, Vienna; Conrad, *Aus meiner Dienstzeit*, IV, 13–87.

the Hungarian House of Deputies and openly hinted of the need for action. His only requirements were that Vienna would present an ultimatum to Belgrade and would pledge not to annex additional Slavic territory.[29]

A further reason for Vienna's delay was more prosaic. Poincaré and René Viviani, the French premier, were scheduled to be in St. Petersburg on a state visit from July 20 to July 23. Understandably, Berchtold wanted the ultimatum presented after the French had left St. Petersburg. As a result, it was finally delivered at 5 p.m. on Thursday, July 23, when the French leaders were at sea.

Vienna used the hiatus of mid-July to mislead the other European governments about its intentions. After July 12 Berchtold restrained press comment about Serbia, and the journals in Vienna and Budapest recounted little about the adjoining state. Conrad went hiking in the mountains; Franz Joseph stayed at Bad Ischl; and the other Habsburg leaders carried out their customary duties. The Danubian monarchy appeared to have returned to normal.[30]

Berchtold had another motive for his deception. In mid-July, he discovered that on July 11 Berlin had informed Hans von Flotow, its ambassador in Rome, about the possibility of Habsburg action against Serbia. Shortly afterward, Flotow conveyed this message to Antonio San Giuliano, the Italian foreign minister; not surprisingly, San Giuliano cabled the information to Vienna. When the telegram reached Vienna, the Austrian codebreakers duly deciphered it, thereby exposing the indiscretion of both Germany and Italy. Berchtold could only assume that San Giuliano had also sent the same information to St. Petersburg and Belgrade. Henceforth, he gave Berlin no further details about his plans, including the text of the ultimatum, until the very last moment. Later, this secrecy would be held against Berchtold as a sign of duplicity; at the time, it appeared to be the only way he could maintain his options.[31]

---

29 Galántai, *Weltkrieg*, 258–271. See also Norman Stone, "Hungary and the Crisis of July 1914," *Journal of Contemporary History*, I (1966), 153–170; *Fremdenblatt*, 16 July 1914.
30 Berchtold used the Literary Bureau of the foreign ministry to help with the press; his efforts were generally successful, but the stock market continued to show signs of uneasiness.
31 Gottlieb von Jagow to Flotow, (tel.) 11 July 1914, *Kautsky Documents*, no. 33; Habs-

The Common Ministerial Council met secretly in Vienna on July 19 to review the ultimatum. Although none present believed Belgrade could accept it, the ministers approved the ultimatum and concurrently affirmed their acquiescence to Tisza's demand that there would be no territorial annexations, only modifications of strategic boundaries in case of victory. Conrad reportedly said, when leaving the meeting, "We will see; before the Balkan war the powers also talked of the status quo—after the war no one worried about it."[32] His cynicism matched the Habsburg approach to war. Vienna wanted war with Serbia in the summer of 1914; for that conflict the leaders were willing to risk a war with St. Petersburg but hoped (and believed) that Germany's support would deter the Russians.

With the ultimatum delivered, Belgrade became the focus of activity. Although the reactions of the Pašić government have never been chronicled in detail, recently published Serbian documents for the pre-1914 years confirm that senior officials in the Serbian government were aware of Apis' conspiratorial activity in May and June and sought to stop it. Yet Pašić's weakened political base made a public confrontation with the Serbian military or with Apis impossible. Apis, behind a carefully constructed non-answer to Pašić's queries about reports of agents being smuggled across the border, essentially went his own way. After the assassinations, Pašić could not, of course, offer Apis to Vienna or do more than proceed as if he and the government had known nothing.[33]

burg ambassador in Rome, Kajetan von Mérey to Berchtold, (tel.) 18 July 1914, *Aussen*, VIII, no. 10364; Berchtold to Mérey, (tel.) 20 July 1914, *ibid*, no. 10418. San Giuliano to Berlin, St. Petersburg, Belgrade, Vienna, (tels.) 16 July 1914, in Italian Foreign Ministry, *I Documenti Diplomatici Italiani* (1908–1914), XII, no. 272.

32   Conrad, *Aus meiner Dienstzeit*, IV, 92. The meeting on July 19 took place at Berchtold's private residence, not at the Ballhausplatz. Conrad came in civilian clothes and in a private car.

33   I am indebted to Dragan Živojinović for help with the documents. Dedijer, who edited the July volume of documents, drew upon them in *Road to Sarajevo*. The volume of documents is Dedijer and Života Anić (eds.), *Documents sur la politique exterieure du Royaume de Serbie [Dokumenti o spoljnoj politici kraljevine Srbije, 1903–1914]* (Belgrade, 1980). For 14 May–4 August 1914, see VII, pt. II. The general series was under the editorial direction of Vasa Čubrilovič. On knowledge of some kind of activity, see Protić (minister of the interior) to Pašić, 15 June 1914, *ibid*., no. 206; report from Sabac county on smuggling of arms across the border, 16 June 1914, *ibid*., no. 209; Apis to Putnik (chief

On one point, however, the Serbian documents are definite—Serbia had no intention of accepting any Habsburg ultimatum that infringed in the slightest on Serbian sovereignty. On July 18 Pašić, probably alerted to Vienna's intentions by the Italian minister to Belgrade, prepared a memorandum stating unequivocally that Serbia would tolerate no infringement of its sovereignty. This defiant tone persisted through the discussions in Belgrade on July 24 and 25. Thus, contrary to earlier explanations which argued that the Russians had acted to stiffen the Serbian will to resist, the Serbian documents reveal a hard-line position in Belgrade that predates the ultimatum. In taking this stance, Pašić and his colleagues were obviously confident of Russian help. In July 1914, the Serbian government showed little willingness to compromise; that stance also contributed to the escalation of the crisis.[34]

Given this new background on the Serbian attitude and the messages sent from Rome, the state visit of Poincaré and Viviani to St. Petersburg assumes new importance. Indeed, some historians have long suspected that Poincaré's talks were more detailed and more relevant to the Balkan situation than either his memoirs or the official memoranda of the visit indicate. Since the Russians probably had broken the Italian code, just as the Austrians had, St. Petersburg must have known of Vienna's intentions.

This assumption in turn helps to explain a series of actions by both French and Russian officials during the crisis, suggesting a coordinated Franco-Russian policy based upon advance knowledge. On July 21 and 22, Poincaré deliberately and abruptly warned Friedrich Szápáry, the Habsburg ambassador to Russia, against any action by Vienna, while indicating strong French support for Serbia. The content of Poincaré's message alarmed the ambassador, the president's tone even more. Given the almost total black-out of news from Vienna about its intentions, Poincaré's warnings were probably prompted by the intercepted telegrams. Certainly, given the anti-Habsburg views of Miroslav Spalajković, the Serbian minister to Russia, the merest hint of

---

of the Serbian general staff), 21 June 1914, *ibid.*, no. 230; Putnik to Pašić, 23 June 1914, *ibid.*, no. 234. On Pašić's attempts to curb the activity, see Pašić to Putnik, 24 June 1914, *ibid.*, no. 254.

34 Pašić to all Serbian missions abroad, (tels.) 18 July 1914, *Documents*, no. 462.

action by Vienna would have prompted overtures to the French and the Russians for strong declarations of support.[35]

Similarly, throughout the crisis, the French apparently never cautioned St. Petersburg to urge Serbia to show restraint. The Russian military preparations on July 25, and thereafter, were those of a government supremely confident of French support; that confidence could have come only from Poincaré and Viviani in a series of discussions in St. Petersburg. Thus, the provocative Russian diplomacy of 1912 would be repeated anew, this time with advance French approval.[36]

In Belgrade on July 23, Wladimir Giesl von Gieslingen, the Austro-Hungarian minister, delivered the forty-eight hour ultimatum. Pašić, campaigning for the general elections in the countryside, returned home to draft a reply. His response stunned even the Habsburgs. He accepted most of Vienna's demands, thus winning European sympathy, while carefully evading the essential demands. Above all, Pašić could not agree to a police investigation of the assassinations, for he knew where such an inquiry could lead. Otherwise, Pašić was so acquiescent that Serbia almost appeared to be the injured party in the proceedings. In any event, the Austrians immediately rejected Belgrade's answer as insufficient and issued orders on July 25 for partial mobilization to begin on July 28.[37]

The senior Russian ministers, meanwhile, met in St. Petersburg on July 24 and 25 to consider their options. Their conclusions can easily be construed as belligerent, provocative, and ill-designed to keep the crisis in check. Furthermore, their decisions were taken before St. Petersburg knew either the Serbian reply or the Austrian response to Serbia. With the czar's approval, the ministers agreed to a series of pre-mobilization measures: military

---

35 See Szápáry to Berchtold, (tels.) 21 July and 22 July 1914, Aussen, VIII, nos. 10461, 10497. On the Russian documents for the Poincaré visit, see Otto Hoetzsch (ed.), Die internationalen Beziehungen im Zeitalter des Imperialismus (Berlin, 1932–1934), V, nos. 1, 2. On the French records for the visit, see Ministère des Affaires Etrangères, Documents diplomatiques français, 1871–1914 (Paris, 1936), X, no. 536 which refers only to Anglo-Russian naval talks; the editors of the volumes indicate that they could find no other records. On this issue, see Albertini, Origins, II, 188–203.

36 Lieven, Origins, makes no mention of the French visit, in keeping with his general view of the lack of Russian activism during the crisis (140–141); cf. Keiger, Origins, 150–152.

37 The ultimatum and the Serbian reply have been frequently reprinted. See Geiss, July 1914, 142–146, 201–204.

cadets were promoted early, protective measures were instituted along the borders, and troops in the east were ordered to prepare to move west. From July 25 to July 30 Serbian officials in Russia sent detailed reports of Russian military measures and referred to them as partial mobilization. Simply put, the Russians initiated a series of military measures well in advance of the other great powers, although Austria-Hungary's partial mobilization came shortly after the Russian initiative. These measures, moreover, were the equivalent of a partial mobilization and accelerated the crisis far more than recent historiography has usually conceded. The Russian measures upset both Habsburg and German assumptions about St. Petersburg's probable behavior in the crisis. Furthermore, the steps disrupted the timetables in Vienna and Berlin, thus reducing the options that were available and, of course, the time to consider them.[38]

The final stage of the third Balkan war began with Austria's declaration of war on July 28 and the desultory shelling of Belgrade that same night. There was little further hostile action for several days. Neither Vienna nor Belgrade showed the slightest willingness to negotiate or to consider half-way measures. Talk of a "Halt in Belgrade" as a Habsburg military objective got nowhere with Conrad, who wanted a total reckoning with Serbia. The once reluctant Tisza now zealously pressed Conrad for action, fearing possible Rumanian movement into Transylvania against the Magyars. Already at war with Serbia, Vienna had risked the wider war that would soon follow.[39]

At this point in the July crisis the diplomatic activity shifted abruptly from eastern to western Europe and to Anglo-German efforts to contain the escalating hostilities. Wilhelm remained as fickle as ever. Returning from his North Sea cruise, the kaiser praised the Serbian response to Austria's ultimatum and suggested

38 Lieven describes some of the measures, *Origins*, 141–151; Snyder, *Ideology*, 183–198; Stone, *Eastern*, 37–60; Ulrich Trumpener, "War Premeditated? German Intelligence Operations in July 1914," *Central European History*, IX (1976), 58–85. Cf. Fischer, *Krieg*, 704–709. On the Serbian reports, see, e.g., Spalajković to Pašić, (tels.) 25, 26, 29 July 1914, Dedijer and Anić (eds.), *Documents*, nos. 570, 584, 673. See also Risto Ropponen, *Die russische Gefahr* (Helsinki, 1976), 180–206.

39 Galántai, *Weltkrieg*, 344–373; Hantsch, *Berchtold*, II, 618–647. Pašić indicated he would concede nothing; note by Pašić, dated 27 July 1914 on telegram from Berlin of the same date (Dedijer and Anić [eds.], *Documents*, no. 588).

a resolution of the crisis. Chancellor Bethmann Hollweg now wavered too; at moments Berlin sought to restrain Vienna, but the German leadership did not abandon Vienna or act responsibly to avert the crisis.

Grey was not much more helpful. Whether a more assertive British policy—action or inaction—would have decisively influenced the crisis has long fascinated historians. It can be argued that the rapidity of the crisis played a major role in the outcome, perhaps a more decisive role than Jervis suggests elsewhere in this volume.[40] Throughout the crisis, Grey failed to appreciate Vienna's desire for war. Accustomed to treating Vienna as an appendage of Berlin, Grey and his hard-line, anti-German associates believed Berlin could control Vienna. But the third largest state in Europe, with a population of fifty million, with two proud governments, and a proud monarch, wanted a resounding defeat of the Serbians. Grey's failure to acknowledge the differences between this crisis and earlier ones constitutes a major failure of perception that severely reduced Britain's ability to manipulate the crisis toward a peaceful solution. In fact, after August 1, the British leaders, like their counterparts on the Continent, sought chiefly to make their actions appear defensive in nature. Just as the Russians obliged the Germans to enter the war, so too the Germans would oblige the British by invading Belgium on their way to France.[41]

In the final days of July, Russia's general mobilization made containment of the crisis an impossibility. Historians have devoted ample attention to Russia's call for general mobilization on July 30. A frequent theme has emerged: why, if the Russians had partially mobilized during the first Balkan war, could they not have done so again? The Serbian documents offer a new interpretation of this issue. A partial mobilization was impossible because the steps St. Petersburg had ordered after July 25 were effectively already those of a partial mobilization. After the preparatory measures, only full mobilization remained. Czar Nicholas agreed to this step on July 29, but on receipt of a letter from Kaiser Wilhelm II, the czar rescinded the order. With difficulty,

40 Robert Jervis, "War and Misperception," *Journal of Interdisciplinary History*, XVIII (1988), 675–700.
41 Steiner, *Britain*, 220–241; also Albertini, *Origins*, III, 521–525; Bridge, *Great Britain*, 211–218.

Sazonov and the generals convinced the czar to reissue the order on July 30. The headquarters' troops allegedly then tore out the telephones to prevent any further delays. With Russian mobilization, Berlin faced the dilemma of a two-front campaign. Wilhelm and his associates proceeded to set in motion their own plans, plans that guaranteed a European conflict.[42]

In Vienna, meanwhile, the war plans unfolded. Conrad remained transfixed with plans for an attack on Serbia. In the north, along the Russian frontier, he planned to leave only minimal defensive forces. He persisted in his intentions despite mounting evidence that the Russians would not stand aside. His southward gaze remains almost inexplicable. Only months before, in the spring, he had worried about the Russian threat and about the implications of recent Russian behavior in the Balkan wars. Yet, he disregarded reports reaching Vienna of Russian preparations, perhaps because of his long-standing distrust of diplomats and his own desire for war. The sooner the troops were engaged, the more likely it was that Conrad would succeed in precipitating the war that he had advocated since the Bosnian crisis of 1908. And the fastest way to engage the troops was to send them south to fight against the Serbian forces. Later, when he could not ignore the movement of Russian troops toward the Habsburg lands, Conrad had to order most of the Habsburg troops to return to fight in Galicia. Not surprisingly, the soldiers were fatigued by the time that they faced the Russian units.[43]

Conrad's desire for war set him apart from most of the other actors in the July crisis. Whereas many would accede to the developing situation with regret or caution, he welcomed the crisis. Anxious to settle scores with the Serbians, the Habsburg chief of staff made a difference in the decision-making process. Of all of the central actors in 1914, Conrad alone could have—by saying no to Berchtold or expressing hesitation to Franz Joseph

42 The Serbian documents report extensive military steps by the Russians after July 25; e.g., Spalajković to Pašić, (tel.) 26 July, 1914, Dedijer and Anić (eds.), *Documents*, no. 585. Albertini summarized the Russian mobilization arguments well in *Origins*, II, 528–581. See also Fischer, *Krieg*, 704–729.
43 Stone, "Die Mobilmachung," 176–184; see also Williamson, "Theories of Organizational Process and Foreign Policy Outcomes," in Paul G. Lauren (ed.), *Diplomacy: New Approaches in History, Theory, and Policy* (New York, 1979), 151–154; Jack S. Levy, "Organizational Routines and the Causes of War," *International Studies Quarterly*, XXX (1986), 193–222.

or accepting some modified "Halt in Belgrade"—brought the crisis to a more peaceful conclusion. Conrad, however, did not, and that raises in stark relief the role of the individual in history. In this instance, Conrad's military ambitions were motivated, possibly, by his own desire to be a military hero and thus be able to marry Gina von Reininghaus, the woman he loved but could not wed because she was already married (and the mother of six children). Between 1907 and their nuptials in 1915, Conrad wrote literally thousands of letters to Gina, many mailed, others not. In several his theme is: if war comes and I am a hero, then I can marry Gina. But first he had to have the war. In the summer of 1914, he finally got his war and a year later his bride.[44]

While Conrad delayed any shift of his forces from the south to the north, Berlin attempted to cope with the Russian mobilization. Those decisions opened the final stages of the July crisis. Faced with the two-front war, the German leadership demanded that the Russians and French cease their preparations. But neither yielded to German pressure. The German high command pointed to unambiguous evidence of extensive Russian military activity; the Schlieffen-Moltke plan demanded action. On August 2, in scenes far distant from Sarajevo, Germany moved against Luxembourg and, one day later, against Belgium. With Germany's violation of Belgium neutrality, Grey pressed the British government to intervene. Thus the third Balkan war became World War I.

The outbreak of World War I saw a fusion of long-term causes with short-run tactical decisions. Although the momentum of the crisis differed from capital to capital, the limited options available to the policymakers are explicable only when the eastern European dynamics are considered. Alliance loyalties, the pressures of the military bureaucrats, and the juxtaposition of different perceptions with personal motivations made the chances of peace extremely remote in the last days of July and early August 1914.

What broader conclusions can be drawn from the July crisis about the origins and prevention of major wars? A few deserve emphasis, even if they are familiar. Nationalism and ethnic arro-

---

44 For a discussion of Conrad's relationship with Gina, see Williamson, "Vienna and July 1914," 13–14. See also Gina Conrad's indiscreet, *Mein Leben mit Conrad von Hötzendorf* (Leipzig, 1935).

gance should never be underestimated. The powerful, emotive forces of prestige and survival press statesmen to take chances that ostensibly rational actors might not take, especially when the civilian ministers fail to comprehend the ramifications of military planning or its illusory nature. Even Berchtold and the other senior Habsburg statesmen, well versed in crisis management after the Balkan wars of 1912 and 1913, never fully probed the logic of Conrad's plans. The offensive ideology swept aside any doubts harbored by the civilian leadership and left them no time to ponder and reconsider.

The alliance and entente structures likewise placed a premium upon action. To be sure, the arrangements seemingly offered protection to their members. The alliances, however, could also coerce a state into taking action simply for the sake of the alliance. Strong, tight alliances may in fact be more dangerous to peace than loose, ambiguous ones where the actors must negotiate among themselves before taking action.

A number of conclusions can be drawn concerning the July crisis. First, "satisficing" as a decision-making process was evident everywhere; the statesmen repeatedly took the first suitable option, not necessarily the best option.[45] An economist model of decision-making was seldom seen during the weeks after Sarajevo; instead, a series of reactive decisions were taken by statesmen in Vienna, Berlin, and St. Petersburg. Cost-benefit analysis, such as occurred during the Cuban missile crisis, may take place if the time parameters of a crisis are known. But such a process is unlikely (and the Cuban missile crisis is not a good guide for decision-making during a crisis), because in most international crises the dénouement can be projected only at an unspecified future time, not at a specific future time. In most crises, this is not possible, and, certainly in 1914, the statesmen had no time carefully to consider their decisions, the Habsburg leadership excepted, once the ultimatum was delivered in Belgrade on July 23.

Second, the events of July reaffirm the power of perceptions and past experience in assessing current situations. In 1914 a group of leaders, all experienced in statecraft, power, and crisis management, deliberately made decisions that risked or assumed war.

45 Graham T. Allison, *The Essence of Decision: Explaining the Cuban Missile Crisis* (Boston, 1971), 72.

Statesmen and generals cast the die because of their fears and apprehensions about the future. No group had less confidence than the Habsburg leaders, who had been battered during the Balkan wars, Serbian expansion, and the loss of Franz Ferdinand, their experienced heir apparent. The Habsburg policymakers desperately desired to shape the future, rather than let events control them. The prospect of domestic disintegration, exacerbated by foreign intervention from the north and south, made war an acceptable policy option. Frustration and fear were a fatal and seductive combination for Vienna and Budapest. The Habsburg decision, backed by the Germans for their own reasons, gave the July crisis momentum and a dynamic that rendered peace the first casualty.

But the willingness of the Habsburg leadership to rescue a sagging dual monarchy by resorting to force had echoes elsewhere in Europe. In each capital, and despite the recent Balkan wars, the policymakers adopted a fatalistic, almost reckless, approach to the crisis. A convergence of offensive military strategies, fears about the future, and an unwillingness to consider other less dangerous options formed the perceptual agenda for the governmental leaders; peace had little chance once Vienna decided war was an acceptable option.

The war of 1914 began as a local quarrel with international ties; those ties converted it into a major conflagration. Therein lies possibly the most salient lesson of the July crisis: a local quarrel does not always remain a local issue. Peace is more easily maintained if one avoids even the smallest incursion into war, for, once the barrier of peace is broken, the process of diplomacy in restoring peace or preventing a larger war is infinitely more difficult. The maintenance of peace requires an aggressive commitment to imaginative diplomacy and to continual negotiation, not spasms of despair and the clash of military action in the hope for something better. Something better is almost always something worse, as all of the European governments discovered in World War I.[46]

46 On the problem of maintaining peace over long decades, see John Lewis Gaddis, "The Long Peace: Elements of Stability in the Postwar International System," *International Security*, X (1986), 99–142.

Charles S. Maier

Wargames: 1914–1919

Are there really lessons of the past?[1] The past is certainly a source of knowledge, our only source of knowledge given the flow of time, but, strictly speaking, it does not teach lessons. By lessons I mean maxims for attaining particular outcomes in the present or future: for example, *Si vis pacem, para bellum,* or it is better for a prince to be feared than loved. Insofar as these maxims seem to offer guidance for policymakers, they are usually psychological, not historical.[2] They supposedly summarize human traits that persist regardless of changing historical contexts. Other examples might include the notion that appeasement encourages aggression or that "military decision makers will tend to overestimate the feasibility of an operational plan if a realistic assessment would require forsaking fundamental beliefs or values."[3] Identification of such allegedly constant traits was the goal of philosophical history and may have seemed an appropriate program for historians during the Enlightenment and their policy-studies heirs. Subsequent historians, however, have usually sought to describe changing societal contexts or outcomes.

Charles S. Maier is Professor of History at Harvard University. He is the author of *In Search of Stability: Explorations in Historical Political Economy* (New York, 1987) and *The Unmasterable Past: History, Holocaust, and German National Identity* (forthcoming).

---

1 With all due respect to Ernest R. May, *"Lessons" of the Past: The Use and Misuse of History in American Foreign Policy* (New York, 1973); and *idem* and Richard Neustadt, *Thinking in Time* (New York, 1986); the real thrust of these exercises is how to avoid simplistic lessons and illusory parallels.

2 Cf. Robin G. Collingwood's critique of Thucydides as the father of "psychological history" in *The Idea of History* (New York, 1956), 29–30. "Its chief purpose is to affirm laws, psychological laws. A psychological law is not an event nor yet a complex of events: it is an unchanging rule which governs the relations between events." Granted, Collingwood's may be an impoverished reading of Thucydides. Moreover, the distinction between relying on general laws to explain specific outcomes and, conversely, using events to "affirm" laws needs closer examination. All historians presuppose some causal "laws"; it is, however, the effort to derive or demonstrate them that distinguishes the sociologist or political scientist from the historian.

3 Jack Snyder, "Civil-Military Relations and the Cult of the Offensive, 1914 and 1984," in Steven E. Miller (ed.), *Military Strategy and the Origins of the First World War* (Princeton, 1985), 137.

This aim means mapping complicated and unanticipated causal chains, not foreseeable individual reactions.[4]

A false dichotomy has been created, it will be objected. The policy scientist can derive genuine lessons from *situational* parallels and not merely psychological constants. Not all elements of a historical situation need to be identical with the present for the past to be instructive. The "controlled case study" presupposes that if sufficient components are congruent, important lessons emerge. But in the "controlled case study," too, many of the lessons are more deductive than historical. Consider: "History indicates that wars rarely start because one side believes it has a military advantage. Rather, they occur when a leader believes force is necessary to achieve important goals."[5] In other words, prospects of success are not sufficient inducement; wars are fought only when belligerents think them necessary. The first clause may be a historical generalization, that is, an empirical rule that we could not know was true or false without consulting the past; the second is simply a proposition derived from the accepted concept of warfare.

Other difficulties attend the controlled case study. Any single new variable or event can change an outcome: is *ceteris paribus* a useful qualification for policymakers if it can never pertain? To control the variables may be precisely to de-historicize. The non-deductive knowledge derived from history must depend upon

4   For German historians from Leopold von Ranke to Friedrich Meinecke, post-Enlightenment *Historismus* justified conceiving of nation-states as analogous to individual personalities, each entitled to pursue its own vital needs and liberated from all imperatives but that of survival. But even the less nationalistic, more systemic, and comparative approaches that emerged, such as Marc Bloch's, also undermined inter-temporal historical analogies. Bloch's comparative method always stressed what was different, not what was similar. See "Pour une histoire comparée des Sociétés européennes," *Mélanges Historiques* (Paris, 1963), I, 16–40. Finally, it should be noted that John Stuart Mill's method of similiarity and method of difference sometimes cited to justify comparison in the social sciences, was specifically held up by Mill as a natural-science procedure. Although Mill aspired to social science, he also stressed the limits on systematic comparison and certibus paribus certainty. See *A System of Logic* (New York, 1881; 8th ed.), 278–284, 586–589, 606–613. Analogical lessons in the modern social sciences must refer to broad contexts or matrices at best, not to individual elements.

5   Richard Ned Lebow, "Windows of Opportunity: Do States Jump Through Them?" in Miller (ed.), *Military Strategy*, 149. For the case study approach, see Alexander L. George and Richard Smoke, *Deterrence in American Foreign Policy: Theory and Practice* (New York, 1974); Smoke, *War: Controlling Escalation* (Cambridge, Mass., 1977); Richard K. Betts, *Soldiers, Statesmen, and Cold War Crises* (Cambridge, Mass., 1977).

history being understood as a process of complex development, not just as a warehouse of examples. It may thus offer insights akin to the mental enhancement provided by good literature or successful psychoanalysis. History provides awareness of layered complexity, warnings of pitfalls, and a feel for the contextual determinants of outcomes; it fills in a sense of human community. At its best, this knowledge can be emancipatory, but not pragmatic.

Does this limitation condemn history to uselessness for policymakers? Only if they approach it as engineers, seeking technological guidance; otherwise, it is indispensable. As Croce summarized history's contribution: "We are products of the past and we live immersed in the past which presses on us all around. . . . Historical thought reduces the past to its own raw material, transforms it into its own object, and history writing liberates us from history."[6]

Let us think further about the process Croce describes. How does written history "liberate" us from being blindly caught up in a stream of events? Accept that it cannot deliver simple, straightforward lessons; how does it provide insight? It does so primarily by virtue of the historian's laying bare its counterfactual implications. The good historian is distinguished by an awareness, which is communicated to his or her readers, that what has come to pass is intensely problematic. Describing what has actually happened, *wie es eigentlich gewesen,* should be like walking on very thin ice. For history to provide insights applicable to present conduct, it must explain why other outcomes did not prevail— not in the sense that they could not, but in the sense that they might well have. The historian cannot establish any given degree of likelihood (except that it be non-trivial) for outcomes that did not occur. But, by exploring what conditions would have been needed for alternative outcomes to materialize, history can assume a heuristic role. It thereby suggests how freedom of action is foreclosed or seized. It allows the assignment of responsibility by revealing the scope for choice.

How should this procedure be applied to World War I? The objective is to construct alternative histories to illuminate the issues that seem instructive for current policy. Certainly the ques-

6 Benedetto Croce, *La storia come pensiero e come azione* (Bari, 1966), 33–34.

tion of origins remains perpetually open for counterfactual exploration. So too is the question of why the war became so major a conflict in terms of duration, intensity (the resources committed by each belligerent), and geographical extension. But equally important, if historians seek to understand the logic of prolonged and extended warfare, they must also ask why wars finally do end. There is inertia or hysteresis in war as well as in peace. Lastly, the nature of the peace settlement helps decide whether other wars must follow. In this article, I address a series of questions that are essential to an understanding of World War I: Was it inevitable? Did it have to last so long? What precipitated its end? Was the Versailles settlement doomed to such a short and troubled life? These issues are perennially engaging, laden with implicit counterfactual demands, and potentially relevant for policy.

A word of caution, perhaps evasion, is necessary: the purpose of this exercise is to test narrative reconstructions and assumptions and to stimulate renewed questioning about some very familiar scenarios. I have conceived it as a *Kriegsspiel* for history. In this spirit, I not only raise some "what if" questions; I also purposely advance some unconventional propositions designed to "deconstruct" the received historical scenarios. Consider first the inquiry on inevitability. The irreversible momentum toward general war in 1914 is usually seen as a result of three factors: the hopeless, long-term instability of the Habsburg empire, the rigid structure of opposing alliances, and the ineluctable pull of military preparations. All three can be overstated. For today's policymaker, the issue of military determinism may seem the most compelling. To what extent did military plans preclude diplomatic solutions? Since German military provisions are usually considered a major factor in the outbreak of war, it is worth testing the proposition that Germany's mobilization schedule, the so-called Schlieffen plan, was in fact irrelevant to the question of the origins of the war.

A second inquiry must ask why a war that seemed so inconclusive and so costly lasted so long. Was it merely a savage nationalism or an unwillingness to lose face that impeded settlement? Or does it not make more sense to assume that for those in charge some compelling logic was at stake, that it was a "rational" war? At least then we are forced to ask what sort of logic pertained, and it becomes evident that the anticipated costs of quitting the conflict outweighed the disadvantages of remaining engaged.

The third and fourth propositions concern the outcome of the war. Germany lost the war *in the form it did* not because of military defeat but because of political collapse. In this sense, there is force to General Erich Ludendorff's thesis, which has long been deemed particularly odious because antidemocratic forces shamefully exploited it during the Weimar republic, namely, that the Germans lost the war because they were "stabbed in the back." But he had the sequence and the perpetrator wrong. Collapse at home and the disorganization that engulfed the army in late October and early November 1918 represented an episode of crisis management that Ludendorff himself mishandled. Finally, this article suggests that, despite its almost universal condemnation, the Versailles Treaty was not a bad peace, and that the outlines of the Versailles settlement were no less unavoidable than was the outbreak of war.

INEVITABILITY AND THE SCHLIEFFEN PLAN   Three clusters of causality are usually cited by those who think that some sort of great war was virtually inevitable by 1914. The first was the internal vulnerability of the Habsburg state, threatened by centrifugal ethnic loyalties. The second was the rigid constraints imposed by the two alliance systems (the Triple Entente and Triple Alliance). The third was the way in which military plans forced the hand of civilian leaders. Although this article concentrates on the third factor, it is useful to challenge each assumption.

Austro-Hungarian Vulnerability   The empire's vulnerability to South-Slav nationalism allegedly led Vienna's leaders to perceive Serbian ambitions as a life-or-death challenge, and therefore rendered at least a local conflict inevitable. Such judgments are often accompanied by assurances that the dual monarchy was an atavistic institution, doomed to collapse. Every reader recalls the sentimental memoirs and spuriously prescient narratives in which rickety, decadent Austria insouciantly waltzes its way to doom. This is history written on the Wurlitzer. If the dual monarchy were so moribund, it might be asked, how could it have withstood four years of war, fielding armies that overcame serious language problems, suffering severe civilian deprivation without disabling conflict at home, and decomposing only a week earlier than the Prusso-German Empire? Did survival of the Habsburg state ultimately require a fight against Serbia? William II hardly thought so when he read the Serbian response to the Austrian ultimatum on 26 July 1914. The issue of nationalities was obviously difficult for Austria-Hungary to resolve, but so was the nationalities question inside the United Kingdom in 1914. Not every irredentist ulcer leads to war. Williamson reveals how bureaucratic organizations, forces of personality, and chance contributed to Habsburg decisions in the summer of 1914.[7] But such a structural analysis only makes it more understandable how miscalculation, vanity, and shortsightedness could be so hard to overcome within the Habsburg regime.

The Alliance System   Or was it the overarching alliance system that proved lethal? On the one hand, the international linkages explain why a local war might develop into a continental struggle. On the other hand, the risks felt by non-front-line allies also worked to contain dangerous escalation. The two alliance systems had allowed German restraint of Austria and French restraint of Russia before 1914. To be sure, each occasion in which one ally imposed moderation might anger its partner, thus making restraint more difficult in subsequent crises. The very admonitions of allies during the Balkan wars of 1912/13 made it more difficult to force partners to be cautious in 1914. Russian, French, and German statesmen might all fear that their partners would see little purpose to the respective pacts were they to serve only as instruments for restraint. It can be argued that it was not the binding nature of the alliances, but the possibility for defection, that proved more destabilizing. Vienna and St. Petersburg sought reassurances beyond the letter of the texts, needed demonstrative state visits, and pursued pledges of support—and, in 1914, extracted them because Paris and Berlin feared that they would seem indifferent. London's stance, as is often pointed out, was so apparently detached that Germany could entertain hopes that English neutrality was possible.

Peace was all the more precarious once each state felt that its own side was becoming more vulnerable. The reciprocal feeling

7 Samuel R. Williamson, Jr., "The Origins of World War I," *Journal of Interdisciplinary History*, XVIII (1988), 749–770.

of vulnerability remains one of the striking components of the 1914 crisis. German strategic planners dreaded the completion of the forward Russian railway network by 1916; Russian statesmen saw German power irrevocably encroaching upon their security in southern Europe: Count A. K. Benckendorff wrote in July 1911 that "at the root of everything, I see the gigantic force of expansion of Germany, which carries along with it its influence and inevitably its flag." Berlin might not mean to be aggressive, but its policy "entails countermeasures on the part of the other powers which always create the danger of conflict."[8]

What does it imply to say that the Schlieffen plan was irrelevant to the question of the origins of the war? The statement means simply that war was neither more nor less likely to occur given German reliance on a strategic concept that envisaged rapid mobilization and deployment of a mass army through Belgium against France. Surely, it is difficult to make this case in light of the frenzied pressure that military leaders imposed on their political leaders. Taylor has written, "When cut down to essentials, the sole cause for the outbreak of war in 1914 was the Schlieffen plan—product of the belief in speed and the offensive. . . . All were trapped by the ingenuity of their military preparations, the Germans most of all." "In the final phase," summarizes Turner, "military considerations were of decisive importance; they accelerated the whole tempo of events and confirmed Count Metternich's dictum: 'When the statesman has to yield to the soldier in peace or war, a people is usually doomed.'" But note the restriction, "in the final phase." Before July 29, there was less reference to its strategic implications. Kennan, by contrast, suggests that, beginning in the 1890s, the militarization of thinking transformed the alliance system into a dangerous time-table.[9]

8 Cited in Dominic C. B. Lieven, *Russia and the Origins of the First World War* (London, 1983), 46. Cf. Lebow, "Windows of Opportunity," 147–186: "When worst case analysis is used by both sides, it means that they will interpret a situation of strategic parity as one of imbalance favoring their adversary" (183). Does it require worst-case analysis?

9 Alan J. P. Taylor, *War by Timetable* (London, 1969), 121. See also 101: "But there was only one decision which turned the little Balkan conflict between Austria-Hungary and Serbia into a European war. That was the German decision to start general mobilization on 31st July, and that was in turn decisive because of the academic ingenuity with which Schlieffen, now in his grave, had attempted to solve the problem of a two-front war." See L. C. F. Turner, *Origins of the First World War* (New York, 1970), 115. Cf. *idem*, "The Significance of the Schlieffen Plan," in Paul M. Kennedy (ed.), *The War Plans of the Great Powers, 1880–1914* (Winchester, Mass., 1985), 198: "the plan strongly influenced the

The Schlieffen plan proposed a solution to the two-front war dilemma that Germany's own policies made increasingly likely, if not inevitable, after 1890. Given the Franco-Russian alliance, German strategy had to decouple the combat in the eastern and western theaters. Whether the Schlieffen plan was feasible tactically—whether it could succeed in light of its demanding timetable and the narrow funnel of Belgium through which so many troops had to pass—can certainly be debated. (Although often criticized, Helmuth von Moltke's decision to shorten the wheel of the German first army so that it turned east and not west of Paris seems a sensible concession.[10] The outer circumference envisaged by Schlieffen would have been totally daunting and exposed.) It is further questionable whether the plan was feasible in a broader strategic sense. Even had the German forces quickly shattered the existing French armies, it is far from certain that a durable German victory would have been ensured. In 1870, France had fought for several months after the defeat of its major armies at Sedan and Metz, and after the German investment of Paris. The French lost because of their diplomatic isolation and lack of an ally as much as their battlefield setbacks.

French national determination was certainly as deep-rooted in 1914 as it was in 1870, when, instead of a broad coalition, the empress had claimed her own *petite guerre à moi*. (And national morale was far more robust then than it would be in 1940.) A France that had its government in Bordeaux would also have had a British coalition partner, perhaps not militarily prepossessing at first, but giving promise of eventual support. In short, even had Paris been taken in 1914, France would have been left in a situation similar to that of Austria in the Napoleonic wars, that is, defeated

---

decisions taken by political and military leaders in July 1914 and must be regarded as a major factor in the chain of events which plunged Europe into war." The major original study was Gerhard Ritter (Andrew and Eva Wilson, trans.), *The Schlieffen Plan* (New York, 1958). See also Gunther E. Rothenberg, "Moltke, Schlieffen, and the Doctrine of Strategic Envelopment," in Peter Paret (ed.), *Makers of Modern Strategy from Machiavelli to the Nuclear Age* (Princeton, 1986), 296–325. George F. Kennan's reflections are in his *The Fateful Alliance: France, Russia, and the Coming of the First World War* (New York, 1984), 248.

10 See Ritter's objections in *Schlieffen Plan*, 57–68. Following other critics, Turner argues that the decision not to invest Paris from the west made possible Joffre's opportunity for the victory at the Marne ("Significance," 212–214). But if Kluck retreated because he feared envelopment east of Paris, how would his being west of Paris (and probably still far northwest) have altered the situation in Germany's favor?

in 1797, 1806, and 1809, but still supported by Britain (except for 1803/04) and capable of participating in an anti-hegemonic coalition. As the elder Moltke understood, no power would be crushed in a single campaign.[11]

Nonetheless, if the Schlieffen plan had been carried out *not* as the prelude to a long war of conquest that Germany must eventually lose because of an Anglo-American coalition, but *only* as a way of avoiding early defeat in a two-front war, then it was a risky but rational tactic. Less explainable was the lack of a fallback strategy. The problem with the doctrines of the offensive was less their increasing the likelihood of war than their belief that an initial military victory resolved all problems. They were concepts *sans lendemain*. This myopia prevailed even for the most successful strategy, for example, blitzkrieg in 1939/40. It may hold true for American plans today.

Whatever the military judgments, many decisive steps during the July crisis took place without particular attention to the implications of the Schlieffen plan. How was the Schlieffen plan supposed to have worked to make war more certain in 1914? Critics from Winston Churchill to Ritter have argued that the focus on the Belgian corridor (and renunciation of a thrust across Dutch Limburg) meant that preparations to storm Liège had to proceed immediately. There could be no mobilization without an immediate offensive because any delay would give French troops time to move northward.[12] Whether or not Moltke was sanguine about prospects in 1914, he certainly felt that the Schlieffen plan was the only possible wager. Turner argues that the failure of Austro-German military coordination made the Schlieffen plan all the more fateful. Since Germany was to commit itself to the west, it urgently needed Austria to threaten to deploy its troops against the Russians on the Galician frontier and not against Serbia. Moltke's concern about Germany's vulnerability to the Russians, Turner maintains, explains Moltke's pressure on Austria on July 30 to move quickly and his reassurances that Germany would ultimately and unstintingly join the combat against Russia. Al-

11 Cited by Turner, *ibid.*, 200.
12 Turner summarizes the argument in *ibid.*, 214–217, and in *Origins*, 108–110. Ritter's argument are in *Schlieffen Plan*; in "Der Anteil des Militärs in der Kriegskatastrophe von 1914," *Historische Zeitschrift*, CXCIII (1961), 71–92; and in *Staatskunst und Kriegshandwerk* (Munich, 1965), II, 239–281.

though these assurances helped Count Leopold Berchthold press for mobilization on July 31, they did not lead General Franz Conrad von Hötzendorf to shift troops from the Serbian theater to the Galician front.

But how does the Schlieffen plan fit? No substantive strategic considerations seem to have influenced assurances from the German civilian leadership to Count Ladislaus Szögyény on July 5; Erich von Falkenhayn was told he need not take any military dispositions and left for vacation.[13] As late as the afternoon of July 29, with news of the partial mobilization by Russia (quickly to be revoked), Theobald von Bethmann Hollweg kept the generals from invoking the measures preparatory for mobilization (the declaration of *drohende Kriegsgefahr*). Moltke even told an Austrian liaison officer the next morning that Germany did not need to mobilize until Austria and Russia were actually at war. Of course, the constellation of wills changed by midday and again during the afternoon and evening. The deprecation of danger on the 29th yielded to the fear of being overrun. By evening on the 30th Bethmann seemed preoccupied more with onus-shifting than with dissuading Austria; the kaiser too had abandoned his view that Austria might well feel satisfied with the Serbian response or even with his own proposal that Vienna merely occupy Belgrade, just across the Danube frontier. And Moltke, whether or not he had confirmed reports of the Russian order for general mobilization, now dropped his caution of the previous day and insisted on German mobilization, which supposedly further entailed the steps against France that were tantamount to general European war.[14]

But consider the crowded events of July 30 through August 1. Even had there been no Schlieffen plan, would any German commander have allowed Russian mobilization without demanding countermobilization? The pressure of time was as critical for standing up to the forces the Russians *alone* might muster as it

13   Sidney B. Fay, *The Origins of the World War* (New York, 1966; 2nd ed.), 211ff.
14   The narrative is provided by Luigi Albertini (trans., Isabella Massey), *The Origins of the War of 1914* (London, 1952–1957), 3 v. Albertini paradoxically blames Russia's partial mobilization—soon revoked—for having "brought Europe to war" because it brought the other powers' military leadership into the decision-making process and subordinated the civilians. However, he still believes Bethmann could have overruled Moltke, insisted that Austria accept a "halt in Belgrade formula," and together with Edward Grey imposed negotiations between Vienna and St. Petersburg (III, 231).

was for taking Liège and moving down the valley of the Meuse. The earlier notion that the Russians would be slow to deploy their troops—a prerequisite for Schlieffen's phased strategy—did not seem so operative a factor in the summer of 1914; otherwise, Moltke need not have been so concerned about Austrian readiness to strike north of the Carpathians. But even if Russia were ponderous and slow in mobilizing, Germany must still have a major force in place within approximately a month to confront the Russians. So long as Austria could not be, or would not be, restrained against Serbia, Russian mobilization became the critical factor in German thinking. And if there was one consistent streak of behavior in the inconstant German responses during July 1914 (indeed the trait that has led Germany to be spotlighted repeatedly as the most culpable for the war), it was its unwillingness to threaten Austria outright with nonimplementation of the 1879 alliance.

But, it will be argued, there could have been mobilization *without* war had not the Schlieffen plan put Germany under such pressure of time. The German rush to war provides the brunt of Albertini's condemnation of the Reich.[15] Although the measures attendant upon Russia's partial mobilization (quickly upgraded to total mobilization) forced the Germans to respond militarily, only the Germans' war plan required that mobilization serve as an immediate prelude to hostilities so that the Reich's enemies could be dealt with seriatim. But was mobilization without war really feasible? As early as 1892, the French and Russians had agreed that mobilization meant war.[16] Only when faced with imminent hostilities did statesmen try to put another firebreak between mobilization and war. This impulse lay behind the celebrated French order to keep troops ten kilometers behind their frontier with Germany. But such an additional step was not easy for Germany, given its two-front exposure. Even had the Germans sought to keep France out of war and renounced offensive operations against that state, given the Franco-Russian alliance, they would have had to keep major forces in the west lest the French

15 *Ibid.*, 230–232.
16 Fay, *Origins*, II, 479–481. It might be argued that, these French notions notwithstanding, France both mobilized and pulled back from its frontiers in 1914. However, France could not have remained in this posture once combat had begun in the east, given the momentum of its political leaders' repeated assurances to Russia.

intervene.[17] That requirement would have meant that they would be seriously outnumbered in the east if they let the Russians complete their deployment. It was not so much the Schlieffen plan for a rapid decision against France as it was the menace of a two-front conflict that made mobilization without war so dubious for Germany. A "phoney war" mobilization seems a plausible strategy only for a one-front conflict.

But, assume further that, rather than yield to war, the kaiser had not backed away from his panicky proposal to Moltke that the Schlieffen plan be dismantled in the crisis and that only a defensive stance be taken in the west. Could mobilization without war have eventually led back to peace? Perhaps: until war actually comes, it can always, in theory, be averted. Nonetheless, might not the next development have been demands by each side that the adversary stand down? Ultimatums were a natural next step: indeed, they were how the British reacted once Belgium was invaded; they were the stepwise procedure used by London and Paris in September 1939.

Was the Schlieffen plan decisive between August 1 and August 4? It justified British entry into the war and allowed Edward Grey to unite the cabinet behind intervention by virtue of its violation of Belgian neutrality. Still, there could have been continental war in any case, and, as Williamson and others have demonstrated, Britain probably would quickly have become involved.[18] In effect, the logic of the Austro-German alliance, the German-Russian antagonism, and the Franco-Russian Entente hardly needed the Schlieffen plan to escalate if not the first, or the second crisis, at least the nth such crisis. The reader may object at this point and claim that such an explanation only reestablishes a causal factor already dismissed, namely the compel-

17 It is worth considering the difference between mobilization in 1914 and the contemporary placing of forces on alert as a means either of pressure or caution. Even today's alerts present grave difficulties, since they can hardly be held in a long-term equilibrium: for example, bombers cannot fly over the Arctic Circle forever. But mobilization required first of all a far more public event, which cut deeply into the civilian labor force, had necessarily to invoke patriotic appeals, tied up rail transportation, and required a day-by-day plan for progressive deployment. Indeed one may ask whether, in fact, rather than doctrines of the offensive being a root cause of the 1914 catastrophe, the half-century development of post-railroad mobilization might not have made such doctrines far more likely to emerge.
18 Samuel J. Williamson, Jr., *The Politics of Grand Strategy: Britain and France Prepare for War, 1904–1914* (Cambridge, Mass., 1969).

ling nature of the alliance system. But the point made was that these alliances were compelling largely because of the need to demonstrate that they would not be abandoned. They bred insecurity, not security, and for that reason they underwent iterated crises. The real lesson of the July crisis is that no system of international and military commitment can deal with iterated crises without moving toward breakdown. Deterrence in the post-1945 epoch has been more robust in good part because it has had to work continuously, not from crisis to crisis.[19]

The Schlieffen plan does not provide the only evidence of military compulsion in the July crisis, but it presents the strongest possible case. Even Sagan, who contests explanations that ascribe enhanced likelihood of war to the "cult of the offensive," accepts the notion that the Schlieffen plan caused the crisis to move out of control.[20] It made the crisis more difficult, but not much more than a Russian decision to mobilize had already made it, a decision that was itself foreseeable in light of German-Austrian behavior between 28 June and 28 July 1914. Perhaps if there had been a powerful outside neutral with bargaining credibility on July 29, diplomacy might still have achieved a forty-eight-hour or seven-day *pre*-mobilization standstill agreement that was binding on all sides. Although success was hardly likely (after all, what had been achieved during the efforts of July 26/27?), in itself the Schlieffen plan would not have precluded such a moratorium on mobilization. The difficulty was that no such outside power was available in 1914: the United States was not yet a relevant actor; and the British could not unambiguously assert pressure from "outside." They, too, were caught up in the crisis as a potential, if uncertain alliance partner. If we envisage the July crisis as a sort of seven-card stud—a few cards held close, the majority on the table—it was not the speed of the game that determined whether players put more chips on the table at each round. It was their unwillingness to fold.

19 The major crises for deterrence included the Berlin blockade (which helped initiate the alliance), the Berlin crisis of 1958–1961, and the Cuban missile crisis, which did not really engage the Alliance as a full partner. Had the tempo of crises after 1945 paralleled that of 1905–1914, an escalation of threat and counterthreat might well have overwhelmed even atomic deterrence.

20 Scott D. Sagan, "1914 Revisited: Allies, Offense, and Instability," *International Security*, XI (1986), 151–175.

This consideration returns the analysis not to *time*, but to *repetition* as the crucial destabilizing variable. To take momentous decisions under the pressure of cascading events, in haste, without sleep, and with a fear of being caught unprepared by the enemy is likely to lead to a deterioration of decision-making. But, even in urgent situations, cool heads can prevail: President John F. Kennedy was faced with a fearsome sequence of developments in 1962 and could still choose to back away from the brink. Iteration is intrinsically more dangerous since each demonstration of resolve must invoke a higher level of threat to achieve the same degree of deterrence.[21]

If the Schlieffen plan did not provide the decisive incremental stimulus, offensive planning did not particularly prejudice the outcome. Indeed, it is hard to see how the alliance structure could have accommodated purely defensive strategies. War might well have come earlier. In the 1930s, for instance, French defensive strategies emboldened Adolf Hitler to force issues in eastern Europe and made war more likely. It might be said that by the 1930s the technological initiative had switched to the offensive, with the result that defensive strategies became inappropriate. (Signs of that transition are evident during the last year of World War I, from the first major application of tanks at the battle of Cambrai to the near success of the Germans on the western front in the spring of 1918.) But technological advantage was not crucial in its own right. Defensive strategies are stabilizing only when all of the powers agree that they are stabilizing and compatible with their alliance obligations. To have one power convinced of the potential for the offensive and others of the capacity of the defensive hardly assures a stable outcome.[22]

---

21 Iterative crises, moreover, break down the distinction between accurate perception and misperception. Jervis' discussion shows why judgment about enemies' intentions is likely to be skewed and thus more dangerous (Robert Jervis, "War and Misperception," *Journal of Interdisciplinary History*, XVIII [1988], 675–700.). But the peril of the international system does not usually arise from such misreadings. Each party's worst fears must be confirmed in the escalation that characterizes repeated confrontation.

22 Defensive strategies promise stability in themselves only as deterrent strategies, not as actual combat concepts. But the strategies of 1914, even had they been defense-oriented, were still concepts that presupposed combat. For the arguments that see the offensive as destabilizing, see *idem*, "Cooperation under the Security Dilemma," *World Politics*, XXX (1978), 167–214; George Quester, *Offense and Defense in the International System* (New York, 1977); Stephan Van Evera, "The Cult of the Offensive and the Origins of the First World War," in Miller (ed.), *Military Strategy*, 58–107. Snyder, *The Ideology of the Offensive*

In 1914, despite the technological factors that Bloch had pointed out, it was not likely that all of the powers could have been converted to the defensive. Their reluctance would have resulted not merely from the way offensive planning corresponded to internal bureaucratic advantages or from the limited cybernetic reasoning capacity of military bureaucracies. Even if French strategic thinking may stubbornly have exalted the offensive (what was more unwise was the specific offensive envisaged by Plan XVII), the German military establishment was hardly in need of offensive concepts to enhance its bureaucratic influence.[23] Snyder cites reasons for an "offensive bias," but Germany chose an offensive strategy *faute de mieux* in a two-front situation. Since German strategy sprang from geopolitical perceptions, it was likely that there would remain at least one power that was not easily to be persuaded by the technological possibilities of the defensive. Germany's choice for an "offensive" strategy would have, in turn, precluded reaching systemic stability on the basis of an international consensus on the advantages of the defensive. Again, we come to the irreducible primacy of political determinants of war: political in the assessment of the respective threats to security (the danger to Austrian statehood or to the two alliance systems) and political in the failure of mediation.

Finally, in the first months of the war, defensive potential hardly outweighed the strength of the offensive. Until the rush to the sea, trench fortifications, barbed wire, and machine-gun emplacements were less decisive than the mass collision of troops. The French sacrificed more men from August through November 1914 than in any other equivalent period (including Verdun). The

---

(Ithaca, 1984), blames less the cult of the offensive in its own right than general rigidity about strategic concepts and the inability to modify them according to circumstances. But he is less concerned with nuance in "Civil-Military Relations," the summarizing article of Miller (ed.), *Military Strategy*, 108–146.

23 Ivan S. Bloch (trans., William Thomas Stead), *The Future of War* (Boston, 1902). The real error was perhaps not a plan for the offensive *per se*, but any rational concept for using the offensive: dazzled by Strasbourg, the French did not have a purposeful strategy for dealing with a Germany whose major political centers (Berlin, Munich, Dresden, and so on) lay far away from the frontiers. The Duisburg-Dortmund industrial area was not easily attainable from the envisaged Lorraine springboard. Riesling, not Ruhr coal, would have been the spoils of success. However, Williamson points out that British unwillingness to have the French maneuver in Belgium made the Lorraine option compelling (given the French conviction that they must take the offensive someplace). See "Joffre Reshapes French Strategy, 1911–1913," in Kennedy (ed.), *War Plans*, esp. 142–143.

Germans, too, lost more soldiers in the five months of fighting during 1914 than in any other equal interval.[24] Trenches and fortifications stabilized the fighting only after the Germans retreated at the Marne and abandoned their offensive. Nor did the Germans lose at the Marne because they encountered entrenched troops. They encountered British troops where they should not have been (between segments of their own line) and, fearing the very catastrophe of envelopment that they had hoped to inflict on the French, they pulled back. In short, they lost because the rapid pace of their offensive made them fear that their army would be split in two and rolled toward each end (Paris and Chalons) by a British and French rush through their center.

THE LOGIC OF A LONG WAR   From the late autumn of 1914, the war in the west settled into a costly stalemate. In effect, the Germans had lost their wager. Why did they not negotiate an end to the war and go home? How irrational that the war should then continue another four years. Or why did not the Russians or French explore peace openly? On the contrary, the logic of the war was persuasive. Reflection shows why extrication was so difficult. For the German leadership to accept the status quo ante while its troops were still deep in enemy territory would have seemed impossible—not even considering that during the heady days of apparent success the regime's civilian and military leadership had generated annexationist objectives. As soon as such plans were stipulated, conservative circles argued that failure to achieve them would severely shake the regime.[25] Voluntarily ceding the major areas of France and of Belgium to return to the conditions seen in 1914 as "encirclement" was out of the question.

Throughout 1915, Germany's peace policy concentrated on approaches to the czar. By the end of that year, the Russian offensive in Galicia had been turned back, the Germans stood over a hundred miles east of Warsaw, the Gallipoli venture had

---

24 Rudolf Meerwarth, "Die Entwicklung der Bevölkerung in Deutschland während der Kriegs- und Nachkriegszeit," in idem, Adolf Günther, and Waldemar Zimmermann, Die Einwirkung des Krieges auf Bevölkerungsbewegung, Einkommen und Lebenshaltung in Deutschland (Stuttgart and New Haven, 1932), 51–57. Michel Huber, La population française pendant la guerre (New Haven, 1931).

25 Hans Gatzke, Germany's Drive to the West: A Study of Germany's Western War Aims in the First World War (Baltimore, 1950), emphasizes this connection. This very useful book was lost sight of once Fritz Fischer published Griff nach der Weltmacht (Dusseldorf, 1961) a decade later.

failed, Serbia had been crushed, and Bulgaria had entered the war on the side of the central powers—but, despite these circumstances, the Russian government did not agree to a separate peace.[26] France was also a possible target of negotiations, but France was not to be moved even if by the end of 1914 it had become clear that no offensive would dislodge Germany. The very fact that Russia and France were hostage to each other's resolution made extrication more difficult for both. The French tried a spring offensive in March and April 1915; when it waned, Russian distress meant they must still send troops to the western front to occupy the Germans and keep their allies from defecting. General Joseph Joffre was convinced that the Russians needed French pressure. The British were convinced that they must aid the French. Horatio Herbert Kitchener told Douglas Haig in August that "the Russians had been severely handled, and it was doubtful how much longer their army could withstand the German blows . . . . he had decided that we must act with all our energy, and do our utmost to help the French, even though, by so doing, we suffered very heavy losses indeed."[27] A fearful symmetry locked the western and eastern fronts together throughout 1915: weakening on one would lead to desperate pleas for diversion on the other.

From the logic of nonextrication, it was a short step to the logic of attrition. In effect, a different war began during the latter half of 1916. The alternatives for flanking action seemed discredited; peace feelers produced no results; and the national economies were harnessed more totally for war (even the Russian economic organization was improved in 1916). In Britain and later in Italy and France, civilian governments became more decisive and streamlined, and, in Germany, military leaders arrogated more general control. This reorganization was carried out so that, as Lloyd George feared, society might "bow its knee to the military Moloch." It was efficiency in service of attrition. Ever since General Ulysses S. Grant's strategy of 1864/65, attrition could tempt commanders. Attrition demanded that one side possess greater reserves than the other, but it was hard to make attrition a strategy

---

26 On this and other German peace offensives, see Lance L. Farrar, Jr., *Divide and Conquer: German Efforts to Conclude a Separate Peace, 1914–1918* (New York, 1978), 13–26.
27 Cited by John Terraine, *The First World War 1914–18* (London, 1984), 91. Cf. Paul Guinn, *British Strategy and Politics, 1914 to 1918* (Oxford, 1965), 95.

for ending the war, any more than it has served to conclude the Iraqi-Iranian war in the past six years. Despite appalling losses, it was hard to prevent replenishment of soldiers. Stone has observed:

> Contrary to legend, it was not so much the difficulty, or physical impossibility of breaking through trench-lines that led to the war's being such a protracted and bloody affair, but rather the fact that even a badly-defeated army could rely on reserves, moving in by railway. The conscription of whole generations, and particularly the enlarged capacity to supply millions of soldiers, meant that man-power was, to all intents and purposes, inexhaustible: even the total casualties of this war were a small proportion of the available man-power.[28]

Table 1 illustrates the depressing truth of this cold-blooded calculation for Germany. In it, we assume that eighteen-year-old males would be inducted into the German army, and then estimate that the male population was half the total and that, as the statistics indicate, about 70 percent would live to adulthood (the figure was improving rapidly).

Germany had one of the most robust population growths of the epoch. It also lost fewer men in relation to its overall population, to the number of males ages nineteen to forty-nine, and to the number of men mobilized than did Serbia, Rumania, or

Table 1   Manpower Available in Germany

	LIVE BIRTHS	MALES ATTAINING 18 (= × 0.35)	WAR DEATHS	SURPLUS
1896	1.915m	670,000	241,000 (1914)	429,000
1897	1.927m	674,000	434,000 (1915)	240,000
1898	1.965m	688,000	340,000 (1916)	348,000
1899	1.980m	693,000	282,000 (1917)	411,000
1900	1.996m	699,000	380,000 (1918)	319,000
1901	2.032m	711,000	—	—
1902	2.025m	709,000	—	—

SOURCE: Meerwarth, Gunther, and Zimmerman, *Die Einwirkung des Krieges*, 18, 51.

28   Norman Stone, *The Eastern Front, 1914–1917* (London, 1985), 265–266.

France.[29] Replenishment would thus be more difficult for France, especially since its slow-growing population had a lower percentage of teenagers and children. (However, by the summer of 1918, about a million United States soldiers had arrived to take a significant combat role on the western front and nearly another million were in France by Armistice Day.) Let us grant also that the problem of replenishment was not eliminated for either side by the simple fact of adolescents growing up sufficiently to be given boots and rifles. Reserves had to be trained; armies had to substitute and reorganize military formations as well as absorb individual soldiers. When severely mauled, whole divisions had to be dissolved. Admittedly, the surpluses above deal with deaths and do not allow for total casualties. By 1918, as a war of movement revived, the number of men injured and taken prisoner grew. Ludendorff's first two (of three) offensives in the spring of 1918 cost the British 240,000 casualties, but Germany lost a million casualties and prisoners by early August.[30] Still, the Germans incurred these sacrifices in a tremendous offensive gamble, not just in the course of holding their positions. Had the supreme command not wagered so desperately, attrition alone was unlikely to terminate the war for the allies within a feasible time frame, that is, before allied as well as German public opinion started to falter.

Why, then, did attrition beckon as a strategy to Falkenhayn, Haig, and civilian leaders as of 1916/17? First, they could always

29

	DEAD	as % mobilized	as % males 15–49	as % popul.
Britain	.723m	11.8	6.3	1.6
France	1.327m	16.8	13.3	3.4
Rumania	.250m	25.0	13.2	3.3
Russia	1.811m	11.5	4.5	1.1
Serbia	.278m	37.1	22.7	5.7
Germany	2.037m	15.4	12.5	3.0
Aust-Hun.	1.100m	12.2	9.0	1.9

SOURCE: J. M. Winter, *The Great War and the British People* (Cambridge, Mass., 1986) 75.

As is evident, the German figures are about 25 percent higher than those listed by Meerwarth, which, I believe, are the more reliable. Revision downward would only make the French, Rumanian, and Serbian losses proportionally greater than the German casualties.

30 Terraine, *First World War*, 168–173.

hope to increase the rapidity with which they killed the enemy. Verdun and the Somme were designed to lead the defending forces to commit more and more men to the meatgrinder. Had the leaders not understood by 1916 and certainly by 1917, the skeptic might ask, that defensive war was relatively economical? In fact, it was not always clear which side was on the defensive. Once a force captured the first line of trenches or outposts, the formerly defensive positions had to be recaptured, and the numerical advantages changed.

Nor was it clear what the relevant "denominators" or manpower pools were when making calculations of attrition. In a coalition war, which numbers are relevant? Today, Soviet/American comparisons do not yield the same results as NATO and Warsaw Pact comparisons. National and allied authorities can each plead that they are weaker than their adversary (in the battle of the budget it pays to be weaker, not stronger); they can each point to their opponents' superiority by including or excluding different categories of weaponry or by including or excluding their allies' weapons. In 1916, which calculation was appropriate? On the one hand, Falkenhayn might have been asked if it made sense to calculate only the proportions between individual countries when combined alliance strength was at stake. On the other hand, if one key opponent was indeed "bled white," might the opposing alliance not simply fall apart and justify the single-country calculus?

Finally, there seemed to be few alternatives in 1916 and 1917. The idea of knocking out the Ottoman Empire came to grief in 1915. Whether Gallipoli could really have had a decisive impact was questionable. Nor did the eastern front yield a decision. Austria could never take a decisive offensive without German reinforcements, but neither could it be subjugated with them. The Germans found that their own advances deep into the czarist empire won territories but did not remove their enemy. As the German military had predicted before 1914, the battle of destiny against the Slavs was to be fought in France. By the end of 1915, it was still being fought there. Granted that the choice of attrition as a tactic might be described as "satisficing" at a very suboptimal level, there was no other promising strategy. As late as autumn 1917, after the disasters of the Somme and the Nivelle offensive, the British embarked on the costly battle of Third Ypres (Passchendaele).[31]

Why was diplomacy not an option? There were several impediments. As noted earlier, the inducements were flawed. Those pursuing a negotiated settlement might well be branded as defeatists and traitors by their domestic opponents. The Germans enjoyed their present domination and were loath to sacrifice it; the allies could hope for future recovery. Austria faced the inverse dilemma. Too weak to prevail on its two fronts without Germany, Austria could not leave the war for fear of alienating Germany. German reinforcements at Gorlice in Galicia had stemmed the Russian's 1915 offensive; German help seemed all the more necessary once the Italian front opened; in 1916, German armies, under August von Mackensen, as at Gorlice, removed the Rumanian threat. Charles, the young emperor who came to the throne in 1916, understood that the pressures of war might well tear his inheritance to pieces, but the alternative of coping without the Germans seemed equally risky. To abandon the war would mean conceding Trent and probably Galicia, perhaps having to countenance Czechoslovakian autonomy and even greater Magyar independence. During 1917/18 Charles found himself in a situation similar to that which Mussolini faced from the autumn of 1943 through the spring of 1945. The Austro-German alliance was truly a death pact. Austria had played on its own weakness to pull its stronger partner into war; Germany was strong enough repeatedly to rescue Austria militarily, but not strong enough to win the war.

Only Britain was in a situation detached enough to explore negotiations, and for this very reason Britain was the power for whom the war was least menacing. Once Britain learned the art of convoying supplies and invoked the aid of its dominions (and

---

31 See the revealing discussion in the war cabinet on whether to send troops to Italy, capture Trieste, and defeat Austria (David Lloyd George's plan), or whether to try again to wear down the Germans (William Robertson and Haig's plan). Documents in Terraine, *The Road to Passchendaele* (London, 1977), 154–182. As Britain's Brigadier General John Charteris reasoned in September 1917, "great though the effort of Great Britain has been, it has not involved her so far as loss in her manhood goes, in any way proportionate to that of France and Germany. But still more important is the argument that if we stop the offensive, Germany will recover and France may give way. The relative advantage of a breathing space is greater for Germany than for her enemies" (275–276).

eventually its former colony, the United States), its statesmen could enjoy insular protection, could dangle Habsburg territory before Italy and Turkish territory before Russia, and could draw on overseas manpower. No wonder that, from the viewpoint of the Germans, Britain seemed to be the spider in the center of the web, manipulating an alliance and exploiting its financial resources to strangle the Reich. Still, by 1917, even Britain had entered an implicit dialogue with Germany. Belgium, however, became the sticking point. The German general staff insisted that it be retained at least as a bargaining chip (and in fact suggested that they wanted to retain portions indefinitely). For London, a German promise to relinquish Belgium was the prerequisite for any talks. The German invasion of Belgium, after all, was not only the cause that had united the Liberals around the war in early August 1914; it also testified to unacceptable German domination of the Continent. If the Belgian issue, moreover, were not enough of an obstacle to negotiations, French insistence on recovery of Alsace-Lorraine further handicapped a diplomatic settlement. When Richard von Kühlmann, the German foreign secretary, declared that those provinces could never be restored, his goal was to separate Britain and France, but, instead, it gave the British another chance to resist rethinking its war aims. As war aims and negotiations became bitterly divisive in each country, for one country to seek negotiations on the part of another meant that it must decisively change the terms of the finely balanced political stalemates within that second country. For Russian or French conservatives to concede negotiations, or for the German right to accept a peace without victory, had great political risks.

From one point of view, the war was "irrational," risking national unity, dynasties, and even bourgeois society. Many of the European statesmen, including Grey, Bethmann Hollweg, and Lord Landsdowne, claimed to understand that such long-term stakes were involved. With the sole exception of Austria, they did not go lightheartedly into the war, and many opined that the war threatened the social order. Nonetheless, they did not think that they were in a position to act upon these long-term forebodings. Rather, they saw themselves confronted with decisions about the next step. Again, the analogy of seven-card stud, in which betting is cumulative, is suggestive.[32] Another way of

32 One might ask whether Bruce Bueno de Mesquita's cumulative utility function has

envisaging the difficulties is to construe decision-making as a non-Abelian process. There may be no way of getting there from here if the steps are taken in the wrong order.

THE OUTCOME OF THE WAR   Why and how did World War I end? The question helps us to think about its larger sequel twenty years later. At the end of September 1918, the German high command asked that an armistice be sought from President Woodrow Wilson. The demand nonplussed even its most ardent supporters, the Prussian conservatives, who had not realized how hollow the German position had become. "We have been lied to and deceived," Ernst von Heydebrand und der Lasa fumed in the Prussian House of Lords.[33] To make Germany a creditable negotiating partner, some degree of political transformation had to take place. What did the generals envisage in terms of an armistice? Was it simply a respite or a military "Title 11" to reorganize their armies, which seemed too exhausted to withstand the allied offensive? In fact, the process of reform in Germany and of negotiation with Wilson, the kaiser's unwillingness to abdicate, and the accumulated civilian hardships began a process of remarkable dissolution. Authority evaporated in Germany by the end of October 1918.

Somewhat like the Tet offensive of 1968, the nature of the German defeat was ambiguous enough to be interpreted differ-

a complex enough heuristic value for the historian. (See *idem*, "The Contribution of Expected Utility Theory to the Study of International Conflict," *Journal of Interdisciplinary History*, XVIII [1988], 629–652.) Does the historian gain by analyzing statesmen as if, in effect, they could cardinalize utility? Different scales seemed to be at stake for short- and long-term consequences. To be sure Bueno de Mesquita would respond that Bethmann or Grey's decisions reflected the fact that short-term utility overpowered long-term utility: there was a high rate of discount. But might the historian not have to think of his protagonists in terms of divided selves, or of undergoing changed mental states? On these problems see Jon Elster, *Sour Grapes: Studies in the Subversion of Rationality* (Cambridge, 1983); *Ulysses and the Sirens: Studies in Rationality and Irrationality* (Cambridge, 1984; rev. ed.).

This writer does not have the mathematical capabilities to provide utility equations for cumulative wagering. But if each decision point puts into play not only the present, but the past chips placed on the table, then, if we simplify the payoffs by ignoring any positive utility to victories except avoidance of the negative utility of a loss and by regarding "folding" or backing down as tantamount to losing; and if we assume further that decision points arrive at regular intervals, then the loss of utility from folding feared at any point should increase at least linearly as a multiple of time.

33 Cited in Hans Peter Hanssen (trans., Oscar Vinther), *Diary of a Dying Empire* (Bloomington, 1955), 319.

ently on both sides. The generals were to claim that years of Social Democratic subversion had undermined the will to resist: strikes at home demoralized the soldiers at the front. This belief was the foundation of the *Dolchstoss Legende*, or the stab-in-the-back thesis that so weakened the Weimar Republic. It was false, although the generals had a point in that final defeat reflected a rapid loss of political will. Political collapse was even more decisive in the case of Austria-Hungary, whose defection, had the war lasted into 1919, would have exposed Germany to a Bavarian front moving north from Italy). But the process of political dissolution had been triggered by Ludendorff and Paul von Hindenburg themselves. After insisting on maximal war aims for so many years, could the supreme command realistically have expected that their reversal would not risk a rapid erosion of civilian and military morale? In any case, they initiated the process of dismantling the war effort with as little foresight of its disintegrative consequences as Bethmann Hollweg and Moltke had initiated a process of military escalation four years earlier. They also seemed unprepared for the foreseeable fact that any armistice would stipulate that the Germans be placed in a situation where they could not resume hostilities at will. Only a more rapid change of leadership and of institutions could have forestalled the November upheaval—but such a change required a foresight and graciousness that neither the kaiser nor the supreme command possessed. The loss of political coherence and military discipline that followed was as remarkable in its way as the disappearance of the German state in 1945.

Ludendorff may have believed his armies were undefeated, but as of November 1918, Germany really had lost, the Reich could not have resisted further, and if Germany was not totally overrun, it was only because of the negotiated armistice. Why, then, did Wilson and the allies agree to the armistice? Why did they not administer a military blow that would have denied credibility to the stab-in-the-back legend? General John Pershing wanted to march to Berlin; and, had the allies visibly defeated the Reich on the country's own soil, much of the aggrieved nationalism that prevailed later might have been precluded—1919 would have looked like 1945. Or would it? Think of the consequences of prolonged fighting.

Germany might well have been able to hold the allied armies from German soil for the remainder of the year (as was the case in December 1944). By November, mud and rains were slowing down the allied advance. The Reich would then have had the winter months to raise a fresh cohort of troops; the combat of the spring of 1919 on German soil might have been particularly sanguinary. The German socialists, who were disillusioned with the war, would still have rallied behind a purely defensive campaign on native ground. Might not the Germans have also more efficiently exploited their puppet state in the Ukraine to assure grain supplies?

At the same time the allied left would also have protested. They had been disgruntled by late 1917; only Wilson's promise of a new world order, as represented in the Fourteen Points and other statements, rallied domestic opinion in France and Britain for a further year of struggle. In effect, by seeming to accept Wilsonian war aims (at least in principle) at the end of 1917, the allied leaders extracted another year of sustained war effort from their own sometimes discouraged populations.[34] If the winter and spring of 1918/19 had been spent in cold and costly assaults on German soil, might not defeatism spread again in the West? Would not the allied left have asked what purpose was gained by forcing Germany to accept unconditional surrender? Would not the manpower costs have been seen as unacceptable in London and Paris?

There was another consideration for British leaders. As Austen Chamberlain wrote his wife, "Our armies must dwindle; the French are no longer fighting; a year hence we shall have lost how many thousands more men? & American power will be dominant. Today we are top dog. *Our* fleets, *our* armies have brought Germany to her knees and today (more than at any later time) the peace may be our peace."[35] Finally, when massive casualties hit the American armies, might there not have been a reopening of debate in the United States? Might not a negotiated settlement have to be reached, say, in the summer of 1919 on the

---

34 Still best on this aspect is Arno J. Mayer, *Political Origins of the New Diplomacy, 1917–1918* (New Haven, 1959).
35 Quoted in Lorna S. Jaffe, *The Decision to Disarm Germany* (Boston, 1985), 99.

line of the Rhine or the Weser? There were good reasons for all parties to settle for the armistice of 1918, especially when it effectively disarmed Germany and rendered the Reich unable to resist allied demands.

The difficulties that lay ahead were no more persuasive than the magnitude of what had already been attained by the time that the armistice had been negotiated. Wilson believed that representative governments were peaceful governments, and he forced the German regime to transform itself into a parliamentary government. Why fight further when this fundamental objective was secured? Indeed, he wired Secretary of State Robert Lansing in London that "too much *success* or *security* on the part of the Allies will make a genuine peace settlement exceedingly difficult, if not impossible."[36]

In one sense the German right was correct. The final collapse was political—it was a loss of will at home as well as in the field. This should not detract from the allies' achievement. Bringing a society to feel that further resistance will be more costly than beneficial is no less a military accomplishment than totally destroying an enemy. Nor should accepting terms on either side be stigmatized. It often means that the calculus of long-term utility, which historians regret was not imposed at the outset, finally does prevail. If the absence of rationality is deplored at the start of wars, its recovery at the end should not be a source of reproach. In sum, the result of World War I was a perfect application of Clausewitzian criteria and should have been satisfactory. The only difficulty was that the Germans did not undergo a unanimous political conversion. Rather, one group of leaders temporarily replaced another, and the nation was left in a state of implicit civil war, to whose final outcome future peace would again be ransom.

Herein lay the difficulty of the peace, which was burdened precisely because the war had ended with a political collapse. It not only depended explicitly on limiting any revival of German

36 Klaus Schwabe (trans., Robert and Rita Kumber), *Woodrow Wilson, Revolutionary Germany, and Peacemaking, 1918–1919* (Chapel Hill, 1985), 88. Schwabe argues that Wilson should have been content with the reformed parliamentary monarchy that the Germans had produced by mid-October 1918, and should not have abetted the final process of decomposition by giving way to domestic demands that he make an armistice apparently conditional upon abdication of the kaiser. Schwabe may overestimate the president's desire for restoring a European balance of power; the president's hope in the League made such calculations dispensable (114).

military potential, but implicitly on keeping the forces of revanchism from gaining power. These objectives proved incompatible. The terms of the treaty that created guarantees were likely to inflame German opinion. Indeed, the political dilemma cut even deeper. To maintain limits on Germany required an Anglo-French consensus on continual containment, especially since Soviet Russia was seen as neither a capable nor a desirable ally. French political forces were not significantly divided over the need for the British connection. By contrast, the British soon disagreed over the opportuneness of supporting France and the treaty precisely because they felt that Paris insisted on holding to its terms too rigidly. The politics of abandonment was to intersect with the politics of revanche.

But was there a promising alternative to the treaty? The Fourteen Points had beckoned to the Germans in September and October 1918 as the basis for a moderate settlement. But the Fourteen Points already stipulated the restoration to France of Alsace-Lorraine, the establishment of a Polish nation with an outlet to the sea, the civilian reparations. Alsace-Lorraine did not prove to be a real grievance, nor did northern Schleswig. However, German nationalists were not prepared to accept the losses in western Prussia, Poznan-Bromberg, and Silesia, and it is uncertain how their resentment would ever be reconciled with the provisions for a Polish state. Reparations became the most difficult tangle and a surrogate throughout the 1920s for trials of military strength between Germany and the allies. But the issue was not settled at Paris, more because of British than French aspirations, and had to be left until 1921 and 1924.[37]

Germany protested the reduction of her army and the temporary occupation of the Rhineland, but, if the primordial task was to give France security against its far more populous neighbor, some limitation had to be placed on the Reich's armed forces. The British always showed themselves far-sighted about the long-term need to reconcile the Germans so as not to drive them into an alignment with Bolshevik Russia or a nationalist reaction. But the British were less successful in devising a peace strategy that could appease Germany and protect the French at the same time.

---

37 See, most recently, Marc Trachtenberg, *Reparation in World Politics: France and European Economic Diplomacy, 1916–1923* (New York, 1980).

Should Paris then have gambled on appeasing Germany, especially if it were reclaiming Alsace-Lorraine? As Georges Clemenceau told the French chamber late in 1918, Wilson could be generous: the United States was far away from the Reich, but France was contiguous.[38]

One can envisage omission of the "prestige" clauses that so galled the Germans: trials for German war criminals became a bitter point, but there were war crimes; in any case, the demand was effectively relinquished. Article 231—the famous war guilt clause—served no good purpose except ostensibly to establish a legal basis for charging reparation. But, with or without Article 231, it was clear that disputes and recriminations about causality would embitter opinion on both sides. The publication of white papers and documents was already underway by the time the treaty was signed, although they were designed as much to discredit previous regimes as to incriminate their enemies. Germany could have been admitted to the League of Nations more promptly—although this decision might well have provided German statesmen with a powerful argument to oust the occupying powers. All in all, those democratic forces in Weimar willing to live with Versailles (but always hoping for piecemeal revision) were distressed but willing to be patient. Those who rejected the treaty were unlikely to be reconciled by any pact that could be achieved. The real case for leniency was that it might have strengthened the former at the expense of the latter. But the French thought that this gamble was speculative at best.

The major difficulty with the settlement of 1918/19 was less the treaty than the fact that the British were generally unwilling to help enforce it and the Americans withdrew completely. If Washington had been willing to connect war debts with reparations, a writing down of reparations would have been easier. If American opinion had accepted collective security, the League might have generated more moral force without being put to military tests it could not meet. The Vienna settlement survived until 1848 or 1856 less because the treaties were so brilliant than because the signatories were bound together by common interests. Britain might not cooperate in extending counterrevolution beyond Europe, but would not oppose the Eastern Courts' re-

38 Assemblée Nationale, *Journal Officiel: Chambre* (1918), 3732ff.

action on the Continent. Russian-Austrian cooperation provided the stability before the 1850s (at the cost of liberal-nationalist pressures that finally undermined the 1815 order) that might have been supplied by Anglo-French agreement in the interwar period.

The framers of the Vienna accords also faced an easier task in regard to their former foe than did the drafters of the Versailles treaty. There was no state that had to be resurrected at the expense of French territory in 1815, but there was one that had to be created at the expense of Germany in 1919. When Belgium achieved independence in the 1830s it seceded only from a small country, the Kingdom of the Netherlands. The potentially disruptive irredenta were in east central Europe, precisely where they remained to handicap peace a century later. Indeed, the collapse of the Habsburg state simply added another major source of irredentism within Czechoslovakia to those that had been created by the Prussian cessions to Poland.

Both Vienna and Versailles represented ideological as well as territorial settlements. Vienna incorporated a conservative bias; it was a peace designed to make the world safe for landed elites that had been severely shaken between 1789 and 1815. When British opinion swung away from its panicked Toryism, one of the major guarantors backed out, but so long as Vienna and Petersburg cooperated (until the Crimean War) the principles could still be enforced. Versailles was intended to make the world safe for democracy. But this result would have required the cooperation of at least two of the three major democratic powers. The British became suspicious of French designs by the end of the war; the Americans repudiated the settlement.

Versailles was also a settlement that implicitly supported capitalist internationalism as a corollary of political liberalism. But the United States was unwilling to pay the price for the international economic order it desired. By so reluctantly accepting responsibility for recycling the international payments Europeans owed to Americans, Washington overburdened the economic framework which internationalist republicans and democrats agreed guaranteed a democratic comity. Had the economic connections between German payments and American investment been established on a less precarious basis than they finally were, then Germany's western orientation, which briefly prevailed under Gustav Stresemann (1924–1929), could have been prolonged.

In effect, such an outcome would have meant that Weimar evolved into Bonn without the intervening regime. Even dismissing such a happy result, had London and Paris at least enforced the military clauses of the treaty in the mid-1930s, they might have avoided the subsequent catastrophe.

The incompatibilities in the international order that lay at the root of World War I were resolved only after World War II. In the long view, the two wars represented a passage of hegemony at the expense of the British and, to a lesser degree, the French, and other European empires. But the original challengers, Germany and Japan, did not have the strength to seize the succession, and instead the Soviet Union and the United States were drawn in. Such great transitions are probably hard to manage peacefully. As late as 1956, Britain was unwilling to yield her privileges peacefully: how could one have expected a bloodless cession in 1914? The Germans showed themselves impatient for grandeur in 1905, 1910/11, and 1914; moreover, they were outfitted with a governing system that encouraged fitfull irresponsibility, and they were tied to an ally whose difficulties would expose them to one crisis after another.

The peaceful transfer of international hegemony was all the more difficult because of the interaction of domestic and foreign politics. The first half of the twentieth century was an era in which Europe's elites differed fundamentally on how to incorporate the industrial working class into politics. Advocates of gradual cooptation were arrayed against those who wished to resist further encroachment, and playing on xenophobic or imperialist sentiments was the major strategy by which groups resisting domestic political concessions sought to rally middle-class majorities. A new class compromise as well as a new pattern of international leadership had eventually to be forged.

These epochal challenges to the domestic and international status quo were bound to make peaceful adjustments difficult at best. Statesmen who were gifted in channeling the currents of reform in mass politics, such as Lloyd George, were not necessarily equally gifted in international politics. And statesmen of earlier generations who are admired for their mastery of the international arena, such as Otto von Bismarck, enjoyed a constellation of forces in which they could exploit smaller wars without the risks of 1914. Nonetheless, these difficulties do not mean that the twin transitions of the early twentieth century had necessarily to be attended by world war. Looking at the political order as of 1914—the vitality of the United States and the modernization of Russia, the thin material base on which the British Empire was run, and the piecemeal concessions being made to working-class claims for a share in capitalism's fruits and domestic political arrangements—one realizes that, had there not been war, the tendencies in place might well have led to an equilibrium similar to the one that followed World War II. The major difference is that, although Russian power would have increased, its scope might have been less oppressive for the peoples east of the Elbe.

The general direction of world history may—only in retrospect, of course—seem foreordained. But the process by which a new order emerges is a contingent one. The world wars were not easy to avoid, but the worst lesson to learn from them would be the pervasive fatalism that so afflicted statesmen during the last days of peace. This caution applies as well to the sophisticated fatalism that the study of large-scale organization tends to impart. Such chastened resignation is perhaps natural after the 1960s, when the tendency was to believe that political and societal constraints at home and abroad were easily overcome. But it would be an incomplete reading of history. When asked how the war had happened, Bethmann Hollweg allegedly sighed, If only I knew. *Er hat es nicht gewollt*: he had not wanted it. The problem was that he had not really wanted the alternative sufficiently.

Jeffrey L. Hughes

The Origins of World War II in Europe: British Deterrence Failure and German Expansionism

Explanations of the origins of World War II tend to emphasize either deliberate, if failed, choices or inexorable processes. The first view indicts Adolf Hitler's aggrandizing choices and preference for violence, and questions the judgment and strategy of the appeasers, personified, correctly or not, by Prime Minister Neville Chamberlain. The second view broadens the focus, pointing to secular changes in relative power between states; to the relation between states' commitments and their ability to uphold and protect them; and to domestic, economic, and cultural dynamics that individually, or in combination, predisposed the situation to conflict. Attention to both dimensions is necessary to appreciate Britain's strategy as the central axis of diplomacy and rivalry with Germany in the 1930s and to distill the "lessons" of the origins of the war.

In the 1930s, Britain took over the mantle of maintaining the status quo vis-à-vis Germany. Chamberlain and his associates faced the classic issue of judging the nature of its adversary's ambitions. Morgenthau captured the dilemma for Britain in this period: "While it would be fatal to counter imperialistic designs with measures appropriate to a policy of the status quo, it would be only a little less risky to deal with a policy [of an adversary] seeking adjustments within the status quo as though it were imperialistic."[1] In an epoch where war's catastrophic destructiveness

Jeffrey L. Hughes is Senior Analyst, White House Situation Staff, National Security Council. He contributed three chapters to Jan F. Triska (ed.), *Dominant Powers and Subordinate States: The United States in Latin America and the Soviet Union in Eastern Europe* (Durham, 1986).

He is grateful for the helpful comments and encouragement which he has received at various stages of this paper from Alexander L. George, Lance L. Farrar, Jr., Robert Jervis, Joseph S. Nye, Jr., Richard Rosencrance, and Richard H. Ullman. The views expressed in this article are those of the author alone.

1 Hans J. Morgenthau, *Politics among Nations* (New York, 1960; 3rd ed.), 63–64. Hitler in 1928 focused on the other horn of the dilemma: "A peace policy that fails leads just as directly to the destruction of a people . . . as a war policy that miscarries." See Adolf Hitler (trans. Salvador Attanasio), *Hitler's Secret Book* (New York, 1961), 7.

282 JEFFREY L. HUGHES

was no longer in doubt, this dilemma of statecraft posed a recurring problem of choice for the British.

Before the end of World War I, Veblen had anticipated a recurrence of imperial challenge to Britain. In the 1920s, Bainville forecast the general lines of conflict and alliances that were to materialize by 1940. By the early 1930s, Wells, Schuman, and others anticipated important specifics of the coming conflict.[2] At the same time, Britain's dependence upon its far-flung empire was increasing, whereas its ability simultaneously to defend it against rising challenges from Japan, Italy, and Germany was decreasing. This tension between threats and British interests posed a second dilemma: inexorable geopolitical trends were making the empire more vulnerable, but wars to defend the British Empire could also imperil its sinews. Opting for war if peace were, in fact, possible was worse than delaying war even if it meant that conditions might become less favorable geographically.

Taking as givens that Hitler was bent on war and that for cultural, economic, and political reasons many Germans were susceptible to follow his lead, important questions still remain. What explains Britain's responses to Hitler's challenges? What was Britain's strategy? Was it flawed not only in execution but also in conception? What effect on the timing and escalation of conflict in World War II did the British strategy have?

Chamberlain recognized and attempted to deal with the dilemmas concerning German intentions and constraints on British power. It is not sufficient simply to indict Chamberlain's failed choices, or to underplay the significance of his strategy by stressing macrotrends. For what is truly interesting in Chamberlain's

2 For example, among the more farsighted accounts, Thorstein Veblen, *An Inquiry into the Nature of Peace* (New York, 1971), 82–85, argued that as a "dynastic empire" Germany, in the absence of an effective League of Nations, would recuperate and try again to achieve their dominion and that "no compact binds the dynastic statesman, and no consideration other than the pursuit of imperial dominion commands his attention"; Jaques Bainville, *Les Consequences Politiques de la Paix* (Paris, 1920), argued that Germany was destined to recover predominance, seek revenge, absorb Austria, subjugate Poland in collaboration with Russia, and continue moving east with the concurrence of Italy; and Frederick L. Schuman, *International Politics* (New York, 1937; 2nd ed.), ix, xiv, 740–746, started making arguments in 1933 that Germany, Italy, and Japan might ally to pursue conquest until stopped by a superior coalition that would materialize only on the brink of a suicidal world conflict, if ever, that Czechoslovakia would be partitioned if not "betrayed," that Germany might attack Russia, and that Russia would ultimately extend its influence in Europe.

strategy as revealed in recent archival research, and what has not been sufficiently appreciated or integrated into explanations for the war's origins, is how Chamberlain's views of air-power strategy were designed to cope with the two above dilemmas.[3]

Conceptions of air power shaped Chamberlain's diplomacy in terms of the means that he believed were available, and the types of threats that he believed he faced. Although British policy was ineffective in deterring the war—in retrospect, war against Hitler probably could not have been deterred—once one comprehends Chamberlain's conception of the nature of air power, it is easier to appreciate that his policies followed from his central premises and were informed by a coherent strategy designed to cope with Britain's central dilemmas. Its primary failure was to assume that Hitler's conception of air power was similar and therefore that threats had a common currency. Chamberlain pursued a coherent strategy—a strategy that had unanticipated diplomatic consequences because of systematic misperceptions caused by the strategic doctrine that he adopted.

BRITISH STRATEGY IN THE 1930S   Fear is one of the most difficult emotions to capture historically, for it leaves little trace when it is over.[4] The image of any future air war was "by the 1930s . . . an awesome, overshadowing presence that preoccupied men quite as much as nuclear arsenals do today." It was anticipated that air power would have decisive consequences, and lead to a sophisticated system of deterrence.[5] The prospect of air war had an exaggerated impact upon Britain because of erroneous extrapolations from the experiences of World War I, the vulnerability of centrally important London, and the publicity it garnered as early

---

3 Archival material and research of the last decade and a half raise new and fundamental questions about the causes and lessons of the conflict. The appearance of new specialized studies of British policy on grand strategy, air strategy, intelligence, the army, cabinet policy and crises, financial constraints, and the dominions provide information that, when combined with a fresh look at older sources, allows us to ask new questions and challenge existing interpretations of British policy and also standard conceptions of the origins of the war.

4 Herbert Butterfield, *International Conflict in the Twentieth Century* (New York, 1960), 81–82.

5 Lee Kennett, *A History of Strategic Bombing* (New York, 1982), 178; Uri Bialer, *The Shadow of the Bomber: The Fear of Air Attack and British Politics, 1932–1939* (London, 1980), 158. See George H. Quester, *Deterrence before Hiroshima: The Airpower Background of Modern Strategy* (New York, 1966), on the genesis of deterrence theorizing.

as the 1920s. It was feared that the next war would start with a German attempt to deliver a "knock-out blow" from the air. Recent studies have highlighted the ways that this "shadow of the bomber" influenced sober British strategists and decision-makers in the 1930s.

Theories of deterrence and conceptions of air-power strategy played a key role in British decision-making in the 1930s. They were more central than appeasement diplomacy in skewing Britain's response to Hitler's challenge to international stability. Britain did not fail to perceive Hitler as a threat in the early 1930s; it was the nature of the threat that was misconstrued. Britain's top decision-makers and military advisers attributed their own assumptions about the significance of air war to Hitler. These conceptions of air power biased their view of Hitler's strategy and perceptions of threats. British strategic policy sought a deterrent capability that could guarantee security in an unquiet age. But the same strategic conception that seemed to promise security could also increase vulnerability; mirror-image assumptions were attributed to Germany, and the prospect of achieving deterrence seemed ever more distant as the 1930s progressed. British conceptions of what would deter Hitler, and their perceptions of the constraints under which their own policy was operating, were a function of their own strategic doctrine. Only by integrating this factor into the better known aspects of British diplomacy can a balanced account of the origins of World War II emerge.

In the early 1930s, Chamberlain consciously sought deterrence through offensive air power. By 1937, Britain believed that its strategy was counterbalanced by Germany's capabilities, and erroneously assumed that their own worst fears of air war were reflected in Hitler's strategy. Britain then switched to a defensive emphasis on fighters, coupled with the threat of an economic blockade to defeat Germany in any long war. Britain believed that its economic threat had proved effective in a number of instances, and that its diplomacy was succeeding. Hitler, however, neither understood the basis of British strategy nor recognized the blockade as a significant British economic weapon. He noted only the decline in the direct and immediate pressure that Britain could bring to bear, which increasingly skewed his perception of British resolve.

Consequently, just as Britain was coming to perceive its economic weapon as its trump card, Hitler became more emboldened to absorb territory in the east that would ultimately enable him to obtain oil and wheat and thereby imperil the efficacy of the blockade. The British guarantee to Poland in 1939 stemmed from its resolve to protect Rumania and deny Hitler such resources. Hitler's surprise that Britain did not renege on this commitment was the result of his failure to understand British strategy and Britain's failure to communicate it. Hitler had not envisioned conflict with Britain or advances toward the west until the mid-1940s. However, when he finally recognized the effectiveness of the British economic threat and its resolve to oppose his limited wars in eastern Europe, he was not deterred. Instead, he resolved to escalate the stakes of war in the short term rather than lose in the long run. The attack on France was improvised on those grounds.

Hitler was bent on some form of conquest. The argument here addresses the timing of escalation, and the degree to which earlier misperceptions by Britain and Germany set in motion the dynamics that led both nations to resolve to go forward out of a sense that inaction meant precipitate decline. War over Poland against Britain was not the war that Hitler had planned to fight. After the fall of France, Britain received the air attacks that it had expected, but for the wrong reason. British deterrence policy had failed, not simply appeasement, which in itself was a rational policy that hewed fairly closely to balance-of-power logic. Chamberlain's strategic assumptions were widely held, and, as late as 1941, Winston Churchill manifested the same confidence as Chamberlain had earlier exhibited concerning the efficacy of air power and economic attrition against Germany.

This article focuses on the conception and formulation of British military strategy and on its effect on Hitler's perceptions and policies in subsequent diplomatic encounters. It addresses how Britain's otherwise reasonable grand strategy for dealing with the changing international balance of power was vitiated by its deterrence strategies, and how this interpretation helps to make sense of a series of classic strategic "puzzles" of prewar diplomacy. It also suggests some new and sobering lessons for the contemporary period.

CHAMBERLAIN'S STRATEGY, 1933–1936   Chamberlain considered himself a realist and believed that diplomacy was a function of power and balancing risks. A recent study drawing on his private papers notes his "cold realism" and his "hard nosed pursuit of *raison d'état.*" By 1933, Chamberlain saw Germany as the central threat to Britain, a view he held throughout the 1930s. Although the chiefs of staff (COS) initially disagreed about whether Japan or Germany posed the greater threat, in November Chamberlain argued that Europe should have priority over the Far East. He warned in 1934 that "we are giving too much attention to the details of disarmament and not enough to security." He opposed the British Disarmament Conventions in 1933 and in 1935. This position was not popular. He endorsed the 1934 Defence Requirements Committee (DRC) report that argued that "deterrence of German aggression was the best long-term safeguard" to keeping Japan in check, recognized Germany as the "ultimate potential enemy," and based its recommendations on the assumption that there would be war by 1939. Soon thereafter, he "invited the Air Ministry to put forward a plan based on the consideration that Germany might become a major threat within five years." Germany was the linchpin of his strategy: if Germany could be held in check, neither Japan nor Italy would confront Britain alone. Conversely, war with Germany could mean war with all three of the nations.[6]

"General" deterrence—reducing the incentives for a potential adversary to consider an attack against oneself or one's interests—rather than "immediate" crisis deterrence—the attempt to dissuade attack where attack is believed to be imminent or seriously contemplated against oneself or a target—was Chamberlain's main focus at this point. His rationale for advocating a dramatic increase in offensive air power concentrated against Germany, at the expense of other defense programs, was general deterrence. Chamberlain also hoped that his deterrence might extend to smaller

6   Keith Feiling, *The Life of Neville Chamberlain* (London, 1946), 253, 312, 319; Arnold Wolfers, *Britain and France between Two World Wars* (New York, 1940), 227–228; Larry William Fuchser, *Neville Chamberlain and Appeasement* (New York, 1982), 35, 44, 49, 161. Malcolm Smith, *British Air Strategy between the Wars* (Oxford, 1984), 126, 133. Charles Loch Mowat, *Britain between the Wars, 1918–1940* (Chicago, 1955), 532–542, 546–556. George C. Penden, *British Rearmament and the Treasury, 1932–1939* (Edinburgh, 1979), 109–110. Keith Middlemas, *The Strategy of Appeasement: The British Government and Germany, 1937–1939* (Chicago, 1972), 50.

countries in Europe. If this bargaining strategy failed to bring about a negotiated agreement, however, Britain would require perpetual superiority to have confidence in its deterrent power since Britain was more geographically compact, and thus more vulnerable than Germany. Like the "massive retaliation" strategy of the nuclear era, this strategy had the disadvantage of being a reactive policy: external challenges drove responses rather than internal decisions. It was the policy of a status quo, rather than a revisionist, power.[7]

Chamberlain backed this strategy as the best available under the circumstances, but noted, in August 1934, "a universal feeling of apprehension about the future." In 1935, Hitler's abandonment of the Versailles Treaty's limitations on ground troops and his claim to have achieved air parity with France confirmed these forebodings. In mid-1935, Chamberlain spoke of the "need for such a recasting of our air programme as would show its truly formidable character and thus act as a deterrent." By early 1936, he expressed concern about matching German rearmament and felt that air deterrence was more important than ever. A proposal for a new air package that involved larger bombers with bigger payloads soon reinvigorated Chamberlain's view that "if we can keep out of war for a few years, we shall have an air force of such striking power that no one will care to run risks with it." His "'enthusiasm' for an air force which, when fully developed, would possess 'terrific striking power' and be 'the most formidable deterrent to war that could be devised'" continued at least through the autumn of 1936.[8] Soon after, military advice tempered Chamberlain's optimism, but did not alter his image of the effectiveness of air power.

Chamberlain's attitude toward the army also needs to be viewed in the context of his image of air power. British policy

7 See Patrick Morgan, *Deterrence: A Conceptual Analysis* (Beverly Hills, 1977), 25–45, regarding the distinction between "general" deterrence and "immediate" crisis deterrence. For Chamberlain's views at the time, see, for example, Norman H. Gibbs, *Grand Strategy: Rearmament Policy* (London, 1976), 106; Montgomery H. Hyde, *British Air Policy between the Wars: 1918–1939* (London, 1976), 304; Penden, *British Rearmament*, 119; Smith, *British Air Strategy*, 135; Michael Howard, *The Continental Commitment: The Dilemma of British Defense Policy in the Era of the Two World Wars* (London, 1972), 109. See W. J. Reader, *Architect of Airpower* (London, 1968), 233–234.

8 Fuchser, *Neville Chamberlain*, 40; Norman H. Gibbs, *Grand Strategy*, 175n, 447n; Penden, *British Rearmament*, 121, 125, 128; Smith, *British Air Strategy*, 164–165; Feiling, *Life of Neville Chamberlain*, 314.

has been criticized for failing to realize that a commitment to France might have acted as a deterrent to Germany. Although the horrors of analogies with 1914 no doubt weighed heavily in many of the decisions that were made by Chamberlain and his colleagues, especially their opposition to developing the army for rapid continental use, Chamberlain had coherent reasons for his policies.[9] In an era of air power, he questioned the army's ability to reach the Continent in time to have an effect and thought that the funds would be better spent elsewhere. Basil H. Liddell Hart had independently made such an argument in 1934; Sir Hugh Trenchard, who was the "father" of the Royal Air Force (RAF), but not averse in principle to the army, Lord Weir, a canny industrial adviser, and even Lord Ismay, the deputy of the Committee of Imperial Defence (CID) from the army, all came to share Chamberlain's position. Theirs was a logical deduction from a shared image of air power.

Bureaucratic Structure, Military Advice, and Air Strategy, 1919–1936 Interservice competition had important effects on grand strategy. As a result of the Ten Year Rule of 1919—supported by Churchill as late as 1928—all of the armed services felt critical shortcomings and had ample reason to perceive multiple threats. As rearmament proceeded, service needs were complicated by technological change, uncertainty as to the nature and timing of the threats, and constraints on resources. In the 1920s, the navy and army waged bureaucratic battles with the fledging RAF to try to integrate it into their own command structures, either as tactical support in a Fleet Air Arm or for troops. The RAF supported its doctrine of "strategic interception" in the 1920s, which involved cooperation with the other services; over time, however, the RAF was driven to proclaim a unique and central role as an independent, strategic offensive deterrent and strike force. Contests over control, heightened by economic stringency, were waged with the navy through 1937. This increased doctrinal stridency decreased interservice coordination, and distracted the RAF from being as self-critical as it might otherwise have been vis-à-vis Germany.

The procedures for processing intelligence and evaluating strategic options had important consequences. At that time, each

9 See Michael Howard, *The Continental Commitment*, 100–101, 111, 115, 118, 125–126, 131, 137, 142, for specific attribution of World War I images.

service had its own intelligence directorate. As a result, analyses were filtered through each service staff's own doctrines, preoccupations, and perceived needs, complicating the integration of information across services. Evaluations of intelligence and strategic capabilities were drafted below the level of the COS and were reported upward in a fashion that led to additive analyses, rather than integrated tradeoffs and assessments across services and theaters. The COS made general recommendations to the political leadership based on these reports.[10] The unquestioned asssumptions used by the air staff led first to an underestimation of the rate of Luftwaffe expansion and then, once it was accurately perceived in 1936, to an overstatement of the offensive bombing threat that the buildup posed. Civilian leaders felt that Britain was falling behind Germany and sought at least to sustain the public pledge of front-line parity, requiring shortcuts that served only to increase the despondency of the air staff's reports.

As the perception of the air threat grew and expenditures increased, the other services also became more pessimistic because their needs were not being met. Intelligence was joined with worst-case capability analyses by the service staffs, which were forwarded to the COS. Some of the threats envisioned by the COS started to materialize at the same time that the COS was receiving lower-level staff reports detailing each service's deficiencies. The British cabinet received a gloomy account of their military position as the diplomatic storm clouds were gathering in Europe.

HITLER'S STRATEGY AND CONCEPTIONS, 1933–1936   Hitler was cautious through 1936.[11] He did not yet have unitary control over

10   Wesley K. Wark, *The Ultimate Enemy: British Intelligence and Nazi Germany, 1933–1939* (Ithaca, 1985), *passim*; Williamson Murray, *The Change in the European Balance of Power, 1938–1939* (Princeton, 1984), 62–64. Chamberlain astutely complained that the COS tended to submit aggregate rather than joint plans around this time, indicating that, although he was not a slave to COS opinions, he studied them closely and was undoubtedly influenced by them. (See David Dilks, "'The Unnecessary War'? Military Advice and Foreign Policy, 1931–1939," in Adrian Preston [ed.], *General Staffs and Diplomacy before the Second World War* [London, 1978], 117.) Chamberlain seems to have given COS opinion more weight as his hopes for an effective offensive deterrent faded and as the prospect of the services actually facing combat increased throughout the decade.
11   The account of Hitler's policy in this and subsequent sections draws particularly on Klaus Hidebrand, *The Foreign Policy of the Third Reich* (Berkeley, 1973); idem, *The Third Reich* (London, 1984); Andreas Hillgruber, "England's Place in Hitler's Plans for World

policy. At that time, his revisionist objectives overlapped those of the professionals in the German Foreign Office, and his policies were consistent with the concerns of the German capitalists. Ironically, just as Britain was identifying Germany as "the ultimate potential enemy" in 1933, Hitler envisioned having Britain as an ally. It is useful to remember in evaluating British strategy that those acquiescing in Hitler's ascension to power thought that they could control him and use him as a front.[12] If German generals could be deceived at close range, one perhaps should laud, rather than indict, the prescience of British perceptions of danger at a time when Hitler sought an alliance with the British Empire. It also suggests the challenge that Britain faced in evaluating the conflicting signals from the various factions even as Hitler's policy took on a more individual cast.

Hitler sought to renounce colonial ambitions in exchange for Britain allowing him a free hand in the east. He believed that Britain would not object to a powerful German state so long as its aims were continental in character and that the basic divergence of their interests would be conducive to a stable relationship. He sought agreement with Britain through "intensive wooing" combined with vague threats. Grander objectives, outlined in *Mein Kampf* in 1925/26, were relegated to a more visionary future.[13] Consistent with his writings, Hitler was pursuing a bilateral agreement with Britain. Britain, in contrast, was pursuing multilateral ones. German withdrawal from the Disarmament Conference and League of Nations in October 1933 was meant to be a prelude to a joint arrangement, whereas in fact it helped to crystallize the British DRC priorities against it. Later, when Britain sought bilateral arrangements, Hitler's objectives had expanded or changed. At different times, both pursued agreements with each other, which were based on erroneous assumptions and led to the disillusionment of both nations. Britain did not behave according to Hitler's plan for them; Hitler's actions confirmed Britain's worst fears.

Domination," *Journal of Contemporary History*, IX (1974), 5–22; *idem, Germany and the Two World Wars* (Cambridge, Mass., 1981). All of these books focus on Hitler's role as a leader but give due attention to domestic and international factors. *Hitler's Secret Book* offers insight into Hitler's views of force and diplomacy.

12   See Gordon A. Craig, *Germany, 1866–1945* (Oxford, 1978), 693.

13   Hildebrand, *Foreign Policy*, 45. See *Hitler's Secret Book*, 146–159; Hitler (trans. Ralph Manheim), *Mein Kampf* (Boston, 1943).

The army was the crucial means of projecting German influence; air power came to be viewed in tactical terms. Hitler regarded his prospective naval buildup as a central threat to Britain. German diplomatic pronouncements about colonies, first put forward by traditional conservative expansionist elements and later taken up by Hitler as a bargaining point with Britain in 1935, were not really of central concern to him. Joachim von Ribbentrop, the German ambassador to Britain from 1936 to 1938, unintentionally helped to confuse the British on this point by earnestly promoting colonial rectification in traditional Wilhelmian fashion, in addition to embracing Hitler's eastern objectives.

Air power was central to British thinking, both as a deterrent to Germany and increasingly as a potential threat to themselves. The British admiralty favored the naval accord of 1935 as a means of meeting the burdens of defense in the Far East rather than as a means to counteract German naval power. British strategists thought that Hitler would not dare run a naval race, and that he would turn to air power.[14] Britain also believed that German diplomatic pronouncements were reliable indicators of Germany's real grievances and took them as a starting point to achieve mutually acceptable changes to the status quo. Both misjudged the central threats presented by the other, their respective sense of vulnerability, and their diplomatic objectives. The prospects for friendship on the terms that Hitler envisioned were destined to be frustrated, and Britain's fears heightened.

It is ironic that Britain's policy later came to be viewed as appeasement when Hitler himself was becoming more antagonistic to Britain at that time because he saw the British as resistant to a bilateral agreement with him. His initial hopes for an unencumbered continental policy were frustrated, leading him to take a harder line with Britain. It is also ironic that British policy was later criticized for failing to support collective security more vigorously in an effort to deter Hitler, when actually Hitler's wrath was generated by Britain's multilateral stance during the mid-1930s. Hitler did skillfully take advantage of Mediterranean dis-

---

14 Chamberlain had differed with the Admiralty's emphasis in 1934 on building more capital ships to confront Japan, favoring bombers against Germany. He argued that only if "the Admiralty were to advise that capital ships would be needed in a war against Germany, he . . . would accept that advice with the expenditure it involved" (Bialer, *Shadow of the Bomber*, 135).

tractions involving the League of Nations and Italy, though at this time rumors of precipitate action by France and Britain were alone sufficient to make Hitler indecisive, causing him almost to cancel reoccupation of the Rhineland. The lack of a British response to this continental action—its unwillingness to escalate to an air war to prevent the Germans from "walking into their own backyard"—and their active response to German plans to exceed the naval agreement, kept alive Hitler's hope that Britain would agree to a division of spoils. The Spanish Civil War was another example of Hitler's probing British reactions, intuitively judging them, and gaining a favorable impression from Britain's lack of intervention. In fact, Britain had made a hard-nosed power calculation that defending Spanish republicanism was not necessary for imperial defense.

CHAMBERLAIN'S STRATEGY, 1937/38   Chamberlain became prime minister in May 1937. He asserted control over his own ministers, but the policies that he advocated in the cabinet were based closely on military advice. Between 1937 and 1938, the German air threat loomed great. Evaluations by military intelligence went from optimism to pessimism; a sense of vulnerability soon pervaded strategic planning and diplomacy. The February 1937 COS Sub-Committee on Planning for a War with Germany assumed that Germany would not only be the aggressor, but would instigate air attacks in the west first in an effort "to exploit her superior preparedness by trying to knock out Great Britain rapidly, or to knock out France rapidly, since she is not well placed for a long war."[15] This expectation of an early air attack in the west raised Britain's threshold in responding to limited German actions: Britain viewed the prospect of any local conflict as tightly linked to escalation to air strikes on their homeland, seemingly leaving them with only two options, capitulation or all-out war. It remained unclear whether Germany, as a challenger to the status quo, was implacable or could be satisfied short of bringing on mutual conflagration.

As Britain's sense of vulnerability increased, her confidence in her economic ability to sustain direct competition in armaments decreased. The "ideal" offensive deterrence strategy was becom-

15 Gibbs, *Grand Strategy*, 283–284.

ing less feasible or credible in the near term, and the process of rearmament itself brought into question how long Britain could sustain the financial stability needed to compete over the long term; an American recession in 1937 seemed to confirm the dangers of an unbalanced budget. Consequently, in early 1937 the cabinet sought to reconcile requests for military funding with what was believed to be economically feasible.

British diplomacy was one way to reduce threats and buy time for rearmament. A second approach examined Britain's economic problems as compared to those of its adversaries, particularly Germany. Policymakers turned to a new source of intelligence outside the traditional COS ambit, the Industrial Intelligence Centre (IIC). Starting in July 1937, the IIC examined Germany vulnerability to economic pressure, and reported that, because of severe constraints on raw materials, an economic blockade could have a crippling effect, although it would not prevent Germany from waging a short war. Like the air staff, however, the IIC also assumed that its own concerns—with economic potential, reserves, and threats thereto—would be mirrored, closely monitored, and evaluated similarly in Germany.[16]

Britain worried that the arms race would not only challenge its own financial stability, but drive Germany and Italy to war. Chamberlain felt Italy's Ethiopian campaign stemmed from a desperate need for raw materials.[17] The Foreign Office now noted discussion in Germany that rearmament was proceeding too fast in light of the available supply of food and raw materials. In 1936 Anthony Eden had argued that Germany was suffering severe economic hardship that could lead to an explosion in war, and therefore that Britain should foster Germany's recovery. In April 1937 Eden received reports of disputes in Germany over the pace of rearmament, with some urging moderation in light of the precariousness of the food and raw materials supply. Hjalmar

16   Wark, *Ultimate Enemy*, 177, 160; Francis H. Hinsley et al., *British Intelligence in the Second World War: Its Influence on Strategy and Operations* (New York, 1979), 63; Gibbs, *Grand Strategy*, 109.

17   See C. A. MacDonald, "Economic Appeasement and the German 'Moderates' 1937–1939," *Past & Present*, 56 (1972), 105–135, and David E. Kaiser, *Economic Diplomacy and the Origins of the Second World War* (Princeton, 1980), 282, regarding the fear of Germany. See Brian Bond, *British Military Policy between the Two World Wars* (Oxford, 1980), 266, regarding Italy. See Ian Macleod, *Neville Chamberlain* (London, 1961), 185, regarding Ethiopia.

Schacht, the German minister of economics, made essentially the same point to Eden in September 1937; Schacht believed that Germany needed raw materials from colonies in order to avoid continental conflict.[18] German economic vulnerability appeared to provide incentives for cooperation with Britain. The premise of Germany's economic vulnerability was unquestioned; only the effect of this financial weakness remained undetermined.

The defense reviews of late 1937 by Sir Thomas Inskip, the newly appointed minister for co-ordination of defence, highlight the confluence of several trends, and show how Chamberlain resolved the tensions facing the faltering offensive strategy. Inskip had to reconcile the ideal with the affordable, and logic with practice. In November, he challenged the latest air expansion program based on the traditional RAF offensive doctrine, arguing that Britain should avail itself of advances in fighter planes and radar that had developed since 1935. Home Defence was to become the priority for the expansion of the army to increase its anti-aircraft capabilities, rather than for deployment on the Continent. Given the image of air power, the possible knock-out blow, and the intelligence reports of the time, this argument was logical and was supported by some of Britain's leading strategists. Chamberlain was now attending to Britain's vulnerabilities as much as the deterrent effects of the bomber. He "was skeptical about any understanding restricting aerial bombardment" and wanted any such agreements to be enforcable; the perception of lapsed deterrence required a conceptual fall-back to defenses.[19]

18 Hinsley et al., *British Intelligence*, 68, 74; Andrew Crozier, "Prelude to Munich: British Foreign Policy and Germany, 1935–38," *European Studies Review*, VI (1976), 361, 365.
19 This interpretation of the change in British strategy differs in important ways from Barry Posen's account in *The Sources of Military Doctrine* (Ithaca, 1984), 141–178. His argument would expect that the RAF, as a military organization, would have favored an offensive doctrine and that only after systemic constraints indicated that the strategy was failing would civilians intervene to institute a more reasoned defensive strategy. But there is evidence that civilian leaders often had a more extreme offensive air deterrent in mind than the RAF and that the 1937 change in strategy was not a rejection of earlier doctrine but an illustration of how much civilian leaders and even critics of air strategy remained prisoners of it, neither reacting to nor constructively influencing systemic factors. In fact, key skeptics who had bureaucratic interests that ran against giving the RAF doctrine emphasis or credence nonetheless did so by 1937. Liddell Hart accepted that limitations would necessarily be placed on the army, Admiral Ernie Chatfield on the navy, and Sir Maurice Hankey, a long-time savant of the cabinet, on both. The irony is that the immediate defensive objective of the defensive air strategy became relevant only after the fall of France, which was not a systemic premise for implementing it.

In late 1937 Inskip coupled this change in emphasis in air strategy with Britain's economic staying power as a deterrent to (and, if necessary, a weapon of) war with Germany. He argued that if the "knock-out" blow could be deterred with anti-aircraft measures, and if, simultaneously, Britain and the dominions could effectively harness their economic capability to beat Germany in a long war, then Germany would not dare go to war in the short run. Chamberlain became enamored of Inskip's argument that Britain's economic stability and potential conveyed a deterrent threat beyond mere numbers of forces. He asserted that not only would it be logical to assume that other governments held this in mind, but that this deterrent would undercut the rationale for attempting a knock-out blow from the air, since such an attack would be the equivalent of engaging in a long war. The cabinet decision endorsing this logic only superficially resolved the dead end to which pursuit of the offensive strategy had led.[20] The strategy was compelling in that it recognized that Britain would not have to be the first to initiate an offensive air strike; the economic base of the three services ultimately rested on the health of the economy and support of the dominions; and that large weapons stocks would be of little use in the event of a crippling preemptive air strike. It also provided a way to draw the dominions in to support Britain and took due note of key German economic vulnerabilities.

At first glance the new approach appears to have been a radical break with the offensive air strategy; in fact it was still hostage to that mode of thinking. It still attributed the strategy of the knock-out blow to Germany and assumed that Germany would pose the gravest danger if it moved west first. Like the offensive strategy, it assumed that the new emphasis on economic war would be accurately perceived by Germany and that it would also affect Germany's air strategy. In fact, Hitler was determined to move east and perceived Britain's economic strategy not as a threat, but as an indication of Britain's declining ability to apply pressure against Germany in the short term. Chamberlain, meanwhile, had anticipated that Austria and Czechoslovakia were next on Hitler's agenda. Although he recognized that Germany wanted

20 Gibbs, *Grand Strategy*, 284. Ian Colvin, *The Chamberlain Cabinet, 1937–1939* (New York, 1971), 80. Bialer, *Shadow of the Bomber*, 116.

to dominate eastern Europe, he believed not only that this could happen peacefully, without territorial incorporation, but also that it could have some beneficial effects on German behavior.[21]

In planning policy, Britain was shifting from its reactive offensive bomber strategy to a less reactive containment plan based upon core British interests. This change in perspective helps to explain the prime minister's diplomacy in 1938. It was not simply a question of fighting now or later, as has been argued, since war with Germany involved assessments of broader threats that involved Italy and Japan as well. Nor was it simply a matter of giving in to Hitler. Rather, given the assumptions about Germany's economy, the issue was how to deter Germany sufficiently to bring it acceptably within the fold without precipitating the very war that they were attempting to prevent. In addition, it was felt that Britian would benefit if war could be delayed.

In early 1938, Hitler's threats and the Austrian government's counterresponse resulted in Hitler's troops being "invited" into Austria, incorporating that nation into the Reich; events outran even Hitler's own initial expectations. Anschluss was sufficiently popular in Austria that there was no chance that Britain or France would resist it by force. Chamberlain concluded that "it is perfectly evident, surely, now that force is the only argument that Germany understands." After Anschluss, the Foreign Office recognized that there were gaps in British strategy. "The Germans are clearly not in a position to fight a great or a long war. . . . But on the other hand neither we nor the French possess the offensive power to prevent Germany from working her will in Central Europe." A COS report noted that Britain would be unprepared for the world war that could arise from a Czechoslovakian crisis, particularly in terms of air attacks. Inskip noted that Germany could still fight a short war and that Britian could lose a short one involving air attacks. Chamberlain concluded that Anschluss made Czechoslovakia's defense militarily impracticable. Defending the Czechs involved a commitment to undertake a long war to resuscitate a state that might precipitate the air

21 *Ibid.*, 118–119; Feiling, *Life of Neville Chamberlain*, 333, 323. See also Middlemas, *Strategy*, 258. See Alan S. Milward, "The Reichsmark Bloc and the International Economy," in Herausgegeben von Gerhard Hirschfeld and Lothan Kettenacker, *Der "Fuhrer-staat": Mythos und Realitat* (Stuttgart, 1981), 377–401. Macleod, *Neville Chamberlain*, 222–223.

attack and short war in the west that Britain was not yet prepared to fight. He wrote privately that such military considerations converted him away from his initial impulse to extend a British guarantee. Diplomacy would have to achieve the best outcome. The military balance in the air would be more favorable a year or two hence.[22]

Anxiety over Czechoslovakia grew, and German troop maneuvers near the Czech border precipitated an atmosphere of crisis. The Czechs may have encouraged this view by mobilizing army reservists in an effort to crystallize British intervention. High tension resulted. France was formally committed to Czech security. Britain privately restrained France while publicly presenting a common front to Hitler. Britain issued general threats to Hitler through diplomatic channels in London and Berlin. Fortuitously, the German troop movements slowed, as had been scheduled for their maneuvers. It appeared to the European press that Hitler had been checked. To the British, the May crisis seemed to confirm both the viability and the risks of a firmer stand against Germany using economic sanctions. In fact, Hitler was so enraged by his perception that Germany had been humiliated that he hastened his plans for subjugating the Czechs.

The first application of the Inskip doctrine by the British confirmed its value, but for the wrong reason. The prime minister averred that "in the end they decided, after getting our warning, that the risks were too great." Since the air balance was seen as negative, the financial weapon had to have been effective. Britain thus undertook a more active economic policy in eastern Europe. Chamberlain even suggested that the opportunity for German domination of eastern Europe might have passed, and he noted the favorable German press reports about him, speculating that the change of tune might be because of their economic situation. By July, even Sir Robert Vansittart, a skeptical anti-German, argued that the more assertive economic strategy, backed by the ultimate threat of a blockade, might be so effective that it could precipitate war.[23] Thus, with excessive pessimism about the air

22 Feiling, *Life of Neville Chamberlain*, 341, 348; Colvin, *Chamberlain Cabinet*, 99, 113; Hinsley et al., *British Intelligence*, 81; Bialer, *Shadow of the Bomber*, 122; Macleod, *Neville Chamberlain*, 224.
23 Newman, *March 1939*, 42; Fuchser, *Neville Chamberlain*, 134; Middlemas, *Strategy*, 239, 256–258, 264.

threat, and excessive optimism about the economic weapon, the Czech crisis approached.

The Munich crisis evolved from decisions and attitudes that had evolved since Anschluss. Chamberlain's dramatic overture of "Plan Z" on September 15, requesting direct discussions with Hitler just as the prospect of German hostilities seemed imminent, led to a meeting with him at Berchtesgaden and a provisional accord over the incorporation of German Sudetens into the Reich. Agreement on this accord, to the relief of the French and the dismay of Edward Benes, the president of Czechoslovakia, was in reach when Hitler escalated his demands on September 22 at Godesberg. Chamberlain was pessimistic on his return home and reluctantly allowed the Czechs to mobilize. War seemed imminent. The cabinet allowed Chamberlain to send a personal communication to Hitler stating that war would mean that France would be drawn in to defend Czechoslovakia and that Britain would follow. In his final authorized appeal to Hitler, Chamberlain noted his incredulity that Hitler would risk world war when his central objectives could be achieved peacefully. Hitler did respond to this overture, probably because the prolonged nature of the crisis vitiated the advantage of military surprise. This response led to the Munich agreement of September 30.

Chamberlain thus prevented war in the near term. He noted to his parliamentary secretary that "if Hitler signed it and kept the bargain well and good; alternatively that if he broke it, he would demonstrate to all the world that he was totally cynical and untrustworthy, and that this would have its value in mobilizing public opinion against him, particularly in America." Chamberlain also convinced Hitler to sign a statement on the basic principles of Anglo-German relations. Chamberlain proclaimed that this agreement represented the second time that peace with honor had been brought back from Germany. (The first time was when Disraeli moderated his antipathy to Bismarck in order to work effectively with him at the Congress of Berlin in 1878.) The imperial past and the future air war were the central images in Chamberlain's calculus as much as fears of another conflict like World War I. He was fully aware that, if his diplomatic effort failed, Churchill and others would suggest that an ultimatum would have succeeded.[24] But he felt that, in dealing with dictators,

24 Fuchser, *Neville Chamberlain*, 164n, 138–139.

the standard diplomatic machinery could not substitute for direct discussions, particularly since dealing through Ribbentrop, now the German foreign minister, posed real liabilities.

Munich was not a craven event for Chamberlain, but one that followed from precise objectives secured at political risk. It tended to moderate the Labour party's opposition to continued rearming, and the policy's critics expressed a more publicly combative alternative to Hitler if he did not deal with Chamberlain. The decision to allow arms programs to continue while leaving open the door to cooperation with Hitler by downplaying the direct public linkage between continuing rearmament and Germany, gave the "Disraeli strategy" a chance to succeed. In time, Hitler did come to see appeasement as buying time for rearming. For Hitler, Munich was an ambiguous confirmation of the more hostile attitude toward Britain that he had adopted since late 1937; by depriving him of martial glory, Chamberlain had increased Hitler's desire to drive Britain into ineffective neutrality in a continental conflict.

After Munich, Britain believed that its economic deterrent was still potent. Chamberlain had refused a draft statement giving a free hand to Germany in eastern Europe. In October, he approved a wheat deal with Rumania, despite the hostile reaction anticipated from Germany. By November, it was clear how completely Chamberlain subscribed to the Inskip strategy, whereby he argued for focusing RAF increases on fighters rather than on new heavy bombers. One could build four fighters for the cost of one bomber.[25] As in 1937, his endorsement did not represent a repudiation of the image of offensive air war but an appropriate distribution of resources to counter threats as he perceived them. Insular defense combined with the economic weapon appeared to be the last viable approach to Germany short of a long war.

Intelligence and Military Advice, 1937/38   Intelligence and military service evaluations became very pessimistic for different reasons, resulting in collective despondency. The RAF was upset over the perceived loss of air parity and the defensive role envisioned for the RAF by the Inskip doctrine, particularly since it now firmly believed that the Luftwaffe was pursuing its own

25 Donald C. Watt, "Misinformation, Misconception, Mistrust: Episodes in British Policy and the Approach of War, 1938–1939," in Michael Bentley and John Stevenson (eds.), *High and Low Politics in Modern Britain: Ten Studies* (Oxford, 1983), 223n; Telford Taylor, *Munich: The Price of Peace* (New York, 1979), 929, 931.

original offensive doctrine. Direct contacts between British and German air force personnel after open German rearmament in 1936/37 led to more accurate information on the expansion of the Luftwaffe. By 1938, when these contacts were severed, there was a shift from the 1933–1935 assumption that constraints on British production were mirrored in German production to the opposite extreme that few of these constraints applied in a dictatorial system and that the Luftwaffe was capable of extremely rapid expansion.[26]

From the Navy's standpoint, because of the nature of refitting and modernization at dock, the effective number of large warships would actually decrease before rearmament could be achieved. The worst period would be in 1938, although the picture would brighten by September 1939.[27] Chatfield, the naval chief, supported a reduction of threats over this period and was opposed to the diversion of resources to a field force. Hore-Belisha, who was appointed secretary of the army in 1937, supported only a limited continental field force in the event of war, whereas the more traditional strategists in that service emphasized the importance of a commitment to France, and were less innovative in terms of contemplating the changing tactics of a land war.[28] The former were despondent over the lack of modern land war equipment, and the latter over the stifling of their proper role; but both groups shared a negative view of their ability to fulfill their mission as they conceived it.

Collectively, the COS were pessimistic, but for different reasons. By 1937, they were arguing that there was an inverse relationship between commitments to Europe and their ability to defend the empire; that the air threat was as prominent as ever; and that an economic blockade was a sensible threat against Germany. Chamberlain's policies often followed closely on the changing military assessments that he received. The Foreign Office, in fact, "became increasingly incensed with the Chiefs of Staff for pessimism in their strategy assessments and took the view that they were exerting too much influence on the formation of policy." But it was understandable that the military analyses

26 Wark, *Ultimate Enemy*, 62, passim.
27 Lawrence K. Pratt, *East of Malta, West of Suez: Britain's Mediterranean Crisis, 1936–1939* (Cambridge, 1975), 50–51, 23.
28 See Bond, *British Military Policy*, 338, passim.

of 1937 emphasized the possibility that commitments in central Europe could outrun capabilities and the need for British rearmament.[29] Sometimes these assessments were in error, particularly regarding the air threat, and biased diplomacy in ways that hindered negotiations with Hitler.

The position of the COS during the Munich crisis followed logically from their assumptions about air war. On September 22, they argued that "from the military point of view the balance of advantage is definitely in favor of postponement . . . we are in a bad condition to wage even a defensive war at the present time." The reality was different. It is even possible to argue that Britain was never behind in effective air power, and that British fears of Luftwaffe attacks were unfounded at the time they were having the greatest effect on their strategic decisions.[30] Cross-channel attacks were not even planned by Germany and were not operationally feasible.

HITLER'S CONCEPTIONS AND STRATEGY, 1937/38   This period was a turning point not only for British strategy, but for Germany's as well. Britain is often criticized for being overly eager to reach an agreement with Germany. Ironically, Hitler became more aggressive toward Britain not because of Chamberlain's quest for agreement, but rather because of an inability to reach agreement on a joint alliance on his own terms. It was difficult for the British to decipher this change. Political intelligence became more complex as various elements in Germany tried to cast their policies so that the führer might adopt them as his own. The German Foreign Office, for example, considered bargaining colonies for an air pact with Britain, and Schacht conceived of negotiating German economic hegemony over eastern Europe in exchange for a stable rapprochement with Britain. Despite its erroneous view of air power, the Inskip strategy was still not far off the mark. However, the dismissal of Schacht in late 1937; Hitler's

29 Hinsley et al., *British Intelligence*, 74, 68.
30 Howard, *Continental Commitment*, 122, 166. Richard Overy, "German Air Strength, 1933 to 1939: A Note," *Historical Journal*, XXVII (1984), 465–471. On the limited threat that the Luftwaffe posed to Britain at the time of the Munich crisis, see Williamson Murray, "German Air Power and the Munich Crisis," in Bond and Ian Roy (eds.), *War and Society* (London, 1977) 107–118; Hinsley et al., *British Intelligence*, 79; Taylor, *Munich*, 865, xv.

decision in early 1938 to put the compliant General Wilhelm Keitel in charge of the army; and the replacement of the traditional Baron Constantin von Neurath by the aggressive Ribbentrop as foreign minister, undercut the groups that had been responding to Britain's grand strategy. In the absence of counterbalancing influences, foreign policy became the extension of Hitler's momentary whim.

Anschluss had not surprised the British, but their lack of opposition kept alive Hitler's hope that Britain would remain neutral. As a result of the Inskip strategy and lack of confidence about an air accord, Britain turned in May 1938 to the indirect application of its economic weapon in southeastern Europe, coupled with flexibility on colonial issues. But British compromises about colonies were not central to Hitler's plans. Increasingly, Hitler's territorial motives in the east clashed directly with Britain's strategies for deterrence and defense. Even after the May crisis, Hitler counted on British neutrality until the 1940s. After Munich, in January 1939, Hitler ordered the construction of a large surface fleet in anticipation of a more global policy—with or without Britain's collaboration—after Germany had subdued the continent.

It is unlikely that Hitler would have been chastened by a vigorous British threat in late 1938. It was not Chamberlain's conciliatory mode of negotiating with Hitler, but Hitler's perception that Britian would continue to meddle in affairs of central Europe, that spurred his resolve to ensure British neutrality. Hitler was determined to realize his expanding continental vision. His own penchant for confronting the Soviets was weighed against Ribbentrop's anti-British policy that was predicated on Soviet neutrality. In 1939 Hitler would continue his pursuit of limited wars in central Europe, and this tension would be resolved by Britain's continuing opposition.

CHAMBERLAIN'S STRATEGY, 1939/40 Chamberlain was not naive about Hitler. By late 1938, British intelligence had cracked ciphers that revealed disparaging remarks by Hitler about Chamberlain and the Munich agreement. Rumors about a possible German move east into the Ukraine were also reported to Chamberlain. Far from being euphoric, Britain was steeled to expect the worst. In fact, "the Cabinet were already braced for war with Germany at the end of January 1939."[31] They had also abandoned hope that Italy would side with Britain.

In January and February 1939, individuals who had previously supplied Britain with accurate intelligence about Germany planted information about possible actions by Hitler in eastern Europe. This effort to precipitate a more active British policy on the Continent helped to cause a war scare in Britain, but war seemed to have been staved off once again. However, with Chamberlain's concurrence, British leaders developed new continental commitments to the Low Countries and France. These commitments were foreshadowed at Munich; Britain had in fact guaranteed the remaining part of Czechoslovakia and concurred on a joint guarantee with France, prefiguring alignments of 1939.

Despite the somber diplomatic feedback after Munich, Chamberlain was temporarily encouraged for a number of reasons. He believed that British rearmament and its deterrent strategy were beginning to impress Hitler. There were reports from Berlin that the moderates were having a restraining influence on Hitler and that important raw materials were in tight supply. The United States was also privately giving him more favorable assurances and focusing more on the Japanese threat. Finally, a major COS military appreciation of February 1939 argued that Britain might actually *benefit* from having Italy hostile at the outset. Using economic warfare, Britain could quickly defeat Italy, thereby striking a penetrating blow at the Axis.[32]

Hitler's move into Prague on 15 March 1939 was not unheralded by British Intelligence, but it flew in the face of a whole set of variables that, from Chamberlain's view, should have convinced Hitler that economic attrition posed a substantial threat to Germany. The decision to guarantee Poland on March 31 did not reflect a drastic revision in the prime minister's view of Hitler or Germany, since it was issued as a deterrent. It guaranteed Polish independence, but not its precise borders (for example, Danzig could be compromised), and was a warning to Hitler. It was an effort to achieve "immediate deterrence" on the model of the 1938 May crisis, rather than letting matters rest with "general deter-

31 Watt, "Misinformation," 224, 226.
32 *Ibid.*, 227–230. *Idem*, "Britain, France and the Italian Problem, 1937–1939," in Centre Nationale de la Recherche Scientifique, *Relations Franco-Britanniques de 1935 à 1939* (Paris, 1975), 286–287.

rence." The optimistic February COS military appreciation needs to be considered as background to put Chamberlain's views in context; otherwise, his sanguine attitude in July 1939 seems even less comprehensible than it had been prior to Prague. An oft-quoted remark is: "The longer the war is put off the less likely it is to come at all . . ." But Chamberlain did not believe Hitler was changing, only that the arms balance was improving. He continued: ". . . as we go on perfecting our defences, and building up the defences of our allies . . . You don't need offensive forces sufficient to win a smashing victory. What you want are defensive forces sufficiently strong to make it impossible for the other side to win except at such a cost as to make it not worth while."[33]

The question of pursuing a Soviet alliance was raised seriously in the cabinet after Hitler's march on Prague. Britain expected Rumania to be the next state threatened. Rumania had resources Germany wanted. However Poland, an ally of Rumania, would not cooperate with Britain if the Soviets were involved. The Soviets were considered as a possible ally for Rumania, but Poland was deemed a first priority. France agreed. The Soviet's strength was looked upon negatively, at different times, by different foreign policy bureaus: first by the COS, and later in the spring of 1939 by the Foreign Office. Consequently, "The COS [had] put no resistance in the way of a guaranty to Poland alone" in late March as long as they were assured that Poland would resist and that France would back it as well.[34]

Chamberlain shared the negative view that the COS held of Soviet offensive capabilities. He also maintained his increased confidence in Britain's attrition capability, particularly since he was privy to information not given to others about eventual United States support. If the attrition strategy had to be implemented, it would require coordination with Poland and other central European states; an alliance with the Soviets was not worth the risk of driving Central European nations to strike a separate deal with Hitler. The prime minister also shared the view of the Foreign Office that an alliance with the Soviets would drive Hitler toward the very conflict that they were trying to avoid. An agreement with the Soviets, they feared, could limit the impact

33 Dilks, "'Unnecessary War'?" 127.
34 Wark, *Ultimate Enemy*, 276, n. 90.

of the economic deterrent or stimulate Hitler to attack in the west first. Nevertheless, Chamberlain reluctantly agreed in May 1939 that the possibility of an alliance should be examined as a precautionary measure.[35]

These were not arguments based upon ideological hostility. To the extent that 1914 was considered analogous, the lesson Chamberlain drew was that Britain had to make its position clear so that there would be, as he wrote to Hitler, no "tragic misunderstanding" in this instance; he noted that Britain was "resolved and prepared to employ without delay all the forces at their command, and it is impossible to see the end of hostilities once they are engaged."[36]

Chamberlain expected a war of nerves with Hitler to occur in late August 1939. Britain believed it had implicitly stated its resolve by means of its North Sea fleet movements in August and September, the fleet clearly being a central threat to Germany in any long war. Indeed, British intelligence reported that Hitler had cancelled his anticipated August 25 attack on Poland. Chamberlain's "delay" in declaring war on September 3 in response to the September 1 attack on Poland was not because he considered reneging on his guarantee. The standard view that Chamberlain lived up to British honor only under pressure is misleading.[37] In the main, any delay was a consequence of his attempt to give deterrence more time to work. His position was not absurd, since on August 22 "Hitler declared that the Reich was being forced by economic factors among others into making war." British strategy tried to play on this German weakness without forcing the issue to war, where they felt vulnerable. Coordination with France also complicated the final declaration of war, because France wanted to achieve maximum mobilization before any official declaration.[38]

35 See Robert Manne, "The British Decision for Alliance with Russia, May 1939," *Journal of Contemporary History*, IX (1974), 3–26, for a critique of Chamberlain. However, he overstates the degree to which the COS favored an alliance with the Soviets and sees too much divergence between Chamberlain's position and the military advice that he received.
36 See Dilks, "'Unnecessary War'?" 127–128. *Idem*, "Appeasement and Intelligence," 166.
37 See, for example, John Lukacs, *The Last European War, September 1939/December 1941* (New York, 1976), 39.
38 Hildebrand, *Foreign Policy*, 89. See R. A. C. Parker, "The British Government and

Intelligence and Military Advice, 1939/40   A number of factors moderated service rivalries and resulted in improved assessments of threats. A major changeover of staff serving the COS in January 1939 led to more balanced analyses of British and German strengths and weaknesses. Optimism in the RAF was renewed by a reevaluation of Luftwaffe deficiencies that had been ignored during the two previous years, indicating that production was peaking. Consequently, in February the COS concluded that Britain's defenses would improve dramatically by 1940.

Chamberlain's views were influenced accordingly. In July 1939 he suggested that Hitler could be deterred because "Hitler has concluded that we mean business and that time is not ripe for a major war. . . . Though at present the German feeling is not worthwhile *yet*, they will soon come to realize that it never *will* be worthwhile, then we can talk." The extent to which IIC optimism was allowed to become the cornerstone of British strategy by 1939 has been criticized in retrospect. Yet, by July 1939, the British Treasury also argued that time was now working against Britain: investors, feeling that war was coming, were removing assets, thereby weakening Britain's long-run reserves.[39] There was ambivalence here. Although optimism about Germany's vulnerabilities bolstered the deterrence strategy so long as war was staved off, the prospect of declining finances reinforced Britain's resolve to resist in the short term if deterrence failed. The latter case may have increased Chamberlain's willingness to risk all-out war, for Germany could obtain piecemeal replenishments by conquest, an option Britain did not have.

HITLER'S STRATEGY AND DIPLOMACY, 1939/40   By 1939 Hitler contemplated the possibility of conflict with Britain in the early stages of his expansionist program rather than in the indefinite future. Britain's continuing opposition to his eastward expansion

the Coming of War with Germany, 1939," in M. R. D. Foot (ed.), *War and Society* (New York, 1973), 1–15.

39 Wark, *Ultimate Enemy*, 71–72. Patrick Salmon, "British Plans for Economic Warfare against Germany 1937–1939: The Problem of Swedish Iron Ore," *Journal of Contemporary History*, XVI (1981), 68. Parker, "Economics, Rearmament and Foreign Policy: The United Kingdom before 1939—A Preliminary Study," *Journal of Contemporary History*, X (1975), 637–647.

of March 1939 made Poland a likely turning point. Hitler privately reiterated that his primary objectives still lay in the east, and, with a certain annoyance over British negotiations with the Soviets, suggested that, if the British refused to see that their interests would be best served by cooperating with him, he would have to turn west first. Hitler expected that his diplomatic coup of concluding a Nazi-Soviet Pact on 23 August 1939 would shock Britain into resignation over eastern Europe. He wanted decisively to isolate Poland, leaving no "rational" military option for Britain to save the Poles.

On August 25 Hitler floated the idea of a German alliance with Britain after the Polish problem had been resolved: Germany would hold sway on the Continent, and Britain at sea. An alliance of convenience remained a genuine objective. Hitler disclaimed interest in colonial issues, although this concession seemed dubious to the British, given their knowledge of Hitler's prospective naval buildup. However, Hitler did not perceive how central Poland was in the context of Britain's strategy of economic attrition, which had the disadvantage that it could be proven only in the process of implementation. The Nazi-Soviet pact did not deflect British strategy any more than the British economic strategy deterred Hitler. Hitler's buildup increased Britain's resolution to stand firm, the opposite of Hitler's intention, and Britain's calculations of Germany's air power deterred Chamberlain but did not faze Hitler.

Hitler was surprised, therefore, when Britain signed a formal alliance with Poland on August 25. Mussolini also startled Hitler, when he indicated that he reluctantly would have to stand aside at the outset of war. Hitler first ordered, then canceled his attack on Poland upon receipt of this news, informing his chief of staff that he needed more time for negotiations. Britain did not accede to his overtures as expected. "To his [Hitler's] mind, the European war that came on September 3 was as incomprehensible as it was contrary to his aims," for he "found himself in a general war, which he had intended neither for that time nor in that set of alignments."[40] Hitler had crossed the line that Chamberlain had drawn, unifying the forces against Germany.

40 Alan J. P. Taylor, *Origins of the Second World War* (London, 1961), 326. Hillgruber, *Germany and the Two World Wars*, 77, 74.

CHURCHILL AND CONTINUITY IN BRITISH STRATEGY, 1940
Churchill was actually much closer to Chamberlain's strategic thinking than is usually recognized.[41] He shared Chamberlain's faith in the bomber and the potency of the economic weapon against Germany. Britain's misperceptions about Germany's air power and about the effectiveness of their economic weapon as a deterrent had made the British appear weaker and less resolved to Hitler than they had been prior to 1939. Ironically, in 1940, the same underlying assumptions resulted in some functional misperceptions that made Britain feel stronger than it was, and bolstered its resolve to continue. British intelligence supported the optimistic view in 1940 that the German economy faced many shortages and constraints. Even after the fall of France, it was incorrectly assumed that Germany's economy was on the brink of disrepair. German production was seen as already at its peak.

Churchill believed that the bomber combined with a blockade could force Germany to seek a negotiated solution. Without these assumptions, the British cabinet would have been more despairing, having just lost its continental ally. The United States was reluctant, even after the fall of France, to declare war (validating Chamberlain's earlier skepticism). But Churchill retained his hope for early support, based partly upon his misperception of the nature of American attitudes toward Britain and the American party system. His positive attitude helped to bolster others. Churchill and Eden's criticism in the 1930s of Chamberlain for not securing United States support earlier was shown to be unfounded. Nor had Chamberlain's concern about financial capability been misplaced, for Britain had to pay for most of her arms at this critical time. As Churchill lamented in late 1940, "We have not had anything from the United States that we have not paid for, and what we have had has not played an essential part in our resistance."[42]

41   The first two paragraphs of this section draw heavily upon David Reynolds, "Churchill and the British 'Decision' to Fight on in 1940: Right Policy, Wrong Reasons," in Richard Langhorne (ed.), *Diplomacy and Intelligence during the Second World War* (Cambridge, 1985), 147–167.
42   Chamberlain wrote in 1934, "we ought to know by this time that the U.S.A. will give us no undertaking to resist by force any action by Japan, short of an attack on Hawaii or Honolulu." The United States Neutrality Act of 1935 and its extension in 1937 confirmed Chamberlain's pessimism on this score (Feiling, *Life of Neville Chamberlain*, 253, 165).

Churchill basically shared the same strategic presuppositions as Chamberlain, but in other respects he was not so prescient. Chamberlain, using untested assumptions about air power and deterrence for guidance, had had to navigate through ambiguous peacetime conditions when war might or might not occur; Churchill, with the benefit of the programs instituted under Chamberlain, faced the more focused, concrete, if equally daunting problem of their actual application in wartime. The faith in the bomber and economic weapon kept hope alive and Britain fighting when the situation was, in fact, dire. Had Hitler not invaded Russia in 1941 and declared war on the United States, linking a European war to a world war, these assumptions might have been clearly disproven. Arguably the same assumptions about economic deterrence and a quest for an insular, if not offensive, deus ex machina, would again form the backdrop, but in a less effective fashion, in Churchill's Mediterranean strategy of attempting to penetrate the "soft underbelly" of Europe first, where more rapid results were expected from economic attrition than proved possible in practice. Churchill, like Chamberlain, was also trying to preserve the empire. His efforts postponed the opening of the "second front," thereby continuing Britain's reluctance to engage in a land war on the Continent.

STRATEGIC PUZZLES OF PREWAR DIPLOMACY   I have discussed the interactive effects of differing strategic doctrines, and their consequences for misinterpretation of intentions, signals, and resolve, and ultimately for deterrence. This argument is strengthened to the extent that British strategy can be shown to have been reasonably conceived. British balance-of-power strategy faced inherent tensions, and the British Empire, because of its commitments, was overextended and vulnerable. Nevertheless, it can be shown that Chamberlain, starting in the early 1930s before he became prime minister, had a reasonably conceived strategy to address the world-wide threats that Britain faced.

Theories concerning balance of power provide a guide to the constraints that diplomacy faces, but they cannot reduce the possible courses of action to the point that the perceptions of state decision-makers can be neglected. Many realist theories offer different interpretations of the period, and there is no shared conception of how structural elements translate into political outcomes. It is necessary, therefore, to factor in the strategic beliefs of the British decision-makers in order to make sense of their balance-of-power strategy and to evaluate why it foundered. A series of questions often raised about British grand strategy and the origins of the war are addressed below. They flow logically from British beliefs about air deterrence and economic strategy and merge with questions about alliances and the timing of decisions to go to war.

Why was there no British continental commitment before it was too late? Through 1936, British air power deterrence seemed to make continental commitment unnecessary. From 1936 to 1939, because the perceived German air threat made Britain feel vulnerable, such a policy also seemed too costly. Finally, when the commitment of army troops to the Continent was made in 1939, it was less an effort to deter Germany by threatening the Ruhr, as analysts often suggest, than the result of implementing the long-war attrition strategy that had been adopted in 1937. By then, the offensive air deterrent strategy seemed impossible because of financial constraints that seemed insurmountable because the British were overawed by the Luftwaffe capabilities.

British diplomatic strategy was conducted with one eye on the Continent, and the other on imperial defense. In 1934, the COS emphasized the importance of not simultaneously facing a hostile Japan in the Far East, Italy in the Mediterranean, and Germany in Europe. Chamberlain concurred. The admiralty wanted to focus first on the Japanese threat. Chamberlain differed, wanting a two-prong strategy of reducing tension between Britain and Italy, and between Britain and Japan, while rearming to deter Germany in Europe. Germany was the linchpin: if that nation could be held in check, neither Italy nor Japan would confront Britain. Conversely, war with Germany could in effect mean war with all three countries. Britain, at one time concerned that France would commit Britain to initiatives on the Continent not in its interest, in the mid-1930s correctly came to believe that France would not take the offensive, but had secure defenses. A deterrence strategy in concert with France based on land forces might have significantly affected Hitler, but it was not central to the threats and responses that Britain believed took priority. European diplomacy and air deterrence were therefore critical in Europe.

Britain's attempt at rapprochement with Italy was a continuing saga from 1934 forward. Chamberlain wanted to keep Italy separate from Germany, leaving Britain with influence over both. Despite German-Italian rivalry, a number of contingencies impeded Anglo-Italian relations, which degenerated into a stand-off concerning League of Nations sanctions over Ethiopia, and later concerning intervention in the Spanish Civil War. Mussolini kept Italy diplomatically active, but now his primary motive was to string the British along as a counterweight to Hitler. Britain turned its initiative back to Germany from 1936 to 1938, thereby addressing its strategic problem at its source. Chamberlain knew that, if he could reach agreement with Germany, Britain would then hold sway between Germany and France and could side with either against Italy. Hitler had wanted an alliance with Britain on his terms, a failing prospect. The Pact of Steel between Germany and Italy was, in some respects, second choice for both nations.

When diplomatic overtures with Hitler seemed ineffective in 1937, the COS pushed for new Italian overtures to reduce the Mediterranean threats. Progress on this front in early 1938 may have even prompted Hitler's Anschluss. It can be argued that Eden's resignation in early 1938 opened the possibility for closer Anglo-Italian ties that were of great concern to Hitler and gave impetus to his Austrian policy. From Chamberlain's standpoint in February 1938, the failure of negotiations with Italy would mean the loss of Austrian independence, the swallowing of Czechoslovakia, and the division of the Balkans. Hitler may have moved in March 1938 to preempt Anglo-Italian rapprochement from becoming an obstacle to Anschluss. The prime minister believed that, had the Italian negotiations taken place sooner, Anschluss might have been prevented.[43] Therefore, even apart from the issue of air power, the reasoned pursuit of restraining alliances, complicated as they were to implement, did not offer a clearly defined ground-based deterrence strategy that was consistent with Britain's diplomatic objectives from 1934 to 1938.

The remilitarization of the Rhineland in 1936 signaled the total failure of France's post-Versailles approach to Germany: in the absence of an American, and thus British, guarantee, France

43 Macleod, *Neville Chamberlain*, 214, 223.

had been insufficiently powerful to control Germany but sufficiently interventionist to alienate its neighbor. Britain had long been developing an approach that was at odds with French policy and was not willing to prevent Germany "from walking into her own backyard." In place of French supremacy over Germany, Britain sought to support German recovery up to the point that Germany would check France, be a satisfied power, and leave Britain to hold sway over both. Unfortunately, Britain did not anticipate that Belgium would be intimidated into discontinuing work on the extension of the Maginot line, thereby undercutting the integrity of the defense against Germany.[44] Such unexpected events made the success of British strategy less likely and increased the consequences of the failure of deterrence.

It was because of the air threat that Britain's army focused on home defense. Defense of the empire accented Britain's perception of its vulnerability and planning dilemmas; but, in the main, the dominions did not divert actual resources from home defense or even from a potential continental force and were an important source of supply in war.[45] Britain responded on the Continent only when it believed that the attrition strategy was threatened by Hitler's conquests in central Europe.

Why was Britain willing to go to war in 1939 and not in 1938 when, in some respects, it would have had stronger alliance support on the Continent? The argument that Britain should have declared war and aided Czechoslovakia against Hitler in 1938 often focuses on the strength of the land forces on the Continent, comparing them before and after Munich.[46] The prime minister argued that Czechoslovakia was militarily indefensible on the ground. Hungary and Poland were waiting as predators in the wings. Both France and the Soviet Union were too distant to offer timely help. Nor was there any expectation that the Poles would let Soviet troops transit their territory. Munich saved Czechoslovakia from immediate dismemberment, avoided the certainty of war in the

---

44 Wolfers, *Britain and France*, 248–249. Taylor, *Munich*, 54–548.
45 Howard, *Continental Commitment, passim.* See Penden, "The Burden of Imperial Defence and the Continental Commitment Reconsidered," *The Historical Journal*, XXVII (1984), 405–423.
46 See, for example, Taylor, *Munich*, 985–998.

short term (when Britain was believed to be vulnerable), and draw a clear line for Hitler to cross.

Air power, not land power, provided the sinews of British balance-of-power thinking. If Britain itself was threatened by a German air offensive, Czechoslovakia was certainly threatened even more. Focus on ground forces alone overlooks Britain's view that the bomber threat applied to allies as well. However, the status of the air threat and their strategy of economic attrition were more central to Britain than changes in the balance of land forces, for example through the loss of Czech divisions. Bombing would have ruined the Czech Skoda arms works, thereby denying them to the allied cause, or started a war in the west. German gains from controlling part of Czechoslovakia and Skoda were less than the potential costs of war in 1938.

War was not seen as inevitable in 1938. Britain's basic dilemma was, on the one hand, concern over pushing Germany too hard, thereby driving Hitler to pursue external conflict in order to foster domestic unity; on the other hand, Britain realized that Hitler had to be stopped. The information available to the decision-makers at the time favored waiting as against war in 1938, and even to a certain extent in 1939. Pessimistic intelligence colored the interpretation of the military balance in 1938 and weighed against action; by early 1939 the predictions were that the balance would again favor Britain. Air defenses were improving. It was believed Britain could still deter war. Although the Luftwaffe was much weaker than it appeared, it is too great a leap to suggest that Britain therefore should have gone to war in 1938. Even in retrospect, the case for 1938 is not clear-cut. For all of the conceptual problems of British air strategy and the difficulties of communicating it, Britain did not end up with obsolete weapons by limiting its options too early, as Germany did to some extent; had war with Germany been delayed a year or so longer, Britain's deterrence policy might have succeeded.

Historians know that World War II occurred and in what time frame. However, a policy that advocates fighting a war at a particular time, say September 1938, will often differ from a policy of deterrence with a longer or open-ended time frame. Britain wanted to deter war in order to maintain the status quo, not in order to win the war. The omniscient analyst's implicit argument is not so much that another strategy would have deterred Hitler, but rather that Britain should have considered war inevitable and, had it done so, been able to fight an earlier and more effective version of World War II. This is tantamount to saying that if British decision-makers had had different objectives, expectations, and perceptions of strategic capabilities—ones the analyst believes they should have had—they could have taken advantage of a strategic opportunity that is discernible in retrospect. The real question, however, should focus on why British decision-makers believed war necessary at a certain time—in 1939 and not 1938—and why they held these beliefs, rather than on the merit of particular military strategies.

Why did Britain guarantee Poland rather than strike an alliance with the Soviets? Chamberlain's preference for an alliance with Poland in lieu of agreement with the Soviets was discussed above. He feared that Britain could lose its eastern front if it did nothing, and that, if Britain allied itself with the Soviets and forced the central European states to choose between the Soviet and the Nazi sphere, many would choose the latter. Either outcome would have compromised the potency of the attrition strategy.

In the context of late March 1939, the concern that Poland or Rumania might independently come to terms with Germany was legitimate. If Germany absorbed Rumania without a struggle, Britain would be faced with the dilemma of initiating war, rather than responding to aggression. Conversely, if Britain were allied with the Soviets, and eastern Europe then turned to Germany, Britain would have had no allies there to support the attrition strategy; and, since the Soviets would remain on the defensive, the prospect of German continental hegemony by a move east was even greater. Furthermore, an alliance with the Soviets, traditionally Hitler's main enemy, might have given Hitler the incentive to strike to the west sooner rather than later since Britain saw itself as Hitler's most formidable opponent and knew that the Soviets could not effectively project their power to the west.

Because the British objective was containment, not the defeat of Germany, the guarantee to Poland was a reasonable strategy. To have a deterrent effect, the guarantee had to be issued prior to any move by Hitler. Negotiations with the Soviets during the summer of 1939 were a supplementary deterrent card to be kept in play against Hitler. The criticism that an alliance with the

Soviets would have been advantageous militarily relies too heavily on hindsight by assuming that war was inevitable, and that the Soviets would have been a potent long-term ally in the war. Britain did not then assume that war was inevitable. It wanted to preserve peace through deterrence. Since the British considered central Europe important from their own perspective, they were not suspicious, as the Soviets may have been, that the guarantees were designed to set off conflicts between Germany and the Soviet Union, which in turn may have helped stimulate Soviet overtures to Germany. Nor could they have foreseen that some unfortunate remarks by a cabinet member might erroneously have confirmed to Joseph Stalin that Britain was set on appeasing Germany, rather than resisting Hitler in his move east.

Why was there no allied attack in the west in September 1939? Some scholars maintain that the real unfought battle was the failure of the British and the French to undertake an offensive in September 1939, while Hitler was dealing with the Poles. Since the British knew that they were involved in a war with Hitler, why did they fail to take advantage of a second front in Poland to move into the Ruhr and deal Hitler a decisive blow?[47] Logistical difficulties of coordinating such action with the French aside, what are other plausible explanations? First, the economic weapon was still believed to be potent. With the taut Germany economy, Britain believed it could defeat Hitler by increasing internal unrest. This viewpoint favored delaying direct offensive action and allowing the indirect offensive to take effect. Second, by September 1939, RAF estimates of Luftwaffe production had again become inflated: its total strength was overestimated by one sixth; the long-range bomber component by one third; and reserves, indicative of Germany's capacity to wage extended air war, by at least 500 percent. These estimates would have chastened any Brit-

---

47 See Jon Kimche, *The Unfought Battle* (London, 1968); Nicholas Bethell, *The War Hitler Won: The Fall of Poland, September 1939* (New York, 1972); Nicholas Fleming, *August 1939: The Last Days of Peace* (London, 1979). John J. Mearsheimer, *Conventional Deterrence* (Ithaca, 1983), 67–98, makes a strong case for why Britain and France refrained from taking on Germany on the Continent from March 1939 to May 1940, with a particular focus on the balance of forces and the nature of strategy on land. Indeed, from this viewpoint, it is clear Britain and France were unprepared for offensive operations in the short term, and in retrospect, even had they been more prepared, would have been hard pressed to engage Germany in conflict had not the issue been forced in May 1940.

ish offensive plans. Furthermore, there were plans for a marked increase in British offensive forces during 1940. A total of 7,940 aircraft were to be produced by Britain in 1939, compared to 15,049 projected for 1940. Medium bombers increased over the period by a factor of three.[48] On the defense, deployment of British radar, operationally feasible, would benefit from more time to construct coastal warning sites. Assuming that France remained secure, the defense-offense balance therefore would improve if Britain waited. Third, although British diplomacy achieved its end in respect to Italy by avoiding simultaneous Atlantic and Mediterranean wars at the outset of hostilities, Mussolini's decision to stand aside at the start of the war meant that waging economic warfare would be seen as a hostile action, not a defensive move. Therefore, it is not surprising that Britain paused instead of taking the offensive.

Why was Hitler willing to go to war with Britain in 1939, even though the German navy would not be ready for some years? Once war was declared, Hitler perceived the British attrition potential as had been intended, but with the opposite effect. "Hitler made a bid for peace with the Western Powers—but was rebuffed. Meanwhile he was growing afraid of what he had started—and of his temporary partners. He expressed the view that a long, drawn-out war of attrition with Britain and France would gradually exhaust Germany's limited resources, and expose her to a fatal attack from behind by Russia. As Hitler said, 'Time is working for our adversary. . . . We have an Achilles' Heel—the Ruhr. . . . If Britain and France push through Belgium into the Ruhr, we shall be in the greatest danger.'" The menace must be removed by striking first. German power would be turned westward. British influence would be driven from the continent. The attack on France was a highly risky endeavor, capitalizing on military and diplomatic weaknesses partly sown by Britain's exaggerated air fears, resulting, paradoxically, in a confirmation of them by attacks on Britain from the Low Countries in the Battle of Britain. Hitler still expected some sort of partitioning arrangement with Britain after the fall of France in May 1940. Throughout the

48 Hinsley et al., *British Intelligence*, 75, 299–300. Michael M. Postan, *British War Production* (London, 1952), 73, 484, App. 4.

summer, Hitler was disappointed by the British. Hitler's attack on the Soviet Union was undertaken with an eye to showing the British that there was no makeweight to provide hope for continuing the war.[49]

The unconsummated rapprochement between Germany and Britain was pursued by both sides at different times and for different reasons, and helped both to escalate their conflict and to bring Hitler down. The British got the war they feared, for the wrong reasons, and Hitler got the war he did not expect, but deserved for good reason.

In the 1930s, Britain had to assess the appropriate balance of deterrent threats and conciliatory overtures to a revisionist state, and uphold mutually interdependent, world-wide commitments. British strategies were formulated within this context, and offered temporary solutions that imposed new conceptual constraints. Britain pursued a series of deterrence policies based upon assumptions about air power; it relied on a variety of deterrent threats, preferring economic cooperation, but proposing to turn economics to warfare if challenged. Hitler, relying on intuition, believed that his will could overcome and forge outcomes, over and above the mere balance of forces, and that all economic strategies were zero-sum from the start, ruling out the status quo as biased against him.[50] Britain's deterrence strategy at first seemed to solve its dilemmas, and seemed to buy time, security, and flexibility; later the strategy seemed to pose new dilemmas, and leave them vulnerable with few choices. In the end, its own misperceptions and will helped them to persevere.

ON APPEASEMENT, DETERRENCE, AND THE MUNICH ANALOGY   The British consciously attempted a policy of "strategic deterrence" in the late 1930s, and this strategy failed. Britain tried to couple the rewards of appeasement with threats of deterrence. One cannot simply conclude from this case that appeasement leads to war. The sobering issue concerns how divergent military doctrines can

49 Hart, The Other Side of the Hill (London, 1951), 141, 146–147. Hildebrand, Foreign Policy, 101.
50 For this contrast with Britain's perspective, see Hitler's Secret Book, for example, on his views of will over matter in politics (25, 42, 119, 143), acceptance of risk-taking (40–41), and the zero-sum conflictual basis of trade (8, 21–23).

skew the issuance and reception of diplomatic and military signals and affect the timing and even degree of escalation of a status quo state in rivalry with a revisionist one. Therefore, not only is the familar "Munich analogy" susceptible to inappropriate application by decision-makers; it also is based on inadequate analysis. One cannot thereby conclude that appeasement cannot lead to war, or that appeasement is never functional.

It is striking that appeasement did not continue after Britain believed that its companion deterrence policy had repeatedly failed. Castigation of "appeasement" alone has begged some of the most interesting issues presented by the 1930s. Having noted that British strategists viewed the consequences of any future air war as we might envision nuclear strikes, attention shifts to the fact that Britain had decided that there were certain circumstances under which these risks and costs would be accepted. Britain's resolve to press forward in 1939 is perhaps the only case we have of a great power going to war when it *believed* that hundreds of thousands of civilians would die from bomb raids. Although the decision to resist Hitler was laudable, it is sobering to recognize that such decisions can be made.

Divergent doctrinal assumptions about the nature of future wars may be as disfunctional as misapplied lessons from past wars. From a common starting point in the 1930s—when arsenals literally went from wooden planes to atomic weapons in a single decade—technological change, misperceptions, and extremism overlaid the standard tensions of international politics in a fashion that favored escalation. In a changing strategic environment, the touchstones for decision-makers may seem small in terms of political-military changes, but nonetheless may be critical in verifying their own view of grand strategy. Furthermore, such apparent silent successes may be more critical than better-known, more dramatic confrontations or policy failures and yet remain unrecognized even by the adversary in question.

Not all strategies that seem to fail in one case can be axiomatically dismissed; nor can successful strategies be rationalized as correct in conception rather than result. That British air defense turned out to be crucial in the blitz was a belated military success stemming from a train of events that had been set in motion by erroneous conceptions of offensive air power. Even those who seemed prescient in predicting outcomes (for example, Churchill and Vansittart) shared erroneous strategic assumptions, and can be seen in retrospect to have advocated plausible alternative strategies for the "wrong reasons." For instance, Eden's advocacy of an army to support France resulted from his loyalty to the League of Nations' efforts to establish collective security in opposition to Italy, rather than prescient realism in opposition to Hitler, with whom he sought accommodation as late as 1938. Also, Churchill's decision to continue the conflict in 1940 was made for the "wrong" reasons.

ON DOCTRINE, CAPABILITIES, AND SIGNALING   To the extent that one can generalize meaningfully from the enduring crises of the 1930s, several factors were conducive to strategic surprises of the worst kind on both sides. Chamberlain and Hitler "saw what they expected to see" in their adversary's military doctrine; assumptions about their adversary's doctrine were simply mirror-imaged. Given that general perception, however, errors by decision-makers—who "saw what they wanted to see"—were important in discounting the risks in pursuing their own strategies to influence their adversary and in capitalizing on the perceived vulnerabilities of their adversary.[51] Both Britain and Germany tried to pursue strategies that would transcend their own inherent vulnerabilities. Chamberlain sought to build air power to intimidate Hitler, even though Britain would be more vulnerable if the strategy failed. Hitler threatened a buildup of naval vessels to menace Britain, even though Germany was more vulnerable to a blockade. The naval agreement was tactical for Britain, whereas the air pact discussions were tactical for Germany. The vulnerabilities that each projected onto its adversary were a function of their own ultimate preoccupations. Front-line bombers dominated British consciousness, whereas Lebensraum preoccupied Hitler. Ironically, Britain's appreciation of Germany's land and tank power and Hitler's appreciation of Britain's economic weapon were realistic only late in the day.

    With all its faults, a strategy may nonetheless effectively communicate the right thing to the wrong people, rather than the

51   See Richard Ned Lebow, *Between Peace and War* (Baltimore, 1981), and Robert Jervis, "Perceiving and Coping with Threat," in *idem,* Lebow, and Janice Gross Stein, *Psychology and Deterrence* (Baltimore, 1985), 13–33, on "unmotivated" and "motivated" bases of decision-making errors.

critical ones, without generating feedback until it is too late. Senior German officials were often influenced by British deterrence policies in the way that Britain intended;[52] but influencing Hitler was a much less straightforward matter. It is useful to assume a unitary actor for deterrence analysis; by the same token, all may be deterred except the unitary actor.

A strategy may be conceptually plausible but the weapons capabilities may be produced, refitted, deployed, or publicized too late to have the desired restraining effect. Britain kept secret the development of a prototype heavy bomber in late 1938 to avoid stimulating a crash effort by Germany to develop a similar plane; Britain was therefore unable to use it as a threat at that time. When Hitler finally perceived Britain's economic strategy and prospective heavy-bomber production, it served as an incentive to preempt rather than as a deterrent.

Conversely, an adversary's strategy can be perceived where none exists, with decisive consequences. The British would have been stunned to realize that the Luftwaffe staff considered their ability to inflict damage on Britain during Munich as "pin pricks" and "completely inadequate" even as late as May 1939.[53] The Germans would have been stunned by the calculus driving British diplomacy.

Assumptions by a deterrer about his capabilities may diverge from the actual composition of the forces that are available for deployment, to the surprise of both parties. It is extremely difficult to coordinate one's own doctrine, intelligence and hardware in respect to an adversary in order to achieve stability. For example, in late 1937 Britain started making decisions that were ·based on a new emphasis on defensive fighters over offensive bombers, combined with economic attrition. The new doctrine affected its diplomacy. Although there were qualitative innovations in radar and fighters, many earlier programs for bombers

---

52 In May 1938 "two senior staff officers of the German Admiralty and the Luftwaffe [discussed] the prospects of a successful blockade of Britain, which concluded gloomily: 'The war against the Anglo-Saxon Powers would in all probability lead both opponents, as in the World War, to complete exhaustion. Germany is not strong enough for a naval and air force arms race against Britain'." Watt, "Hitler's Visit to Rome and the May Weekend Crisis: A Study in Hitler's Response to External Stimuli," *Journal of Contemporary History*, IX (1974), 31. Britain's attrition threat was intended to pose this type of calculation.

53 Murray, "German Air Power," 115–116.

still went forward, and the actual ratio of fighters to bombers did not change greatly in 1939/40. The new doctrine continued to affect British diplomacy, but by the time that Hitler had seriously pondered probable British opposition, he saw that by 1940 Britain would have both a potent offense and a real defense, with a continental field force imminent.

Munich was the result of the dilemmas attending the considered use of immense destructive power—which the British were among the first seriously to confront in its modern form—rather than a simple failure of a will to power. As a metaphor, "Munich" might better stand for the dilemmas attending the conceptual and ideological fragmentation of the modern world in possession of immense, rapidly changing, destructive capabilities.

Scott D. Sagan

The Origins of the Pacific War

"Whom the Gods would destroy they first make mad," declared Congressman Hamilton Fish on December 8, 1941, the day after infamy. Minutes before, Franklin D. Roosevelt had asked Congress to declare war on the nation that had just launched the "unprovoked and dastardly" attack on Pearl Harbor, and Fish, an ardent isolationist, rose to support the president's request. "The Japanese," he said, "have gone stark, raving mad, and have, by their unprovoked attack committed military, naval, and national suicide."[1]

Although others did not quote the classics, this madness theme was echoed throughout American newspapers that day: "sublime insanity" declared the *New York Times*; "the act of a mad dog" the *Los Angeles Times* announced; "an insane adventure that for fatalistic abandon is unsurpassed in the history of the world" argued the *Philadelphia Inquirer*. In December 1941, most observers agreed with Winston Churchill's statement that, since American military potential vastly outweighed Japan's, the Tokyo government's decision to go to war was "difficult to reconcile . . . with prudence, or even sanity."[2]

This belief that the Japanese must have been irrational to attack the United States continues to plague our understanding of the origins of the Pacific War and the lessons that modern strategists draw from that tragic occurrence. In the Pentagon, for example, the events of 1941 have inspired the dominant scenario for nuclear war: a lingering concern that can be described as *hormephobia*, the fear of shock or surprise, has haunted American strategic planning since Pearl Harbor. The nuclear arsenal of the United States has long been postured to respond promptly to an unlikely, peacetime Soviet surprise nuclear attack. Moreover, the increasing dissatisfaction with the policy of deterrence today can,

Scott D. Sagan is Assistant Professor of Political Science at Stanford University. He is co-author of *Living with Nuclear Weapons* (Cambridge, Mass., 1983).

1 *Congressional Record*, LXXXVIII, Pt. IX, 9521.
2 The newspaper editorials are reprinted in *ibid*, 9509–9513, 10118.

in part, be viewed as stemming from the belief that even the most stable and robust deterrent will fail if the United States is confronted with an irrational adversary. Indeed, when historical analogies are referred to by military and civilian officials in private Pentagon meetings, the "crazy" Japanese decision to go to war in 1941 is often used to support the development of strategic defenses in order to protect the American people from potentially irrational acts by the Soviet Union or other nuclear powers.

Many scholars have also succumbed to the "insanity plea" when explaining the Japanese decision to attack the United States. Among modern academic strategists, there is a widespread tendency to treat the Japanese decision as a crazy aberration: the government in Tokyo behaved irrationally and therefore was "beyond deterrence."[3] For many, this view is perversely comforting. If deterrence fails only in the rare occasion when an adversary is irrational or suicidal, then surely nuclear deterrence between the superpowers is likely to remain stable.

The persistent theme of Japanese irrationality is highly misleading, for, using the common standard in the literature (a conscious calculation to maximize utility based on a consistent value system[4]), the Japanese decision for war appears to have been rational. If one examines the decisions made in Tokyo in 1941 more closely, one finds not a thoughtless rush to national suicide, but rather a prolonged, agonizing debate between two repugnant alternatives.

In the months preceding the attack on Pearl Harbor, the United States had placed an embargo on oil exports to Japan and had demanded that the Japanese accept defeat in the war in China and withdraw their forces from the mainland. Although the Tokyo government believed, in the words of Nagano Osami, the navy chief of staff, that we "must never fight a war that can be avoided," by December 1941 Prime Minister Tojo Hideki could report to emperor Hirohito that "our Empire has no alternative

3 Colin S. Gray, *Strategic Studies: A Critical Assessment* (Westport, 1982), 87, 180, n. 10. Other arguments emphasizing, in different degrees, the irrational nature of the Japanese decision include Bruce Russett, "Pearl Harbor: Deterrence Theory and Decision Theory," *Journal of Peace Research*, IV (1967), 99; Robert Jervis, "Deterrence and Perception," *International Security*, VII (1982/1983), 7, 30; A. F. K. Organski and Jacek Kugler, *The War Ledger* (Chicago, 1980), 3; Glenn H. Snyder and Paul Diesing, *Conflict among Nations* (Princeton, 1977), 301.
4 Thomas C. Schelling, *The Strategy of Conflict* (Cambridge, Mass., 1960), 4.

but to begin war."[5] In the eyes of the Tokyo decision-makers, the decision to attack the United States was compared, not to an act of suicide, but rather to a desperate but necessary operation given to a man with a terminal disease. This was Admiral Nagano's explanation to the emperor:

> Japan was like a patient suffering from a serious illness. He said the patient's case was so critical that the question of whether or not to operate had to be determined without delay. Should he be let alone without an operation, there was danger of a gradual decline. An operation, while it might be extremely dangerous, would still offer some hope of saving his life.[6]

In order to understand the origins of the Pacific War and to draw appropriate lessons for the modern world, one must focus beyond the insanity plea and examine how the Tokyo government found itself in a desperate position in which starting a war that all agreed was not likely to end in victory was considered the least repugnant alternative. The origins of the Pacific War are best viewed as a mutual failure of deterrence. The Japanese government wanted to expand into Southeast Asia, but sought to do so while deterring American intervention in support of the European colonial powers. The United States attempted to prevent Japanese expansion, but sought to do so without precipitating war in the Pacific. The basic policy of both governments failed on 7 December 1941. This essay traces the decision-making process in 1940 and 1941 in Tokyo and Washington which led to the Pacific War and explains why the Japanese government chose to go to war against an enemy whose military power and potential were so vastly superior to its own.

Most deterrence theorists argue that the destructive potential of nuclear weapons and the immense size of current superpower arsenals are a source of strategic stability, since rational leaders in neither the United States nor the Soviet Union believe that victory

---

5 Imperial Conferences, Sept. 6, 1941; Dec. 1, 1941. Nobutaka Ike (ed.), *Japan's Decision for War: Records of the 1941 Policy Conferences* (Stanford, 1967), 140, 263.

6 Nagano Osami's words as recalled by Prime Minister Prince Konoe Fumimaro. Konoe's memoirs are translated by the Language Section G-2 of the U.S. Strategic Bombing Survey, as printed in *Pearl Harbor Attack Hearings before the Joint Committee on the Investigation of the Pearl Harbor Attack* (Washington, D.C., 1946), Pt. XX, 3985–4029. The quote is from 4005.

is at all likely in a nuclear war. A historical case in which a government launched an attack knowing that the probability of victory was low and the costs of defeat extremely high is, therefore, particularly challenging to contemporary strategy. Indeed, since it is difficult to imagine a decision to go to war in the nuclear age which, if it escalated to a total war between the superpowers, would seem rational in retrospect, it is what appears irrational in the past that can best illuminate the future that we seek to avoid.

FIRST STEPS: EXPANSION AND MUTUAL DETERRENT BLUFFS   On 3 November 1938, more than a year after the war between China and Japan had begun, the Foreign Ministry in Tokyo proclaimed "a new order in East Asia" and announced that its goal in what was euphemistically called the "China incident" was "to perfect the joint defense against Communism and to create a new culture and realize a close economic cohesion throughout East Asia."[7] The desire for Japanese hegemony in East Asia was nearly ubiquitous in Tokyo in the late 1930s. But there is often a considerable difference between an accepted political desire and an immediate policy objective. Although the "New Order" had been announced in 1938, it was only after Hitler had achieved his unanticipated victories in Europe in 1940 that the Japanese government saw an opportunity to achieve its goal. By the summer, the Dutch government, which controlled the oil of the Dutch East Indies, had gone into exile; the new Vichy regime controlled French Indochina; and the British government was fighting for its existence in the Battle of Britain. On June 25, Hata Shunroku, the army minister, expressed the widespread view in Tokyo when he urged his staff to "seize this golden opportunity! Don't let anything stand in your way."[8] The key question for Japan was how to take best advantage of the war in Europe to advance its goals in Asia.

In July 1940, a new government under the leadership of Prince Konoe Fumimaro was formed explicitly to "expedite the settlement of the China Incident" and "solve the Southern Area problem." The Imperial Army feared that a sudden British collapse might diminish its strategic opportunities. It began to make

---

7 *Foreign Relations of the United States* (henceforth *FRUS*) *Japan: 1931–1941*, I, 477–478.
8 As quoted in Hosoya Chihiro, "The Tripartite Pact, 1939–1940," in James W. Morley (ed.), *Deterrent Diplomacy: Japan, Germany, and the USSR, 1935–1940* (New York, 1976), 207.

plans for an immediate surprise attack against British possessions in the Far East. When the army staff approached the navy staff to coordinate planning for an operation aimed against the British colonies, however, the navy insisted that a war in Southeast Asia could not be limited to the European powers alone and that American intervention must be expected.[9] How did the Imperial Navy arrive at this assessment?

The navy position was based largely on its view of the United States' capabilities, not intentions, and it appears to have been crystallized by the navy staff's large-scale strategic map exercises between 15 and 21 May 1940. The purpose of these meetings was to determine whether a military occupation of the Dutch East Indies was possible. In the exercise, the Imperial Navy launched a surprise attack against the Borneo oil fields and the nickel mines of Celebes. The Japanese attack, launched under the pretext of guaranteeing the neutrality of the Dutch East Indies, succeeded in its preliminary stages, but then the hypothetical potential enemy, the American fleet at Pearl Harbor, counterattacked. What had been designed as a "quick-grab" of the resource-rich islands became a prolonged war with the most feared enemy. The navy's official report, therefore, reached devastating conclusions. As the navy had depended significantly on American oil for the running of the fleet since its conversion from coal after World War I, a total war against the United States would be a disaster:

1. If U.S. exports of petroleum are totally banned, it will be impossible to continue the war unless within four months we are able to secure oil in the Dutch East Indies and acquire the capacity to transport it to Japan.

2. Even then, Japan would be able to continue the war for a year at most. Should the war continue beyond a year, our chances of winning would be nil.[10]

9 "The Main Principles for Coping with the Changing World Situation," July 27, 1940, in Hattori Takushiro, *Daitoa Senso Zenshi* [*History of the Greater East Asia War*] (Tokyo, 1953). See unpub. trans., U.S. Army Center for Military History (Washington, D.C., n.d.), I, 33–38. Arthur J. Marder, *Old Friends, New Enemies: The Royal Navy and the Imperial Japanese Navy. Strategic Illusions 1936–1941* (Oxford, 1981), 154; Tsunoda Jun, "The Navy's Role in the Southern Strategy," in Morley (ed.), *The Fateful Choice: Japan's Advance into Southeast Asia* (New York, 1980), 247–248.
10 Tsunoda, "Navy's Role," 246.

With the army and navy positions so divergent, the governing Liaison Conference could only agree to a very ambiguous compromise policy: to make initial plans and preparations for both the desired attack against the European colonies alone and the undesired war against the United States. The navy, however, refused to agree to an attack against the British and Dutch territories unless it was clear that the United States would not intervene militarily. It was left to the Japanese Foreign Ministry to find a way of reducing the likelihood of American involvement in a war in Southeast Asia.[11]

Which was more accurate: the view that the United States was unlikely to go to war over European colonial possessions, or the navy's position that American intervention was too probable to make the "southward advance" an advisable policy? If one examines the available evidence, it is difficult to avoid the conclusion that the United States would not have gone to war in the summer of 1940 had the Japanese restricted their attack to the British and Dutch colonies. Unbeknown to Tokyo, on 23 May 1940 the United States' senior political and military officials reviewed strategic policy in light of the anticipated German victory against France and determined (according to General George Marshall's notes of the meeting) that "we must not become involved with Japan, that we must not concern ourselves beyond the 180th meridian, and that we must concentrate on the South American situation."[12]

The Roosevelt administration, nonetheless, sought to prevent Japanese expansion into Southeast Asia through the use of the two diplomatic tools it had available to influence Japan: the threat of an oil embargo and the threat of military intervention. After considerable debate and confusion, the administration decided in July 1940 not to impose an oil embargo on the grounds that such a drastic step might provoke the very action—a Japanese attack on the oil fields of the Dutch East Indies—that the United States sought to deter.[13] With respect to military threats, however, the

11 "Political Strategy Prior to the Outbreak of War," in Donald S. Detwiler and Charles B. Burdick (eds.), *War in Asia and the Pacific* (New York, 1980), II, 18–19.
12 As quoted in Mark S. Watson, *Chief of Staff: Prewar Plans and Preparations* (Washington, D.C., 1974), 105–106. It cannot be known whether the United States would have reversed this agreed-upon position in the event of an actual attack against the European powers.
13 The best discussions are Jonathan G. Utley, *Going to War with Japan 1937–1941*

United States was willing to let the Japanese believe that the United States Navy was poised to interfere in any Japanese move south. In May 1940, the United States fleet was ordered to remain at Pearl Harbor rather than return to its regular, less vulnerable bases along the West Coast. The private explanation given for this action, by Admiral Harold Stark, chief of naval operations, to Admiral James O. Richardson, the commanding officer, deserves to be quoted at length:

> Why are you in the Hawaiian area?
>
> Answer: You are there because of the deterrent effect which it is thought your presence may have on the Japs going into the East Indies . . .
>
> . . . Suppose the Japs do go into the East Indies? What are we going to do about it? My answer to that is, I don't know, and I think there is nobody on God's green earth who can tell you.
>
> I would point out one thing, and that is even if the decision here were for the U.S. to take no decisive action if the Japs should decide to go into the Dutch East Indies, we must not breathe it to a soul, as by so doing we would completely nullify the reason for your presence in the Hawaiian area. Just remember that the Japs don't know what we are going to do, and so long as they don't know, they may hesitate or be deterred.[14]

KEEPING THE JAPANESE GUESSING   In September 1940, the Japanese government took two major steps toward a confrontation with the United States. First, the decision makers in Tokyo put significant pressure on the French colonial authorities in Indochina to permit the Imperial Army to station troops in Tonkin Province and use its airfields in the war against China. The Imperial Navy had agreed to this policy of limited intervention on the grounds that Japanese movement into the northern province of the French colony would be unlikely to produce an American oil embargo, but they did believe that "the probability of a strengthened embargo on Japanese shipment [of oil] would increase if we invaded

---

(Knoxville, 1985), 83–101; Irvine H. Anderson, *The Standard-Vacuum Oil Company and United States East Asian Policy, 1933–1941* (Princeton, 1975), 126–143.
14 *Pearl Harbor Attack Hearings*, I, 259.

the whole of French Indochina."[15] The French backed down when threatened with Japanese intervention and allowed the limited incursion to take place peacefully. The United States' response was limited to an embargo on scrap metal.

Second, on September 7, the Foreign Ministry began secret negotiations with General Heinrich Stahmer, the personal emissary of Joachim von Ribbentrop, Germany's foreign minister, to form a tripartite alliance with the Nazi and Italian Fascist regimes. Matsuoka Yosuke, the Japanese foreign minister, sought an alliance with Germany, in which all parties agreed to go to war against any nation that attacked another member of the pact, in order to reduce the likelihood of American intervention if Japan pushed southward. Stahmer agreed with this assessment.[16] Matsuoka was unable, however, to persuade the navy to accept such a commitment, the naval officials being fearful that Germany and the United States would engage in hostilities in the Atlantic before Japanese naval power was prepared for a war in the Pacific. Naval authorities therefore agreed to the Tripartite Pact only after Matsuoka added a secret protocol (with the concurrence of Germany's Ambassador Eugen Ott, but without the knowledge of Stahmer) that allowed each party to determine independently when its ally had been attacked by an adversary. Thus, the Japanese government entered into the Tripartite Pact in late September in order to prevent the United States from supporting the British and the Dutch in the East Indies, but it was fully prepared to back away from its stated commitment to join a war if German-American hostilities began. If Washington was bluffing with the fleet at Pearl Harbor, Tokyo was bluffing with the alliance with Hitler.[17]

The United States' reactions to the Tripartite Pact and Japanese actions in French Indochina were constrained by three fac-

15 "Study Concerning Policy for Indochina," in *Gendai Shi Shiryo: X, Nicchu Senso, Pt. 3, Misuzo Shobo* (Tokyo, 1964), 369–371. (Translation provided by Howard Stern.)
16 Stahmer argued on September 7 that "a strong and determined attitude, unequivocal and unmistakable, on the part of the three nations, Japan, Germany and Italy, and the knowledge of it by the U.S. and the world at large at this juncture, that alone can only be of a powerful and effective deterrent on the U.S. A weak, lukewarm attitude or declaration at this juncture will only invite derision and danger." *International Military Tribunal of the Far East (IMTFE)*, exhibit 549, reprinted in *Documents in German Foreign Policy* (Washington, D.C., 1949), Series D, xi, 57.
17 See Hosoya, "The Tripartite Pact"; Marder, *Old Friends, New Enemies*, 105–135.

tors. First, American public opinion did not support actions that would risk war in the Pacific, and Roosevelt, in the midst of an election campaign, was under great pressure to pander to isolationist sentiment. The second constraint on American policy continued to be the fear that actions taken to deter further Japanese expansion might backfire and provoke rather than prevent aggression. The third constraint was a tension between the actions which civilian authorities supported to signal America's resolve to Japan and preparation for future combat requested by military authorities. Throughout this period, the military leadership in Washington feared that actions to support minatory diplomacy, such as stationing the fleet at Pearl Harbor or sending it to Singapore, would reduce combat effectiveness if war did break out.

For example, on October 4, Churchill sent Roosevelt an urgent telegram requesting that an American naval squadron, "the bigger the better," be sent to Singapore to have a "deterrent effect upon a Japanese declaration of war upon us." Although both Ambassador Joseph Grew in Tokyo and Henry L. Stimson, secretary of war in Washington supported such a move, Admiral Stark and General Marshall strongly opposed it as provocative. On October 8, Admiral Richardson even requested that the fleet be sent back to the continental United States, arguing that stationing ships at Pearl Harbor was "just window dressing," since full training and provisioning could take place only at the Pacific Coast bases. Roosevelt, confronted with contradictory advice, compromised. The fleet was kept at Pearl Harbor, but no visits to Singapore were approved.[18]

In response to the signing of the Tripartite Pact, Stimson, Harold Ickes, and Henry Morgenthau renewed their push for tougher United States economic sanctions against Japan. Secretary Cordell Hull, as well as General Marshall and Admiral Stark, continued to oppose such actions and Roosevelt strongly criticized Morgenthau for pressuring him on the embargo issue, sharply reminding the secretary of the treasury that the president and

18 Warren F. Kimball (ed.), *Churchill and Roosevelt: The Complete Correspondence* (Princeton, 1984), 74; Joseph Grew, *Ten Years in Japan* (New York, 1944), 333; Joseph Lash, *Roosevelt and Churchill* (New York, 1976), 226; Watson, *Chief of Staff*, 117; *Pearl Harbor Attack Hearings*, I, 265–266; James O. Richardson, *On the Treadmill to Pearl Harbor* (Washington, D.C., 1973), 333, 424–436.

secretary of state were "handling foreign affairs."[19] Roosevelt's concerns about provoking Japan continued to make him follow a very cautious policy of limited sanctions:

> The President's position [according to Breckinridge Long's account] was that we were not to shut off oil from Japan or machine tools from Japan and thereby force her into a military expedition against the Dutch East Indies but that we were to withhold from Japan only such things as high test gas and certain machine tools and certain machinery which we now absolutely needed ourselves; that there was to be no prodding of Japan and that we were not going to get into any war by forcing Japan into a position where she was going to fight for some reason or another.[20]

This cautious policy continued until the November elections, but, following Roosevelt's victory, the British pressured Washington to make it clear to Japan that the United States would react to any further Japanese aggression. Roosevelt informed Lord Halifax, the new British ambassador, on February 8, 1941 that he was "through with bluffing" Japan and promised to warn Ambassador Nomura Kichisaburo that the southward advance might lead to war with the United States. At the same time, however, he told Halifax that he did not think that the country would, in reality, approve of entering the war if the Japanese attacked only British or Dutch possessions.[21]

Despite this belief, the United States government began a concerted effort to persuade the Japanese government that America would intervene in such a contingency. "On February 14, Roosevelt was, he told Adolf Berle, 'really emotional' when he warned Nomura [against further aggression:] while everybody here was doing their best to keep things quiet, . . . should the dikes ever break (three sobs), civilization would end." On the same day, apparently on his own authority, Eugene H. Dooman, consul of the American embassy in Tokyo, directly warned the Japanese that an attack on Singapore might bring the United States into the war. Perhaps most important, the United States entered

19 Morgenthau Diary, October 2, 1940, as quoted in William F. Langer and S. Everett Gleason, *The Undeclared War* (New York, 1953), 35.
20 Fred L. Israel (ed.), *The War Diary of Breckinridge Long* (Lincoln, Neb., 1966), 140.
21 Llewellyn Woodward, *British Foreign Policy during the Second World War* (London, 1971), II, 122.

"secret" military talks with the British and the Dutch in order to coordinate contingency plans in case the United States did enter the war. American officials believed, correctly, that Japanese intelligence would soon learn of these "secret" talks among American, British, and Dutch military officers and thus such "signals" might be passed to Tokyo without arousing isolationist opinion in the United States. Finally, the president, against the advice of the United States Navy, approved a State Department request to send *part* of the fleet on a visit to Australia and New Zealand. "I just want to keep them [American ships] popping up here and there," Roosevelt told Stark, "and keep the Japs guessing."[22]

THE SUMMER OF 1941: NORTH OR SOUTH? In April 1941, Matsuoka signed a neutrality pact with the Soviet Union, thereby enhancing his own prestige and his ability to persuade the Japanese military to support military action in Southeast Asia. Before a decision could be made, however, the Germans invaded the Soviet Union, surprising the Tokyo government and producing a prolonged reassessment of the southern advance policy. Should Japan take advantage of Barbarossa and, following German advice, attack the Soviet Union immediately? Or should Japan continue the slow but steady preparations to expand into Southeast Asia?

Throughout the summer of 1941, the Japanese leaders were involved in what Roosevelt (who followed the debate through Magic decrypts) described as "a real drag-down and knock out fight among themselves . . . to decide which way they are going to jump."[23] Matsuoka called for an immediate attack on the Soviet Union, but the army and navy commands favored a policy of waiting to see how the German-Soviet war progressed. Under this "principle of the ripe persimmon," the Japanese military preferred to prepare for both the southern and northern advances and to postpone deciding when to attack until they knew which front presented the most ripe fruit for the picking. In the mean-

22 Beatrice Bishop Berle and Travis Beal Jacobs (eds.), *Navigating the Rapids: From the Papers of Adolf A. Berle* (New York, 1973), 359–360; *FRUS, Japan 1931–1941*, II, 137–138; Herbert Feis, *The Road to Pearl Harbor* (Princeton, 1950), 190; Marder, *Old Friends, New Enemies*, 206–207; James R. Leutze, *Bargaining for Supremacy: Anglo-American Naval Collaboration, 1937–1941* (Chapel Hill, 1977), 216–252; *Pearl Harbor Attack Hearings*, Pt. XVI, 2163.
23 Harold L. Ickes, *The Secret Diary of Harold L. Ickes: III, The Lowering Clouds 1939–1941* (New York, 1954), 567.

time, however, the Tokyo government decided that moving troops into southern Indochina was a safe initial step, which increased their ability to attack the British and Dutch colonies later if necessary.

The Imperial Navy's greatest concern continued to be the possibility of an American oil embargo. Japan imported approximately 80 percent of its fuel supplies from the United States and efforts to develop alternative sources of supply—from both domestic synthetic fuel programs and other minor oil producers—had been a failure. The navy authorities accepted the decision to move into southern Indochina, however, because they believed that it would not result in an American oil embargo, since Washington "knew well enough" that such an embargo would force Japan to attack the Dutch East Indies. On 2 July 1941, the Imperial Conference approved the decision to prepare for either a northern or southern contingency and to take the limited incursion into southern French Indochina, Matsuoka reporting to the emperor that "a war against Great Britain and the United States is unlikely to occur if we proceed with great caution."[24] This claim was, however, a severe miscalculation.

THE AMERICAN EMBARGO "DECISION"   Due to the Magic codebreakers, senior officials in the United States knew about the impending Japanese occupation of southern Indochina, and the ensuing debate within the administration about how to respond to this aggression once again revolved around whether an oil embargo would provoke a Japanese attack on the European colonies. The United States Navy strongly advised the president against a full embargo; the Japanese made an explicit warning that such an act would force them to obtain oil elsewhere; and the president, both publicly and privately, maintained his earlier position that a complete embargo "would simply drive the Japanese down to the Dutch East Indies."[25] Yet, despite these misgivings,

24   Hattori, *Complete History*, 131; Asada Sadao, "The Japanese Navy and the United States," in Dorothy Borg and Shumpei Okamoto (eds.), *Pearl Harbor as History* (New York, 1973); Ike, *Japan's Decision*, 87.
25   The quote is from John Morton Blum (ed.), *From the Morgenthau Diaries: II, Years of Urgency, 1938–1941* (Boston, 1965), 377. Roosevelt explained this position publicly on July 24, 1941. See *FRUS, Japan 1931–1941*, II, 223. For Japanese warnings see *ibid.*, 501, 502–532. On Navy warnings see *FRUS, The Far East 1941*, IV, 836–841; James H. Herzog,

by the end of July the United States had stopped all shipments of oil to Japan. Why?

Previous studies of 1941 as a case of deterrence failure have treated the embargo as simply the United States playing its trump card, and many traditional histories of the origins of the Pacific War have done likewise.[26] This argument ignores one of the most critical aspects of the events of 1941. The President of the United States did not originally want a total embargo to be placed on oil exports to Japan but unintentionally allowed this provocative action to come into being.[27]

On July 24, the cabinet met in Washington and decided to freeze all Japanese assets in the United States. In response to a question as to whether this action might force Japan to make further moves, Roosevelt answered that the freeze order would require only that a license for oil exports be approved on a case by case basis by the United States Treasury and that he was "inclined" to grant such licenses. The benefit, he explained, was flexibility, since the amount of oil going to Japan could now be directly controlled by the administration. The president's calculation was recorded, with bitterness but considerable insight, in Ickes' private diary:

> Notwithstanding that Japan was boldly making this hostile move, the President on Thursday was still unwilling to draw the noose tight. He thought that it might be better to slip the noose around Japan's neck and give it a jerk now and then.[28]

Despite the president's approval on July 31, that export licenses be issued to Japan up to the 1935/36 oil export level, after Roosevelt left on August 3 to meet with Churchill off Argentia,

---

"Influence of the United States Navy in the Embargo of Oil to Japan, 1940–1941," *Pacific Historical Review*, XXXV, (1966), 317–328.

26 Hosoya Chihiro, "Miscalculations in Deterrent Policy," *Journal of Peace Research*, V (1968), 110; Russett, "Pearl Harbor," 97. Among the historians, see Marder, *Old Friends, New Enemies*, 166; Robert J. C. Butow, *Tojo and the Coming of the War* (Stanford, 1961), 223; Gordon W. Prange, *At Dawn We Slept* (New York, 1981), 169.

27 Two recent works have emphasized the "unintentional" nature of the embargo decision: Anderson, *Standard-Vacuum Oil Company*, 158–192; Utley, *Going to War with Japan*, 151–156. See also *idem*, "Upstairs, Downstairs at Foggy Bottom," *Prologue*, VIII (1976), 17–28. For a contrary perspective, see Waldo Heinrichs, *The Threshold of War: Franklin D. Roosevelt and American Entry into World War II*, forthcoming.

28 Blum (ed.), *Morgenthau Diaries*, II, 378–379. Ickes, *Secret Diary: III*, 588.

Newfoundland, the self-proclaimed hawks in the administration were able to ensure that no further oil was exported to Japan.[29] Acheson, assistant secretary of state and head of the Foreign Funds Committee (FFC), which had sole authority to release frozen funds, strongly favored a full embargo of oil: such an action could not provoke a war in the Pacific, he maintained, since "no rational Japanese could believe that an attack on us could result in anything but disaster for his country." Despite protests from the State Department's Far Eastern Division and the Treasury Department, Acheson therefore refused to release FFC controlled funds in early August and, when Roosevelt returned from Argentia, the noose that he had put around Japan's neck had been pulled so tight that he could not loosen it.[30]

Evidence on precisely when Hull and Roosevelt found out about the de facto embargo or on why they accepted the policy is not available in the records. One can speculate, however, on a possible factor that may have played an important role in the president's acceptance of Acheson's actions. Once a provocative move is taken, it may appear more dangerous to change course than to stick to the unintended policy. It is probable that by the time Roosevelt returned from the Argentia conference, any retreat from what was by that time widely believed, in both Japan and the United States, to be a full oil embargo would have been perceived as appeasement—as giving in to Japanese aggression. Roosevelt had in 1940 opposed moving the fleet from Pearl Harbor to the West Coast, because to the American people and the Japanese government it might appear that the United States was "stepping backward."[31] It is possible that similar fears overcame Roosevelt's earlier concerns about provocation in the waning days of the summer of 1941.

29 *FRUS, The Far East 1941*, IV, 846–848.
30 Dean Acheson, *Present at the Creation* (New York, 1970), 43, 46, 52. Acheson explained his motives in his memoirs: "But if President Roosevelt lacked decisiveness in the degree his successor possessed it, he had a sense of direction in which he constantly advanced. It seemed to those in government that our most useful function was to increase, so far as we could, the rate of that advance."
31 It is clear that Hull did not believe that an embargo was in place on Aug. 2, 1941. On Aug. 27 and 28, Roosevelt told Nomura that the Japanese could still purchase oil, and Hull admitted that he "had not checked fully into the matter." It is possible that both men were, at that point, trying to reduce the provocative nature of the action. *FRUS, The Far East 1941*, IV, 359; *FRUS, Japan 1931–1941*, II, 567, 572; *Pearl Harbor Attack Hearings*, Pt. I, 265–266.

TOKYO'S REACTION   Prior to August 1941, the Japanese government did not face the necessity of choice: military preparations for the southern advance and the war against the Soviet Union could take place simultaneously without a decision on what direction, if any, future Japanese expansion would take. The American oil embargo, intentional or not, changed the calculus and added immense time pressures on Tokyo. Japan produced only 10 percent of its fuel supply and, most important from the military perspective, was without a secure source of oil for the Imperial Navy; estimates suggested that the entire Japanese fleet could not operate for more than one to one and a half years in wartime conditions. Each day that passed meant that Japan's limited oil reserves were being depleted and Admiral Nagano was privately brought before the emperor at the end of July to explain the predicament. Nagano reported that, given the oil situation and the growing American military buildup, the navy was in an increasingly disadvantageous military position. Yet even if Japan began the war immediately, Nagano reported, "it was doubtful whether or not we would even win, to say nothing of a great victory as in the Russo-Japanese War."[32]

This deep sense of desperation hung over the Liaison Conference meetings in Tokyo in August and September. Even the most slender hope of a naval victory over the United States would dissipate if war were not begun soon. Naval officers argued that, without fuel supplies, their battleships would soon be mere "scarecrows" and, in September, Nagano compared Japan to a critically ill patient: a desperate operation offered the only hope of saving his life.[33] Two alternatives to this risky operation existed: the possibility that negotiations with the United States would produce the life blood that the patient needed (that is, a resumption of oil exports); or the acceptance of the risk of what Prime Minister Konoe Fumimaro called "gradual exhaustion" (that is, living with the military danger Nagano sought to avoid).

In the Liaison Conference meetings, only Kido Koichi and Konoe appear to have been willing to consider acceptance of the latter alternative: accepting a desperate peace rather than fighting

---

32   Kido Diary, *IMTFE*, transcript, 10,185–10,200; 30,940–30,941.
33   Marder, *Old Friends, New Enemies*, 167; Konoe's memoirs, in *Pearl Harbor Attack Hearings*, Pt. XX, 4005.

a desperate war. Although other decision-makers called for continued negotiations with the United States, they warned that Japan would eventually be defenseless if the embargo continued. The nation was like a fish in a pond from which the water was gradually being drained away: Japan would "finally be reduced to a crippled condition" without oil.[34] Therefore the two critical questions in the eyes of most of the Liaison Conference members were: first, what would Japan be willing to give up in order to end the unbearable oil embargo; and second, how long could Japan negotiate without endangering her survival?

With respect to the first question, the Tokyo government decided that it would demand that the United States and Great Britain cease to support the Chiang Kai-shek regime in China and resume oil supplies in return for a Japanese promise not to advance further south and to withdraw forces from French Indochina "after a just peace has been established in the Far East." With respect to China, the government's position was that it would "insist on stationing our troops [in China] under a new agreement between Japan and China. However, we have no objection to affirming that we are in principle prepared to withdraw our troops following the settlement of the incident."[35] In short, Japan would abandon the southern advance, but would insist on reaping the minimum rewards of the "China incident," by having a puppet regime come to power on the mainland.

With respect to the second question, Japanese leaders, especially in the navy, were concerned that the United States would deliberately prolong negotiations in order to improve its military preparations and, in early September, the Liaison Conference members agreed that a decision for war had to come by October 10 if there were "no prospect" of Japanese demands being met through diplomatic negotiations. The materials prepared for answering the emperor's questions, however, display the desperate character of Japanese military strategy if war were chosen:

> A war with the United States and Great Britain will be long, and will become a war of endurance. It is very difficult to predict the termination of war, but it would be well-nigh impossible to expect

34 The fish metaphor appears in Butow, *Tojo*, 245. The "crippled condition" statement is by Nagano at the Sept. 6, 1941 Imperial Conference: Ike, *Japan's Decision*, 138–139.
35 *Ibid.*, 136.

the surrender of the United States. However, we cannot exclude the possibility that the war may end because of a great change in American public opinion, which may result from such factors as the remarkable success of our military operations in the South or the surrender of Great Britain.[36]

The emperor, at the Imperial Conference on September 6, broke with tradition and spoke in favor of peace. Admiral Nagano responded by promising that "diplomacy would be stressed: war would be chosen only as an unavoidable last resort." The hopes for peace were placed on the possibility of a meeting between Konoe and Roosevelt to negotiate a settlement.[37]

Despite knowledge from the Magic decrypts that the Tokyo government had decided to "pin our last hopes on an interview between the Premier and the President," the American government decided in early October that no such meeting would take place. Two factors determined this negative response. First, Hull feared that the Japanese negotiators would simply try to find "a formula that would satisfy [the American] desire and determination in principle, while still giving [the Japanese] an outlet for their ambitions" and therefore insisted that the Japanese present concrete proposals before the summit.[38]

Second, this view was strengthened by the knowledge, again gained through Magic decrypts, that any agreement to withdraw Japanese troops from the mainland after the "China incident" was resolved, had been interpreted in Tokyo to mean after the Chiang Kai-shek regime was eliminated. The United States, however, strongly supported Chiang Kai-shek and wanted a complete withdrawal of Japanese troops from China. Although Konoe had planned to have the emperor intervene in order to ensure that the

36 Ibid., 135, 153.
37 Ibid., 151; Butow, Tojo, 259.
38 U.S. Department of Defense, The "Magic" Background of Pearl Harbor (Washington, D.C., 1979), III, A-45. A detailed examination of the complex negotiations with the Japanese and between bureaucracies in Washington is beyond the scope of this study. For discussions which are favorable to the American refusal, see Feis, Road to Pearl Harbor, 271–281; Langer and Gleason, Undeclared War, 693–731. For the contrary view, see Grew, Turbulent Era (Boston, 1952), II, 1309–1373; Paul W. Schroeder, The Axis Alliance and Japanese-American Relations (Ithaca, 1958), 200–216. The details of the negotiations can be found in the memoranda printed in FRUS, Japan 1931–1941, II, 561–661; FRUS, The Far East 1941, IV, 389–494. Hull, The Memoirs of Cordell Hull (New York, 1948), II, 1024, 1025, 1031.

army would agree to an unconditional withdrawal from China, Americans in Washington did not anticipate this plan and when Nomura admitted that the Army leadership was the stumbling block to an agreement, Hull only asked "why the Japanese Government could not educate the generals."[39]

THE "CLEAN SLATE" DEBATE   As the mid-October deadline approached with no prospect of a diplomatic breakthrough in sight, Konoe despaired and met privately with Oikawa Koshiro, minister of the Imperial Navy, to seek a solution to the domestic crisis. The navy leadership agreed that negotiations in Washington should continue and that, given the prospects of a desperate war, Japan "in principle" should accept the American demand for a complete withdrawal from China. The navy refused in the Liaison Conference, however, to go further than to state that the prime minister alone must decide whether Japan should continue negotiations or go to war. Oikawa was unwilling to state publicly that the navy lacked the strength to attack the United States Navy, because (as he stated after the war) "if we were to say that we were not able to carry out operations against the United States, it would have meant we had been lying to the Emperor when presenting operational plans for war." In addition, Oikawa felt that "the Navy could not solve the problem that even the Prime Minister could not solve," apparently fearing an army coup d'etat attempt. Army Minister Tojo had insisted that withdrawal from China "would not be in keeping with the dignity of the Army" and that, in any case, backing down to Washington's demands would only cause the United States to be "more arrogant and more overbearing." Konoe, faced with strong army opposition to continued negotiations and only equivocal navy support, resigned on October 16 rather than take responsibility for leading Japan into a desperate war against a militarily superior enemy.[40]

39 *Pearl Harbor Attack Hearings*, Pt. XVII, 2791; Konoe to Max Bishop, Nov. 7, 1945, as quoted in Langer and Gleason, *Undeclared War*, 707. Konoe had told this plan to Grew, but there is no record of Grew reporting the information to Washington. Grew, *Turbulent Era*, II, 1329; FRUS, *Japan 1931–1941*, II, 651.
40 Marder, *Old Friends, New Enemies*, 175–179. See, also Butow, *Tojo*, 268–270, 273–274; Asada, "Japanese Navy and United States," 255–256; Agawa Hiroyuki, *The Reluctant Admiral: Yamamoto and the Imperial Navy* (Tokyo, 1979), 226.

The emperor appointed General Tojo to lead the next government but, again intervening without precedent, requested that Tojo accept the position *without* being bound to earlier agreed upon decisions and deadlines. There was to be what was called a "clean slate" debate: all policy issues were to be decided anew. Yet, although the new government may have had a clean slate, the same clock on the wall relentlessly ticked away. For each day that passed without petroleum imports, Japan consumed an estimated 12,000 tons of oil and each month an estimated 4,000 allied soldiers reinforced British and American garrisons in the Far East. The military services, the Foreign Ministry, and the Imperial General Headquarters agreed that war, if it could not be avoided through negotiations, had to come in early December if Japan were to have even the slightest hope of victory.[41]

Three questions were paramount in the clean slate discussions: first, should Japan accept the American demand for complete troop withdrawals from China? Second, could British and Dutch territories be attacked to acquire the needed oil supplies, without American intervention? Third, how could Japan win a war against the United States?

The Imperial Army maintained throughout the clean state debate that a complete withdrawal from China was unacceptable. Historians disagree on the causes of the army's insistence on maintaining troops in China and not allowing the "China incident" to end in complete defeat. Some emphasize the Japanese military officers' code of honor: to back down or surrender was worse than death and, thus, a humiliating end to the "China incident" was simply psychologically impossible. Others have been less charitable, arguing that the Japanese army used the old jargon of honor and defensive intentions in China to cover their aggressive ambitions.[42] Both views accurately represent the views of many army officers, but it is important to note that many naval officers and civilian officials agreed with a third argument against total withdrawal made by the Imperial Army: agreement to end

41 Butow, *Tojo*, 243, 289–309; Togo Shigenori, *The Cause of Japan* (New York, 1956), 54–55; Detwiler and Burdick (eds.), *War in Asia*, II, 89, 90.
42 See Hosoya, "Twenty-Five Years after Pearl Harbor: A New Look at Japan's Decision for War," in Grant Goodman, *Imperial Japan and Asia: A Reassessment* (New York, 1967), 58; Schroeder, *Axis Alliance*, 175–176. For a less charitable view, see, for example, Butow, *Tojo*, 326.

the "China incident" might not bring a lasting peace. Indeed, it might merely delay a war against the United States to a later date, which would be more disadvantageous to Japan.

Admiral Nagano, for example, had earlier argued against accepting a false peace like that after "the Winter Battle of Osaka Castle," the Japanese equivalent of "a Munich Settlement." The Liaison Conference under Konoe had accepted a similar position:

> Even if we should make concessions to the United States by giving up part of our national policy for the sake of a temporary peace, the United States, its military position strengthened, is sure to demand more and more concessions on our part; and ultimately our empire will lie prostrate at the feet of the United States.[43]

Thus, the Japanese government did not view the troop withdrawal issue in isolation. Given the prevailing belief of American hostility and the massive American arms buildup, many naval and army leaders felt that conflict was inevitable in the long run and that it was better to go to war now than in the future.[44] Under the threat of the foreign minister's resignation, however, the military agreed that the United States would be told that troops in China would be withdrawn after a period of approximately twenty-five years. No further concessions were to be made at the Washington negotiations.

The second issue—could a war be limited to an attack on the European colonies—was critical, since the key target for Japanese expansion was the oil fields of the Dutch East Indies. The government in Tokyo was not the only group debating this issue. In Washington, the American military was split on the question of whether operational considerations would allow the Japanese to bypass the Philippines if they attacked to the south. The German Embassy in Tokyo also urged precisely such a policy so that "the United States can be saddled with . . . this difficult decision about entering the war."[45]

43 Ike, *Japan's Decision*, 140, 152.
44 For example, Nagano argued on Nov. 1 that "we might avoid war now, but go to war three years later; or we might go to war now and plan for what the situation will be three years hence. I think it would be easier to go to war now." *Ibid.*, 201–202.
45 In July 1941 a naval study argued that "if Japan should take military action against the British and the Dutch, she would also include military action against the Philippines." As quoted in Herzog, "Influence of the United States Navy," 327. In Oct. 1941, General

In the Imperial Navy, strong disagreements arose between the leading members of the Navy General Staff and Admiral Yamamoto Isoroku, Commander in Chief of the combined fleet, who had created a new operational plan for a surprise attack on the Pearl Harbor fleet. Vice Admiral Kondo Nobutake, for example, maintained that Japan should attack Malaya and the Dutch East Indies only, and numerous high-ranking officers opposed the Pearl Harbor plan. The traditional navy strategy had been defensive: forcing the American fleet to cross the Pacific; attriting the fleet through submarine attacks during its voyages, and attempting to win what was expected to be the decisive battle near Japan. Yamamoto, who favored concessions to avoid war, nonetheless argued that a surprise attack against the United States in Hawaii and the Philippines was preferable to awaiting American actions because "we cannot rule out the possibility that the enemy would dare to launch an attack upon our homeland to burn down our capital and other cities."[46]

Under the threat of Yamamoto's resignation, the navy leadership agreed to his secret Pearl Harbor attack plan. All naval presentations in the Liaison Conference, however, stressed the need to avoid exposing the Japanese flank to an attack from the Philippines only, and the army concluded at the Liaison Conference on October 28 that "if it is impossible [to separate the United States from Great Britain and the Netherlands] from the point of view of Naval strategy, then it would be the same for the Army." The Foreign Ministry prepared a paper for the Liaison Conference which reinforced this position. The conclusion was that there was a Western "Anti-Japanese Joint Encirclement" policy and that secret agents had learned "from American sources" that the Western allies had agreed "to declare war against the aggressor in case the aggressor invades Dutch East Indies or Burma."[47]

Leonard Gerow, Acting Assistant Chief of Staff, reported to General Marshall that is was not clear whether the Japanese would include the Philippines in an attack southward. Operations Division, War Department, General Staff, Box 14, 3251–3281, RG 165 Modern Military Branch, National Archives; *Documents in German Foreign Policy*, XIII, 399, 544, 784, 956.

46 Prange, *At Dawn We Slept*, 17, 284–285.

47 Ike, *Japan's Decision*, 193; "On the Formation of the Anti-Japanese Joint Encirclement by Great Britain, United States and the Netherlands," *IMTFE* exhibit No. 3566; "The Anglo-American Policy of Encirclement against Japan in the South Pacific Ocean," *IMTFE* exhibit No. 3567; Togo, *Cause of Japan*, 215.

On 1 November 1941, the Liaison Conference meeting lasted for a record seventeen hours, frequently erupting into angry arguments, but eventually a decision was made. Togo and Finance Minister Kaya Okinori voiced their support for continued negotiations to reach a peaceful settlement; the army called for an immediate decision for war; and the navy argued that, because British and American defenses were improving and the number of enemy warships increasing, "the time for war will not come later."[48] By the early morning of November 2, the majority opinion was clear: Japan should make preparations for an attack which would take place in the first week of December, unless last-minute negotiations were successful. Togo and Kaya, the dissenters, eventually agreed to accept the majority opinion. The negotiators in Washington had less than a month to reach a settlement, while the Japanese military prepared for war.

HOW COULD JAPAN WIN?   On November 15, the Liaison Conference approved a statement spelling out Japan's plan to "destroy the will of the United States" to fight a prolonged war (Box 1). The Tokyo leadership accepted that complete victory over the United States was not possible, but sought, by a series of quick victories in the Pacific, to set up a defensive barrier and persuade the United States that a painful war of attrition was simply not worth fighting. Efforts were to be started, the document stated, to point out "the uselessness of a Japanese-American war . . . [and] American public opinion will be directed toward opposition to war." Japanese agents in the United States had already been instructed to make contact with individuals and organizations whom the Japanese government believed would hinder "unity in the United States": labor unions, the Communist and Socialist parties, "influential Negroes," "German and Italian Fifth Columns," and "other anti-Roosevelt movements." The Japanese government had also already explored the possibility of the Vatican playing a role in negotiating peace. The limited war strategy, given the overwhelming military power of the United States, was the only way in which Japan could win a Pacific war.[49]

48 Ike, *Japan's Decision*, 198–202.
49 *Ibid.*, 248–249; U.S. Department of Defense, *"Magic" Background*, I, A-93, A-99; David J. Alvarez, "The Vatican and the War in the Far East, 1941–1943, *The Historian*, XL (1978), 508–523.

Box 1   How Japan Planned to Win a Limited War

Japan, Germany, and Italy will cooperate and endeavor to deal with Great Britain, and at the same time endeavor to destroy the will of the United States to fight.

(a) The Empire will adopt the following policies: (1) In dealing with the Philippines, for the time being the present policy will be continued, and thought will be given to how it can hasten the end of the war. (2) An all-out attempt will be made to disrupt commerce to the United States. (3) The flow of materials from China and the South Seas to the United States will be cut off. (4) Strategic propaganda against the United States will be stepped up; emphasis will be placed on enticing the American main fleet to come to the Far East, persuading Americans to reconsider their Far Eastern policy, and pointing out the uselessness of a Japanese-American war; American public opinion will be directed toward opposition to war. (5) Attempts will be made to break the ties between the United States and Australia.

While paying full attention to changes in the war situation, the international situation, and popular feelings in enemy countries, we will endeavor to seize the following opportunities in order to bring the war to a close: (a) conclusion of the principal military operations in the South; (b) conclusion of the principal military operations in China, especially the capitulation of the Chiang regime: (c) favorable developments in the war situation in Europe, especially the conquest of the British Isles, the end of the war between Germany and the Soviet Union, and the success of the policy vis-a-vis India.

For this purpose we will step up our diplomatic and propaganda activities directed against Latin America, Switzerland, Portugal, and the Vatican.

The three countries—Japan, Germany, and Italy—agree not to sign a separate peace agreement; at the same time, they will not immediately make peace with Great Britain when she surrenders, but will endeavor to use Great Britain to persuade the United States. In the planning to promote peace with the United States, attention will be paid to supplies of tin and rubber in the South Pacific region, and to the treatment of the Philippines.

SOURCE: Ike, *Japan's Decision*, 248–249. Note that this approved document does not include the Pearl Harbor attack plan.

It has been argued that this vision of a limited victory and a negotiated settlement was the result of wishful thinking on the part of desperate leaders.[50] Yet, anyone who has lived through the war in Vietnam cannot easily dismiss the possibility that the United States public and elite opinion might have decided that the costs of continuing a war in Asia were greater than any possible gains to be made. Moreover, the American military leadership believed, before December 7, 1941, that such a limited Japanese victory in the Pacific was likely if deterrence failed. For example, on September 11, General Marshall and Admiral Stark reported to the president that it was "probable that Japan could be forced to give up much of her territorial gains [in a war], *unless she had already firmly established herself in such strength that the United States and its Associates could not afford the energy to continue the war against her.*"[51]

What neither the British nor the Americans had anticipated, when making their predictions of a limited Japanese victory, was the galvanizing effect that the surprise Pearl Harbor attack would have on American public support for the war effort. Thinking that the war would most likely begin through a limited Japanese attack in Southeast Asia, probably including the Philippines, the allied officers had not foreseen the critical effect of the "day of infamy." This same blind spot also existed within the Japanese government. Contrary to the common assumption that the Pearl Harbor attack was caused by the Tokyo leadership's ethnocentric misperceptions of the American people, the available evidence suggests that the root cause of this problem was that *the full Liaison Conference was never informed of the Pearl Harbor plan.* The strategic contradiction at the center of Japan's war plan—a war dependent on a negotiated settlement was to begin with a surprise Sunday morning attack on the American fleet—was never resolved, be-

50 Lebow has argued that Japanese leaders "convinced themselves, for no other reason than their need to, that the United States would fight such a [limited] war." Richard Ned Lebow, *Between Peace and War* (Baltimore, 1981), 274. See also, Jervis, "Perceiving and Coping with Threat," in Jervis, Lebow, and Janice Gross Stein, *Psychology and Deterrence* (Baltimore, 1985), 26.

51 Sept. 11, 1941, Joint Board Estimate, quoted in Robert Sherwood, *Roosevelt and Hopkins* (New York, 1948), 415 (emphasis added). British naval authorities shared this view, arguing in early 1941 that, even if Germany were defeated in a global war, it was "at least highly problematical" that the status quo could be restored in the Far East. See Marder, *Old Friends, New Enemies*, 193.

cause it was never raised at the highest levels of the Tokyo government.[52]

Discussions of the strategic and political implications of the Pearl Harbor attack were limited to the inner circles of the Japanese navy. Naval officers who opposed the plan did stress that it would have a disastrous effect:

> It would be impossible [argued Onishi Takijiro] in any war with the U.S. for Japan to bring the other side to its knees. Going to war with America without this ability means that we must consider ways to bring it to an early end, which means in turn that at some time we'll have to reach a compromise. For that reason, whether we land in the Philippines or anywhere else, we should avoid anything like the Hawaiian operation that would put America's back up too badly.[53]

Admiral Yamamoto overruled such arguments, however, and the navy's desire for strict operational secrecy meant that many members of the Liaison Conference believed that the December 7 attacks would be limited to the Philippines and European colonial territories. "There was no necessity to talk of the attack on Pearl Harbor," Admiral Nagano explained after the war, since "it was only a naval operation and did not involve strategy but tactics."[54] Thus, although the Pearl Harbor attack destroyed part of the American fleet, the Imperial Navy's secrecy also ensured that the Liaison Conference never discussed whether such an attack was strategically wise. The attack on Pearl Harbor was a two-way surprise.

FINAL MOVES   There was little room for maneuver in the Washington negotiations after the Japanese decisions of early November. The United States government had, without being fully aware of the consequences, moved from a policy of deterring the

---

52 This interpretation does not mean that all Japanese officials understood the psychology of the American people, but only that the central decision-making body never was informed of the Pearl Harbor plan and therefore never debated the dilemma of the U.S. response to the attack. The Nov. 15 statement (Box 1) specifically stated that "emphasis will be placed on enticing the American main fleet to come to the Far East." See also, Togo, *Cause of Japan*, 197–198.
53 Agawa, *Reluctant Admiral*, 229.
54 Nagano USSBS Interrogation, Mar. 29, 1946, 5, Library of Congress microfilm collection.

southward advance to a policy seeking to gain a complete withdrawal from China in exchange for a return of oil exports. The Japanese government was unwilling to agree to such humiliating terms that might merely result in an even more disadvantageous war in 1942 or 1943.

The Roosevelt administration attempted, nonetheless, to stave off what appeared to be an imminent Pacific conflict in November 1941. If peace could be maintained until February or March 1942, the Joint Board of the Army and Navy reported to the president on November 5, a large force of B-17 flying fortresses could be deployed in the Philippines "to the point where it might well be a deciding factor in deterring Japan in operations in the area south and west of the Philippines." Although Roosevelt and Hull immediately rejected Tokyo's comprehensive proposal on the China issue, believing that it would leave Chiang Kai-shek at the mercy of Japanese aggression, the president agreed to an alternative Japanese proposal for a *modus vivendi*, in which, in return for resumed United States exports ("some oil and rice—more later"), Tokyo would pledge not to send further troops into Southeast Asia, not to invoke the Tripartite Pact if the United States entered the European war, and, in Roosevelt's words, to "talk things over" with the Chinese.[55]

Although Roosevelt, Stimson, Stark, and Marshall all believed on November 25 that such a *modus vivendi* would be offered to the Japanese, later that night Secretary Hull, without consulting the military, decided to "kick the whole thing over," scuttling the temporary agreement and substituting a statement of United States "principles" to give to the Japanese ambassador. Chinese and British opposition to the *modus vivendi*, as well as the fear of adverse public reaction in the United States, tipped the scales against such an agreement in Hull's opinion. Roosevelt approved Hull's decision the next morning, apparently after having received intelligence that a Japanese naval squadron was moving into the South China Sea, and believing that this "was evidence of bad faith on the part of the Japanese." On December 6, the president issued a final direct message to the emperor, calling for a with-

55 Joint Board memorandum, Nov. 5, 1941, reprinted in Langer and Gleason, *Undeclared War*, 845–846. On the B-17 threat, see Daniel F. Harrington, "A Careless Hope: American Air Power and Japan, 1941," *Pacific Historical Review*, XLIII (1979), 217–238. Roosevelt to Hull memorandum, undated, *FRUS, The Far East 1941*, IV, 626.

drawal of forces from Indochina and warning that the situation was "a keg of dynamite." The message was received by the emperor at 3 a.m. on December 8 (Japanese time), when their attack force was in the air over Oahu.[56]

There was almost no possibility of avoiding war, however, after the failure of the *modus vivendi* effort and Hull's issuance of the statement of principles. The Tokyo leadership believed that the principles were tantamount to an ultimatum issued by the United States "knowing full well that they were unacceptable." Tojo even feared that the United States might be planning to strike Japan first. The emperor was informed on December 1 that the hardening American position "not only belittled the dignity of our Empire and made it impossible for us to harvest the fruits of the China Incident, but also threatened the very existence of our Empire." Hara Yoshimichi, president of the Privy Council, speaking for the emperor, approved the decision to go to war. "At the moment," Tojo concluded the meeting, "our Empire stands at the threshold of glory or oblivion." The Pacific War had begun.[57]

LESSONS FROM THE ORIGINS OF THE PACIFIC WAR   Deterrence theory emphasizes the twin requirements of capability and credibility for successful deterrence. Military *capabilities* must be sufficient, even under the most adverse conditions of having been struck first, to threaten to inflict unacceptable costs on an enemy. Such threats must also have sufficient *credibility*; execution of that threat must appear *probable* enough to make the risks of attacking unacceptable. Most deterrence theorists assume that if the potential costs of war are extremely high and the probability of having to pay those costs is high (or, in traditional terms, the probability of victory is low), then deterrence ought to be secure.

The events of 1941 should serve, however, as a demonstration of how a policy of deterrence can fail even if the force capabilities are robust and the threats are credible. The potential levels of destruction expected by the government in Tokyo may

56 *Ibid.*, 665–666; Hull, *Memoirs*, II, 1081–1082; Stimson Diary, Nov. 26, 1941, appendix to statement of Henry Stimson, Pearl Harbor Liaison Office, Box 30, General Record of the Navy Department, Record Group 80, Modern Military Branch, National Archives.
57 Detwiler and Burdick (eds.) *War in Asia*, II, app. 3; Tojo testimony, *IMTFE*, exhibit 3655, 185; Ike, *Japan's Decision*, 263, 283.

not have been the same as those faced by statesman in the nuclear age, but they were nevertheless apocalyptic. Japanese newspapers, for example, predicted that a war against the United States would be a "holocaust," and Admiral Yamamoto envisioned the possibility of Tokyo being "completely destroyed by fire three or four times" by American bombers.[58] With respect to credibility, the Tokyo government believed that the United States *might* be persuaded to accept a negotiated settlement rather than fight a total war. But this assessment was more a hope than an expectation, and Japanese leaders chose to attack the United States despite being highly pessimistic about the prospects of victory.

Deterrence failed in 1941, despite the anticipated "unacceptable" costs of war to Japan, because the costs of *not* going to war were considered even higher. The possibility of a similar occurrence today—the inadvertent provocation of a nuclear adversary to execute a desperate attack—is often given inadequate attention by political scientists and defense analysts. Among advocates of an "assured destruction" nuclear deterrent posture, this tendency is most strikingly seen in Waltz's tenet of deterrent faith that "no country will goad a nuclear adversary that finds itself in sad straits." Among more hawkish strategists, the denigration of the possibility of provocation can be seen in Gray's arguments that the United States' possession of a "theoretical first strike threat" against the Soviet Union would not increase the likelihood that the Moscow leadership would strike first, out of fear of being attacked, in a crisis. As Gray puts it, "Why the Soviet Union would be interested in starting a war that it would stand little, if any, prospect of winning is, to say the least, obscure." Yet although it may be true that no statesmen will *intentionally* goad a nuclear adversary into attacking, it is possible that one could *unintentionally* do so. And, although the capability to deny the Soviet Union an ability to achieve even costly victories is critical for deterrence, avoiding forces and operations that could be perceived as provocative is nonetheless necessary.[59]

58   Quoted in Prange, *At Dawn We Slept*, 13, 279.
59   Kenneth N. Waltz, *The Spread of Nuclear Weapons: More May be Better* (London, 1981), 20. An exception is Jervis, who both focuses on the problem of provocation and uses the 1941 case as an example. See Jervis, "Why Nuclear Superiority Doesn't Matter," *Political Science Quarterly*, XCIV (1979/80), 633. Colin S. Gray, "Nuclear Strategy: The Case for a Theory of Victory," *International Security*, IV (1979), 87.

The nature of the process by which *unintentional* provocation of Japan took place in 1941—through the de facto oil embargo and the intense American pressure to withdraw from China—could easily be repeated under different circumstances in the nuclear age. First, just as Roosevelt allowed an unguided bureaucracy to impose a complete embargo against his wishes, a future president, inadequately in control of complex military operations in a crisis, could allow provocative missions to take place. Actions which lead the Soviet leadership to believe that war is imminent and unavoidable could undercut even the most overwhelming deterrent. In a crisis, if the Soviets came to believe that their only choice was between preemptively striking first or retaliating, preemption might appear to be the least unattractive option. Certainly, it is critical that the United States maintain adequate nuclear forces and operational plans to provide robust deterrence. But it is also critical that the United States avoid taking military measures in a crisis that could increase the probability that the Soviets would believe a nuclear first strike to be imminent. In particular, reconnaissance missions near the Soviet Union and dangerous nuclear alerting measures must be carefully controlled by central authorities to ensure that unintentional provocations do not occur.[60]

Second, the temptation to believe that strong coercive actions will not lead to war, simply because the consequences of such a war would be "unacceptable" to an enemy, is especially strong in the nuclear age. It may be true that the horrifying prospect of nuclear escalation has engendered considerable caution among Soviet and American leaders when they have been confronted with the prospect of direct armed conflict. Yet it would be a tragic irony if success in managing the dangerous superpower crises of the past should lead to overconfidence in crises in the future. If both governments believed that they could safely escalate a crisis because the other side would back down, both would be wrong.

In 1941, the complacency of power was poignantly seen in the attitude of Stanley Hornbeck, the State Department's leading Asian expert, who dismissed a younger colleague's fears that Japan might risk a disastrous war, one that it was unlikely to win,

60 For historical and speculative examples, see Sagan, "Nuclear Alerts and Crisis Management," *International Security*, IX (1985), 99–139.

because of its desperate situation after the oil embargo. "Tell me," Hornbeck asked, "of one case in history when a nation went to war out of desperation."[61] The young foreign service officer was speechless; the question went unanswered.

The origins of the Pacific War should serve as a constant reminder to future strategists that a nation, if provoked sufficiently can launch a dangerous, even disastrous war, out of desperation. A repetition of the tragic events of 1941 is by no means the only path by which a nuclear war could begin. But it is an important one which we ignore at our peril.

61 James C. Thomson, Jr., "The Role of the State Department," in Borg and Okamato (ed.), *Pearl Harbor as History*, 101.